D0926169

SPIRIT-WRESTLERS' VOICES

Honouring Doukhobors on the Centenary of their migration to Canada in 1899

Compiled and edited

by

Koozma J. Tarasoff

AC ET
CI LE
PE GE

LEGAS

New York   Ottawa   Toronto

© 1998 LEGAS No part of this book may be reproduced in any form, by print, photoprint, microfilm, microphiche, or any other means, without written permission from the publisher.

Canadian Cataloguing in Publication Data

Main entry under title:

Spirit -Wrestlers' Voices; centennial papers in honour of Canada's Doukhobors

Includes bibliographical references.
ISBN 0-921252-74-9

1. Dukhobors—Canada. 2. Dukhobors—Canada—History.
I. Tarasoff, Koozma J., 1932-

FC106.D76S68   1998   305.6'89071   C98-900484-8
F1035.D76S654   1998

For further information and for orders:

LEGAS

P. O. Box 040328
Brooklyn, New York
USA 11204

68 Kamloops Ave.
Ottawa, Ontario
K1V 7C9

2908 Dufferin Str.
Toronto, Ontario
M6B 3S8

TABLE OF CONTENTS

Part III: Learning and adapting

Part IV: Stories remembered

Part V: Through others' eyes

Part VI: Stretching the future

ACKNOWLEDGEMENTS

Most of the papers in this volume were originally prepared for use in the Canadian Museum of Civilization's publication honouring Canadians of Doukhobor heritage. Mainly because of financial cuts, only half of the papers were actually used in the museum's edition.

As guest editor of both volumes, I wish to thank all the contributors for their patience in waiting for their papers to be published. Your inner voices speak to the hearts and minds of what it means to be a Doukhobor today and why the Doukhobor spirit is, more than ever before, relevant to the times in which we live.

I offer my special thanks to the Canadian Museum of Civilization for allowing these papers to be published in their entirety.

My thanks also go to John Woodsworth of the University of Ottawa's Department of Modern Languages and Literatures for working with me in preparing the final draft for the publisher. It was none other than John's grandfather, J. S. Woodsworth (founder of the CCF), who in 1939 dared to lobby in Parliament against Canada's participation in World War II. One of the CCF leader's supporters was slapped in the face by an alderman when he advocated a similar position in the Saskatoon Municipal Council chamber. The supporter in this case was the distinguished Doukhobor lawyer, Peter G. Makaroff, whose own opposition to war was rooted in the centuries-old Doukhobor philosophy of non-violence — a feeling evidently shared by at least one prominent Canadian statesman.

Introduction

Koozma J. Tarasoff

Non-violence, active pacifism and anti-militarism has been the hallmark of the Doukhobors during their 300-year history. Their Burning of Firearms on the night of 28–29 June 1895 was the first organised mass act of pacifism in world history; for them it was the single most important event of their movement. As pacifists and seekers of the spirit of truth, the Doukhobors discovered that there is a spark of love, beauty and God in every person (hence their name, *Doukhobors,* which in English means *Spirit-Wrestlers*). Because each man and woman has this divine spirit within them, it is therefore wrong to kill another human being, they argued.

Out of that simple truth, some 7,000 activists from three separate Doukhobor settlements of Transcaucasia collected all of their guns, swords and sabres and, in the manner of the famous Biblical metaphor, converted their 'swords into ploughshares'. They placed guns, wood, coal and kerosene into a pile and lit the whole. As the wood of their weapons burnt and the metal changed shape, the Russian peasants formed a circle around the fire and sang songs of love, disarmament and a new era of humanity on earth.

This event of the spirit eventually led to the death of many, the persecution of others, and the exile of thousands of Doukhobors. In 1899 one-third (7,500) took their flight to Canada. The other two-thirds, less affected by their radical stance, largely thanks to more friendly local authorities, stayed behind and are today Russian, Georgian and Ukrainian citizens. The noted world writer Lev Nikolaevich Tolstoy and a number of Russian intellectuals, along with Quakers and other humanitarians, helped with the migration.

Today some 30,000 Doukhobors reside in Canada, 500 in the USA, and some 30,000 in what was the Soviet Union. Wherever they make their homes, the pacifist Doukhobors have maintained and developed their friendly philosophy in order to survive in the wider society. Their philosophy and traditions are founded on a deep-rooted belief system that is strikingly relevant today.

With the continuing nuclear threat to our global community, the eruption of nationalistic and religious wars, environmental concerns and Third-World problems (including violence, wars, hunger, disease, crime, corruption, illiteracy, unemployment, inflation and a growing world debt), the nations of the world are being forced to make radical changes in their thinking and behaviour. Herein the Doukhobor values of non-violence, cooperation, internationalism, hospitality and hard work have come of age. These values are a beacon for the future.

For many of the Doukhobors who contributed to this volume, the book has stimulated them to rediscover themselves and their family roots. Six of them have described various *material and artistic achievements* by representatives of their people. After her research on Doukhobor women, *Annie Barnes* was encouraged to plan an international Doukhobor women's conference to be held in 1999; as well, she has written a play about her grandmother which premiered at the Canadian Learned Societies Meeting in Calgary in 1994. In this volume, she presents the inner voices of Doukhobor women who until now have not had a chance to reveal their societal worth as homemakers and career people. Indeed, Doukhobor women have come of age. They are now speaking out and have a feeling of belonging to the group as well as to this world.

In her first published work, artist *Jan Kabatoff* features other prominent artists such as Frederick Nicholas Loveroff, whose landscapes and forest scenes were influenced not only by his Doukhobor heritage, but also by his own experience in logging and farming and by the Canadian Group of Seven. Also included are William Perehudoff, whose painting as an abstract artist has become a way of life and a daily ritual, and sculptor Bill Koochin, who says that 'craftsmanship is one of the reasons for being an artist'.

Former educator *Peter F. Chernoff* begins with recollections of the early days of sports amongst the Doukhobors like *v gilki* (resembling baseball), soccer and hockey. Out of this spirit of physical and mental health evolved several world level champions. Peter Knight was a North American saddle-horse bronco-riding champion for years — until his tragic accident in the 1930s. Debbie Brill was a champion high-jumper. In her view, jumping is not about winning or losing; it has to do with bringing out something out of yourself, something that is your great strength and purpose, the expression of yourself'. National Hockey League all-star goalie Tim Cheveldae is mentioned, as is Jon-Lee Kootnekoff, Olympic basketball player and university coach. As a coach consultant, Jon-Lee believes that a person needs to look inside himself or herself and heed the voice of the subconscious mind, the God within, to find happiness, health and prosperity.

Marilyn Verigin was surprised to discover the wide range of entrepreneurship that she found among her people. In a personal survey,

2

she cites examples of success in the last century covering 86 cities and towns across Canada and the USA, including the large industries of fruit-growing, logging, woodworking and construction, as well as smaller businesses dealing with food, clothing, books, sports and recreation, hotel and motels, restaurants, a tourist complex in St Lucia in the West Indies, television, photography, jewellery, insurance, car sales, co-operative games and much more. The study is a tribute to the courage of the Doukhobors in overcoming opposition from elders who believed in the basic economic structure of the communal system. Excessive profitmaking was viewed with abhorrence as the exploitation of one person over another. At least some of the effective Doukhobor entrepreneurs have found that honesty is the best policy; and repeated business occurs when you are fair and square with your customer.

Successful entrepreneur *William Kanigan* pays tribute to the determination and strength of the Doukhobor elders' who helped him understand who he is. They taught him the virtues of hard work and responsibility as well as the need for a positive attitude and outlook on life. They instilled him the importance of experimentation which challenged him to reach out beyond normal expectations, yet not neglecting the Golden Rule of treating people as equal and worthy human beings.

James and *Nina Kolesnikoff* have chosen to write about the poet Ivan Sysoev who came to Canada on a cattle boat at the age of five. Before he died in 1967, Sysoev chronicled Doukhobor history with more than 1,000 poems, many of them with melodies for hymns. He recalled vividly the long sea voyage, the first difficult years on the Saskatchewan prairies, and much later his relocation to the interior of British Columbia. His parents composed melodies to Doukhobor hymns and psalms — thereby creating new songs for Doukhobor choirs. Right to his dying days, Sysoev felt it was his sacred duty to speak the truth so that sooner or later people would listen to his call. The burning of firearms and the refusal to do military service were, in his view, the most shining examples of Doukhobor heroism.

A second group of contributors have looked at a number of *Doukhobor traditions* that have been *preserved in emigration. Fred Petroff* found that, given the newcomers' ignorance of English and of Canadian institutions, their limited resources and lack of a leader, the communal or co-operative arrangement was necessary for the initial survival of the Doukhobors in the new land. Unfortunately, much communal land was lost because of government pressure toward individual conformity. In spite of this, many Doukhobors became Independents and prospered as successful farmers to this day.

Since the mid-1950s, every summer during the annual weeklong exhibition in the city of Saskatoon, local and area Doukhobor men and women bake bread in brick ovens as their ancestors did during the pioneering era on the Canadian prairies. The fresh bread is sold in loaves or in slices. Saskatoon member *George Stushnoff* writes that this project has been an effective way of organising and funding the local Doukhobor Society, as well as supporting community and charitable causes.

The pacifist beliefs of the Doukhobors, discrimination against them and their general mistrust of government authority had a significant influence on their history, according to *Peter P. Podovinikoff* of Vancouver. In spite of this, Doukhobors contributed significantly to the building of co-operatives and credit unions in Canada at the provincial and national levels. Podovinikoff worked in the co-operative and credit-union movements in Grand Forks for two decades before moving to the coast as a professional expert in this field. Twice the co-operative business in Grand Forks was destroyed by arson (in December 1946 and again in the mid-1970s), and ended in foreclosure in 1986. The lesson: It is difficult to maintain a successful retail enterprise while adhering to the narrow interpretation of the Doukhobor movement. Even the city tried to bar the co-operative retail store from operating its business by cancelling its trade licence; when the appeal process went to the Supreme Court of Canada, the city suddenly gave in and re-issued its licence.

Steve Malloff describes how the Community Doukhobors have been helping to preserve Doukhobor identity in multicultural Canada through the use of modern audio-visual facilities. Since the 1960s, Doukhobor activities such as annual youth festivals, peace manifestations, special anniversaries, meetings and interviews, have been recorded on video and shown on local cable-TV channels.

Finally in this group, *John J. Semenoff*, working from the basis of the Doukhobors' conviction of the sacredness of life, briefly highlights their leadership role in peace manifestations in western Canada during the 1960s.

The next four articles show how Doukhobors have *learnt to adapt* to the ways of their adopted land. For example, the movement of youth to larger centres for education and work has led to more opportunities for intermarriage. *Vera Kanigan* writes that those who feel a loss of their cultural background through intermarriage can look at the situation differently: you have not lost your children, but have given them to the world. That is what Doukhobor philosophy and its universalism is all about: You have lost them only if they cease to love you and only if they take no cherished values into the world.

Educator, artist & inventor *Jim Deacove* has pioneered a 'cottage industry' of games for children and adults based on the principle of co-operation in place of competition. Inspired by the spirit shown by his Slavic grandparents, Jim describes how players help each other climb a mountain, build a community, bring in the harvest or complete a space exploration. He shows how the challenge of the game, like the challenge of life, shifts from 'striving to be number one' to working together constructively to attain mutual goals. Participating in joint decision-making is a powerful tool for bringing about a caring civilisation.

Finally, two Grand Forks (B.C.) residents write briefly about important aspects of learning. *Peter J. Popoff* describes an experiment in public participation where people learn through monthly research symposia. *Paul Seminoff* describes a Doukhobor outreach project which for several decades has built bridges of understanding between the communist East and the capitalist West.

Our fourth group of contributors draw upon the traditional Doukhobor art of *storytelling*. After going through a period of denial, fear and anger, *Vi Plotnikoff* discovered the use of fiction to tell the story of the Doukhobors in a sympathetic and unembarrassing manner. This was the beginning of her transformation towards being a boni-fide human being in Canada. She was able to feel comfortable with psalm singing, the Russian language, Sunday Schools, writing bilingual lessons and being a Doukhobor. And she was able to overcome the stigma of the media when it failed to place into perspective the worth of the larger population of the peaceful Doukhobor peoples in the Canadian context. The violence and roadblocks in the Kootenays, she realised, was just an aberration of a tiny extremist fringe minority within the British Columbia community.

Writer *Eli A. Popoff* tells a true story about his grandmother (*Babushka*) Siminishcheva-Popova. Babushka came to Canada along with a group of a hundred and fifty Siberian exiles in 1905 and was soon reunited with her extended families on the prairies. The forces of individual and communal farming were in full play as Babushka helped to bridge the difficult years of adaptation at the family level where this story is fully told. With 'a smile and a sparkle in her eyes', she showed her boundless stamina and dedication, and revealed her inner soul.

An ode to Grandmother Dunia Berukoff who came from Russia as a small child of one-and-a-half years is told emotionally by *Natalie Voykin*. With no prior education and a peasant background, Dunia had a heart of gold as she lived through the difficulties of resettlement, first in Saskatchewan and then in British Columbia. She participated in the experimental community of Hilliers on Vancouver Island from 1946 to 1950, after which she moved back to the interior of B.C. to settle in the 'zealot' community of Krestova. She read psalms to her granddaughter and discussed them with her. She connected her belief in God with practical everyday life. She often used home remedies to cure her ills. And like a modern psychologist, she used the power of her natural intelligence to change her state of mind (from negative to positive) and produce good health. When the zealots went on a trek to the coast in 1962, she followed them, carrying only a bundle containing the sum of her earthly possessions. When she died in a Vancouver hospital, she was dressed in the traditional clothes she was carrying with her.

In 1915 *Michael Verigin*'s grandfather, Simeon Ivanovich Verigin, who was then living in Brilliant, British Columbia, was asked to establish a settlement in Alberta. The Doukhobors cultivated the soil, seeded, constructed houses, barns and grain elevators and a flour mill and acquired three hundred horses, including ten pure-bred Perchern stallions. Thirteen villages were established, which in 1924 had a combined population of 300. The enterprise continued to serve the needs of British Columbia Doukhobors until its collapse during the foreclosure proceedings of 1939. Another community in the Mossleigh area, known as the 'Lord's Settlement' or 'Anastasia's Village', formed by Anastasia Golubova following the death of her companion Peter V. Verigin in 1924, was disbanded in the 1940s.

In addition to presenting articles written by Doukhobors themselves, we also asked seven external observers of the Doukhobor scene to share their perspectives with us, *'through others' eyes'*. Russian scholar *Nadezhda Grigulevich* describes how Georgian Doukhobors, who were exiled from the Milky Waters [*Molochnye vody*] of Russia one hundred and fifty years ago to an inhospitable mountainous country — where even in summertime the temperature rarely rises above 15°(C) — were able not only to survive in these harsh conditions, but managed to prove the incredible strength of their spiritual power, their courage and their proud allegiance to their ideals. A team of scholars who studied the group in 1988 reported, for example, that traditional dishes such as *lapshá, pirogi, blintsy, kalachí, vareniki* and *borshch* have continued to this day.

Canadian folk-art collector *Jim Shockey* discovered a great treasure when he saw the work of Wasyl Zubenkoff, a personal guard to Lukeria Kalmykova during the Golden Years in Russia when the best singers and best riders accompanied the leader around the Caucasian villages. The guards were given time to practise their individual talents. Wasyl built wagon boxes and was famous for painting flowers on them. In Canada, the best-known piece that has been preserved is a mirror and frame he built; on top of the frame are two eagle heads carved in wood and painted. As a folk artist, Wasyl has helped us understand the life of the Doukhobors.

Another Russian scholar, *Seraphima Nikitina,* studied the oral tradition of the Doukhobors of Dzhavakhetiia (as the former Doukhobor settlement in Georgia was renamed). Sixty of the 360 psalms in the Doukhobor *Book of Life* are of the question-and-answer type. In most cases, the questions asked refer to concepts, especially the concept of the Spirit-Wrestler. 'We serve God with our soul... we fight with our spiritual sword.' Oral transmission is a common method of passing text from one generation to another. It protected the early Doukhobors from the corrupting influence of the outside world which written sources could bring. The fact that the verbal text was incomprehensible to the uninitiated proved useful during periods of persecution. In this sense, Doukhobor singing is analogous to a coded professional language. The printed *Zhivotnaia Kniga Dukhobortsev* is just a written version of the living *Book of Life* of the Doukhobors. Since the Doukhobors preserve their teachings by way of a collective oral memory, a dispersal of the population can be damaging for them.

Legend has it that *stranniki* (holy men, religious wanderers) used to visit an isolated idyllic settlement on Vancouver Island not far from Nanaimo. It was there that contributor *Arnie Weeks* was born. Later he met a group of zealots who had moved there in 1946 from the Kootenays. The author notes the antagonism shown by neighbours towards these people because of the different lifestyle they followed and their refusal to send their young men to war. He cites examples of how this antagonism was overcome to some degree through personal acts of hospitality and friendship — through simply getting to know each other. Here the author rediscovers the lifestyle and values that he had deeply admired, but had lost in the hustle and bustle of the money-oriented materialistic world in which we live.

Kenneth Peacock, the first musicologist to notate the music to Doukhobor hymns and psalms, describes the unique *a cappella* singing of the Doukhobors, which he claims stems from forms dating back to ancient times. Doukhoborism has resiliency for the future.

In her paper on war in the teaching and life of the Russian Doukhobors, *Svetlana A. Inikova* reveals how their self-identity as internationalists or as Russians was reflected in their relations to the state. She cites documents showing that Doukhobors were 'not so much anti-Russian as anti-state in character'.

Rounding out the series of non-Doukhobor contributions, a paper by *John Woodsworth* of the University of Ottawa chronicles recent and current scholarly activities concerning the Doukhobors in the Ottawa academic community. These include (among others) two volumes touching on Lev Tolstoy's relations with the Doukhobor movement being prepared by John's colleague Prof. Andrew Donskov, the translation of the correspondence between Tolstoy and Peter V. Verigin and of the diaries of the writer's son Sergei Tolstoy who accompanied the Doukhobors to Canada, the cataloguing of documents on the Doukhobors from the Imperial Russian archives, and Doukhobor studies undertaken by students at Ottawa universities.

Setting the scene for examining the *future prospects* of the Doukhobor movement, *Koozma J. Tarasoff* draws upon his more than forty years of research to look at the issues of citizenship, multiculturalism and the rise of a new Doukhobor spirit at the threshold of the third millenium. He points out certain 'fault lines', or crisis points, that mark the Doukhobors' dealings with the federal government over the years: military service, land ownership, public-school education, heritage language and culture, and the co-operative communal ethic. The emerging forces of multiculturalism and the ever-changing times have given Doukhobors new opportunities to express themselves, to stand up and be counted. One institution that has taken the lead in a long overdue recognition of this small Canadian minority is the Canadian Museum of Civilization.

Another perspective on the future is provided by consultant *Norman K. Rebin*. Because God is love for the Doukhobors, both heaven and hell exist right here in the secular world in the way we live our lives. The Doukhobors of tomorrow must not only proclaim, but act on their love. They must be activists in the universal cause of the world's survival. They must learn the art and science of motivation, management and marketing, and must become proficient in the use of the media. The Doukhobors of the future need to be audacious, articulate and adaptable. 'Reaching is teaching, and that's our true business', he states. The inner voice must sing out into the next millennium.

Former Olympic basketball player *Jon-Lee Kootnekoff*, writes about imaging the future, taking into account ourselves and our ecology. Co-operation, teamwork and harmony is the way.

Last but certainly not least, three poets touch our hearts with their several contributions: *Virginia Svetlikov's* 'Silent woman' is a prophetic call to action, proclaiming: 'I am woman, silent no more', while *Kathryn Soloveoff Robbie,* in her first publication, points the way to the future by making us see and feel our connection with the past and the present. *Larry A. Ewashen* rounds out the poetry section with 'The Spirit of '95', which takes a new and dramatic look at one of the most traumatic experiences in Doukhobor history: the burning of arms in the Caucasus in 1895.

In sum, these papers join together like a chorus of voices that ring out for truth, beauty, peace, love and universalism. The message is similar: by acknowledging and acting upon the spirit of love and God within each of us, we then open the door to a whole new world of possibilities. Now let us listen to the voices of the spirit.

Part I

Material
and
artistic
achievements

Doukhobor women in the twentieth century

Annie B. Barnes

Prologue: a new beginning

The *S.S. Lake Huron* steams toward Grosse Isle, the 'Quarantine Island' in Québec on 21 June 1899. The girl's hands grip the ship's rail tightly. Twenty-seven days earlier she left the port of Batum on the Black Sea. Her home in the village of Terpenie in Kars province is a world behind her. A strange land lies ahead. What promises does it hold for this thirteen-year-old Doukhobor girl? The immediate future will mean an additional twenty-seven days in quarantine because of a smallpox out-break during the voyage. She looks for reassurance from her mother be-side her: are they really in Canada?

The future will be living with a Mennonite family in Manitoba where her father and older brothers find work. It will be some time before they can proceed to the village of Nadezhda in the South Colony of the North-West Territories (now the province of Saskatchewan). While living with the Mennonites, Annie will spend only one glorious day at school with her brothers. Despite her tearful pleas to remain, despite the urging of her Mennnonite teacher, she will stay at home. She is needed to gather wheat kernels in the field and to knit woollen stockings for her father and brothers for the winter. Her father says girls do not need to go to school. The future holds no opportunity to learn to read or write.

The future will be marriage at eighteen years of age, formalised only by receiving the blessing of both sets of parents. She will give birth to five children at home and strive to allow each one of them some formal education. There will be many years of hard work on the farm, the death of a son and a husband within a four-year period, and finally a peaceful ending to her life on 17 April 1964.

The girl at the ship's rail was *Annie (Hlookoff) Zarchikoff.* The Hlookoffs and their six children were on the last of the four ships that brought approximately 7,500 Doukhobors to Canada, of which only a fifth were male. Over 12,000 remained in Tsarist Russia.

In 1990 Annie's great-great-granddaughter, Hannah Barnes, was born in a modern hospital in Edmonton, Alberta. Vaccination programmes had eliminated the scourge of smallpox. She lives with her parents and

13

brother in a condominium and has a library of picture-books and videos. She attends school and ballet classes and education is certain. She travels by car and jet airplane. Doukhobor history is a pleasant folk-tale related by her Baba. Her future seems secure. But her parents worry about the escalating violence in city schools, the immorality and the growing crime element. They plan to eventually flee the pressure and pollution of the big city. They, like the Hlookoffs nearly a hundred years ago, want a better future for their children.

Every Doukhobor woman today has an ancestor who felt the biting lead tip of the Cossack whip and who had the courage to leave a homeland of persecution. The ancestors believed that freedom from having to bear arms against a fellow human being and the right to worship in their own way would be worth the unknown hardships they would have to endure.

Introduction

Material for this story was taken from many sources (see Bibliography) and from a questionnaire distributed throughout Canada (see Appendix).

The questionnaire invited women of Doukhobor ancestry to participate. It is impossible to determine how many questionnaires were circulated as many were photocopied by the recipients and further distributed. This article is not to honour a chosen few, nor to be exclusive to any group. There was no attempt to include everyone and no attempt was made to contact select people or groups. In retrospect, this may have been a mistake, as Doukhobor women are very modest and reluctant to come forth and be recognised in any way. 'Oh, don't put me in the book! I am not important, I haven't done anything!' is a common response.

Eighty-four questionnaires were returned. Of the twentyeight respondents who chose to remain anonymous, 66% belonged to a group or society.

Although much of the historical Doukhobor material identifies three main groups — (1) Orthodox or Community Doukhobors, (2) Independent or Farm Doukhobors, (3) Sons of Freedom or Zealot Doukhobors — today many Doukhobor women belong to sub-groups or societies, e.g., the Canadian Doukhobor Society, the Union of Spiritual Communites of Christ, the Doukhobor Society of Saskatchewan, the United Doukhobors of Alberta, the Christian Community & Brotherhood of Reformed Doukhobors, the Union of Doukhobor Youth, the Doukhobor Fraternal

Society, the Doukhobor Benevolent Society, the Sons of Freedom, the Doukhobor Historical Society, the Doukhobor Cultural Association and others. Thirty-five percent of the respondents did not belong to any group at the time of the survey, although about half of that percentage did belong to a group at one time.

Some have embraced other religious beliefs. A piece in the Toronto Star of 23 December 1990 tells of *Vicky Obedkoff,* a minister at the Bloor Street United Church in Toronto, who 'grew up in the West Kootenay mountains of British Columbia in a communal Russian Doukhobor family'.

A woman from Manitoba writes:

> I am quite disgruntled with Sunday-morning Christianity though a member of the United Church. I am too much of a feminist and anarchist to fit into the Doukhobor faith, but respect and cherish many of the [Doukhobor] values.

In the 1991 Statistics Canada census 2,525 females identified themselves as *Doukhobor* by religion. Given the choice to list their priorities of home, health, spiritual belief, career and community standing, 75% ranked *home* number one; 13% listed *spiritual belief* as most important; 10% chose *health* and for 2% career was the number-one priority.

The way we were

Like many early Canadian immigrants, Doukhobor women set up housekeeping that first winter in 1900 on the barren Saskatchewan prairie, some in caves dug into the banks of the North Saskatchewan River. 'They lived like gophers', *Masha Kalesnikoff* tearfully recalled to June Callwood in 1984. Unlike other Western Canadian women immigrants, however, Doukhobor women were not isolated. The village or communal lifestyle provided support and companionship. They did not bear children alone. Every village had some woman with midwifery experience. There was always an auntie or a grandmother to look after the babies.

As villages prospered, young women sewed and embroidered linens for their hope chests. The hope chest was a portrait of the talent of the hopeful bride; it was often a reflection on the entire family. Many a poor girl was scorned for lack of a well-filled hope chest. After marriage, the young bride and groom often moved in with the groom's parents where, if the mother-in-law was kindly, she took the young bride under her ample wing and taught her the intricacies of caring for a family.

Not all mothers-in-law were kindly, however. Sharing a cup of tea in a spotless Calgary kitchen on 17 October 1992, I listened to this story: A woman married at the age of 16 years. She was petite, less than five feet [= 150 cm] tall. Her husband, a big, strapping man, was advised not to marry this tiny woman. After all, what help could she be, his mother wailed? He should marry a strong woman, a large woman, one who could carry a heavy pail of water in each hand. The marriage lasted six months before this child-bride, subjected to many taunts, went back to her parents' home. Not many Doukhobor women in the first half of the twentieth century had this courage.

Another story of a woman's courage was related to me in August 1993 by a Ponoka (Alberta) woman. In 1908 her grandmother, a Community Doukhobor, was moving to British Columbia to the new settlement established by Peter V. ('The Lordly'[1]) Verigin. Her sister-in-law, whom she loved dearly, was married to an Independent Doukho bor farmer; they were staying in Saskatchewan. She wanted to say good-bye to her sister-in-law but was forbidden by her husband and the community to speak to the Independent group of Doukhobors. No Community Doukhobor man would drive her to this farm. She secretly hired an English-Canadian with a team of horses to drive her to the farm so she could say good-bye.

Doukhobor *Anastasia (Verigin) Cazakoff* (1888–1979) describes her dismay upon visiting her neighbour and noticing that her hair had been shorn. The neighbour woman reluctantly admitted that she had followed Peter V. Verigin's orders that women must cut their hair short and surrender all objects of vanity — mirrors, combs, watches, 'even irons, everything was put in a pile and taken away'.[2]

> The Doukhobor woman is a housewife. She does not believe that her home is a jail, and that her babies are the turnkeys. Like Solomon's virtuous woman, she 'seeketh wool, and flax, and worketh willingly with her hands' [Prov. 31:13]. On the other hand, she is a housewife only. She is not expected, as our AngloSaxon women are, to be a combination of Mary, Martha,
> Magdalen, Bridget and the Queen of Sheba.

This observation was written by Emily (Ferguson) Murphy in her book in 1910.

Very quickly the Doukhobor woman came to face even more pressure than her non-Doukhobor peers. Sometimes employed full-time on the farm or outside the home, she maintained a house to perfection, grew huge gardens, freezing and preserving the produce for the winter, provided a heavily laden table of traditional (mostly vegetarian) Doukhobor fare, sewed costumes for her daughters, participated in community events, both Doukhobor and non-Doukhobor. She often looked after grandchildren while their parents worked or took on the responsibility of her own or her husband's aged parents.

Anastasia Feodorovna Holuboff (= Golubova) (1885–1965) had aspired to succeed Peter V. Verigin as leader of the Orthodox Doukhobors after he was killed in a train explosion in 1924. 'The majority of Doukhobors were not in agreement with her wish' (favouring instead Peter's son — Peter P. Verigin — still in Russia). 'Naturally Anastasia was very disappointed; after all, it was she who knew Verigin's teachings better than anyone else. Had she not been at his side for twenty years?' (Friesen and Verigin, 1989). In 1926 she founded a small colony of Doukhobors in Shouldice, Alta. By 1945 all had left the colony except for Anastasia and her faithful friend and servant, Fedosia Verigin.

Fig. 1. Maria L. Savenkoff and Doris V. Verigin, stand at the commemorative plaque unveiling at Shouldice, Alberta on October 29, 1988.

Anna Petrovna Markova (1902–1978) came to British Columbia from the Soviet Union in 1960 to be with the family of her son, John J. Verigin,

Honorary Chairman of the Union of Spiritual Communities of Christ, and his wife Laura. Anna was described as a woman who was 'quick, open and spoke her mind'. She brought with her a Russian hymn, 'The Holy Temple of the Living God', whose text beautifully illustrates some of the fundamental beliefs of the Doukhobors. Two of the verses are translated as follows (Peacock, 1970):

> Why, with walls so high and rigid,
> Has hate divided the hearts of men;
> From brethren making them adversaries,
> Their hearts be hardened to condemn.

> Material gains but serve to blind us,
> Lust obscures God, His truth to hide.
> With pompous rites we are distracted,
> Our conscience hate has stupefied.

Anna Markova left a legacy of hymns. She and Peter P. Legebokoff compiled and published an important collection of Doukhobor psalms, hymns and songs in 1978, a collection described in the *Castlegar News* as 'ranking only with that of the Russian scholar Bonch-Bruevich'. Through her efforts a Womens' Group was formed and money was raised for the building of the Doukhobor Cultural Centre in Brilliant, B.C. — just one of her many projects during her short time in Canada.

Kamsack, Saskatchewan, 19 July 1992

Sitting in Agnes'[3] immaculate kitchen, snacking on her delicate *pirogi*, we discussed parenting in the 1930s. She recalled proudly how her grandson shares in the parenting of his children. I asked if men helped bathe children in the 'thirties.

'Bathe children? Men didn't ever bathe children', she said matter-of--factly. 'I hardly remember them holding children!' They were farmers, hard-working men. Work was their contribution to the family: bread on the table, a threshing machine in the shed, stern discipline and farming advice.

It was the women who nurtured, comforted, compensated, cried and held the children. We spoke about education. 'My girls, I had to plead with their father so they could have time to do their homework. He insisted they help me with chores.'

We talked openly about marriage, living with the in-laws.

'Oh sure, it was hard… you moved in with the in-laws when you got married.' There was little privacy; sometimes the bedrooms didn't even have doors, just curtains. She sighed. 'The happiest time of your life was often spent in suppressed silence. Then', she continued with a rueful smile, 'when the in-laws got old, they moved in with you.'

These are the women who now brush away an imminent tear for what might have been, for what they could have done, saying 'Ah, that's the way it was in those days!' — leaving the listener to imagine if there is anguish or regret in the voice. In her novel *The Fragile lights of earth* Gabrielle Roy (1982:31–32) writes:

> When in July 1942 I found myself among Doukhobors, what struck me about them was their disappointment, their feeling they had missed their destiny?

What were the choices for Doukhobor women in 1942? The 1943 British Columbia and Yukon Directory (a listing of names, addresses and occupations) lists the following Doukhobor women in the workplace:

> *New Westminster, Vancouver & Burnaby, B.C.*
> Perverziff Annie CW lumber
> Maloff Mrs. Betty Edmunds & Walker
> Kondrat Helen factory worker
> Koochin Mary grader Pacific Veneer
> Kabatow Pauline waitress
> Zarchikoff Annie passer Burrard Dry Dock
> Cheveldave Pauline employee Boeing
> Bloudoff Nettie asst cook Monarch Lodge
> Chernoff Anne helper Leonards cafe
> Chernoff Elizabeth Dominion Bridge
> Horkoff Mary operator Gault Bros.
> Kazakoff Mildred presser Peerless Laundry
> Koochin Ann operator Jones Tent
> Lactin Mary helper H. Mattson
> Markin Nettie winder British Ropes
> Masloff Pauline passer Burrard Dry Dock (shipyards)
> Popoff Ann waitress Central Cafe
> Popoff Lilian clerk Vancouver City
> Popove Marion nurse
> Rezansoff Elizabeth operator Bownman's Apron
> Reiben Pauline waitress Empire Cafe

Reiben Dora waitress Leonards Cafe
Vanin Florence waitress Coast fish frying
Waselenkoff Vera bus girl White Lunch
Holuboff Helen prop. Laurel Beauty Salon

Nelson, B.C.
Markin Nellie waitress Standard Cafe
Osachoff Polly baker Canadian Bakery
Pankoff Annie maid for H. Burns
Popoff Annie waitress Star Cafe
Verigin Mary cook McDonald Jam

Trail, B.C.
Kabaatow Mary maid I. Marder
Hrooshkin Hazel student
Zarchicoff Mary maid Dr Coghlin
Zoobkoff Alice maid Lazereff & Co
Verigin Florence maid
Rizansoff Pauline housemaid
Podmarow Anne presser Dollar cleaners
Fofonoff Pauline waitress Trail Cafe
Osachoff Lucy asst. W.E. Marshall
Ozeroff Mary bookkeeper Riverside Apartments

Grand Forks, Castlegar, Brilliant, Blewett and many other Kootenay and Okanagan communities had no listings for Doukhobor women. As a matter of interest, there were very few listings for women of any nationality or culture in these smaller towns. Shoreacres is an exception: 'population 800, including Doukhobors' — forty-seven Doukhobor men are listed, two Doukhobor women.

The way we are

A sampling from the 1992 questionnaire returned by Doukhobor women reveals a rather different range of professions: *Irene Maloff* of Grand Forks, B.C., is an educator; *Abbe Ewashen* of Vancouver is in the legal field; *Vi Hegan* of Blueberry Creek, B.C., is a nurse; *Kae (Kazakoff) Harvey* of Yorkton, Saskatchewan, recently retired from a nursing career; *Dr Shirley (Cheveldayeff) Perry* of West Vancouver is an educator and music scholar; *Moneca Ryon (Barieso) Cox* of Vancouver is in health-care and the arts; *Nadya (Konkin) Tarasoff* of Baysville, Ontario, is a social-worker turned research and planning consultant; *Shelley (Strilioff)*

Craig of Outremont, Québec, is a mixer for the National Film Board; *Florence Turnbull* of North Battleford, Saskatchewan, is a homemaker; *Gloria (Pozdnikoff) Wyse* of Gloucester, Ontario, reads and writes in English, Russian, Italian, Spanish and French; *Hazel Samorodin* of Nelson, B.C., is a home-maker and works in agriculture; *Vera Strelaioff* of Benito, Manitoba, is a home-maker; *Laura Verigin* of Benito, Man., worked as a nurse's aide for twentythree years (in 1992 she was director of the Benito branch of the National Doukhobor Heritage Village at Verigin, Saskatchewan); *Katie Slastukin* of Grand Forks, B.C., is a home-maker; *Malonie Zaremba* of Saskatoon (in the '60–75' age category) has two degrees from the University of Saskatchewan; *Verna (Berukoff) Kidd* of Nelson, B.C., is an educator and co-author of a published novel; *Polly Chernoff* of Castlegar, B.C., is a recently retired marriage commissioner for the Province of British Columbia; *Margo Trofimenkoff* of Calgary, Alberta, is an interior designer.

Laverne Bonderoff of Castlegar, B.C., is a nurse; *Nora (Trofimenkoff) Muise* of Ottawa is a registered nurse with management training; *Carol Stevens* of Medicine Hat is a pharmacy technician; *Margaret Zumik* of Fort MacLeod, Alberta, is a cook; *Mabel (Soloveoff) Verigin* of Montrose, B.C., is a master weaver; *Eva Varabioff* of Castlegar is in management; the *Canora Courier* of 23 December 1992 mentions *Annette Zeeben* of Yorkton, Sask., as having won a Canadian Society of Laboratory Technologists award; *Polly Vishloff* of Mission, B.C., is a home-maker and sends a photo of her craft: hundreds of freshly baked *pirogi;* the September/October 1990 issue of *Harrowsmith* features *Louise Konkin* of New Krestova, B.C., in an article on Canadian gardens; the 18th edition of the *Doukhobor Society of Saskatchewan Newsletter* congratulates *Mary Fofonoff* of Verigin, Sask., on her Canada-125 Anniversary award; the *Canadian Doukhobor Society Newsletter* (vol. 1, n°2) advises readers that *Elizabeth Semenoff* of Grand Forks, B.C., was appointed editor of the USCC publication *Iskra,* which she served until the autumn of 1996; *Mary Oglow* of Castlegar and her husband were honoured as Citizens of the Year. It would be impossible to list all the Doukhobor women who have 'accomplished something' because without the hard work and guidance of Doukhobor women, very little might have been 'accomplished'. 'A household, church, community would be non-functional had it not been for our hardy, willing, resourceful women, past and present', writes *Laura Verigin* of Benito, Manitoba.

Today some Doukhobor women are marching for peace. In its 29 January 1992 issue *Iskra* published a picture of the Castlegar Peace Group, including *Polly Malekow, Nat Voykin* and *Linda Stoochnoff.* Seventy-two percent of the women surveyed for the same issue believed 'strongly' that Doukhobors must be pacifist. 'The welfare of all nations is not worth the life of one child', reads a Doukhobor motto. Doukhobor women now speak out openly against pornography and decry the mental and physical abuse of any human being.

Lukeria Vasilevna Kalmykova (1841–1886) was a Doukhobor leader in Transcaucasia after her husband's death. Under her strong and benevolent twenty-two-year leadership the Doukhobors lived peacefully and prospered. Folk tales say she punished men who abused their wives by having them spend a night on public view in the village chicken-coop! *Lily J. (Konkin) Nowak* of Fort Saskatchewan, Alta, writes: 'Even though she lived 100 years ago, Lukeria Kalmykova is still a model for the modern Doukhobor woman.'

Women too often work quietly within the shadow of their partners or the male members of the community. *Lisa Semenoff*, formerly of Grand Forks writes: 'They [Doukhobor women] work mostly behind the scenes, unrecognised and overworked.' *Edna Wright* of Saskatoon expresses her frustration when she notes: 'After serving three years [on the Board], I left with a feeling of frustration that the women's place was [only] for cooking and serving.'

Tina Jmaeff, a member of the Sons of Freedom, was serving a term at the Burnaby (B.C.) Correctional Centre for Women. One woman, who asked to remain anonymous, said of the female members of this sect:

> No one ever explained to me their belief in non-materialism, and that's why they burned their houses and disrobed, to remind supposedly the rest of us of our addictions to our possessions. I was embarrassed by them, the women, because their pictures were in the papers and in the books. Then I recently read in the Bible (Prov. 23:4): 'Do not toil to acquire wealth; be wise enough to desist.'4

Another woman expresses her resentment as follows:

> Yet being from that background [Doukhobor] often left me with much explaining to do because of the Sons of Freedom activities. They have coloured public perception of my people and I will always resent this.

They were so eager, interrupting each other, laughing, when there could have been tears. They were anxious to share some old hurts in a safe place, with other women who understood, in an atmosphere of love and acceptance. As *Verna (Berukoff) Kidd* writes, 'In a group we still seem to find each other and ask about our ancestors.'

Lola (Vatkin) Cheveldave was brought to this gathering by her husband because she was in a wheel-chair, one leg in a cast, the other ankle bandaged — the result, she laughs, of a 'stupid fall'. Lola spoke assertively and confidently, with pride in her heritage. She admitted that, like almost all women between fifty and seventy years of age, she experienced discrimination, but assured us:

> I sure let them know that my feelings were of pride. I have always told everyone off (that said anything about the 'dirty douks') and I didn't care what profession or nationality they were.

When Lola went to work for a local businessman in the 1950s she was cautioned about speaking in Russian to any of the Doukhobor customers. At the risk of losing her new job, she stood her ground, saying that if anyone spoke to her in Russian, she would answer them in Russian and that was that. Not everyone had the same confidence. One woman, a teacher, bright, a natural-born story-teller, laughing at herself, admitted she had to work twice as hard to get half as far at university. After finishing her degree and at her first school posting, even the janitor felt he could call her by her first name, taking a liberty he would not have dared to take with any of the English-Canadian teachers.

But within these women was there not a yearning to do more — perhaps to paint the scene blooming outside their kitchen window? Artist *Jan Kabatoff* of Bragg Creek, Alta, spoke of her struggle to find acceptance for her talent within the community. Was there ever time to write a story? *Vi Plotnikoff*, a writer living in Castlegar, B.C., author of *Head Cook at weddings and funerals*, spoke almost apologetically about making time for her writing, 'letting my house self go'. A poet apologised for her beautiful poetry because nobody had given her piece a stamp of approval by paying money for it:

> Even parents didn't recognise our efforts until some member of the English community recognised our worth. They remembered when Mr Pitts or Mrs Downtown praised us to them; suddenly we were worth something.

Verna (Kanigan) Keraiff eagerly awaits the first signs of spring at her home in Castlegar. To plant her garden? Yes, that too, but she waits for her 'first love' — ball season.

> I think back to when I lived in Brilliant, B.C., as a twelve-year-old; my first love was playing softball. I would hurry and get my chores done so I could race down the hill where everybody was gathering and start playing.

To her credit, Verna never gave up on that love; to this day she and her husband Bill, now both retired and 'fifty-something', play in the 'A' Division of the B.C. Seniors' Softball League. 'We give it all we got', she laughs.

In August 1993 I had a telephone conversation with eightyyear-old *Polly (Hrooshkin) Romaine* in Castlegar. Polly was the first woman of Doukhobor descent to teach in the British Columbia school system. She completed her teaching education in 1931 at the Victoria Normal School and at the age of eighteen was assigned to Brilliant School №4 to teach Grades 3–8 inclusive. She thanks her father for encouraging her in her education. 'Father yearned for education' at great personal sacrifice. Sensing unfairness within the community where they lived at Brilliant, her father left to find work in Grand Forks.

Because Father left the community, Mother and I were isolated; Mother could not eat with the rest of the people. Finally she wrote to Dad to come and get her. They [the community] wouldn't let her bedding be taken out the door so she threw it out the top window. We moved to Trail when I was three and Dad worked for the smelter. Later we went to Blaine Lake [Saskatchewan].

When asked how she was received as a teacher in a Doukhobor community in the 1930s, she replied: 'I was honoured and respected by all.'

Fig. 2. Louise E. Zaitsoff, Manager, Accounting Kootenay Savings Credit Union in Castlegar, BC and member of the Doukhobor Centennial Coordinating Committee.

Louise E. Zaitsoff, Manager (Accounting) with the Kootenay Savings Credit Union in Castlegar and a member of the Doukhobor Centennial Co-ordinating Committee, has concerns with many Doukhobor people who have

...sidestepped from the mainstream of Doukhoborism.. I believe it stems from the language barrier. We must examine our spiritual programmes and develop workshops specifically for this purpose. Getting our youth to participate is very important, but it may have to be in the English language.

Louise sent this note with her picture in February 1993:

What I would like to have photographed is to be at my place of employment surrounded by the modern technology, reading business material, attempting to read a story book to my grandchildren perched on my knees. Why? Because this is the way my life really is. As working Moms or grandmothers we have so much on our minds that we forget to take time for ourselves.

Fig. 3. Hellen (nee Bariesoff) Pullem, New Westminster, BC,
historian and publisher.

Hellen C. (Bariesoff) Pullem of New Westminster, B.C., an historian and publisher, wrote on 14 January 1993:

I began writing local history about 20 years ago. In 1975 I selfpublished a little book about the Queensborough area. In 1985 another one about very early New Westminster. The latest (about how cemeteries began in New Westminster) I published last year.

'Writing is easy', Hellen quips, 'You just open a vein!' On being a Doukhobor she had this to say: 'I know that as I age, my heritage becomes more precious to me and I find myself admitting to being of a Doukhobor background more often.'

Virginia Svetlikov of Vancouver is a Russian interpreter, free-lance writer and a lifelong student of holistic medicine. She writes:

> I knew as a child that I would never be satisfied to just sit back and watch the years go by so with a very young child and [being] a single parent I went back to school and got a degree in business administration.

In 1970, when she felt a need to rejoin her heritage ('the tugging on my heart never ceased'), she returned to the Kootenays. Through her involvement with a theatre group, a man from the Soviet Union asked if she would consider studying theatre in Moscow. She remained in Moscow for two years, where 'doors opened for me that I had only dreamt about'. Through one of these doors Virginia went to Japan, where she was asked to tour universities with a Japanese professor who was studying Doukhoborism.

Fig. 4. *Virgina Svetlikov of Vancouver, BC, interpreter, writer, and communications officer.*

She then signed on with a Soviet vessel as an interpreter, sailing all over the world.

> I saw children die of malnutrition and even babes barely out of diapers selling drugs and themselves on the streets in order to survive. If someone were to ask me what I would have done differently in my life, or would I have made the same choices, I would have to say the only change I would like to have made is to have started questioning my role as a woman, as a Doukhobor, earlier in life. We all have the same opportunities, it's just that we [Doukhobor] women don't push hard enough.

Mae (Chernoff) Popoff of Saskatoon is a mother, teacher and librarian. Mae traces the evolution of education and career in her family — from

her maternal grandmother, who was a self-taught homemaker with no formal education, to her mother, also a homemaker with limited (Grade 6) education, to herself, a teacher and homemaker with both a Bachelor's and Master's degree, and finally to her daughter Lori, a musician with a Bachelor's, a Master's and a Doctor's degree.

She feels that more literary publications — both factual and story — depicting Doukhobor characters are necessary for global awareness of Doukhobors. No children's books on peace are authored by Doukhobors.5

Fig. 5. Mae (nee Chernoff) Popoff, Saskatoon, Saskatchewan, mother, teacher, librarian.

Fig. 6. Mary A. Green of Winnipeg, Manitoba, pictured with Dorothy Burnham (Curator Emeritus of the Royal Ontario Museum), on the occasion of the opening of "Unlike the Lilies", an exhibit of Doukhobor textiles and tools onthe 19 January 1989, Museum of Man and Nature in Winnipeg.

Mary A. Green belongs to a Seniors' Writers' Group in Winnipeg, Manitoba. She writes:

> I have always wanted to write something about my grandmother who lived at Kamsack, Saskatchewan, and how her Doukhobor ethics influenced my own life, even though I never practised the religion. At the stage of my adolescence when I had begun to think of my first pair of nylons, my maternal grandmother, Tanya Podovinnikoff, presented me with a pair of black woollen stockings. They were thigh-high and a masterpiece of craftsmanship, hand-knit in a fine rib pattern. She had done all the work herself: washed the fleece, carded the wool, spun it into a length of yarn, dyed it and then knitted it up on thin steel needles. I don't think I ever wore them. I don't have them today but I do possess a clear memory of their maker, the gentle lady in a yellow kerchief who sang as she spun and sewed and knitted to create raiment for her family.

Caroline Podmoroff of Grand Forks writes:

> In order to be a 'good' Doukhobor, I feel it is important to believe and to live accordingly. No individual can choose the wrong path in life if they follow and live by the excellent guideline noted in the [Doukhobor] psalm 'Be Devout'. Because of this I feel that one can be a Doukhobor, believe and live anywhere in the world. Once these basics are learned, understood and incorporated into our lives, we should progress with little problem..

Fig. 7. *Caroline Podmoroff of Grand Forks, BC.*

Not only this, but by our good deeds others will notice and soon we will become their role models. My only hope is that I can do as good a job in bringing up my daughter (Sierra) as my mother has done with me. Since the mother figure plays such a predominant role in the nurturing of her children, Doukhobor women will have an enormous impact on whether or not the Doukhobor ways will be preserved or slowly forgotten.

Judi (Wishlow) Thomas of Surrey, B.C., writes:

I believe it is very possible and very important for Doukhobor women to aspire to goals in the modern world while maintaining a strong spiritual and traditional base. In fact, it is that base which makes us most successful.

Fig. 8. Judi (nee Wishlow) Thomas of Surrey, BC, with son Sean at her parent's farm in Creston, BC.

Agatha: the 'free spirit'

Agatha (Pereverseff) Phillips was born 1 January 1904 in 'Gorelovka Village' (an early Doukhobor settlement near Prince Albert, Saskatchewan named after a village in the Caucasus) and currently resides in Regina, Saskatchewan. The following account by her son is taken from *Roger F. Phillips* of Regina, entitled *Then and now: a Pereverseff family history.*

> Few fit the description free spirit better than Agatha. She has crowded into her four score and ten years more activities, more travel and more experiences than most people chalk up in a very full lifetime. From an early age her avowed purpose in life was to make the world better. This intent stemmed from the profound influence her Doukhobor parents had on her. She was a vegetarian most of her life, never drank nor smoked nor deviated from her self-ordained paths of honesty and strict morality. She became a teacher because she thought this vocation offered a pulpit from which she could influence mankind. She wrote stories for newspapers and other periodicals that were morally uplifting, hoping readers would profit from the lessons implied. Blessed with a remarkable memory, she

still pictures vividly in words scenes from early childhood in Gorelovka Village before 1914, when the Pereverseff family moved to a farmstead two miles east of the village. It was a small lake bordering the village that provided Agatha with her first 'entertainment' — in her own words: 'deer stealing to the water's edge in the evening to drink, the twilight chorus of loons and frog song, the colours of sunset splashed on the water...' She remembers her Father and Grandfather struggling desperately to free a horse from a nearby bog and finally succeeding. Memories linger of her Mother and Grandmother sewing and embroidering colourful blouses and shirts for visiting gypsies in exchange for a handsome horse that turned out to be a real rogue, of 'boot skating' on the slick snow-packed village street in the winter.

A few years hence and another memory surfaces. This time the setting is the Jack and Louise Lewis home in Prince Albert, where Agatha stayed while attending Grade VIII. A 'country bumpkin' in a broadcloth dress and squeaky boys' shoes, she was shunned by her school's 'English classy girls'. A kindly, intuitive woman, Mrs Lewis immediately outfitted her with 'nice girls' patent shoes and a smart cream-coloured dress with a blue sash'. She recalled what happened: 'The next day the English girls who paraded up and down the hall at lunchtime and recess hooked their arms into mine and I was accepted from then on to parade with them daily.' The style-conscious 'twenties spawned the flamboyant 'flapper' craze and Agatha fell into step with a 'smashing' blue dress and matching blue cane (fancy ladies' canes were all the rage then). Later on Agatha would cite these as examples of the superficiality she came to abhor.

Switching from university to Normal School, she received her teaching certificate in 1924 and immediately got a school northeast of Lloydminster in the rural community of Tangleflags. In the fall of 1924 she accepted a teaching position at neighbouring North Gully but gave that up at Christmas time to marry Frank Phillips. A son Roger was born in 1926 and a daughter Lorna in 1928. A sudden illness claimed this pretty, fair-haired child in 1933. This tragic event coloured Agatha's feelings about the Tangleflags farm with the result that she and Frank 'sold out' in 1935 and moved to her parents' home west of Blaine Lake.

Uncomfortable in surroundings that seemed to rob him of a sense of control, Frank felt a growing compulsion to return to his native England, and did so in late 1935. He and Agatha talked of getting back together again but they never did. In the years that followed, a good part of North America and Europe became Agatha's 'back yard'. She travelled to London, Paris, New York, Los Angeles, the American South-west, the Bahamas, from coast to coast in Canada. She taught in a military academy in California, worked as governess and private nurse in Hollywood, served stints with newspapers in Canada and abroad, taught English at the [Soviet] Embassy in Ottawa, headed a press-clipping bureau in

Vancouver, worked for the MacleanHunter Publishing Co. in Toronto, pitched in as a library volunteer in Prince Albert and wrote articles for the CCF6 [paper] Commonwealth. She worked as a doctor's assistant, a free-lance writer and tutor. She spoke English and Russian fluently and counted Russian expatriates as far away as Aldershot, England, among her friends.

She steered her own course in life, going where she pleased when she pleased — 'free as the breeze', as a line in a well-known song goes. Widely read and a quick study in sizing up people and situations, she was in some ways a perfectionist and looked for perfection in others. She inherited her Father's intolerance of ineptitude and deceit and her blunt, naked honesty earned her enemies as well as admirers. She had an unquenchable thirst for philosophical discussion, using it as a vehicle to propagate her ideas about how people should be and how the world should function. Gandhi and Tolstoy topped the list of her heroes.

Almost a century of life has given Agatha much to remember — the bitter and the sweet. Today she sees a yawning gap between what she thinks the world should be and what it really is, and this preys heavily on her mind. Still, she struggles on, finding some solace in a kind of philosophical resignation.

Calgary, Alberta, 21 October 1992

Mary Tamelin of Castlegar had just returned from having cataract surgery when I knocked on the door of her hotel room at the Quality Inn. Mary is a poised, extremely well-spoken seventy-five-year-old woman.

For thirty years she and her husband were members of a forty--member Brilliant choir, which produced three long-playing records. We talked about being a Doukhobor. 'I cannot deviate from my way of life; Doukhoborism is our way of life; our faith is our way of life.' She spoke about the Doukhobor doctrine being 'like a thread' joining us to our ancestors who fought to keep the spirit. And about the Doukhobor love of song: 'They sing when they are happy. They sing when they are sad, at work, in prayer, at festivals and peace rallies and manifestations.'

Mary recalled a particular event that took place on Sunday, 27 June 1965: '...speeches, and such singing in the rain; now we can only reminisce'. Koozma J. Tarasoff (1969: 272) writes of that event:

> At that time some 1,500 persons stood or sat in the rain for four hours in a bid for a non-violent approach to peace. The peace vigil, or manifestation

as it had also been called, was held at the picnic grounds a mile south of the Royal Canadian Air Force radar base at Dana, Saskatchewan, 45 miles northeast of Saskatoon.

Fig. 9. Mary Tamelin of Castlegar, BC.

'The Doukhobor singing is beautiful. I sing to myself a lot of old songs; I still remember most of the words, but with no one to talk to [in Russian], I find myself forgetting words I used to know', laments *Diane (Lacktin) Law* of One Hundred Mile House, B.C.

Epilogue

As the singer starts the closing hymn of the Doukhobor Youth Festival on 17 May 1992, three women at the rear of the Brilliant Cultural Centre rise and join hands. One of them does not understand a word of the hymn. A second remembers the melody and one or two words, while the third is singing. It does not matter, for they are three new friends sharing a common Doukhobor heritage.

An Autobiographical note

My offer to write 'Doukhobor women in the 20th century' is a continuation of the journey started by my grandmothers. They came to Canada with strong Doukhobor beliefs. My mother Tena was born in 1913 to Nicholas and Anastasia Kazakoff and grew up in a Saskatchewan Doukhobor village. As a young woman, she became disillusioned with the integrity of the leaders and their interpretation of the faith, but her trust in God remained very strong. I took that strength with me on my journey to find my reality and my spirituality. The spiritual path is a long and lonely journey; where it begins is not as important as where it ends.

Fig. 10. *Group of Doukhobor women (with author of article, seated far right), in Castlegar, B.C., May 1992.*

This article is a celebration, a weaving, a quilting, an embroidery, a mosaic, a palette, a bouquet, a poem, a hymn for descendants of Doukhobor women, with gratitude for their participation. I am especially grateful to those who wrote and spoke from the heart, knowing some readers may misunderstand or criticise them. My understanding is with those who replied anonymously and with those who did not feel safe enough in our society to respond at all. One woman wrote:

We've never seemed to be free enough to express our opinions, be our real selves. We always wonder, what would mother or mother-in-law or grandmother say? Would my husband approve? Would other Doukhobors approve? Some of us have been so injured by an uninformed segment of society we are afraid, embarrassed or both, to acknowledge our culture.

I urge all women to read, enquire and learn our history. Once we have learned the history, we can pass accurate information to the next generation. We do not want them to hide behind changed names and apologetic excuses. We will learn to be more tolerant and forgiving of one another. We will learn to judge less harshly, to love more unconditionally, to say more often: 'There but for the grace of God go I.' We will then see our heritage for what it is: not perfect, but worth preserving and perhaps even visionary. We will know what it means to be a Doukhobor woman in the 20th century.

Bibliography

British Columbia and Yukon Directory (1943). Vancouver, B.C.: Sun Directories Ltd.

Burton, Claudette (1990). 'From Russia with love, Doukhobor traditions in Canadian gardens'. *Harrowsmith*, vol. 15, nº 93.

Callwood, June (1984). *Emma. The True story of Canada's unlikely spy.* Toronto: Stoddart Publishing.

Canadian Women's Educational Press (1976). Toronto: The Women's Press.

Friesen, J.W. and Michael M. Verigin (1989). *The Community Doukhobors: a People in transition.* Ottawa: Borealis Press.

Holt, Simma (1964). *Terror in the name of God.* Toronto: McLelland & Stewart.

Kootenay Historical Society (1979). 'Trust fund to support archives'. *Castlegar News* (Castlegar, B.C.), 26 July 1979.

Langlois, W.J. (1977). *Toil and peaceful life. Portraits of Doukhobors.* Victoria, B.C.: Provincial Archives.

Murphy (Ferguson), Emily (1910). *Janey Canuck in the West.* London, England.

Peacock, Kenneth (1970). *Songs of the Doukhobors*. Ottawa: National Museums of Canada. Bulletin nº 31, Folklore Series nº 7.

Phillips, Roger F. (1993). *Then and now: a Pereverseff family history*. Regina, Sask.: private publication.

Plotnikoff, Vi (1986). 'Aunt Sophie and the soldier'. *Journey to the interior*. Kimberley, B.C.: Kimberley Writers' Group.

Plotnikoff, Vi (1994). *Head Cook at weddings and funerals and Other stories of Doukhobor life*. Vancouver: Polestar Press Ltd.

Popoff, Eli (1992). *Stories from Doukhobor history*. Grand Forks, B.C.: Union of Spiritual Communites of Christ.

Roy, Gabrielle (1982). *The Fragile lights of earth*. Toronto: McLelland & Stewart.

Schmidt, Jeremy (1986). 'Spirit Wrestlers. The Uneasy life of the British Columbia Doukhobors. *Equinox*, vol. 5, nº 25.

Stupnikoff, Sam George (1992). *Historical saga of the Doukhobor faith*. Blaine Lake, Sask.: Stupnikoff.

Sulerzhitsky, L.A. (1982). *To America with the Doukhobors*. Translated by Michael Kalmakoff from the 1905 Russian edition. Regina, Sask.: Univ. of Regina Canadian Plains Research Centre.

Tarasoff, Koozma J. (1969). *Pictorial history of the Doukhobors*. Saskatoon, Sask.: Western Producer/Prairie Books.

———— (1982). *Plakun trava. The Doukhobors*. Grand Forks, B.C.: MIR Publication Society.

Voykin, Natalie (1995). *A Gift of peace*. Illustrated by Harold Rezansoff. Vernon, B.C.: Bytan.

Appendix

QUESTIONNAIRE

Please circle, in ink, the answer that best describes you.

1. (a) I wish to answer this questionnaire but please respect my wishes to remain anonymous and allow my thoughts to be used in general and nonidentifying comments only.

   (b) As well as answering this questionnaire, I am interested in this volume on Doukhobor Women, feel it is important for me to aprticipate in a more active way and I am willing to be inter viewed for possible publication.

My name is: _____

Address & telephone number: _____

My thoughts on 20th-century Doukhobor women: _____

_____

_____

2. I am (a) under 25 years (b) 25–40 years (c) 40–60 years (d) 60–75 years (e) 75 years and over.

3. I was born in (a) B.C. (b) Alberta (c) Saskatchewan (d) Manitoba (e) Ontario, Québec or Maritimes (f) USA (g) USSR (h) Other

4. I now live in (a) B.C. (b) Alberta (c) Saskatchewan (d) Manitoba (e) Ontario, Québec or Maritimes (f) USA (g) USSR (h) Other

5. I am single, widowed, married, common-law, divorced, separated

6. My mate is/was Doukhobor: yes   no

7. I (a) finished Grade 12 (b) left school in Grade __ (c) went to college
   (d) have a university degree (e) am self-taught

8. My occupation is in the field of (a) education   (b) health care
   (c) arts   (d) agriculture   (e) management   (f) English
   (g) other_____

9. I speak (1) Russian (b) English (c) other _____

10. I have travelled (a) no further than outside my province (b) no further
    than outside my country (c) to countries other than North America

11. I belong to the following formal Doukhobor organisations:
    (a) Doukhobor Society of Saskatchewan (b) United Doukhobors of
    Alberta (c) Union of Spiritual Communites of Christ (d) Christian
    Community & Brotherhood of Reformed Doukhobors (e) CCUB (f)
    Doukhobor Historical Society (g) Peace groups (h) No group (i) did
    but left for personal reasons.

12. Circle any of the following 'Doukhobor culture elements' you practise:

    (a) I attend Moleniye (often) (sometimes) (not at all).

    (b) I teach   (a) Doukhobor Sunday school   (b) choir
    (c) kindergarten.

    (c) I sing in a Doukhobor choir (regularly) (occasionally) (not at all).

    (d) I can recite (many) (few) (no) Doukhobor prayers.

    (e) I (sometimes) (regularly) attend religious ceremonies of a
    different faith.

    (f) I believe (very strongly) (I don't believe) that Doukhobors must
    be pacifist.

    (g) I own (none) (one) (several) Doukhobor costumes.

(h) I believe (strongly) (slightly) (not at all) that the Doukhobor faith means no meat, alcohol or tobacco consumption.

(i) I believe (strongly) (slightly) (not at all) that Doukhobors should marry other Doukhobors to preserve the culture.

(j) I cook Doukhobor dishes, such as borshch, perogy, lapsha and bake bread (regularly) (if time permits) (for special occasions only) (don't know how).

(k) In my teens, I was (very proud) (not concerned) (embarrassed) about my heritage.

(l) I was taught to (knit) (crochet) (sew) (cook) (garden) (embroider) (weave) (can) (sculpt) (paint) (write poetry) (sing) (read for pleasure)

(m) If I have children/grandchildren I (am) (will) (don't plan) to teach them Doukhobor history and language.

13. While (in school) (in the workplace) (in the community) (with members of the opposite sex) I (often) (sometimes) (never) felt discrimination or harassment.

14. Rank in order of importance to you (#1, #2, #3, #4):

( ) My career and occupation

( ) My spiritual belief

( ) My standing in the community

( ) My home and family

( ) My health

Thank you for taking the time to answer these questions. If you did not wish to participate, please don't destroy, but pass on to other women.

[1]The Russian is *Gospodnii,* which actually means 'belonging to the Lord'—*ed.*

[2]This incident was related during a tape-recorded interview with Al Konkin on 25 June 1975 (transcribed with permission from Anastasia's daughter Florence (Cazakoff) Konkin of Kamsack, Saskatchewan).

[3]Not her real name.

[4]In the Authorised ('King James') Version this verse reads: 'Labour not to be rich: cease from thine own wisdom' — *ed.*

[5]In 1995 Natalie Voykin authored *A Gift of peace.*

[6]*CCF* — the *Co-operative Commonwealth Foundation,* a national political party founded on the Canadian prairies in the 1930s by J.S. Woodsworth. In 1961 it formed an alliance with the trade-union movement and was renamed the *New Democratic Party* (NDP) — *ed.*

Artists of Doukhobor heritage

Jan Kabatoff

Introduction

Art has been called the heart and soul of nations and of cultures, mirroring people's religious beliefs, political ambitions, aspirations and hardships. What is experienced as an inspiration of the 'inner', creative world, is made manifest in the 'outer' material world, through music, literature and the visual arts.

Art serves to educate us not only about the lives of people in ancient times and in other cultures, but also about ourselves. The absence of certain art forms and the inclusion of others speak to us of the influences and lifestyles of the past, as well as the present.

Since the present is built upon the past, we would not gain a complete picture of Canadian artists of Doukhobor heritage without the benefit of an historical and cultural context for their work. No matter how hard the Doukhobors have struggled to maintain a unique and autonomous cultural identity, they have inevitably been affected by both Russian and Canadian history and culture.

Long before the Doukhobors emigrated to Canada in 1899, Russia experienced two streams of artistic expression: folk or decorative art and religious art. The techniques and motifs of *folk art* (primarily comprising wood-carving, metal-work, ceramics, embroidery and weaving) were handed down from one generation to the next. These traditions were maintained as long as villagers depended on each other for both the necessities and the adornments of life, and as long as they remained isolated from Russia's major cultural centres and from western European influences.

While the decorative arts were known as early as 4,000 B.C., the beginning of Russian *religious art* is customarily associated with the advent of Christianity, adopted from the Greek Orthodoxy of the Byzantine Empire in the tenth century. This conversion and Byzantine influence led the Russians into a new world of visual and spiritual creativity in architecture, icon and mural painting, mosaics and relief sculpure. The *icon*, in particular, was an art form venerated by both rich and poor, and occupied a special corner in their homes and a prominent place in their churches. It served not only to educate the predominately illiterate population about the Gospels and the teachings of Christ, but also as a source of contemplation about the mysteries of life, heaven and man's relationship to God.

The Russian people were passionate in their religious beliefs and not afraid to question or to doubt. Perhaps because of the many hardships they encountered, they looked to religious art for strength, spiritual guidance and inspiration (Alpatov, 1967).

The Doukhobors, one of many sects whose roots can be traced back to social and religious upheavals during the 17th century, rejected church ritual, clergy, veneration of icons, the Bible and the historical Christ--figure. They aspired to live the simple and self-sufficient life of the early Christians, believing that God existed as spirit within every human being.

Like most Russian peasants, the Doukhobors were hardworking and competent wood-carvers, embroiderers and weavers. As Doukhobor belief spread and believers came from different regions of the Russian empire, they brought with them a variety of styles and traditions. Furthermore, the persecutions and subsequent relocation of the Doukhobors from Ukraine and central Russia to Transcaucasia brought them into close contact with Turkish, Armenian and Iranian rug-making techniques and designs.

Perhaps because of the variety of influences on their handcrafts, no specific motif or style emerged that specifically represented their religious beliefs, although certain colours and designs were preferred over others. It is this creative process of assimilation and adaptation of utilitarian handcrafts and decorative motifs which seems to embody the Doukhobor spirit and unique characteristics of their lifestyle and is identifiable in their work to this day.

In 1899 these skills, crafts and designs were brought by the Doukhobors to Canada, where over time Canadian influences and tastes would also be assimilated.

Industrialisation, which affected the centuries-old folk art and handcrafts in Russia, had a similar effect among the Doukhobors in Canada. As the Doukhobors prospered and their communal way of life gradually dissolved, traditional handcrafts were discontinued in favour of Western styles, ready-made garments and store-bought mass-produced items. Very little attempt has been made to revive the earlier crafts of wood-carving, quilting, weaving and embroidery, and very few artisans remain to uphold those traditions today.

During the 1700s, when Doukhobors were asserting their identity in Russia, another art form began to emerge, which, being neither religious nor traditional, was termed *secular*. Russian artists were sponsored for training abroad, foreign artists were commissioned by the tsars, art schools were fashioned after the *Académie française* and a mass collection of European art began.

In addition to depicting the Russian landscape and the lifestyles of the different classes, art served as a tool in helping ordinary people achieve educational, economic and social emancipation. The tumultuous times of the late 1800s were reflected in a popular, moralistic art which aspired to social and political reform. Artists represented life realistically and sympathetically, taking particular interest in the lives of emancipated peasants who, upon relocation to major urban centres, were subjected to the most squalid conditions.

Within this milieu a considerable moral influence was exerted by the literary artist Lev Nikolaevich Tolstoy, whose numerous writings reflected his own sympathetic attitudes toward the peasants. Deeply moved by the Doukhobors' plight, especially the persecution they endured following their burning of arms in 1895, Tolstoy helped organise their emigration to Canada, funding it with the proceeds of his novel *Voskresenie (Resurrection)*.

It was the Doukhobors' association with Tolstoy that first brought them into contact with artists, notably with Leopold Sulerzhitsky, an artist who later became a legend of the Russian theatre. An avowed humanitarian, Sulerzhitsky was chosen by Tolstoy to accompany the first contingent of Doukhobors on their journey from the Black Sea port of Batoum to their new homes in Manitoba and Assiniboia (now Saskatchewan).

The Doukhobors who emigrated in 1899 were far from Russia's struggles and still largely unaware of Canada's own development. They became occupied with establishing their homesteads, pressing their land claims and dealing with a major split in their community. In 1907–08 the split resulted in some 5,000 Doukhobors removing to the interior of British Columbia; later a colony of 300 took root in Alberta.

Whereas the Saskatchewan government had honoured the educational wishes of minorities, the British Columbia government attempted to enforce a standard of education on all school pupils. The threat of assimilation and loss of cultural identity created much conflict and distrust amongst the Doukhobors. It was not until the end of the 1930s that the Community Doukhobors accepted public education in British

Columbia (Tarasoff, 1982:130), and it was only in 1959 that the so-called 'Freedomite' zealot faction acquiesced to the government's demands and sent their children to school. Higher education was not encouraged for many years, least of all an education in the arts. While traditional handcrafts were produced for some time, lack of exposure to the outside art community as well as a philosophy that favoured more practical, survival skills, inhibited all but the most determined of Doukhobor artists.

In the meantime, Canadian artists, encouraged to study in Europe, brought back with them styles of the French Impressionists and the Dutch school of painting. These styles and themes were looked at critically, however, since they had little if anything to do with the Canadian experience of vast northern landscapes, ever-changing seasons and the struggles that immigrants faced in taming the land.

The search for the 'essence' of Canada ultimately led to the formation of the 'Group of Seven' and a 'national' school of art, which changed how we viewed the Canadian landscape. These artists, believing that Canadian art could find sufficient sustenance in Canada alone, succeeded in depicting the vastness of our lonely and mystic northern landscape.

Frederick Nicholas Loveroff

An associate of the Group of Seven, J.W. Beatty, who was an avid traveller and painter of the Canadian landscape, had a direct influence on one of the first known Canadian Doukhobor artists, Frederick Nicholas Loveroff (1890–1959).

Here is a sad yet fascinating story about one of Canada's overlooked artists. *Frederick Nicholas Postnikoff* was born in Russia and came to Canada as a young boy with his family during the mass Doukhobor migration in 1899. He later took his mother's maiden name (Loveroff) in order to distinguish himself from the many Postnikoffs among the Doukhobor community.

Young Frederick attended school in Pennsylvania for three years, with the help of the Quaker Society of Friends. It was during this time that his artistic ability was first recognised. In Saskatchewan, his small watercolour paintings, which he did in the evenings after the farm chores were done, were discovered by the principal of the Normal School in Regina, a Colonel Perret, who persuaded industrial magnate D.A. Dunlop of Toronto to sponsor Frederick Postnikoff's four years at the Ontario College of Art.

Described by his friends as a 'youthful prodigy of the Ontario College of Art', Frederick Loveroff had established his reputation by his third year of study, when he exhibited with the prestigious Royal Canadian Academy. His success during the 1920s was further facilitated by such notable purchasers as the National Gallery of Canada, Hart House at the University of Toronto and two Saskatchewan universities, as well as many private indiviuals.

Fig.1. Frederick Nicholas Loveroff's painting "The Backyard". Oil on panel, 26.7 x 30.5 cm.Collection of the University of Saskatchewan. Photo courtesy of the MacKenzie Art Gallery, Regina, Sask.

While Loveroff's consistent themes were landscapes and forest interiors, he included many references to his Doukhobor heritage and his own experience, portraying men involved in logging and farming along with vendors at the market. One major canvas entitled *Toilers of the land* shows a group of men and workhorses, fatigued at the end of the day, silhouetted against a pattern of clouds at sunset.

Even though Loveroff denied any similarities between his work and that of the Group of Seven, he was undoubtedly influenced by them after arriving in Toronto in 1913, where he associated with J.E.H. MacDonald and J.W. Beatty. Loveroff shared with the Group an enthusiasm for the north country and had travelled far and often. During the 1920s his commercial and critical success even surpassed that of his more famous contemporaries.

Unfortunately neither recognition nor commercial success prevented Loveroff from making a decision that was to bring his painting career to an abrupt and mysterious end. For some fourteen years he and his wife May had had a 'commuting marriage' — she worked in Cleveland, Ohio, while he lived with their son in Toronto. But when she moved to California in 1931, he, perhaps reluctantly, decided to join her. There he worked for a seed company and raised chickens until his death in Redwood City in 1959. He never painted again (see Forrest, 1981a&b).

After the Second World War the Group of Seven exhausted its influence on young Canadian artists, who, in an attempt to establish their own national identity, began to depict a wider variety of subject matter, including still-life, traditional landscapes, seascapes and academic portraiture.

For many years following the war, Canada experienced both a wave of new immigration and a major population drift toward the cities. The latter movement prompted new government support for the arts and a flurry of cultural activitiy in the 1950s and 1960s.

Many Canadian artists, however, tended toward the new international avant-garde movement, and began gravitating to New York as the new art centre and to American abstract art as a model which was neither populist nor regional. Embracing an optimistic, experimental and modern world and brushing aside both its wartime associations and its ties with its European past, it became 'art for art's sake', emphasising the surface qualities of painting: colour, brushwork, texture, overall pattern and gestural movement.

William Perehudoff

An artist who broke from traditional landscape painting to pursue an abstract stream, William ('Bill') Perehudoff established himself as a major Canadian modern painter during the 1960s. He was born in Langham, Sask., in 1919, to a Doukhobor family that remained to farm the

Saskatchewan prairies with thousands of other 'independent' Doukhobors after the split in 1908.

Doukhobor families at that time did not favour higher education, encouraging boys to quit school at age fifteen and begin helping on the farm.

Young Bill's determination, however, won out: he managed to reach Grade 12 with the help of a particular teacher who took an interest in him. Some forty years later that same teacher witnessed with pride Perehudoff's success as a Canadian modernist at a Vancouver art exhibition.

Interested in art and history at a young age, Perehudoff gradually developed his artistic abilities during the late 1940s and 1950s, travelling to the United States to study in Colorado Springs and New York, in between harvesting and seeding crops on his farm. A trip to Europe further exposed him to French Impressionists and Cubists. But the most significant period of his career was associated with his many visits to the Emma Lake Artists' Workshop in northern Saskatchewan during the late 1950s and early 1960s, where he came into direct contact with such notable American abstract painters as William Barnett, Kenneth Noland and Jules Olitski, as well as art critic Clement Greenberg, all of whom were guests of the Workshop (Fenton, 1984).

Fig. 2. William Perehudoff.
Acrylic on paper, 1994. 30"x 22".

Perehudoff's horizontal bands and muted colours of the early 1960s seemed to 'reference' the prairie landscape. Gradually, however, he began to shift from nature to culture, moving further away from natural subjects and more toward the abstract, until his work embraced non-referential, surface-oriented horizontal and vertical bands of intense colour — more like musical chords (for which Perehudoff had an affinity) than landscapes (Grenville, 1990).

In spite of the criticism that abstract painters encountered during the 1960s for their abandonment of Canadian nationalism, along with the lack of support from Perehudoff's own community, his perseverance was eventually rewarded with success and recognition. He has exhibited in major centres across Canada as well as in New York and London, and has been written up in many books, magazines and newspapers in both Canada and the United States.

Perhaps one of the most rewarding highlights of Perehudoff's career was a touring retrospective exhibition in 1994; he had already been described as (Fenton, 1993) 'one of the most influential senior abstract painters working on the prairies today'.

Bill Perehudoff lives with his wife Dorothy Knowles, also a prominent Canadian landscape artist, on their farm in Langham, overlooking the North Saskatchewan River valley and just across the highway from one of the original Doukhobor settlement sites. In typical Doukhobor fashion Bill is extremely supportive and hospitable toward aspiring artists, encouraging them to 'paint, paint, paint'. Painting for the Perehudoffs has become a way of life and a daily ritual, as they head out to their respective studios each morning. Their daughter Catherine is also an established artist (see below).

Bill Koochin

Bill Koochin was born in a Doukhobor community in Brilliant, British Columbia, in 1927. He attended school in Brilliant but was not encouraged to seek higher education. Expected to learn a practical and lucrative trade, he worked in construction for a time. Perhaps it was this early experience in working with his hands that eventually led him to a career in carving, sculpting, tool-making, cabinet-making, stonemasonry and draughtsmanship.

Bill Koochin's art education began at an early age when his drawings were noticed by teachers at school. Some time later he attended the Vancouver School of Art (now known as the Emily Carr Institute of Art and Design), and then went to Paris to study drawing at *La Grande Chaumière* as well as ceramic sculpture at Sèvres. Returning from France, he settled in Ottawa, where he produced many large welded steel structures, three of which were installed in the Canadian pavilion at the 1958 Brussels International Exposition (B. Reid, 1980).

In 1961 he moved to the west coast, where for the next seventeen years he taught sculpture at the Emily Carr College of Art & Design (as it was known at the time), all the while developing his own art practice. He also explored the rich cultures of the surrounding area, including that of the west-coast native peoples.

While touring Russia in the 1970s Koochin became fascinated by a type of carved wooden ladle (or *kovsh*) in the shape of a swimming duck or goose, whose head and bill constitute the handle, not unlike the early Doukhobor wooden ladles. The kovsh had many uses, from a practical drinking-vessel to a ceremonial object, and ranged from a simple wooden carving to one of ornate metal. Koochin subsequently executed a series of intricately carved wooden kovshes in the shape of geese, roosters and ducks.

In spite of the fact that sculpture in Canada has not received the same attention as painting, Koochin has successfully exhibited in many places across the country and won significant acclaim. His work is in private collections in Canada and the United States, and has received critical attention in numerous articles, as well as in a 1963 CBC television documentary entitled *The Hand and eye,* produced by Arla Saare. His commissions include a full-length wood-carving of Saint Alphonsus Ligiori for Redemption College in Edmonton, ornamental iron gates for Vancouver's Bayshore Inn, the Vancouver Festival's famous 'Talking Stick', masks used in the Festival's production of *Peter Pan* and a cere-monial steering paddle for the opening of the Dragon Boat Festival.

Bill Koochin has transformed bronze, marble, steel plate, stone and wood into bulls, calves, peacocks, ducks, swans and sensuous nudes. More recently, he has begun a series of portrait masks which are first painstakingly modelled in clay, then cast in bronze; the bronze model is used together with photographs to carve a likeness out of wood. The finished product resembles something between folk art and high realism (Tippet, 1990).

Perhaps his most challenging undertaking was a recent commission for a granite sculpture of Rick Hansen in a wheelchair one and a half times life size, in commemoration of the tenth anniversary of his world tour, to be displayed at GM Place in dowtown Vancouver.

Koochin's connection to peasant life, folk art and a Doukhobor culture which prides itself on its craftsmanship can be seen in his masks of ordi-nary people, his carved doors and his replicas of Russian ladles. He has been quoted as saying: 'Craftsmanship is one of the reasons for being an artist', and this ethic has earned him the reputation of a master craftsman in a 'high-tech' world where hand-crafted objects are quickly disappearing (Graham, 1991).

Fig. 3. Bill Koochin. "Rooster", 1989. 17 1/2" by 9 1/2". Alder wood.

Bill Koochin lives with his wife Eileen in West Vancouver, B.C., where he also has his studio. He has retired from teaching but not from learning, and continues to challenge himself as he explores the medium of sculpture.

William Nicholas Seminoff

William (Bill) Seminoff, born in Willow Point, B.C., in 1933. is a wood sculptor whose work can be traced to the traditional Doukhobor strength in the art of woodworking.

Seminoff's was first influenced by his carpenter-father who recruited him at age fourteen to help with building and carving pews for a United Church in Nelson. Later he was taught the basics of carving by by Mike Sarchinko, an accomplished carver of Russian wooden spoons, with whom he established a lifelong friendship.

After twenty years as a mining consultant in the Philippines and an overall world traveller, Seminoff turned to carving in earnest, deriving satisfaction from working with a variety of woods, While he prefers the natural warmth and unique characteristics of wood, he has also carved in various stones. His earlier exposure to many different cultures has supplied him with a wide variety of subject matter: Japanese masks, totem poles, wildlife and Doukhobor trunks. His work is now to be found in collections around the world.

Primarily self-taught, and following in the Doukhobor tradition of fine craftsmanship, Seminoff has been a successful award-winner in numerous carving competitions throughout Canada and the United States. He won first prize at a 'Sculptures and Designs in Wood with Natural

Finish' competition in South Carolina. He also holds first-prize standing in both east- and west-coast competitions in North America.

In the past few years Seminoff has been judging competitions and working on commissions. His most notable commission was a half-life-size wood sculpture of Elvis Presley for a museum in Baltimore, Maryland.

He currently resides with his wife Jean Barnes in Vancouver, where he continues to work, teaching carving out of his studio and producing wooden objects such as hope-chests, boot boxes and Doukhobor *babushkas*.

Fig. 4. William Nicholas Seminoff. "Great Blue Heron", 1991. 38" high.
Dao wood, also known as New Guinea walnut, with natural oil finish.
Glass eyes and forged iron legs.

I think that I was born with a desire to create. For me, real art only happens when I can transfer my feelings to a piece of wood or stone. — *Bill Seminoff*

Mabel Verigin

Mabel Verigin (*née* Soloveoff) was born in 1935 at a Doukhobor commune in Pass Creek, B.C. She received her early education in a rural school and completed high school in Trail. A keen learner, the young child quickly absorbed the traditional Doukhobor techniques of sewing, needlework, spinning and weaving taught in her village. She was knitting and embroidering by age six and sewing her own clothes by age twelve. Her passion for weaving was undoubtedly influenced by her maternal grandmother, an accomplished master weaver recognised for her skills both in and outside her immediate community.

Mabel Verigin's interest in fibre and textiles led her to a varied career in teaching dressmaking and needlework, designing leisure wear and lingerie, and establishing and operating a sewing factory originally aimed at helping Asian refugees and other immigrants by providing employment in the recycling of used clothing. Although Verigin has sold her share of the business, the factory, now relocated to Ontario, continues to uphold her original vision and aim.

Having begun weaving in 1986, a year later Verigin attended her first weavers' conference, where other participants, recognising her talent and potential, inspired and encouraged her to study with the Canadian Guild of Weavers. In 1993 she obtained her Master Weaver's Certificate — one of only twenty to be awarded up to that point since 1946.

Fig. 14. George Koochin. "Birth", 1995. 200 cm. x 200 cm. Oil on canvas.

Verigin's special interest and area of study has been the Doukhobor weaving of British Columbia. A meticulous observer and accomplished craftsperson, she has retraced the Doukhobor process of dyeing, spinning and weaving, and has even experimented with growing her own flax fibres. In her research of the traditional weaving techniques she was surprised to discover how complex and intricate much of the work was, in spite of the simple and sometimes crude equipment used by the early Doukhobor women. In spite of a general decline in interest in the production of Doukhobor textiles, Verigin continues to teach traditional weaving techniques, and hopes to document her research in the form of a video.

In 1995 she was invited to present her thesis at a Northwest Weavers' Guild conference in Prince George. This self-published monograph, entitled *Forgotten weaves*, traces the history of Doukhobor textile-making in British Columbia. It is available at the Doukhobor Heritage Village gift shop in Castlegar.

Currently president of the Selkirk Weavers' Guild, Verigin participates in group exhibitions, conferences and weaving projects. At the moment she is striving to complete a series of rag rugs warped on a loom in the 1930s by her great-grandmother.

Mabel Verigin lives with her husband Lawrence in Montrose, B.C.

> My maternal grandmother's family was an extremely knowledgeable and productive group of weavers and spinners, as well as tailors and needle-workers. I clearly remember my grandmother's loom. I own three of the old spinning wheels. My weaving skills came much later — 1986. It was then that I realised how talented my forebears were and I became compelled not to let this part of my heritage be forgotten.
> — *Mabel Verigin*

Elaine Rathie

Elaine Rathie (*née* Troubetzkoy) was born in Saskatoon in 1943, but moved to Calgary with her family three years later.

Like most young Doukhobor girls, Elaine was taught the textile crafts of her culture, and actively participated in Doukhobor community events until her early teens. Her love of traditional crafts (sewing, knitting, quilting, embroidery and crochet) fostered a fascination with the rich and varied textures, patterns and colours of textiles — a fascination that is still evident today in her multi-media creations.

An exceptional student, Elaine was encouraged by her family and teachers to pursue a strictly academic career, and never dreamt she would eventually become an artist. After receiving her first degree she spent two years as a social worker, subsequently completing a M.Sc. degree in psychology.

Noticing her disillusionment with her chosen profession, her brother encouraged her to do something stimulating and different. She decided to take an art course, which opened up a whole new world for her. A series of art classes followed: textile studies at the Alberta College of Art and Design, classes in sculpture, design and drawing at the University of Calgary and an art-history study tour of Europe. In art, Rathie had finally found her own voice, receiving a B.F.A. degree (with distinction)

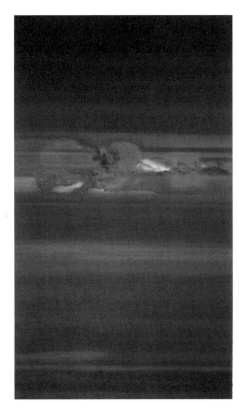

from the University of Calgary in 1979. During the years that followed, she painted, exhibited and sold her work in major centres such as Vancouver, Calgary, Toronto and New York, and today her works are to be found in both private and corporate collections in North America and Europe.

Fig. 5.*Elaine Rathie. "For Gail", 1994.*
58" x 34". Acrylic on raw canvas.

Two serious motor-vehicle accidents only a few years apart meant a significant setback in her art practice. Unable to work with heavy materials during her period of recovery, Rathie turned to writing. As a freelance writer, researcher, editor and photostylist, she has written and published more than 170 articles on fashion, homes, beauty, health, nutrition and other topics of general interest.

Today this remarkable woman and dedicated artist is finally beginning to resume her original career. She considers art a gift to herself, a door to personal reflection and discovery. She is currently working with acrylics and mixed media on raw canvas, employing staining techniques originally developed by New York artists of the 1950s and 1960s. Staining allows her to achieve a layering and control of colour intensity, from the gentlest of hues to the deepest, most 'brooding' colour saturations The texture and weightiness of the unprimed canvas she uses takes her back to her Doukhobor roots and her childhood love of working with textiles.

Since 1984 she has been working out of her home studio in Vancouver, where she lives with her husband Bob and their three children.

The wonder I feel as the sun quietly slips beneath the horizon; the peace that settles on me as our boat glides through the sea; the rush I get from a raging storm — these are the feelings I try to convey on canvas. If I can reach someone and share this joy, I will have made a difference.
— *Elaine Rathie*

Fig. 6. Elaine Rathie. "Precipice", 1987. 30" x 40". Acrylic on raw canvas.

John Kalmakov

John Kalmakov was born in 1945 and raised in a Doukhobor community in Grand Forks, where he received his early education. He later pursued a degree in fine-arts education at the University of British Columbia.

Kalmakov's earliest childhood creative influence came through his grandfather, a skilled blacksmith and wood-carver. While John was initially inclined toward building technology and architecture, a teaching degree with a fine-arts specialisation seemed more attainable at the time, and enabled him to teach art at the high-school level for more than twenty years.

But this art teacher also developed his skill as a professional artist. Inspired by such realist painters as Andrew Wyeth and Richard Estes, Kalmakov, with his keen sensitivity to detail and an inherent interest in geometric forms, worked out a 'highrealism' approach to painting, exploring such media as acrylics, egg-tempera and watercolour. His nostalgic paintings portray 'cultural artifacts' reminiscent of rural life and the small towns of the 1950s: abandoned buildings, vehicles and rusty farm equipment. Perhaps among his most successful works are his depictions of a typical small-town centre in *Main Street* and an empty 'diner' lunch-counter in *Milkshake*, with everything rendered in acute detail and precision, implying human presence and yet conveying a sense of abandonment and loneliness.

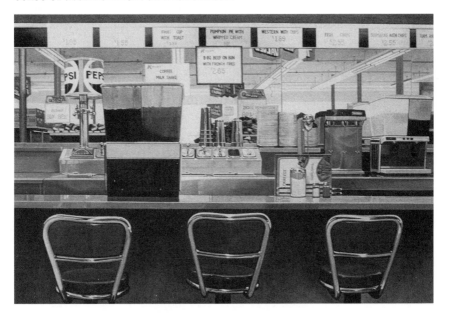

Fig. 7. John Kalmakov. "Milkshake", 1982. 36" x 48". Acrylic on canvas.

Kalmakov's involvement in the Doukhobor community has led to numerous commissions for illustrative art and consulting material, which inspired him to produce an extremely successful commemorative print in honour of the Doukhobor Centenary of the Burning of Arms in 1995. He currently resides with his wife Luba and their two children Mathew and Mia in Ooteshenie, near Brilliant, B.C.

> The perceptual process in visual art has always intrigued me. A casual drawing can be the result of a simple eye-to-hand reflex action — a graphite trail on paper re-enacting the path of the artist's eye. It is our tampering with this reflex process, the deliverate intervention of our minds, however, that gives us infinite joy. — *John Kalmakov*

Peter Potapoff

Peter Potapoff was born in Nelson, B.C., in 1948. He grew up in the Doukhobor community of Ooteshenie, attending school in nearby Castlegar. Even though he pursued a career as a forestry technician, he admits to always having had a 'deep-down urge to draw and paint'. He persevered as a self-taught artist and has since earned himself a solid reputation as a wildlife painter.

Potapoff is one of the few artists who has been able to successfully combine his love of painting with a non-artistic career. His many years of working for the government of the Northwest Territories and the Arctic College Renewable Resources Programme exposed him to the northern wilderness and its wildlife and inspired many of his paintings. He has travelled extensively from Baffin Island, Resolute Bay and Victoria Island to the southern regions of the Upper Taltson River, photographing and sketching the wildreness for future paintings. Potapoff considers his field studies, rendered in pen and ink, pencil and watercolour, to be his most important tool in capturing the initial, intimate connection with the natural world.

Fig. 8. *Peter Potapoff. "Alphine Grandeur - Big Horn Sheep", 1994.*
17" x 22". Acyrlic on masonite.

Inspired by such notable landscape and wildlife artists as John Seerey-
-Lester and Robert Bateman, Potapoff developed his own unique realistic
style. His success encouraged him to produce two limited-edition prints:

Morning solitude—Moose, the
subject of significant public
acclaim, and *Late-morning
getaway,* a sold-out print
depicting a 'bush plane' in
the North. Since then, he has
produced several more successful prints, such as
Sandhill Crane, which earned
him the title of the B.C.
Wildlife Federation's 1997
'Artist of the Year'. His
prints have been purchased
by private collectors in Canada, America and Europe.

*Fig. 9. Peter Potapoff. "Twilight Admirer —
Sandhill Crane", 1996.
24" x 18". Acrylic on masonite.*

All this success enabled Potapoff to relocate with his family to the
Kootenays in 1989. He continues to depict local wildlife to help make
people more aware of the need to protect the natural environment and its
creatures. He was recently chosen 1998 Artist of the Year by Ducks Un-
limited Canada for his portrayal of a pair of Canada geese entitled
Snowed in.

Peter Potapoff lives with his wife Eleanor (and their two children
Katie and Ian) in Castlegar, where he juggles his time between family,
forestry work and painting.

> As a visual arist, I am most influenced by what I see and experience in na-
> ture. I'm forever fascinated with the seemingly endless forms, textures and
> designs that surround me everywhere I look. With constantly changing

light conditions, there is no end to the possible compositions out there to challenge my creativity. — *Peter Potapoff*

Jan Kabatoff

Born in Nelson, B.C. in 1948, Jan Kabatoff (*née* Janet Gevatkow) spent her early childhood years in a Sons-of-Freedom community in nearby Krestova, and later attended school in Castlegar.

As a young girl, Jan was taught basic needlework skills by her aunts and grandmother. Even at an early age, however, she preferred the freedom of drawing on any surface she could find, rather than follow a prescribed pattern. At age thirteen she received her first set of oil paints from her father, Joe Gevatkow, who supported her persistent interest in art. The encouragement and support she received from her teachers at school motiated her to develop her art over the years through numerous evening classes and summer workshops in British Columbia, Alberta and Saskatchewan.

After moving to Alberta in 1972, Kabatoff pursued a career in respiratory technology, receiving a diploma from the Southern Alberta Institute of Technology in 1976. While she intended to go on to art school at some point, it was not until 1991, after raising a family, owning and managing a gift shop in Bragg Creek (just outside Calgary), where she received considerable acclaim for her exquisitely rendered nature studies in watercolour, that she finally enrolled as a painting major at the Alberta College of Art and Design in Calgary. A recipient of several scholarships and awards, she graduated with a Diploma in Fine Art in 1995, and a Bachelor of Fine Arts degree in 1996.

Among the many influences on her art, she is especially cognisant of the support she received from the arts-and-craftsoriented community of Bragg Creek. In particular, the encouragement she received from Stan Parrott, a local artist and retired Dean of the Alberta College of Art, greatly increased both her confidence and her resolve to become a serious artist, and eventually led to her enrolment in art school.

Drawing upon the intensely creative and supportive academic environment, Kabatoff was finally able to realise her dream of depicting her Doukhobor heritage in a contemporary way. She produced a series of large linen wall-hangings honouring the textile skills of Doukhobor women and the oral tradition with which she grew up. Using her own hand-dyed linen and incorporating stitched photographic images, needlework and text into her creations, Kabatoff told her own story about the Doukhobors' roots in the Russian language, their emphasis on prayer, their relationship to nature and their strong sense of community. In 1995 this body of work became part of a four-woman touring exhibition she co-curated, entitled *Our Doukhobor Heritage/Contemporary Reflections.*

*Fig. 10. .Jan Kabatoff. "I remember, I forgot...", 1996. 22" x 30".
Mixed media on paper.*

Jan Kabatoff lives in Bragg Creek with her husband Alex and their two children Tara and Mathew, who share their mother's interest in art. Working out of her home studio in a variety of media, she continues to portray the local natural surroundings for which she has always had an affinity, along with her Doukhobor heritage, sometimes touching upon issues of cultural change.

> One of my biggest challenges has been to honour my creative impulse and trust my innter guidance, amidst life's many distractions and responsibilities. It is in that moment of creativity and total focus that I feel most connected to self and the Divine in all things. — *Jan Kabatoff*

*Fig. 11. Jan Kabatoff. "Toil and Peaceful Life", 1995. 4' x 6'.
Silk screen on linen. Hand-dyed textile.*

Volga Wright

A native of Nelson, B.C., (b. 1954), Volga Wright (*née* Jmaiff) has spent most of her life in the Doukhobor community of Krestova. After completing high school in Crescent Valley, B.C.,Volga went on to take a secretarial course, but continued to pursue her love of painting, portraying the Doukhobor feminine form as a personal and emotional expression.

In the late 1980s Wright had an opportunity to experiment with glass. She immediately felt a kinship and a familiarity with this medium and with the support of her husband and family set up a studio in her home. Primarily self-taught, she produces of variety stained-glass works, from small ornaments and suncatchers to lamps, clocks, windows and doors. She has also been successful in integrating glass with painting, devising her own unique method of sandwiching a painting between two sheets of glass.

Over the years Wright has earned herself a solid reputation in the Doukhobor and Kootenay communities, leading to an expanded studio, hired help and numerous commissions from both Canada and the United States. Currently working with an architect on designing large-scale projects for various points on the continent, she also participates in solo and group exhibitions in the Kootenays.

Volga Wright continues to live in Krestova with her husband Jim (who serves as her mechanical/technical assistant) and their two children James and Kenneth.

Fig. 12. Mabel Verigin. All wool hand-woven tapestry (palas) inspired by Doukhobor rug motifs, on linen warp, 1993. 26" x 43".

James Fillipoff

James Fillipoff was born in Penticton, B.C., in 1960. Interested in art at a very early age, young James was first influenced by Marvel comics and later, as an art student, by Michelangelo. In 1982 he was awarded a Bachelor of Fine Arts degree by Mount Allison University in Sackville, New Brunswick.

Fillipoff has proved himself a highly skilled artist in both watercolour and drawing, capable of expressing the finest degree of detail. He has been successful as a commissioned illustrator of heritage buildings, nautical themes and townscapes. More recently he has been exploring figurative work through the medium of clay, which has earned him an ward at the National Capital Fine Arts Festival in Ottawa.

Most of his commissions come from Ontario, some from the United States. He is currently exhibiting in Ontario and British Columbia, as well as abroad in Boston and New York.

James Fillipoff maintains his studio in Lanark, Ont., where, as a dedicated family man, he lives an idyllic country life with his wife Shelley and their four children.

With the world changing so fast, it seems as though a pause, a thoughtful moment, might be interpreted as negative, inactive. I try to capture that peaceful, reflective and often provocative time and condense it into something essential. If I'm successful, the result will open the eye, much like good music opens the ear, and frees the soul. — *James Fillipoff*

Fig. 13. *James Fillipoff. "Harvard"*
Lowell House Tower, 1992.
18" x 72". Water colour.

George Koochin

George Christopher Koochin was born in Castlegar, B.C., in 1966. He grew up in the Doukhobor commu nity in nearby Brilliant, where from an early age he participated in community cultural traditions.

His artistic bent was evident even in his youth, when he explored different ideas and media by constructing objects out of wood and other materials. But when he began his post-secondary education at Selkirk College (Castlegar) in 1984 , he was actually thinking of making a career in the sciences, in particular, astronomy.

After his first year at Selkirk, however, he decided to study Russian at the Kiev State Pedagogical Institute in Ukraine. It was here, surrounded by masterpieces of Slavic and Western European art, that he discovered his true passion for painting. After returning to Canada and graduating from the Graphic Communications Programme at Selkirk College, he worked for a time as a graphic artist in Vancouver. Later he decided to go to Russia and enrol in the Repin Institute of Painting, Sculpture and Architecture in St-Petersburg, receiving a 'Candidate's' art degree (Master's equivalent), with a specialisation in painting, in 1995.

Koochin's total immersion in Rus-sian culture and its secular, folk and religious art, along with the rigorous discipline of the classical training he received, has enabled him to produce a number of exceptional figurative

works, especially in the portrayal of the female nude. Currently, he is rediscovering the local Kootenay landscape. Both his paintings and pen- -and-ink drawings seem to have captured the depth and richness of his natural sur- roundings, as well as the area's history.

Fig. 14. George Koochin. "Birth", l995. 200 cm. x 200 cm. Oil on canvas.

George Koochin lives with his Russian bride, Irina, in Brilliant, where he continues to develop his career in art, participating in both local and provincial exhibitions.

The form is the content — art must be able to speak for itself. I am interested in art that offers something of long-lasting value to the Universe, and strives to make it better. — *George Koochin*

Polly Faminow

Born in Victoria in 1953, Polly Faminow has spent most of her life in and around Vancouver. Both she and her sister *Megan* showed a childhood interest in art, no doubt influenced by their mother, *Frances Faminow*, an American-born artist. In 1976 Polly received a diploma in print-making from the Vancouver School of Art (now the Emily Carr Institute of Art and Design) and subsequently completed two years in Fine Arts at the University of British Columbia. Since then she has been the recipient of several grants and scholarship awards.

Polly Faminow's expertise lies in the highly technical process of lithography, which is often very laborious and timeconsuming. Her prints, filled with dream-like plants, animals and people, have a unique and imaginative quality. Inspired by such artists as Kandinsky, Picasso and Klee, Faminow derives her imagery from the natural world of organic shapes and colours.

More recently she has begun to explore her Doukhobor heritage. One result has been a series of finely crafted, life-size *papier-mâché* skirts, styled after early Doukhobor designs. These skirts, along with pastel drawings of early Doukhobor pioneers in the province, were included in a group exhibition entitled *Our Doukhobor Heritage/Contemporary Reflections*, which toured British Columbia in 1995–96.

Fig. 15. *Polly Faminow. "Skirt for Fenya", 1995.*
Height 40".
Paper mache sculpture.

Faminow's work has been shown in many other group and solo exhibitions both in British Columbia and Ontario, and is now in a

significant number of private collectors. As an Outreach Instructor with Vancouver's Emily Carr Institute of Art and Design, she has spent many years conducting workshops in printmaking and drawing for adults and children in remote parts of the province. Since 1994 she has been teaching children's art at the Shadbolt Centre for the Arts in Burnaby (near Vancouver).

Polly Faminow currently resides just outside Vancouver in White Rock, where she works out of a home studio in a variety of media.

Fig. 16. Polly Faminow. "Waiting", 1995. 20" x 15". Charcoal and pastel drawing.

A lot has been written about the Doukhobors, but very little has been said about them in visual terms. Creating new images around the Doukhobor heritage at this point in time could have a great deal of impact in creating a bridge for more understanding to occur regarding a group which has been widely misunderstood. — *Polly Faminow*

Catherine Perehudoff

Catherine Perehudoff was born in Saskatoon in 1958 to two distinguished artists: Dorothy Knowles, best known for her portrayal of the Saskatchewan landscape, and William Perehudoff, whose career in abstract art is detailed above. From an early age she seemed destined to become an artist in her own right.

Her educational credentials include a B.F.A. in Art History from the University of Saskatchewan, a teaching certificate from the University of Alberta, numerous art courses and workshops in Alberta, Saskatchewan and Norway, as well as Museum studies throughout Europe, the Middle East and the United States.

Perehudoff has received considerable acclaim for her ethereal land-scapes, most of them painted on site in Saskatchewan, Alberta and British Columbia in watercolour or acrylics. She has successfully exhibited in solo and group shows since 1979, in major cities across the country as well as abroad in Chicago and New York. Her progress has been favourably reviewed over the years by a variety of publications.

Fig. 17. *Catherine Perehudoff. "Birch Bay", 1994. 30" x 40".*
Acrylic on canvas.

Fig. 18. *Catherine Perehudoff. "Annie", 1994. 18" x 24". Acrylic on canvas.*

More recently, Perehudoff participated in a four-woman group show entitled *Our Doukhobor Heritage/Contemporary Reflections.* Her contribution was an extensively researched and poignant documentary film on five Doukhobor women, entitled *Write it on the heart,* celebrating the Doukhobor Centenary of the Burning of Arms. The five women speak as mothers, whose views on pacifism have a universal appeal to all parents of children threatened with conscription. The portrait paintings supplementing the video further evoke the sensitivitiy, pride and pensive mood of each woman. Together with her partner in the project, June Morgan, Perehudoff received Best Documentary and First Production awards at the 1995 Saskatchewan Film and Video Showcase.

Catherine Perehudoff is not alone in carrying on her family's artistic legacy: she has also participated in several group shows with her sisters Carol and Rebecca. Having earned an M.F.A. at the University of Alberta, *Carol Perehudoff* won a business scholarship to Yonsey University in Seoul, South Korea, where she has remained to teach English and develop her painting career. *Rebecca Perehudoff* has both a Bachelor of Arts and a law degree from the University of Saskatchewan; now living abroad in Chicago with her husband and daughter, she has been painting full time since 1987, and has shown her work extensively in both countries.

A recipient of a number of awards and commissions, Catherine Perehudoff is appreciated by collectors in Canada, the United States and Europe. Most notable are federal and provincial gifts to Her Majesty Queen Elizabeth II, the Queen Mother, the Lord Archbishop of Canterbury, Mrs Andrei Gromyko and Mrs Laurent Fabius.

Catherine Perehudoff currently resides in Saskatoon with her artist-husband, Graham Fowler, and their young son.

Alana Kapell

Alana Kapell is a native of Canora, Sask. (b. 1948). Raised in a Catholic and Doukhobor environment, she received her education in Regina, obtaining a Bachelor of Arts degree and a teaching certificate from the University of Regina in 1971. She subsequently moved to Kingston, Ontario, where she spent many years teaching at a community college and recently became one of the founders of the Kingston School of Art.

Her Doukhobor grandmother, *Ann Hoodecoff,* as well as her Doukhobor aunts, inspired Kapell to incorporate Doukhobor culture into her art work. She has attempted to integrate Doukhobor philosophy with her Catholic upbringing, addressing such issues as the power of symbols in both religions. Her portrayal of the garden, for example, speaks of the meditative and spiritual qualities of gardens and their importance in her own life as well as in Doukhobor culture.

Kapell works comfortably in a variety of media, such as beeswax, oil paints, watercolour and wood. She also did a personal exploration in video, depicting her grandmother's Doukhobor traditions of needlework, textiles and foods.

Fig. 19. Alana Kapell. "Baba Yaga Makes Borshch", 1995. 30" x 57". Mixed medium.

Alana Kapell has participated in several cross-Canada group shows, including *Our Doukhobor Heritage/Contemporary Reflections,* which toured British Columbia in 1995–96. Her recent solo exhibition in Kingston, entitled *Baba Yaga Flies Over Saskatchewan,* was especially well received.

> In my current work I focus on the interplay of traditional and folk art with non-traditional and contemporary visual arts. Colour is of prime importance. The texture of mixed media — e.g., tin, fabric, wood, needlepoint — contrasted with the two-dimensional surface of watercolour, fascinates me.
> —*Alana Kapell*

Brad Chernoff

Born to Doukhobor and Italian parents in Burnaby, B.C., in 1963, Brad Chernoff has spent most of life on the west coast. He studied at Fraser Valley College and majored in painting at the Emily Carr College (now 'Institute') of Art and Design in Vancouver. His interest in his Doukhobor ancestry and especially the Doukhobor concept of spirituality has been a contributing factor in his paintings, which deal with architectural symbols of the past and present and their relationship to modern architecture. His large-scale acrylic paintings reflect contemporary times

as well as political issues such as the replacement of religious and spiritual centres by monolithic corporate structures, along with the disappearance of heritage buildings. His strong abstractions of urban ar-chitecture convey an urgency to examine the rapidly changing urban environment and a need to integrate the new with the old in a meaningful way.

Fig. 20. Brad Chernoff. "West Coast Energy", 1991.
51" x 48". Acrylic on canvas.

Over the years these powerful works, shown in numerous group exhibitions in and around Vancouver, have established Chernoff as one of the city's finest emerging artists.

More recently Chernoff has begun to explore the history of Doukhobor quilting and folk art, incorporating fragments of paintings and photographs into a cohesive collage, over which he subsequently applies paint.

After owning and managing a successful gallery and framing/art-supply business for many years, Brad Chernoff has scaled it down to just a framing service, in order to devote more time to his family and his art, especially to the artistic exploration of his Doukhobor heritage. He lives with his wife Doris and their young children in Vancouver.

Tamara Ewashen

Tamara Ewashen was born in Calgary in 1965, where she received all her education, including a diploma in painting from the Alberta College of Art in 1987. She has since done extensive museum tours to London, New York and San Francisco.

Her work involves a variety of materials — wood, metal, paint, wax, photocopies, ink etc. — which she applies over a period of time to create organic layers of colours, images, textures and words. This labour-intensive process constitutes a type of narrative and exploration of various concerns playing in the artist's mind, triggered by particular happenings or observations. The subtly manipulated, sensuous objects that result from this process are designed to evoke unexpected thoughts and questions in the mind of the viewer.

Ewashen has had numerous local exhibitions of her paintings, and has been critically reviewed in several publications. Her work may be found in private collections throughout Alberta.

Fig. 21. Tamara Ewashen. "Memory",
1991. 13 cm x 13 cm x 2 cm.
Wood, metal, acrylic, acetate, graphite.

Ewashen has been actively involved in Calgary's art community for many years. For five years she was an artist's model at the Alberta College of Art. She has also served as coordinator of exhibitions at the Night Gallery Cabaret, and administrator of the Second Storey Gallery.

Tamara Ewashen recently relocated to Vancouver, where she continues to pursue her love of painting, while volunteering at artrelated events.

> Throughout the process of building these objects, I am exploring a sensibility derived from the colloquial, the local, the actual. My work is tied to the specificity of my own life. It draws from my experiences and my varied perceptions of them: from the music, the art and the books that I respond to; and from the people I know; rather than from an abstracted or generalised intent. — *Tamara Ewashen*

*   *   *

Photography

Since the mid-nineteenth century photography has provided artists with a substitute for carefully executed field sketches, which can then be translated onto canvas in full detail in the studio. In this role it has had a profound effect on painting, from impressionism to photorealism.

In addition, it has become not only a significant recording device but also an art-form in its own right — in both cases one of the most powerful tools of communication in the world today. Despite the fact that it is generally taken for granted, it has had a profound influence on our society: it has revealed to us 'moments of truth' and preserved for us a sense of history, along with entertaining and educating us (Arnason, 1986).

Koozma J. Tarasoff

Koozma J. Tarasoff was born in 1932 to parents of Doukhobor background living on a farm in the Langham district of Saskatchewan. After completing school in his native province, he obtained a Bachelor of Arts at the University of Saskatchewan in Saskatoon, and then went on to the University of British Columbia, where he later completed an M.A. in Sociology and Anthropology.

He has since become a leading historian on the Canadian Doukhobors. His writings and photographs portray to the world the Doukhobor spirit of community, peace and hard work, and constitute an invaluable textual and pictorial resource for future generations.

Koozma's early introduction to the art of photography came through his father, who worked with a folding Eastman camera and also did darkroom processing. Primarily self-taught, Koozma Tarasoff developed his skills in photography as editor of the first Doukhobor English-language publication — *The Inquirer* — in the mid-to late 1950s, and while working as an anthropologist/ethnographer.

In his role as an historian, Tarasoff collected old Doukhobor photographic prints. These, together with some of his own pictures of Doukhobor society, comprise the Tarasoff Photo Collection on Doukhobor history in the B.C. Public Archives in Victoria, the largest of its kind. In 1994 he donated another collection of old photos, manuscripts and tape-recordings documenting Doukhobor history to the Saskatchewan Public Archives, where they are known as the 'Tarasoff papers'.

Tarasoff's avid interest in both photography and Doukhobor history have led to several pictorial publications: *Pictorial history of the Doukhobors* (1969), *Traditional Doukhobor folkways* (1977) and *Plakun trava. The Doukhobors* (1982). Tarasoff has authored a significant entry on the Doukhobors for *An Encyclopædia of Canada's peoples* and served as one of several historical consultant for an hour-long film on the Doukhobors: *In Search of Utopia*. He has also served as Associate Guest Curator of the Doukhobor exhibit at the Canadian Museum of Civilization near Ottawa, where he resides.

Fig. 22. Koozma J. Tarasoff, "Jim Deacove, founder of Family Pastimes Co-operative Games", Perth, Ontario", Sept. 12, 1981. Photograph in black and white 8" x 10".

In his many writings and talks across Canada and abroad, as well as in his photographic career, Koozma Tarasoff continues to prove an eminent spokesman and champion of the Doukhobor cause, their philosophies and spiritual convictions.

What is art? For me, art is passion, art is enjoyment, and art is a creative combination that works. Art brings together elements that we see, hear or feel so as to give colour and meaning to the spirit of life.— *Koozma Tarasoff*

Edward Chernoff

Edward (Ed) John Chernoff was born to a Doukhobor family in Vancouver in 1951, but grew up in the Okanagan Valley. After graduating from high school there, he spent a year at the University of Victoria before enrolling in Ryerson Polytechnic Institute in Toronto. He completed three years of media studies there, including film-making and photography, receiving his Diploma in 1975.

Edward's early interest in photography was inspired by his artist-

mother *Florence,* and later solidified by a trip to Europe in the early 1970s. He found himself fascinated by the ability of the still camera to capture the 'decisive moment', as well as by the power of a documentary photograph to convey a personal testimony or to tell a story. He owes his greatest inspiration to such photographers as Henri Cartier-Bresson, Eugene Smith and Denis Reggie (a celebrity wedding photographer with whom he took a workshop in 1995).

Fig. 23. Ed Chernoff. "Anna Markova and Friends", August 17, 1975. Photograph in black and white 8" x 10" silverprint.

Naturally drawn to the Doukhobors' history and their sense of community spirit, Chernoff moved to the Kootenays in 1975, where, while working as a programme manager for community television, he began a photographic project on the Doukhobor community. This work is still in progress as he continues to photograph or videotape various Doukhobor events throughout the Kootenays. He focuses primarily on the 'human condition', endeavouring to capture on film the personal strengths and weaknesses of his subjects.

Chernoff is frequently consulted for his professional expertise by people in the community. In addition to working for Shaw Cable, he has operated his own photography and video business for the past fifteen years. His home studio is equipped with a darkroom and a video-editing suite.

Ed Chernoff lives with his wife Denise and their children Chris and Aimie in Ooteshenie (near Castlegar).

Donna Guillemin

Born in Claresholm, Alberta, in 1957, Donna Marie Guillemin moved to the Kootenays with her family when she was eight. While attending school in Castlegar she sang in the local Doukhobor youth choir. Her post-secondary education began with an arts-and-science university transfer programme at Selkirk College, followed by a B.A. in English from the University of British Columbia, specialising in twentieth--century poetics and semantics.

Donna's early-childhood influence in art was provided by her mother, *Mabel Plotnikoff,* who was extremely creative with needlework, baking and gardening. Her grandmother, *Nora Plotnikoff,* accomplished in the art of weaving, gardening and folk medicine, contributed significantly to her later interest in gardening and plant essence. She eventually earned a Master Gardener certificate from the Van Dusen Botanical Gardens in Vancouver, and studied plant--essence medicine in the American state of Washington.

As a primarily self-taught photographer, many years ago Guillemin undertook an ongoing documentary study of the Doukhobor people and the richness of their culture, seeking and acknowledging the divine spark in all people and things. Preferring black-and-white photography for its simplicity, directness and ability to communicate the unspoken, she captures, among other subjects, the female Doukhobor form in all its intimacy and vulnerability.

Fig. 24. Donna Guillemin. Three women in traditional costumes, 1984. Photograph in black and white.

Guillemin has shown her work in numerous solo and group exhibitions in British Columbia, as well as abroad in California. Her most notable exhibit, entitled *What You Need, Gain Through Work,* was shown in several B.C. locations in conjunction with the touring art exhibition *Our Doukhobor Heritage/Contemporary Reflections.*

Donna Guillemin lives with her husband Bart and their two sons Yuri and Kai in Delta (just south of Vancouver). As an avid gardener interested in exploring local native plants for their healing qualities, she strives to live in harmony with nature through prayer, song and gratitude.

> I remember walking through a field one day, like Alice in Wonderland, simply following my nose. I climbed through a broken piece of fence and was surprised to hear someone ask, *Ch'ia?* (Who are you?). Because the Russian voice momentarily displaced me from my English identity, I answered, without thinking, in Russian: *Ty znala moyu babushku, Nastiu Plotnikovu?* (Did you know my grandmother, Nora Plotnikoff?) Any barrier that might have existed, simply disappeared. In that moment, I gratefully received the gift of ancestorship and what it meant to belong to a people. — *Donna Guillemin*

Other artists and artisans

The artists profiled in this paper, some of whom are more prominent than others, represent only a fraction of the many creative and talented people of Doukhobor heritage. Unfortunately, time and space did not allow more of them to be described; those whose creative efforts also merit acknowledgement include the following:

- *Florence (Chernoff) Lymburner,* of Seattle (Washington), USA, who has taught painting for many years. One of her more notable works, entitled *Spring 1900,* portraying Doukhobor women pulling a plough, was painted to commemorate the 1995 Centenary of the Burning of Arms.

- *Ginger Webster* (née *Vera Ann Malakoff*), of High River, Alberta, a self--taught painter and creator of realistic hand-made dolls, fashioned out of recycled materials to represent certain human characteristics and personalities (for example, a Doukhobor couple in traditional costume).

- *John Kabatoff* of Calgary (originally from the Kootenays), a wedding photographer who now photographs wildlife and supplies an agency with stock photos of nature.

- *Harry Soloveoff,* of Castlegar, an architectural designer trained at the Emily Carr College (now 'Institute') of Art and Design in Vancouver. A painter in his spare time, he has designed numerous buildings in the Kootenay area using Doukhobor historical motifs.

*　　　　*　　　　*

Summary

This research on artists of Doukhobor heritage has taken me to many studios and other interesting places, and I have always been welcomed with that warm Doukhobor hospitality. Even in conducting interviews with artists by telephone, I felt that same sincerity and willingness to tell their story. Through this project I have met many a kindred spirit and have formed deep and lasting friendships. I feel privileged to share what I have learnt about these artists' abilities and achievements with others.

I found it both fascinating and heartwarming to discover that the effect of the Doukhobor culture has left its imprint on even the most 'remote' Doukhobors—that is, those who have been away from Doukhobor communities for many years who have had just one parent of Doukhobor background.

The Doukhobor philosophy of 'toil and peaceful life' continues to prevail in these artists, who, for the most part, are pacifists, humanitarians and spiritual thinkers, greatly appreciative of their heritage and history. Invariably, they exhibit a strong work ethic and strive for excellence in their chosen field.

As with our Doukhobor ancestors, whose folk art assimilated and adapted outside influences, my research has not uncovered any specific art form that is uniquely Doukhobor. Taken collectively, however, the work of these artists speaks of the ability to adapt to a variety of influences, from a strong ethnic culture to mainstream society. Their styles range from nonreferential abstract expression to landscape and portraiture and the recording of their ethnic and cultural heritage, and involve many kinds of media: sculpture, painting, video, stained glass, photography, textiles and printmaking.

By presenting a brief (albeit simplified) historical background I hope I have provided a glimpse into some of the influences on the careers of Doukhobor artists living today — influences that have come both from Doukhobor culture itself and from the process of adapting to a broader dominant society.

Influence, of course, can work in both directions. As one artist expressed it:

By living in the mainstream society I have not robbed the Doukhobor culture as much as I have shared it with those that I have come in contact with.

Acknowledgements

I am grateful to Koozma Tarasoff for giving me this opportunity to connect with fellow-artists of Doukhobor heritage and for his confidence in my research capabilities. I also thank Amy Gogarty and Amy Garneau (both artists and instructors at the Alberta College of Art and Design), as well as Elaine Rathie (a kindred spirit), for editing various parts of the manuscript. In particular, I wish to thank my husband Alex and my children Tara and Mathew for the support and patience they have shown me — both during my travels and over the many hours I have spent at my desk.

Bibliography

Alpatov, M.W. (1967). *Art treasures of Russia.* New York: Abrams.

Arnason, H.H. (1986). *History of modern art — painting, sculpting, architecture and photography,* 3rd ed. New York: Abrams.

Bird, Alan (1987). *A History of Russian painting.* Boston: Hall.

Bringhurst, Robert, Geoffrey James, Russell Kezière and Doris Shadbolt (1983). *Visions.* Vancouver: Douglas & McIntyre.

Burnham, Dorothy (1986). *Unlike the lilies — Doukhobor textile traditions in Canada.* Toronto: Royal Ontario Museum.

Fenton, Terry (1984). 'Western Canada and the Emma Lake Workshops'. *Update* (magazine of the Edmonton Art Gallery), Jan/Feb 1984.

Fenton, Terry (1993). *William Perehudoff.* Saskatoon: The Mendel Art Gallery.

Forrest, Kevin (1981a). 'The Paintings of Frederick Nicholas Loveroff'. Exhibition catalogue, Norman MacKenzie Gallery, Univ. of Regina.

——— (1981b). 'F.N. Loveroff — Legend of the twenties revisited'. *Artswest* (Calgary), vol. 6, nº 10.

Graham, Archie (1991). 'The Recovery of the well-crafted piece'. *North Shore News,* 19 June 1991.

Grenville, Bruce (1990). 'William Perehudoff — paintings of the sixties'. *Show catalogue.*

Reid, Bill (1980). 'Bill Koochin'. *Show catalogue,* Burnaby Art Gallery (Burnaby, B.C.)

Reid, Dennis (1988). *A Concise history of Canadian painting,* 2nd ed. Toronto: Oxford.

Sulerzhitsky, L.A. *V Ameriku s dukhoborami.* Moscow: Posrednik, 1905. English translation by Michael Kalmakoff: *To America with the Doukhobors.* Regina: Canadian Plains Research Centre, 1982.

Tarasoff, Koozma J. (1969). *Pictorial history of the Doukhobors.* Saskatoon: Western Producer/Prairie Books.

————— (1977). *Traditional Doukhobor folkways. An Ethnographic and biographic record of prescribed behaviour.* Ottawa: National Museums of Canada. Series: Canadian Centre for Folk Culture Studies, Paper n° 20.

————— (1982). *Plakun trava. The Doukhobors.* Grand Forks, B.C.: MIR Publication Society.

Tippett, Maria (1990). 'Focus on Bill Koochin'. *Canadian Art* (summer issue).

Doukhobor stars in the sports world

Peter F. Chernoff

It is logical to assume that among the Doukhobors the first sports to develop were a natural outgrowth, or extension, of everyday living. For example, horses were raised for power and transportation. The Doukhobors always took pride in their agriculture and animal husbandry. They owned many fine animals. Quality animals, careful training and superior horsemanship were assets in co-existing with their frontier neighbours. One can easily imagine how equestrian sports developed and became accepted. As rodeos increased in popularity in the Canadian West, Doukhobors also entered the competitions. In fact, in the 1920s and 1930s a Doukhobor saddle-bronc rider in North America won the World Championship four times.

All settlements need access to water, and lakes and rivers provide a natural venue for aquatic sports. Even recreational swimming often takes on a competitive aspect. My grandmother, *Polly Konkin* (*née Chutskoff,* from Spasovka village), told many stories of winning swimming races in the 1890s.

> Sometimes, [she would say,] someone would bring a swimmer from a far-away village, or even from a non-Doukhobor community, supposedly to visit. I always knew they really came to have a race. Often you heard that a particular visitor was reputed to be an exceptional swimmer. But I always beat them all!

She raced males and females, informally, using the breaststroke. Almost a hundred years later, a great-grandson of hers, *Rob Chernoff,* set Canadian records in breastroke and represented Canada and the Olympic and Commonwealth Games, as well as at the World Championships and many other international swimming competitions.

Running races and jumping were natural pastimes during picnics. Sprinting skills were also very useful for pacifistic survival. Old Doukhobor men told a story of particular interest from pre-emigration days. Pasture land in the Caucasus was often located near Tatar settlements, and when cattle or horses would inadvertently stray too near someone's garden, the owner would run out to apprehend their youthful herders. The latter in time developed a skill for survival: a horse was trained so that a youth could grab hold of its tail, set it to running, and then sprint to escape from his pursuers. To be caught meant severe punishment. No medal was needed to encourage a good performance!

An early favourite group game was called *v gilki*. It was played with a bat or a suitable willow stick called a *gilka,* and any convenient ball, like a softball. Home-made balls were made by stuffing a canvas cover with horsehair. Any number of players participated and any playground or pasture made a good playing field. Two circles eight to ten metres apart were scratched into the ground (these served a similar purpose to 'home plate' and 'first base' in baseball). There were no teams. While two players were at bat, the remainder comprised a designated catcher, a pitcher, a first-baseman and any number of fielders. The game began with a batter inside one circle, to whom the ball was pitched, through the circle (as in 'slow-pitch' softball). Once a 'hit' was made, the batter could score a point by running to the other circle, touching the ground (with the bat) and then running back to the first circle. More than one point might be attempted if the ball had been hit sufficiently far.

The batter was 'out' if a flyball was caught, if he was tagged by the ball, if he was struck by a thrown ball while running between bases, or if he was forced out at either circle. If the ball was thrown at the runner, he could protect himself using the bat. In case of a short 'hit', a runner could wait in the second circle until the next batter brought him 'home'. Once the batter was 'out', he went to the last outfield position. Everyone moved up a place. The catcher became the new batter, and so on. Anyone could join the game, even after it had begun, by becoming the last outfielder. The game went on until everyone had a turn at bat, or it became too dark to play, or it was time to go home. *V gilki* lost its appeal as the games of softball and baseball were adopted in Canada.

Over the years many primarily Doukhobor teams have distinguished themselves in various sports. One soccer-football team from Langham, Saskatchewan, entered a tournament in Saskatoon (probbably in the 1920s or 1930s). The Doukhobors did not even have team uniforms, while their opponents were a smartly-attired Winnipeg bunch, full of self-confidence — the league leaders back home. Needless to say, the work-conditioned farm boys from Langham gave a sound licking to the Winnipeg side.

Spring sports days were sponsored by many towns and villages in Western Canada, and Doukhobor groups often entered the baseball tournaments which were organised as part of the festivities. To this writer's knowledge, no exclusively Doukhobor leagues were ever set up, and any local non-Doukhobors were always welcome to join a team. The Doukhobors won their fair share of exhibition matches which were sometimes arranged with touring teams, including some from the United States of America. Our editor, *Koozma Tarasoff*, along with his brother, father and uncles, formed the nucleus of one such baseball team in the 1940s. An indication of the high skill-level developed by many of the team participants is that some of them were invited to attend training camps sponsored by the National and American baseball leagues. While attending the training camp of the Pittsburgh Pirates, Koozma once met the famous Ty Cobb.

Hockey and curling were natural winter sports, and many individuals took up both games. One notable curler, *Mike Chernoff* of Calgary, played third on a team skipped by Ed Lukowich, but threw 'last rocks'. In 1978 this team won the Macdonald Brier Canadian Curling Championship and then went on to play in the final at the World's. While they lost that game by a small margin, Mike was selected the outstanding third on the all-star team.

In Canada, the Doukhobors, who have not migrated for ninety years, have prospered as never before. Athletes of Doukhobor descent have pursued their interests and aptitudes in every sporting activity imaginable. While there are many teams and individuals that deserve mention here, accurate documentation is difficult, and often impossible, to obtain. Those described below are Doukhobor athletes who have reached a particularly high level (sometimes world-class) in their chosen sport.

Peter Knight — world champion saddle-bronc rider

Pete Knight (my father's first cousin) was born 3 May 1903 in Pennsylvania. When he was still a small boy, his family moved to a mixed farm and stock ranch near Crossfield, Alberta, where one of his youthful pastimes was to saddle up the work-horses and make them buck. When one stopped, he would try another, sometimes riding as many as eight or ten in one afternoon. When a horse was bucking vigorously, Pete would often jump off, almost always landing on his feet. Before he turned twelve he had 'broken' his first saddle-pony, and was soon breaking horses for the neighbours.

Pete was described as a modest man who possessed the grace of a cat and the strength of Atlas. There was no horse that he ever feared, and he could easily calm the most nervous animal. Handling a six-horse team was no problem for him. He was not a big man; at age twenty he is reported by neighbours to have weighed 156 pounds [= 71 kg] (Davis, 1976: 11).

Pete's nephew Ray is quoted as saying (*ibid.*, 29):

> Pete was always a real stickler for being in top physical condition. He used to carry a set of chest expanders in his suitcase. The average person could stretch them out a time or two. Pete could pull them all the way a hundred times.

Norman Edge, a rodeo contestant, comments on Pete's physical conditioning and strength (*ibid.*, 27):

Fig. 1. World champion saddle bronco rider Pete Knight. 1930s.

Not many men can chin themselves with one hand — using either the right or left — but Pete could. He would reach above a door, catch the frame with only the tips of his fingers, and chin himself 5 or 6 times — not showing off, just doing the exercise.

Frank Sharp also recalls (*ibid.*, 19):

I'll tell you what Pete had. He had strong arms. He could chin himself with one hand 'til you got tired of watchin' him. I don't think there ever was a guy his size that had strength in his arms like he had.

In addition to staying in top physical condition, Pete stayed away from alcohol. He is quoted by his neighbour as saying: 'I hate whisky. I hate beer. I hate milk and I hate cows' (*ibid.*, 14).

Pete had a very positive attitude about winning. He *knew* he was going to ride every horse. The following tribute by Eddie Woods bears this out (*ibid.*, 27):

He was a bronc rider who just knew he was going to win. There never ever was any doubt in his mind. And danged if he didn't almost make believers out of all of us other bronc riders. ... Over the years I won second place behind Pete so many times that after a while, I quit counting. One year — while I was still counting — I was in for second behind Pete sixteen times.

Pete was also known to be a generous and extremely honest man. He never turned down a pal in need — he believed that there had to be contestants around in order to have a good rodeo. His honesty is evidenced during one of the Crossfield rodeos in the early 1920s. As the judges were debating about Pete's ride, one of them proposed putting the question to Pete himself: 'Did you lose a stirrup on that last ride?' 'Yep', came the answer, 'I sure did' (*ibid.*, 24).

Pete's rodeo career began in 1918 when he entered his first rodeo at Crossfield at age fifteen. He won second-place money of $60 on each of the two days, adequate pocket-money for a young lad. Between 1918 and 1923 he mainly worked on the family ranch and entered only local rodeos.

In 1923, while riding at one of the five rodeos he entered that year (he won all five), he was spotted by Calgary Stampede manager Guy Weadick. Accepting an invitation to participate, Pete went to Calgary and rode in the opening parade. But on leaving the parade his horse spooked and slipped on the freshly hosed-down intersection of Ninth Avenue and Centre Street, breaking Pete's ankle against the curb, denying him even a single ride in the Stampede that year. He returned the following year (in spite of a still stiff ankle), but though his final ride on a horse called 'Alberta Kid' made him a clear winner in the eyes of the spectators, the judges, much to everyone's consternation, awarded the trophy to a rival with a score of 89.73 to 89.70 (Gray, 1985; Weadick, 1944).

In 1925 Pete rode well at the Stampede, but losing a stirrup in his final ride meant splitting the first and second money. The same year he won his first-place trophy — a belt with a gold buckle and a cash prize of one thousand dollars.

For the years 1925–27 Pete Knight agreed to ride at all six of Pete Welsh's Alberta Company Shows. Welsh owned the top stock, and had hired top riders to appear in shows across North America (Winnipeg, Ottawa and Toronto, as well as Buffalo in New York and Columbus in Ohio).

In 1926 Pete Knight rode to his first North American Championship in Winnipeg, when he successfully rode six outsanding bucking horses in a row. He won fifteen hundred dollars and a silver mounted bridle presented by the Hollywood star Tom Mix. Writer Fred Kennedy indicates that after 1926 Pete was universally recognised as Champion of the World (Kennedy, 1952) — a title which was not officially established by the Rodeo Association of America until 1929. At the 1927 Stampede he easily won both the Canadian and North American Saddle-Bronc Riding titles, becoming the first Canadian to win the North American title.

Later that summer, promoters arranged for the reigning World Champion, Bobby Askins of Montana, to come to Canada. Only Askins and Knight qualified for the Saturday night saddle-bronc finals. Askins, having drawn a horse called 'Midnight'(who had not been ridden in two years), had a wild, hair-raising ride that lasted about eight jumps. Pete drew 'Tumbleweed', and rode the big spotted 'outlaw' to the finish. Two weeks later Pete drew 'Midnight' in the finals of the Montréal show; while he got a terrific shaking-up, he managed to stay aboard long enough to win first money (Davis, 1976: 33).

In 1928 Pete did not compete at all. His father had died (as had his mother two years earlier), and Pete stayed on the ranch looking after family interests. The next year, however, Pete rented out the place and set out to compete in all the rodeos he could find. He entered practically every big event on the continent, placing 'in the money' in just about all of them. He won firsts in both Vancouver and Moose Jaw, and in the United States at Pendleton (Oregon), Roswell (New Mexico) and New York City's Madison Square Garden. Pete again won the Canadian titles in 1930 and 1931, and the following year he once more became not only Canadian but also North American Champion.

The year 1932 also included a special event, an invitational saddle--bronc riding competition staged in Reno, Nevada, whose prize was a beautiful cup presented by ex-world heavyweight boxing champion Jack Dempsey. Only the four outstanding competitors from the 1931 season were invited: Frank Studnick, Gene Ross, Earl Thode, and, of course, Pete Knight.

The first day of competition, Studnick was bucked off a big black horse named 'Steamboat' who, it was claimed, had never been ridden. Knight drew 'Cannonball', a large white horse that had a habit of standing up on his hind legs and then falling to one side, only to break into a vicious buck, giving the rider the impression the horse was about to fall on him. Pete gave the audience a sensational ride. The second day Ross was bucked off 'Steamboat' and Thode off 'Cannonball', leaving Pete Knight to be declared the winner.

In 1933 Pete continued his string of firsts all over North America. He won the open, the Prince of Wales Cup and the North American Championship, and became the first-ever three-time winner of the Canadian Championship in saddle-bronc riding at the Calgary Stampede. It was to be his last appearance there.

The following year he declined to defend his title, embarking instead on a Commonwealth tour which took him to England, New Zealand, Australia (where he was dubbed 'World Champion of Buck Jumpers') and several South Pacific islands. In 1935, however, he reclaimed both the North American and World titles, and repeated this achievement a year later.

He was well on his way to winning a fifth World title when a tragic accident took his life 23 May 1937 in Hayward (California). The following eye-witness account was reprinted in *The Calgary Herald:*

> Pete Knight died a champion's death Sunday. He was riding Duster (also known as Sundown), the best bucking horse in the world, and he was winning.
> The 5000 spectators were cheering him and there wasn't one of the boys, not even those who had ridden against him, who wasn't pulling for him to win. It was the last event of the day and Pete had ridden another hourse earlier in the day and had given the crowd plenty of thrills.
> The horse was bucking like an eel, but Pete was riding him high, wide and handsome and trying to get Duster to pitch even harder. The judges had written him down already as a winner.
> Then it happened.
> Nobody knows why it happened, I guess. Duster was just a little too good that one second. It didn't look as though Pete was in any trouble when suddenly he was just out of the saddle. He went over the horse's head and the dust just spurted a little as he fell on his back and lay there for a hundredth of a second. He didn't have a chance to move.
> When we got to Pete's side, he was still. Duster's hoofs had landed square in his stomach. A doctor in the crowd called an ambulance, but when we got to the hospital, Pete was dead.
> We're going to bury him Wednesday with the Cowboy's Funeral. They'll sing him the cowboy songs he loved to sing and they'll sing them well because they'll be for one of the finest guys in the world.

Harry Knight of Colorado, a very good friend of Pete's (not a relative) and the last man to hear his voice, recalls (Davis, 1976:49):

> The day he was killed I ran out to him. When I asked if he was hurt bad, he said: 'Sure, I am', but he got up anyway. That broken rib must have pierced a vital spot.

Even the doctor who signed the death certificate admitted that Pete might have had a chance of surviving if he had not tried to get up and walk away (*loc. cit.*).

There is no lack of tributes to this Doukhobor cowboy turned world champion. Among them was an article in the *Canadian Cattlemen* by former Stampede manager Guy Weadick, which concluded as follows (Weadick, 1944)[1]:

> And so ended the riding career of one of the greatest exponents of clean cowboy bucking horse riding that has ever been in the professional contest business.

Debbie Brill — World champion high-jumper

As a young girl in Mission, B.C., Debbie Veregin (daughter to Eugene Veregin) enjoyed jumping, which she found to be a natural activity for her.

By the time she was fourteen (1967) she was jumping 1.5 metres (4 ft 11 in.). A year later she cleared 1.71 metres and competed in her first international meets in Norway and Britain. The following year she came out a winner. At the Star Games in Toronto in 1970 at age 17 she became the first North American woman to clear 6 feet (1.83 m) and in 1971, after winning gold at both the Commonwealth Games in Edinburgh and the Pan American Games in Cali, Colombia, was named Canadian Female Athlete of the Year.

Fig. 2. World champion high jumper Debbie Brill.
Credit: National Health and Welfare Canada.
1971. Pan Am Games, Cali, Columbia.

When she started competing, she and her coach developed a style that evolved into a revolutionary reverse jump that is now used by all jumpers. Her talent and her competitive spirit combined to give her a twenty-year reign as a world-class high-jumper, and made her unquestionably Canada's greatest track-and-field athlete. These are some of the other highlights of her career:

1977   Silver medal at World University Student Games in Bulgaria, bronze at the World Cup in Düsseldorf. Named Outstanding University Athlete of the Year.

1978   Silver at Commonwealth Games in Edmonton.

1979   World Champion high-jumper at the World Cup in Montréal, clearing 1.96 metres to beat out both the reigning Olympic champion and the reigning world record-holder.[2]

1980   Second World Championship in Switzerland, clearing 1.97 m. Denied opportunity (by international boycott) of competing at the Moscow Olympics, where the gold medal was also won at the 1.97-metre mark. Named British Columbia's Athlete of the Decade.

1981   Birth of first child, son Neil, in August; a brief maternity leave followed by renewed training.

1982   24 January cleared 1.99 m at an Edmonton meet to establish a world indoor high-jump record; later in the year took gold at Commonwealth Games in Australia. Inducted into Canadian Amateur Sports Hall of Fame. Gradually increasing physical problems.

1983   In spite of injuries and constant pain, continued jumping (1.95 m indoors and 1.9 outdoors), ranked 6th in world. Received Award of Excellence at the Tribute of Champions. Made an Officer of the Order of Canada.

1984   5th-place performance at Los Angeles Olympics, hampered by severe ankle injury; later jumped up to 1.98 m in Europe, defeating reigning Olympic champion.

1985   Jump of 1.97 m second highest in world.

1989   Inducted into the B.C. Sports Hall of Fame.

By the time she retired from competition in 1988 Debbie Brill had represented Canada at four Olympiads, four Commonwealth Games and three Pan American competitions. She had set seventeen Commonwealth high-jump records and eight indoor World marks equalling or bettering the record — the most for any athlete in any event. She was twelve times Canadian high-jump champion and twice won the U.S. championship. She won medals at more than sixty-five national and international competitions along with a series of coveted trophies.

In her book (Brill, 1986:138) she sums up the sport of high-jumping as follows:

> It is not about winning and losing, it has to do with bringing out something of yourself, something that is your great strength and purpose, the expression of yourself.

Tim Cheveldae — NHL all-star goaltender

The most notable of many Doukhobor hockey players, Tim Cheveldae hails from Melville, Saskatchewan, where he divided his spare time in high school between hockey and badminton. After a year of playing hockey with the Yorkton Terriers (a Triple-A team), in 1984 he joined his home-town Millionaires hockey club and the following season began an outstanding three-year stint as goaltender for the Saskatoon Blades. Completing his final year there with a record of 44 wins, 19 losses and 3 ties, along with a 'goals-against' average of 3.71, Cheveldae was invited to join the first all-star team in the East Division of the World Hockey League.

Fig. 3. N.H.L All star goaltender Tim Cheveldae.

He had already played with the Adirondacks, the #1 farm club for the Detroit Red Wings, who took him on in 1990 as their regular goalie. That October he earned the first 'shut-out' of his NHL career in a game against Vancouver. By the end of the season he had achieved an average of 3.55, another 'shut-out' and a stunning thirty victories (third in the whole of the NHL for that year).

Even greater success awaited him in the 1991–92 season, when he achieved a 3.20 average and tied with Glenn Hall for the third-best win total in Red Wing Club history. He was eventually selected to play on the All-Star team, and more than once has been named Player of the Week.

Jon-Lee Kootnekoff — Olympic basketball player and coach

Born on a farm near Canora, Saskatchewan, at age 6 Jon-Lee moved with his family to Mission, B.C., where he was introduced to basketball in primary school. He soon became totally infatuated with the game, playing everywhere he could — at school, in his back yard, in the hayloft of an old barn nearby.

In Grade 10 Jon-Lee was voted Most Valuable Player on the Mission High School basketball team, which placed second that year in the B.C. Provincial Championships, repeating this distinction two years later, scoring 20 of his team's 40 points in a narrow victory over a powerful opponent from Vancouver.

Upon completing high school in 1954, 19-year-old Jon-Lee decided to 'strike out on his own' to work in Alberni, having accepted an invitation to join the Alberni Athletics basketball club. During his first year there his team won the Canadian Men's Senior 'A' Championships. The following year he was elected to the B.C. Senior 'A' Men's League's first all-star team, and while his team lost in the finals, he came second in the league's scoring race.

In 1956 Kootnekoff was awarded an entrance scholarship at Seattle University in America. In his second year he made their basketball team, which went all the way to the U.S. National Championships, losing the final game by only 12 points.

After graduating in 1960, Jon-Lee was one of twelve players selected for Canada's Olympic basketball team, which narrowly missed qualifying for the Rome event at a pre-Olympic tournament in Bologna (Italy). That autumn he returned to Seattle to undertake a Masters' programme in physical education; his busy schedule involved not only study and practice teaching, but two part-time jobs and playing basketball with two local teams (Kootnekoff, 1990:81–82). He subsequently immersed himself in basketball, coaching and teaching in Seattle high schools.

He returned to Canada in 1966 to accept the position of head basketball coach at the newly opened Simon Fraser University, the first academic institution in Canada to grant athletic scholarships. His teams consistently outplayed their natural rivals from UBC and won not only major CIAU tournaments but most of their games with nearby American colleges.

An initial attitude of ambition and aggressiveness[3] gradually gave way to more communication and consultation with his team. He introduced innovative training methods, including creative dance to loosen muscles, and visualisation. His satisfaction with the sport began to improve, as did his win-loss record.

His obsession with basketball diminished as he began attending seminars on human potential and joined groups for yoga, meditation, jogging and creative dance, and he decided to forsake his regimented life-pattern to pursue a quest for truth, new ideas and patterns of thought. Resigning his position at Simon Fraser, in 1975 he established the Horizon Positive SelfImage Institute. As a coaching consultant he conducts clinics on the psychology of sport and game strategy, speaking out on his beliefs whenever he can. He advises athletes to look inside themselves and heed the voice of the sub-concious mind — the God within — to find happiness, health and prosperity (*ibid.*, 110).

Ron Cherkas — Defensive tackle, Canadian Football League

Ron Cherkas grew up in Kamsack, Saskatchewan, where he was an outstanding player in the football programme at the Kamsack Collegiate Institute. In 1971 he joined the Regina Rams Junior Football team, which won all of their fifteen league games as well as the Canadian Junior Football Championship; Ron was named Rookie of the Year.

From 1971 to 1975 Ron played American football while studying in the United States — first at Gavilan Junior College in California and then with the University of Utah.

Upon his return to Canada, in 1976 he was selected to join the Saskatchewan Roughriders, where he served six seasons as an outstanding defensive lineman. He also played three seasons with the Winnipeg Blue Bombers and two with the B.C. Lions.

After ten years of professional football Ron retired from the CFL to coach and to teach physical education and science in Regina, where he is also head coach of the Johnson Wildcats football team.

Bibliography

Brill, Debbie, with James Lawton (1986). *Jump.* Vancouver: Douglas J. McIntyre.

Davis, Jim (c. 1976). *We remember Pete Knight.* Calgary: Canadian Rodeo Cowboys' Association.

Gray, James H. (c. 1985). *A Brand of its own — The 100-year history of the Calgary Exhibition and Stampede.* Saskatoon: Western Producer Prairie Books.

Kennedy, Fred (1965). *The Calgary Stampede story.* Calgary: T. Edwards Thonger.

Kootnekoff, Jon-Lee (1990). *From Kooty with love: Self-discovery through the games of life.* Vancouver: Horizon Positive Self-Image Institute.

Weadick, Guy (1944). 'Pete Knight, champion rider of the rodeos'. *Canadian Cattlemen,* vol. 7, nº 1 (June 1944).

Appendix

Riding High in the Hand Hills
by Ferg James
Dedicated to the 53rd Annual Hand Hills Stampede
11 June 1969

He came out of the chutes
On a wall-eyed brute;
And he raked him fore and aft.
Then they sunfished high
In the bright blue sky
And I think they both went daft.

His hoofs resound
As they hit the ground,
You could hear that cayuse squeal,
With his ears laid flat,
Then he went to bat
When he felt the cowboy's heel.

He flipped and turned
As the ground he churned,
And his hind hoofs grazed his neck.
It was nip and tuck,
But the cowboy stuck,
And still remained on deck.

Then the whistle blew
And the pick-up crew
Closed in to do their stuff.
And the crowd went wild

When the rider smiled,
For they know that his ride was rough.

It was years ago,
That we watched this show,
And I'll never forget the sight
Of a bronc plumb mad
And that carefree lad,
For that boy was young Pete Knight.

Hanna, Alberta
26 May 1969

[1] Authors of other tributes include Barry Tibbit of the Canadian Rodeo Cowboy's Association and Canada's famous 'Yodelling Cowboy' Wilf Carter (see Davis, 1976:49–51). A memorial poem by cowboy Ferg James of Hanna, Alberta, is given in the Appendix at the end of this article.

[2] In her autobiography (Brill, 1986:138) she describes the event as follows: 'It was one of the great competitive battles of my life. I went into a tunnel of concentration... I wanted this as badly as I'd wanted anything in my career... I felt strong and confident... The moment of victory was wild exhilaration... I'd achieved what I'd set out for that year. I was the best in the world.'

[3] In his book Kootnekoff comments on this period of his life as follows (*ibid.*, 106): '...winning was an obsession with me... I was an ambitious coach, but not much else. I was a ... workaholic — the complete one-dimensional person'.

Doukhobor entrepreneurs

Marilyn Verigin

Introduction

Migration to Canada has bonded Doukhobor beliefs and strengthened the basic need for togetherness. The sheer necessity for survival in a new and strange land dictated a continuation of their communal way of life.

However, to supplement the income and stabilise the economy of the community in the new land, many members took work outside its boundaries, pooling their earnings to share with the community as a whole. Some were hired by non-Doukhobor farmers while others worked in lumber camps or constructing railroads.

But not all who went out to work wanted to return to the community. Doukhobors who dealt with foremen and superintendents were quicker to acquire a working knowledge of English and Canadian business practices, and many of these left the community with their families to integrate with the Englishspeaking populace.

This trend was particularly noticeable among Doukhobors who stayed behind on the Canadian prairies after 1912, by which time most of their fellow sect-members (approximately 6,000 in number) had moved to British Columbia. Most who did not join the trek west were obliged to procure individual homesteads and become independent entrepreneurs.

*   *   *

By definition, an *entrepreneur* is one who organises and manages a business undertaking. He or she is a person of energy and initiative, always searching for positive change and willing to venture into new projects, full of hope for success but aware of the ever-present threat of financial failure.

Most Doukhobor businesses began as small, single-family operations requiring little capital investment. Often the entire family would become involved, finding satisfaction in working together to provide an income for the household. Children would use their work experience to carry on the family business or to start one of their own.

Entrepreneurs have a genuine interest in working to help others. They may provide a new product or service or improve upon those already available. Talented individuals are able to exercise a particular skill, and younger family members have an opportunity to put their education to immediate use. Working independently offers a harmonious lifestyle for those who find it difficult to be dependent on others.

The appearance of individual Doukhobor entrepreneurs was met by considerable opposition from other Doukhobors, however, especially on the part of the elders, for whom the basic communal structure of their society with its equitable distribution of wealth left no room for capitalistic attitudes or affluence. They were abhorred by the very thought of excessive profit-making, which they associated with the exploitation of one person by another. In their eyes, time should be spent in the pursuit of spiritual development rather than material comfort. They adhered consistently to a greatly revered Doukhobor motto: *Toil and peaceful life* (which loosely translates into: *Work as hard as possible and be content with as little as possible*).

An extensive research project has yielded information on hundreds of Doukhobor business undertakings in eighty-six cities and towns in both Canada and America over the past seventy years. While it is unfortunately not possible to include all the interesting accounts of the start-up struggles received or list all those who have been in business, this article aims to provide a representative sampling of Doukhobor enterprises in various economic sectors, with a special focus on unique ventures.[1]

Agriculture

Farming is the most predominant type of self-employment on the prairies, and Doukhobors are renowned for their effective farming techniques. Though not usually thought of as entrepreneurs per se, farmers must possess business skills, and they do organise and manage what amounts to a business enterprise. Examples of Doukhobor undertakings in the agricultural field are as follows:

- In Grand Forks, B.C., *Paul Abetkoff* provides much-needed yearround employment for planters, weeders, harvesters, sorters and packagers in his vegetable market gardens.
- *Larry* and *Elsie Berisoff* of Asquith, Saskatchewan, supplied fresh milk to Saskatoon dairies in the 1940s from their modern dairy farm with its refrigeration equipment.
- *Fred* and *Anne Conkin* ran a chicken farm (known as Broadview Farms) from 1960 to 1977 near Aldergrove, B.C.

- In Thrums, B.C., two *Koodrin* families (*Paul* and *Nina, Mike* and *Mable*) have operated Blue Crop Farms for the past decade. With the help of as many as twenty employees they grow thousands of kilograms of huge blueberries each year.
- In the 1930s the *Peter Maloff* family in Thrums produced firstgrade apples which sold for $1 per box and hay which sold for $12 per ton. Around the same time the *George Popoff* family of Shoreacres, B.C. raised fruit, vegetables, clover, grains and timothy grass.
- *Mike* and *Pauline Nazaroff* (formerly owners of Pardman's Furniture in Castlegar, B.C.), decided to take on fruit farming in Oliver in the Okanagan Valley. Their sons *Arnie* and *Terry* grow fruit, vegetables and seedlings. Further up the valley in Kelowna, orchards are kept by *George* and *Polly Voykin* and by *Bill* and *Judy Horkoff.*
- *Nicholas Plotnicove* of Richmond, B.C. specialised in fruit-tree care and became known as a 'fruit-tree doctor'.
- Two Alberta families — the *Peter Saliken* family of Lundbreck and the *Alex A. Vishloff* family of Okatoks — were involved in ranching operations with horses and cattle, an activity requiring heavy physical demands from all family members.
- *Alex* and *Harry Verishine,* brothers and joint farmers in Langham, Saskatchewan, offered a 'custom farming' service to their neighbours in the 1950s, helping other farmers who were not able to complete planting or harvesting within the required time frame.
- *Harvey Verishine* (Harry's son) decided to diversify from traditional grain-crop farming and become a hay grower and broker.

Forestry

The forest industry, including logging, milling and woodworking, has always held a positive attraction for outdoorloving Doukhobor males, a number of whom have become successful entrepreneurs. The Kootenay and Boundary areas of British Columbia are dotted with logging operations owned by Doukhobors, for example:

- Former Saskatchewan famer *Peter M. Bloodoff* owned a sawmill in Passmore, B.C., in the 1940s and 1950s, while *Paul Koochin* and *Alex Tamelin* set up their sawmill in Pass Creek, B.C.; *Fred Maloff* ran a shake mill at Krestova, B.C.
- In Slocan Park, *Walter Demoskoff* owns and operates the Dinlo Logging Co., while *Alex* and *Jack Voykin* have been running Voykin Bros Ltd since 1956, employing as many as twenty-five men. The latter also own

and operate cranes and other heavyduty machinery. They acknowledge their success as stemming from their commitment of long hours, hard work and fair treatment of their employees.

- In 1951 *George, Peter, Nick* and *Fred Hadikin* started their logging /milling business with nothing more than 'strong backs, a couple of wedges and a hammer'. Their efforts produced over 100,000 fence posts and 6,000 telephone poles. Despite several moves and losses due to fire, this family operation lasted thirty years and at its peak employed 147 people.
- In 1940 *Peter Kalesnikoff*, who had been in the lumber business since the age of fourteen, started the Kalesnikoff Lumber Co. in Tarrys, B.C., running one of the larger sawmills in the Kootenays and employing logging contractors as well as sawyers. Serving a broad range of clientèle from global lumber brokers to domestic carpenters, the company has taken great pains to work together in harmony with environmentalists. Peter's son *Ken* is carrying on the family business.
- In the 1940s *Nick Poohachow* had a logging company, sawmill and general store at Winlaw, B.C.
- *Peter Popoff* of Grand Forks was one of the original planners and initiators of a particle-board mill known as Parta Industries.
- In the 1930s the *John W. Sherbinin* family (including *John Jr*, his wife *Helen*, along with *Gus, George* and *Eli*) of Midway started the well-known Boundary Sawmill which employed hundreds of local workers.
- The Zeeben Lumber Co., owned by *Max Zeeben* of Ymir, B.C., operated from 1946 to 1968 with thirty employees, producing shingles and lumber. Mr Zeeben later ran a service station in Nelson.
- *William Zaitsoff* and his sons *George & Bill* produced cedar fence posts at Robson, B.C., which sold throughout the western provinces.

There were also a few families who operated sawmills in Saskatchewan, including *Bill* and *Mary Chernoff* at Kamsack and *Sam Rebalkin* at Blaine Lake. Other prominent B.C. families on the logging scene were the *Evins* of Robson and the *Strelioffs* of Castlegar.

Construction: general contractors

Doukhobors are said to excel in the construction field. Noted for being master craftsmen in their trades, they seem to possess a natural, inherent skill when working with building products. Most prevalent are general contractors, which include the following:

- *George Rilkoff* and *Alex Hoodicoff Sr* of Raspberry Village, B.C.
- *Bill Pepin* and *Harry Lazaroff* — well-known builders who joined forces a few years ago to construct a beautiful condominum complex called the Grand Forks River Park Estates;
- *Michael Popoff* of Grand Forks, who operates Mr West Construction, offering residential, commercial and industrial building.
- *Mike Semenoff* of Castlegar, whose company, Woodland Construction, has built many exclusive custom homes;
- *Paul Semenoff* (Mike's son), a 'new-generation' entrepreneur, head of Nu Tech Construction, which won an award from B.C. Chamber of Commerce as one of the top five new ventures in its category in the province for the year 1987.
- *Lawrence* and *Russel Verigin,* who started Verigin Industries Ltd in Trail in 1955, later joined by their brother *Elmer*. Begun on a 'shoe-string', the company specialised in custom homes and later expanded with the addition of a sash-and-door/millwork shop. In 1986 the company moved to Vancouver under the name of Marbella Pacific Construction Ltd, where it built over forty buildings for the Expo '86 Worlds Fair, along with schools, arenas, care centres and seismic upgrades of older structures.
- *Peter Savenkoff* of Coquitlam, a partner in Tynan Construction Ltd, which built schools on the B.C. Lower Mainland; he also ventured to construct a hotel complex in the West Indies.
- *Peter Rezansoff,* of Intertech Construction in Vancouver; his work ethic, commended by architects and owners alike, is reflected in his company's motto: 'Quality work — on budget — on time'.

Other general contractors in B.C. include *John Androsoff* and *Ken Gorkoff* in Castlegar, *Peter Jmaeff,* operator of Jaemar Construction Ltd in Delta, *Jack* and *Anna Konken* in Grand Forks, *N.F. Ogloff* in Robson, *Nick Plotnikoff* in Creston, and *George & Phil Soukeroff* in Fernie. Outside the province *Ron Zarchikoff* is a general contractor in Kamsack, Sask. and *Phil Zaitsoff* in Whitehorse, Yukon. At least one Doukhobor contractor is known to operate in the United States: *John Kazakov,* who contracts in Salem, Oregon.

Several general contractors in the Castlegar area have also run building supply stores: *Mike Popoff* and *Peter Gorkoff* owned P&G Builders while *Alex* and *Bill Plotnikoff* operated Kootenay Builders, and *John Negraeff* owned Castlegar Building Supplies. *Pete Konkin* together with his sons *Peter, Sam* and *Ed* started as contractors, but later opened Pete Konkin & Sons Building Supplies in Trail.

Construction: sub-contractors

Doukhobors are also active in sub-contracting businesses; the following are representative of their respective categories:

- **Concrete & interiors:** *Fred P. Chernoff, Peter P. Chernoff, Peter Horkoff, William E. Kootenekoff, Ignace P. Makaeff, Joseph Ogloff, Nick Ozeroff, Eli Popoff* and *Fred Popoff* were all shareholders in Interior Cement Works of Grand Forks, which contracted residential and commercial work, supplying cabinets, windows, doors and concrete blocks in the area from 1955 to 1975. *Wayne Trofimenkoff* and *Michael Vereschagin* assembled and marketed kitchen cabinets from their shop in Saskatoon. A concrete-testing service is offered by *Allan Morozoff* through his two Calgary companies: Almor Testing and Geo-Grout Inc. *Harry Wasilenkoff* owns Versatile Concrete in Shoreacres, B.C.

- **Drywall, plaster & stucco:** *Peter, Harry* and *John Voykin* in Pass Creek, B.C.; *Mike, Walter* and *Larry Sapriken* in the Okanagan and the Kootenays; *Andy & Don Savinkoff* as well as *George & Cecil Pereverseff* in Castlegar; *Pete* and *Anthony Stushnow* in Grand Forks; *Alex Reznasoff* in Thrums.

- **Electrical:** *Michael Zeeben* in Canora, Sask.; *Joe Vereshchagin, Gary Sherstobitoff* in Langham, Sask.; *John Sirota* in Saskatoon; *Alex Bojey* in Appledale, B.C.; *Pete Drazdoff* in Castlegar; *Gordon Planidin* in Christina Lake. *Mike Saukerookoff* in Kelowna and *Sid Saukerookoff* in Calgary both own electric motor rewinding shops.

- **Excavation:** *Gerry Evin* in Robson, B.C.; *John Hlookoff Jr* in Crescent Valley; *John Salekin* and *Eli Sopow Sr* in Castlegar; *Larry Swetlikoff* in nearby Brilliant; *Preston Zeeben* in Nelson.

- **Land surveying:** *Alex Cheveldave* is a land surveyor in Castlegar.

- **Landscaping:** *Murray* and *Peter Khadekin* in Yorkton, Sask.; *Mike Kalesnikoff* in Castlegar, B.C. runs Grass Roots Gardening. In America, *Paul Voykin* of Deerfield (Illinois) has published a book called *Ask the Lawn Expert*.

- **Masonry:** *Mike Laren* is a masonry contractor in Thrums, B.C.

- **Millwork:** *Alex Hoodicoff Jr* in Raspberry Village, B.C.; *Peter Demoskoff* in Tarrys; *Harry Maloff* in Harrop; *Walter Katelnikoff* in Appledale.

- **Fuel & oil:** *Jakob Kalmakoff* started an oil refinery in Kamsack, Sask.; *John Fedosa* in Henrietta, Sask., *Alex W. Cheveldayoff* in Blaine Lake, Sask. and *Sidney Popoff* in Grand Forks, B.C., are all (or have been) bulk fuel distributors. In Calgary *Allen Markin* owns an oil exploration company, while *Harry Vanjoff* owned Plains Construction.

- **Painting:** *John Pankoff* in Grand Forks; *Alex Gleboff & Peter Woykin* in Castlegar; *John W. Popoff* in Langham, Sask. *Fred Stushnoff* in

Shoreacres, B.C. sandblasts and paints bridges; *Allan Verishine* painted aircraft in Saskatoon and Calgary (in addition to being a commercial artist—see below); another painting contractor is a firm owned by *Bill & Jack Dergousoff* in Grand Forks (who also market sport cards—see below).

- **Plumbing & mechanical services:** *Bill Strookoff* in Christina Lake, B.C.; *Hank Tarasoff* in Cranbrook; *Andy Boolinoff, Gordon Grieves, Sam Soukeroff* and *Mike Tomlin* in Castlegar; *Philip Novakshonoff* in Grand Forks.
- **Road construction:** *Peter Nemanischen* and sons in Langham, Sask.; *John Hlookoff* and *Colin Sherbinin* in Crescent Valley; *Peter* and *Jack Kabatoff* in Ooteshenie (near Castlegar).
- **Trucking:** *Gary Malakoff* of Pelly, Sask.; *George* & *Paul Markin* of Raspberry Village, B.C.; *Wayne Voykin* of Passmore; *Jim Postnikoff* & *Andrew Strelioff* of Castlegar; *Angus Verishine* of Victoria, who also did carpentry under the name 'Have Hammer, Will Travel'.

Automotive & Machinery: sales & service

Doukhobors are involved in a number of ventures selling and/or servicing vehicles and mechanical equipment, including:

- **Automotive repairs:** *John* and *Bill Harelkin* ran a collision repair shop in Arlee, Sask.; in Castlegar *Andy Poohochoff* has operated Trail Auto Body for several decades while *Jason Chernoff* and *Kenton Holoboff* did automobile repairs; *William P. Sherstobitoff* of Saskatoon fixed cars most of his life.
- **Bicycles etc.:** *Peter Gorkoff* purchased Markin Equipment in Nelson from founders *Walter* and *Fred Markin*, selling small equipment such as motorbikes, snowmobiles, lawn mowers and chain-saws; similar services are provided by *Bill Tomilin* of B&F Sales in Grand Forks, where *Fred Astoforoff* runs Silver Barn Bike & Board; another bicycle sales & repair shop was operated by *Fred Nazaroff* in Castlegar.
- **Heavy-duty machinery:** In South Slocan, B.C., *Bill Areshenkoff* supplies heavy-duty machinery as well as small equipment at his business called Playmor Power, while at Interior Fabweld such machinery is repaired by owner *Joe Podovinikoff*, who together with Fred Padowinikoff provides sawmill maintenance through I&I Installations.
- **Vehicle dealerships:** *Koozma J. Tarasoff Sr* had a vehicle dealership in Henrietta, Sask., in the 1940s; *Pat Picton* rents and sells vehicles in Castlegar, where *Kevin* and *Rick Sherstobitoff* operate Shersty Motors.

Retail sales: General stores

During the 1930s and 1940s the *general store* was an integral part of rural Canadian communities. Besides providing a wide variety of merchandise from clothing to candy to horse collars, it also became a gathering place where local residents socialised. The first Doukhobor to open an independent general store was *Vassili Potapoff* of Verigin, Sask., in the early 1920s (he had previously managed the community store at Station Verigin). In British Columbia two generations have operated the *Bloodoff* Store in Brilliant, the *Kooznetsoff* Store in Glade and the *Polovnicoff* Store in Thrums. Other general store entrepreneurs include the following:

- *George* & *Lucy Cheveldave* of Cheveldave Mercantile in Castlegar regularly shipped supplies on the paddle-wheeler *Minto* to customers as well as other stores at Renata and Deer Park, B.C.[2]
- *John Demoskoff,* who offered an interesting display of merchandise at his store in Environ, Sask.
- *Jim Legebokow,* who opened a store in Grand Forks in 1946. In winter, upturned wooden soft-drink cases were set up around the wood heater to serve as seats for customers who would sing, tell stories and enjoy buying and eating roasted, homegrown sunflower seeds prepared by Jim's wife *Lucille*. In summer, teen-agers would bring their guitars and accordions and provide entertainment for those who wished to 'dance in the streets'. This family operation included sons *Fred* and *Sam* who looked after the family's income-producing orchard, and daughter *Irene* who assembled apple boxes and from the age of eight waited on customers.
- *Sam* and *Mary Markin,* proprietors of a combination motel, trailer court, service station and general store in Grand Forks.
- *Joe* and *Mabel Shukin,* proprietors of a store in Nelson from 1956 to 1967.
- *William* and *Martha Stooshinoff,* whose store in Appledale, B.C. was equipped with a post office, as many were in the 1940s and 1950s.
- *Mike* and *Mary (Vereschagin) Terichow,* who owned and operated a general store at Arrowood, Alta., from 1930 to 1943.
- *Pete* and *Helen Verishine,* owners of the Maple Leaf Store in Crescent Valley, B.C., which provided neighbouring communities with food, fuel, footwear and friendship.
- *Nicholas S. Zibin,* who established the Zibin General Store in a strategic location near the Columbia River ferry dock in Robson, B.C. At one point during its forty years of operation it was taken over by Nicholas' sons *Philip* and *Moses*.

Still other general stores have been owned or run by *Pete & Mary Aborssimoff* in Thrums, B.C. and the *Pete Polonicoff* family in Grand Forks; there is also the *Kanigan* Store in Kylemore, Sask.

Retail sales: Clothing & fabric enterprises

Owning and managing a clothing store holds special challenges. Merchandise must be selected to meet an ever-changing fashion market. Doukhobor retail clothing enterprises include:

- **Children's wear:** a children's clothing store in Nelson run by *Ann Poznikoff.*
- **Consignment:** shops owned by *Kate Varabioff* and *Martha (Popoff) Grieves* in Castlegar and by *Michael* and *Val Verigin* in Kamsack, Sask.
- **Custom design & tailoring:** Doukhobor ladies' suits created upon request by *Emma Kavaloff* in Blueberry Creek, B.C.; wedding finery crafted by *Elsie Rezansoff* in Vancouver.
- **Embroidery, drapery & upholstery:** Ladies shawls are embroidered by *Helen Katasonoff* in Vernon and *Dorothy Shkuratoff* in Winlaw, B.C.; *Netti Sookochoff* fashions home-made quilts, as does *Alma Hadikin;* in Calgary, *Marion Steeves* of Steveplan Services Ltd, who (until her retirement in 1990) travelled across Western Canada selling top-of-the-line upholstery and drapery fabrics. In America, *Donna (Maloff) Henderson* ran an upholstery shop in Marion (Illinois).
- **Fabric and dry goods:** stores run by *Harry* and *Helen Hoodicoff* in Castlegar and by *George Vereschagin* in Meacham, Sask.
- **General clothing:** a store in North Battleford, Sask., owned by *Fred, John* and *Barry Conkin.*
- **Ladies' and men's wear:** the Kootenay Klothes Kloset in Trail and JJ's in Castlegar, both run by *Joe* and *Ruby Streloff;* also His and Her Fashions in Grand Forks, run by *Peter Perepelkin.*
- **Ladies' wear shops:** two in Nelson, B.C., run by *Karen (Laktin) Schacher;* two in Blaine Lake, Sask., owned, respectively, by *Julie Perverseff* and *Tina Popoff.*
- **Recreational wear:** CABA Fashions, a manufacturing plant in Grand Forks, is owned and operated by *Florence Vatkin (née Ogloff).*

Retail sales: Miscellaneous

Other sales outlets owned or operated by Doukhobors include the following:

- **Antiques & auctions:** An impressive line of furniture and collectibles is displayed by *Alex Ewashen,* owner of Jual Auction in Creston, B.C., who also hires out his services as an auctioneer; *Paul Reban* and *John J. Androsoff* have served as auctioneers in Blaine Lake, Sask.
- **Department Stores:** *Peter Vatkin* co-owns and manages West's Department Store in Castlegar, reputed to be 'the best stocked department store in the Kootenays'.
- **Floor coverings:** These were supplied and installed by two dealers in Saskatoon: *John Atamenenko* and *Mike Semenoff* (later John sold his carpet business and until recently operated a successful bingo hall in the same city).
- **Flowers:** *Helen Golay* sold beautiful arrangements from her store in Kamsack, Sask.; *Maureen Hadikin* used innovative approaches to flower--arranging in her Tulips Floral Co. in Castlegar, a store currently owned by *Kathy Soloveoff*; also in Castlegar *Katherine Kalmakoff* sells 'everlasting florals'; *Alex* and *Nellie Plotnikoff* sell flowers and gifts from their Grand Forks shop.
- **Furniture:** Dealers include *Bill Kanigan, Cecil Kanigan, Jim Barabanoff* and *John Popoff* in Saskatoon, *Nick Kanigan* in Prince Albert.
- **Hardware:** Stores supplying household needs were operated by *Bill Maloff* and *Sarge Rilkoff* in Grand Forks, *Jim* and *Helen (Halisheff) McKelvie* in Wells, B.C., *Harry Verishine* in Langham, Sask., *Pete* and *Angeline Papove* in Watson, Sask., *Alex Plaxin* in Buchanan, Sask. and *Bill Semenoff* in Saskatoon.
- **Janitorial supplies:** These are sold by *John Kazakoff* of Castlegar.
- **Jewellery:** Doukhobor dealers include *Al Demosky, Fred Popoff* and *Peter Fredericks* in Grand Forks, *Bill Ozeroff* in Castlegar and *Mike Pictin* in Calgary.
- **Pharmacies:** *Ken Konkin* was resident pharmacist in a drug store he owned and operated in Vancouver.

Service industries: Food and accomodation

There are at least twelve *hotel/motel* complexes owned by Doukhobors, the best-known of these being the Yale Hotel in Grand Forks, renowned for its Russian food. Eventually destroyed by fire, it had been owned by *Paul Makortoff, Harry Berisoff, John Chernoff, Ed Plotnikoff, John Vatkin, Bill Faminoff, Pete Plotnikoff, Mitch Chernoff, Alex Semenoff* and *Harry Berisoff.* Another prominent hotel-owner is *Nick Troubitskoff,* formerly of Vancouver, who operates a large tourist complex in St Lucia, West Indies. *Pete &*

Christina Koochin left their Saskatchewan farm to operate Mom's Motel in Grand Forks, B.C.

Doukhobor-owned *restaurants* abound in Canada, and run the gamut from fast foods to fine dining, all with superior fare and service. These include *Delores Pepin*'s bistro in Grand Forks, *Debbie Mallow*'s coffee shop in Krestova, *Rose Legebokoff*'s cappucino bar in Nelson and *Pat Rilkoff*'s eatery in Castlegar.

Many Doukhobors have become *food service providers*. Records show at least thirty-six grocery, confection and convenience stores across western Canada. Doukhobor food service providers supplying either Russian or Canadian food items include the following:

- *Liz Arishenkoff*, who operates a health-food store in Grand Forks, as does *Mickey Tarasoff* in Castlegar; also *John* and *Mary Tarasoff*, *Mike Hlookoff* and *Wayne Savinkoff* (all in Nelson, B.C.).
- *Fred* and *Pearl Bondaroff*, who ran Cut-Rate Foods, and *Mike* and *Mabel Bonderoff*, who operated Central Food Mart, both in the Castlegar area.
- *Cyril* and *Hazel Demoskoff*, owners of Playmor Foods in Playmor Junction, B.C.
- *John Evdokimoff*, who started Johnnie's Bakery in Nelson.
- *Pauline (Meakin) Isaac* of Langham, Sask., *Polly Tokaryk* of Saskatoon, *Mary Abrossimoff* of Thrums, B.C. *Edna Sapriken* and *Violet Popoff* of Slocan Park, all of whom cater feasts for groups numbering from twenty to two hundred.
- *Alex* and *Nettie Jmaeff*, who operate well-established bakeries in Castlegar and Creston, B.C.
- *Sam Kalesnikoff*, former owner of Blue Top Burger in Castlegar, and his successor *Nadia Stoochnoff*.
- *Mabel Koorbatoff*, who provides Russian baked goods to numerous stores from her home-based bakery in Slocan Park, B.C.
- *Vi* and *Phil Kurenoff*, owners of P&V Borsh Ltd in Kamsack, Sask., who make & distribute province-wide two types of Russian borshch.
- *Bill Ozeroff*, who ran a bakery in Saskatoon.
- *Ann Popoff*, who runs a popular bake shop in Christina Lake, B.C.
- *Terry* and *Valerie Rilkoff*, who owned a market and garden centre in Grand Forks.
- *Alona Zeiben*, who uses her creative abilities to delight customers of her A Zee Cake Decorating business in Kamsack, Sask.

Service industries: Arts & leisure

A number of Doukhobors have established enterprises in the various branches of the arts and recreation world, including:

- **Books:** The largest mystery book store on the west coast is operated by *Christa Deacove* in North Vancouver, while books on every subject are offered by *Tina Salekin* and *Peter Popoff* in the Castlegar Book Shop and by *William Holuboff* at Westgate Books in Saskatoon.
- **Camps & hiking tours:** *Greg Gritchen* of Inland Expeditions in Castlegar welcomes visitors to the Kootenays with guided walks, hikes and tours; *Paul* and *Laura Strelioff* run the Kootenay River Kampground in nearby Ooteshenie.
- **Cinema:** Cinema-theatre owners include the late *Pete Abrossimoff* of Grand Forks and *Paul* and *Laura Strelioff* of Ooteshenie, who owned a drive-in cinema in the Castlegar area.
- **Family games:** *Jim Deacove*'s company Family Pastimes manufactures co--operative games in Perth, Ont., and markets them around the world.
- **Film & video:** Entrepreneurs in this field include *Larry A. Ewashen* of Castlegar, who has made documentary films on the Doukhobors, *Sharon McGovan,* an award-winning film-maker at Blue Heron Media, Ltd, in Vancouver and *Dan Semenoff* of Video Productions in Saskatoon.
- **Fitness & gymnastics:** Castlegar's only fitness parlour belongs to *Gerry Hoodicoff;* three gymnastics programmes for young children and their parents have been started in Calgary by *Kathryn (Markin) McPhail.*
- **Home entertainment:** Pete's TV in Castlegar, owned by the *Pete Zaitsoff* family, offers home entertainment through television and videos, while others in this business include *Bill Doubinin* in Pass Creek, B.C., *Mike Hoodicoff* and *George Bonderoff* in Castlegar and *John Popoff* in Saskatoon.
- **Photography** This particular art-form is pursued by *Ken Strelioff* in Grand Forks and *John* and *Blair Kalesnikoff* in North Battleford, Sask.
- **Pottery:** *Kim Chernoff* of Crescent Valley, B.C., markets her raku pottery from Calgary to Vancouver.
- **Singing/song-writing:** Doukhobor musical artists include: the family of *Frank* and *Ruby Konken* of Victoria; *Serge Plotnikoff,* a singer and song--writer with five albums to his credit, and former part owner and sales manager of CKQR radio in Castlegar for over twenty years; *Ron Kalmakoff,* another singer/song-writer who has released several albums[3] and put on numerous concerts (including many shows at Expo '86 in Vancouver).
- **Sports cards:** *Bill Dergousoff* of Grand Forks, together with partners *Peter Verigin* and *George Sookochoff* owns Columbia Creations, a mar-

keting firm with exclusive rights to certain Canadian Olympic Associa-
tion products, including sports cards and games Bill has invented for
Canada's Olympic athletes (Bill and his brother *Jack* also own Castle
Developments, a product development company as well as a painting
contracting firm—see above). In addition, sports cards are sold by
George and *Willie Perepolkin* of Thrums in their Castlegar shop.

- **Sports equipment:** The *Wishlow* family of Vancouver sells recreational
  sail boats; *Cecil Kanigan* manufactures sport airplanes in Saskatoon; *Bill
  Maloff* of Saskatoon supplied gaming specialties; *Peter Cheveldave*
  owned a sports store at Salmon Arm, B.C., while *Bill Semenoff* had one
  at Castlegar.
- **Studio recording:** *Mike Plotnikoff* of Vancouver is a master sound-
  -engineer who works around the world in the recording industry.
- **Travel:** *Peter Perepelkin* (also proprietor of a clothing store) is a certified
  travel consultant, whose Grand Forks firm, Sun Lite Travel, specialises
  in arranging trips to Russia and other countries of the former Soviet
  Union.
- **Wood-carving:** Wooden spoons and ladles have been beautifully executed by carvers in a number of B.C. towns: *John Chernenkoff* in Salmo,
  Nick Denisoff in Glade, *Harry Hadikin* and *Walter Kanigan* in Shoreacres,
  as well as *Tom & Pete Oglow* in Castlegar.

Service industries: Miscellaneous

A number of Doukhobor individuals and families have started or
maintained enterprises offering various services to the public, including
the following:

- **Commercial art:** Signs, lettering and graphics are produced by *Kathy
  Verigin* in Robson, B.C., *Jason Markin* in Castlegar and *Kim Kanigan* in
  Saskatoon; in Whitehorse, Yukon, *Allan Verishine* uses sandblasting
  techniques to make logos and artwork (in addition to painting aircraft).
- **Computer & business services:** *Ryan Androsoff* in Saskatoon, who runs
  a Doukhobor web page on the Internet; *Peter Perelpelkin* of Biznet and
  Gordon Soukeroff of Kootenay Network are both based in Castlegar;
  Frank Wishlow of Edal Computer Centre in Creston, B.C. and *Laverne
  (Sookochoff) Simpson,* owner of the town office in Grand Forks, offering
  bookkeeping, accounting, word-processing and brochure design.
- **Consulting services:** Personal development seminars are offered by
  Jon-Lee Kootnekoff of New Denver, B.C., president of the Horizon
  Positive Self-Image Institute; media consulting services are provided
  by *Eli Sopow* in Victoria; *Wayne Cheveldayoff* is an economic advisor in

Toronto; *Norman K. Rebin* of Almonte, Ont. (now residing in Saskatoon), founded the Pinehurst Institute in 1976 — a management consulting organisation aimed at helping executives improve their personal and professional performance.

- **Hairdressing:** Beauty shops were/are owned by *Vera Chernoff* in Grand Forks (during the 1950s), *Anne Osachoff, Beverly (Chernoff) Parson* and *Sandra (Elasoff) Samarodin* in Castlegar, as well as *Ella Boki* in Saskatoon; barber shops were operated by *Mike Ogloff* in Grand Forks, *Wesley Gorkoff* in Kamsack, Sask., *Fritz Chernoff* in Verigin and *Eli Hoolaeff* in Blaine Lake.

- **Insurance:** Agencies are owned by *Mike Andrasoff* in Grand Forks, *Walter Antifave* in Saskatoon and *John Chutskoff* in Blaine Lake.

- **Real estate:** Doukhobor real estate agents include *Walter Tymofievich* in Castlegar and *Fred Legebokoff* in Red Deer, Alberta.

- **Shoe repairs:** These are provided by *Bill Antifaeff* in Pelly, Sask., *Pete Zaitsoff* in Robson, B.C., *Wasyl Voykin* in South Slocan, *John Hlookoff* in Grand Forks and *Bill Kolosoff* in Castlegar.

- **Smithies:** Accomplished Saskatchewan blacksmiths, making and repairing metal objects by hammering heated iron by hand on an anvil, included *Fred Makaiff* and *Bill Verigin* in Pelly, *Fred Perehudoff* and *John Shukin* in Verigin, *Steve Antifaev* in Asquith, *John Antifaev* in Henrietta and *Pete Katelnikoff* in Blaine Lake.

- **Transportation services:** These range from air charters by pilot *Fred Strukoff Jr* of Stony Rapids, Manitoba, to *Alex Kalidin*'s school bus fleet in Grand Forks, to *Pete Davidoff*'s taxi service in the same town. Not to be forgotten is yesteryear's means of transport, horses, which were well looked after by several Doukhobor livery stable owners: *Matvei Lebedoff, Nick Chutskoff* and *Aleks Yashenkoff* in Verigin, Sask., *Nikolai Popoff* and *Mike Zarchikoff* in Blaine Lake, as well as by *Mike Hoolaeff* and *Bill Makaroff* in Canora, Sask.

Doukhobor inventions

A number of Doukhobors have applied their acumen to invention as well as business. Among them are the following:

- **Foot-massager:** *Fred Chursinoff* of Brilliant, B.C., has developed a reflex foot massager, whch he and his wife *Ann* are marketing.

- **Garden equipment:** *Bill Voykin* of Slocan Park, B.C., invented a two--wheeled garden cart called the 'Easy Wheeler'.

- **Heating equipment:** *Pete Stupnikoff* of Appledale, B.C. has come up with a wood heater he calls 'Valley Comfort'.

- **Hotel-registration device:** *Sam Conkin* developed such a device, which he marketed along with *Jim Laktin* (see below).
- **Snowmobiles:** *John M. Troubitskoff,* a steel fabricator from Blaine Lake, was reponsible for perfecting a certain type of snowmobile.

Other unique enterprises

Inventions are not the only one-of-a-kind enterprises that attract attention. *Tom Chernoff,* who lived in Fort Lauderdale (USA), had several different enterprises going at once: he employed 750 people in manufacturing quonset-type steel buildings, trained racehorses and owned a muffler shop in Winnipeg, and lectured on the art of selling. The following undertakings by Canadian Doukhobors could also be said to fall into this category:

- **Coffins:** These are manufactured by *Mike Chernenkoff* of Krestova, B.C.
- **Cookbook:** A cookbook under the title *Cooking without Mom* was compiled by a group of friends in Castlegar known as the 'Hen Party' — including *Anne Zibin, Kathy Popoff, Mary Cheveldave, Mary Pictin, Shirley Wanjoff, Lola Sherstobitoff, Nadine Elasoff* and *Margaret Holuboff.*
- **Gold mining:** *Walter Berekoff* of Nelson owns a Yukon gold mine as well as businesses in the United States and Cuba.
- **Gutters:** *Harry Zarchikoff* of Winlaw installs seamless gutters.
- **Leather goods:** During the 1920s and 1930s the family of *Alex Maloff Sr* worked together in their tannery, tanning hides and manufacturing shoes, robes and harnesses.
- **Nursing home:** A nursing home in Saskatoon is operated by *Marion (Tarasoff) Mell.*
- **Office cleaning:** *Marge Semenoff* heads an office cleaning company in Saskatoon.
- **Picture frames:** *John Antifaev Jr* of Blewett, B.C., fashions wood into unique picture frames.
- **Pressure washing:** Such a firm is run by *Michael Nevakshonoff* in Castlegar.
- **Spinning-wheels:** These are carved by *Stanley Petroff* of Canora.
- **Well-drilling:** *Walter Koftinoff* and *John Kanigan* of Ooteshenie drill water wells, as does *Bill Drazdoff* of Nelson.

Generations of entrepreneurs

Sometimes the entrepreneurial spirit seems to flow down through several generations; a number of such family enterprises have already been noted. In addition, the following Doukhobor families are worthy of mention for their respective contributions to the marketplace:

- *Chernoff:* Nick and his sons *Kevin, Nick Jr* and *Harold* specialise in concrete construction and land development; they also operate Trowelex Rentals, one of the largest equipment-rental-and-sales outlets in the Kootenays.

- *Fomenoff:* Business pioneers *Pete* and *Helen* owned both a sawmill and a timber mill, in addition to running a general store in Castlegar in the mid-1920s. Their young sons *Bill* and *Fred* delivered fresh milk to individual homes from their dairy farm and later trucked wood and coal. Bill and his wife *Mary* bought a service station, while Fred and his wife *Anne* owned the Sportsman's Shop. The family owned apartments as well as business premises.

- *Holuboff:* John and *Tina* owned Johnnie's Grocery in Raspberry Village, B.C., while their son *Walter* and his wife *Margaret* helped convert two communal village homes into a care home for senior citizens called Raspberry Lodge. Walter and Margaret have also operated a kitchen design centre as well as the Sandpiper Motel & Trailer Court.

- *Hoolaeff:* Louis was an electrical contractor in Pass Creek, B.C., where *Nila* compiled a gourmet cookbook entitled *Doorway to creative cooking.* Moving to Victoria, they established a fine restaurant called Zhivago's, specialising in Russian food as well as Russian singing for entertainment.

- *Laktin:* Brothers *Peter* and *Jim* have been involved in a variety of business ventures, including a fast-food outlet in Nelson, which they own jointly. Peter and his wife *Doris* have operated shoe stores in both Gold River and Nelson. Jim owned Mitech Business Systems in Nelson along with *Pete Supnikoff* and other partners, and is currently a financial consultant in Castlegar. With partner *Sam Conkin* he marketed a registration device for hotels and motels which Sam had invented. Jim's wife *Katie* operates a licensed day-care centre at Playmor Junction.

- *Lazeroff:* Brothers *Samuel* and *William* and their respective families were part of the Trail business community for more than thirty years. Starting with a sawmill, they opened a huge building-supply store and contracted construction projects, and went on to rent out houses and apartment blocks. *William Jr* owned a building-supply store in Rossland, B.C. and his brother *John* a store in Kinnaird, B.C.

- *Oglow:* Brothers *Bill, Peter, Paul* and *Nick* chose Castlegar as their place of buisness and residence. They started a construction company in 1950 and soon afterward opened a building-supply store. Peter's sons *Peter Jr* and *Ivan* supplied and installed carpets and owned an import gift shop. Paul's sons *Tom* and *David* and daughters *Gail* and *Carole* currently operate Oglow's Paint & Wallcoverings in Castlegar and Grand Forks.

- *Planidin:* *Sam* and *Pete,* along with their father *Paul,* originally hailed from Queenstown, Alberta, where the brothers started the Planidin Bros. enterprise in the mid-1950s, selling groceries, hardware and appliances for twenty-two years. *Nora* Planidin and her husband *John Verigin* (who was also involved in home construction) developed three separate grocery stores in Creston, B.C.

- *Pozdnikoff:* Brothers *Nick* and *John* have applied their energies to a wide variety of business ventures, including an electrical contracting firm and the Monte Carlo Inn in Castlegar, shopping-mall construction and land development. John also operates a pharmacy in Creston, where his wife *Liz* runs a stationers' shop. Nick owns an orchard in Oliver.

- *Soloveoff:* *Pete* and *Tina* of Castlegar have three daughters and a son who have all ventured into the entrepreneurial field in B.C. *Mabel Verigin,* a dressmaker who started a garment factory in Trail, is currently a master weaver as well as a fashion consultant in Montrose. *Helen Taschuk* is part owner of Aquatime Leisure Products, which sells home and patio furniture in Burnaby. *Liska Miller* is a partner in All Seasons Pool and Patio in Richmond, while *Harry* designs & drafts building plans at Solo Designs in Castlegar.

- *Vereschagin:* This family in America (Orland, Calif.) sets an example to which many Doukhobor families aspire — namely, to live and work together in harmony. Beginning with the Vereschagin Ranch in the early 1930s, they expanded to include both a petroleum and farm-implement-sales business along with an appliance store. In their orchards they continue to grow prunes, almonds and olives, as well as alfalfa hay and certified clover seed. The family takes pride in being self-sufficient, clearing their own land, repairing their own equipment and keeping their own books.

Epilogue

Without question, one of the basic ingredients of a successful entrepreneur is strong ambition. Moral support from family, friends and acquaintances can help cushion the 'ups and downs'. A good sense of humour is also mandatory! While necessarily following general guidelines to ensure consumer protection, the ultimate control is the conscience of the business person who desires respect from customers, associates, workers and fellowcitizens in the community.

[1]No reference will be made to trained professionals employed by nonDoukhobor enterprises.

[2]As one of three Commissionaires on Castlegar's first municipal Council, George often supplied food to forest-fire fighters.

[3]**One of Ron's best-loved songs is called 'Toil and Peaceful Life' (after the Doukhobor motto).**

Responsible entrepreneurship: an attitude of the mind

William W. Kanigan

Fig. 1. *Bill Kanigan and his mother doing chores on the farm near Kylemore, Saskatchewan. c. 1940s.*

Editor's note: Born 24 December 1931 to a Doukhobor family in the tiny independent Doukhobor community of Kylemore, Sask., William W. (Bill) Kanigan studied industrial electricity and worked part-time in Saskatoon selling furniture and appliances. He soon found the furniture business so much to his liking that he decided to stay in it. In fact, for twenty-seven years, until his retirement in 1989, he operated Buy-Rite Furniture, which he owned with his younger brother Cecil (b. 1939). This grew into one of Saskatchewan's largest furniture concerns with seven stores in the province and one in Manitoba, employing several hundred people and grossing $21 million in sales in 1987. The business was sold when he retired, although Bill still remains active managing his properties, besides helping his daughter and eldest son in their businesses.

His father, William George Kanigan (1910–1983) and mother Mary (née Makortoff, b. 1909) farmed in Kylemore until their retirement in 1975, when they moved to Saskatoon. As Bill recalls, his father was a gifted

111

singer who frequently officiated at Doukhobor social and religious meetings, as well as funerals. Both parents were strong adherents of the Doukhobor faith. Bill attributes his business success to the deep entrepreneurial values of work and honesty his parents taught him.

'You will understand when you grow up', my parents would say. 'We want you to learn to make something of yourself. Learn hard and work hard, but still enjoy yourself. You have got to get out and become something different, something better. Become a teacher, a lawyer, some kind of professional, maybe even a businessman like Bill Fudikuf, like Cecil Rilkoff.'[1]

Doukhobors were communal as well as private entrepreneurs. They set up smithies, general stores, and so on. They built brick plants, flour mills, sawmills and food processing plants (including jam factories) and marketed their products and skills from Vancouver to Winnipeg. Those who stayed on the land were entrepreneurs too, many of them highly successful.

Unfortunately many communal enterprises failed, not from incompetency or lack of the will to be self-sufficient, but largely because of the squandering of assets by some irresponsible leaders who disregarded the welfare of the people. Not only did they damage their own generation, both culturally and otherwise, but they also abandoned all meaningful responsibility for the generations to follow.

This was in marked contrast to the wisdom and the teaching of the Doukhobor elders. While my farming parents, denied an education themselves, confessed to not knowing exactly what I must do to succeed (beyond 'wearing a white shirt'), they did realise I needed an education, and added these telling words of wisdom:

> But more important, never forget God. Be compassionate and honest, be useful. You may not understand now what we are telling you, but some day you will when you grow up.

As I matured, I began to know how wise my formally illiterate parents actually were, and I desired to become the best I could be, as (I think) did many Doukhobors who elevated themselves to the level of their parents' expectations and beyond, accomplishing things that may have also exceeded much of their parents' comprehension.

Responsible entrepreneurship is the result of learning to be God--fearing, honest and compassionate. It was such moral strengths as these on the part of our elders, and their unfailing determination, that helped me begin to understand who I am, and I honour them by sharing their memories here. They gleaned and passed on to us the best qualities, values and beliefs of our people, and their teachings still influence our lives today. The beliefs and practices they instilled regarding courage, hard work and responsibility are shared not just by Doukhobors, but by all people who believe in non-violence. I am grateful for their teachings and the example they set of a positive attitude and outlook on life which enables one to remain undiscouraged by the prophets of doom.

During my youth my parents encouraged me to try out various small business ventures. While not educated in a traditional sense, they instinctively understood the importance of experimentation in preparation for the broader society and the highly competitive world in which we live. They taught me about brotherhood, the importance of resolving conflicts peaceably and the sense of confidence which whispers: 'I think I can, I think I can'.

My parents clung to their beliefs in the face of not only economic hardship but also religious discrimination, and expected us to follow their example, which we endeavoured to do without exception. It was a very, very hard path to follow, especially since it isolated me from almost everyone in school and in the community, but as time passed, I learnt how to integrate. These difficult lessons helped me survive, gave me the courage to take calculated risks and enabled me to prosper in diversified social and cultural communities. They challenged me to reach beyond my usual expectations. This proved to be a confidence-building process, the beginnings of my entrepreneurial approach to life.

Among other painful (but beneficial) lessons for my business career, I saw first-hand the dangers of harbouring prejudice and felt the stressful effects of being on the receiving end. I was taught the importance of promoting and practising co-operation, how it takes strength to be gentle, to solve problems with thoughtfulness and kindness. I learnt to accept the consequences — good or bad — of risk-taking through the realisation that rights go hand in hand with responsibilities. I recognised the need to create situations suitable for adaptation and adjustment in order to provide service to others. Above all I learnt how to assert myself within my God-given rights.

At home I would frequently hear the Golden Rule: 'Do unto others as you would have them do unto you'. This centuries-old rule is rarely entertained by our contemporary business society. Yet it is the keystone of ethics, even though many wrongly assume it is just for 'losers'. I believe that the truly successful entrepreneurs are those who practise these values.

Fig. 2. Bill Kanigan in three-piece suit, with mother. c. 1950s.

What does *being successful* mean? As I was growing up in the middle of the Great Depression, it meant, for one thing, that I was rarely out of pocket money; my entrepreneurial spirit led me to go out and find something to buy and sell at a profit. This helped me rise fairly easily to challenges and the expectation that I should do well.

In professional terms, success can be thought of as building a company that lasts for many years. Rarely does an organisation survive for any length of time unless it is ethical and guided by ethical leaders. Such people of entrepreneurial temperament frequently take advantage of opportunities to make exceptional contributions to the community in terms of both monetary donations and personal service. Their survival as hardy, positive thinkers in a hectic, competitive world reflect the experience of our ancestors who not only survived but thrived on physical adversity. Ethically guided entrepreneurs have mastered the art of survival, they know how to act when faced with seemingly impossible situations beyond their control (such as an overall economic downturn in society), they can isolate problems and turn them around, and come out winners. They find the open doors that are always there for people willing to look for them, knowing that the most hopeless problem harbours opportunity. They take their minds off what 'might have been' and think about what 'can be', and then go forward with deliberate, positive steps.

An entrepreneur is a manager, a producer, who organises, operates and assumes the risk of business ventures, applying his/her strengths (in order of priority) to the three basic management functions: *marketing* (getting the business), *operations* (policies and procedures) and *finance* (making a reasonable profit). Aware that a business is only as strong as its weakest link, entrepreneurs will recognise their weaknesses and compensate for them with partners, senior employees and/or outside consultants. With both peers and subordinates they will build a relationship based, at least in part, on the consistency and predictability of their actions. Having achieved success (as they usually do) through developing their God-given talents and exerting their energies in an honest and responsible manner, they can then enjoy the fruits of their labour, recognised and respected by people from every walk of life and denomination.

It is true that the entrepreneurial attitude of mind places a rather heavy burden on the individual and extracts a heavy price. It can be worth the effort, especially if one is married to a supportive partner who lives to share in the memories of one's accomplishments. I was fortunate that my family survived with me (only God and my wife know why). In my case, my business prospered, and my accomplishments afforded me a great sense of gratification.

---

[1]*Cecil Rilkoff* — a building contractor from Winnipeg whose firm is still in existence today; one of his projects was St Paul's Hospital in Saskatoon.

Ivan Sysoev:
a Doukhobor 'poet of the century'[*]

James D. Kolesnikoff and Nina Kolesnikoff

Ivan Sysoev was born 4 November 1894 at Rodionovka, a village located in the Caucasus mountains of Georgia. Ivan was the youngest of the six children of Fyodor and Manya Sysoev. Three of his brothers died in infancy; three others survived: Fedosya (b. 1888), Fyodor (b. 1891) and Ivan.

The year of Ivan's birth co-incided with several major events in Doukhobor history. It was in 1894 that exiled Doukhobor leader *Peter Vasilevich Verigin* advised his followers living in the Caucasus to burn their arms in symbolic opposition to all types of killing and wars. A year later, at the end of June 1895, the Burning of Arms took place.

Another important event of this period was the Doukhobors' refusal to do military service. Enlisted Doukhobor men began to proclaim that a true Christian must serve only one master — God — and not the Tsar as well. Those who refused military service were put into a penal battalion, and later sent to Yakutsk in Siberia, while those who burned their arms were banished to Tiflis Province and dispersed in mountain villages among Georgians and Tatars. Deprived of any land and forbidden to associate with their brethren in other places, the newly exiled Doukhobors faced almost certain death from starvation.[1]

Fortunately, the great Russian writer and humanist *Lev Nikolaevich Tolstoy* was informed of the Doukhobors' plight and intervened on their behalf, thus averting what might other wise have been a tragedy. In 1898, with help from Tolstoy[2] and English Quakers, the Doukhobors received permission to emigrate from Russia. The first group left in August of the same year, setting out in a cattle boat first for Cyprus, then several months later for Halifax, Nova Scotia. Three other groups followed, and by the summer of 1899 some 7,500 Doukhobors had arrived in Canada, eventually to settle in Saskatchewan.

When Ivan Sysoev set foot on Canadian soil he was only five years old, but he would later recall vividly the long sea journey in the cattle boat and the first difficult months on the prairies. These memorable events are reflected in his poems 'Long past' [*Davno proshlo*], 'No one knows' [*Nikto ne znaet*] and 'My beginning' [*Ia beru svoe nachalo*].[3]

The Sysoev family settled in the Community village of Uspenie (80 kilometres north of Saskatoon), named by the Doukhobors in honour of the biblical Feast of the Assumption. Settling in, the family began to work the land and from the early age of six Ivan helped plough, feed and graze cattle. Seldom was there much time or energy left after a long day's work, but there were some moments when he would sneak away to a nearby grove and memorise psalms from the *Book of Life* [*Zhivotnaia kniga*].[4]

Ivan's parents had the rare gift of being able to compose melodies to hymns and psalms and in so doing they created new songs for Doukhobor choirs. As Ivan recalls, many people would gather at their home to learn new psalms and hymns. The mystical chants of hymn-singing would fascinate the young poet, though reading was still his fondest occupation. His passionate love for books came through listening to his father read aloud to the whole family during the long winter evenings. After learning the Russian alphabet, Ivan would read any printed material he could get his hands on. But there were very few books among the Doukhobors during their early years in Canada. These were hard times and there was little money for the essentials of life, let alone books.

As if by the grace of God, the Sysoev family acquired the Russian book *Zolotye kolos'ia* [*The Golden Grains*][5] from Tolstoyan friends who apparently lived nearby. The book was a collection of short stories aimed at helping people develop 'a Christian consciousness'. In Ivan's words, *The Golden Grains* was his school, his textbook, for learning both grammar and poetry.

When life improved materially in the Community, the Doukhobors began ordering books from Russia. Among the first books from the motherland which Ivan read were the poems of Pushkin. Lermontov, Nadson and Kol'tsov[6] — poetry which sparked the youngster's interest enough to convince him to test his own skill as a poet.

In 1909, at the age of fourteen, Ivan wrote his first poems: 'Along the pathway' [*Idu tropoi*], 'Awaking early' [*Prosnulis' rano*], 'In the Village of Uspenie' [*V sele Uspenii*] and 'Among the fieldgrass' [*V pole travka zeleneet*], in each of which the central theme is derived from daily impressions of life and from admiration of Nature's beauty. 'Awaking early' describes a ploughing scene in spring, while 'In the Village of Uspenie' and 'Among the fieldgrass' depict the elemental rhythms of Nature. Sysoev's early verses are reminiscent of Kol'tsov's poetry in their admiration for Nature, simplicity of language and melody. Like Kol'tsov, Sysoev was a self-taught poet who had never attended a single day of school (Kol'tsov had spent one year in school).

In 1912 the Sysoevs, along with many other Doukhobors, moved from Saskatchewan to British Columbia. Ivan's initial yearning for his native province, the great expanses of its prairies, the family farmhouse and the little leafy-green grove where he would run off to to write poetry, is expressed in his poem 'Farewell, dear Saskatchewan' [*Proshchai, moi krai*]. Yet it was not long before he began to feel himself at home in the Kootenays, embraced by the beauty of the Selkirk Mountains and their many fertile valleys. What helped him most in adapting to the new environment and people was his meeting, courtship and eventual marriage in 1915 to young *Agafya Popoff*.

While Agafya remembers receiving several love-poems from Ivan, none of them, surprisingly, have been preserved. Except for a few romantic poems written in the 1920s, Sysoev seems to have intentionally shied away from this topic, possibly considering it too trivial for a 'spiritually minded' Doukhobor poet.

In 1919 Ivan and his young family returned to Saskatchewan, settled in the village of Kylemore and began farming again, where, in spite of the seemingly endless toil on the land, he found time to write some of his best poetry. In fact, his poetic career blossomed during the 1920s, when he created such outstanding hymns as 'In the struggle for freedom' [*V bor'be za svobodu*], 'Rise up ye new forces' [*Vstavaite sily novye*], 'Friends, the dawn is breaking' [*Druz'ia, gorit zaria*] and many others which exhort Doukhobors to lead a Christian life and to proclaim the ideals of freedom, brotherhood and love. Many of his songs of this period were adopted into the repertoire of various Doukhobor choirs and are still sung at Doukhobor meetings, concerts and festivals.

The year 1924 marked the end of an era in the turbulent history of the Canadian Doukhobors, when their leader since pre-emigration days, Peter Vasil'evich ('the Lordly') Verigin was killed by a bomb explosion in the railway car in which he was travelling. The news of his death shocked all Doukhobors.[7] Sysoev expressed his own deep sorrow in his poems 'The Great fighter' [*Velikii borets*], 'Westward' [*Na zapad*], 'From the beginning of time' [*Ot nachala mirov*] and especially 'In the poet's eyes' [*V glazakh poeta*], where Verigin is seen not simply as a leader who dies tragically at the hands of an enemy but as a universal fighter for truth. The poet assures the dying leader that the Doukhobors will continue their non-violent struggle for the good of mankind under the guidance of his successor.

The new leader, *Peter Petrovich (Chistiakov)Verigin*,[8] arrived from

Russia in 1927 and established an intimate and lasting friendship with Sysoev, who became one of his most faithful and staunch supporters. The poet began to participate actively in the affairs of the Doukhobor community, and at the request of the new leader became a choirmaster and composed many new songs, portraying the Doukhobors as true followers of Christ who carried the cross of civilisation in the name of brotherhood and love, holy martyrs suffering for the Christian faith. As one illustration Sysoev wrote poems decrying Chistiakov's imprisonment in a Prince Albert jail and the Canadian government's abortive attempt to deport him, and during his confinement sent him passionate verses pledging his loyalty and love. His grief over his beloved leader's tragic death in 1939 is expressed in a series of poems: 'Sad news' [*Pechal'naia vest'*], 'My eyes no longer see him' [*Teper' ne vizhu*] and 'Two years pass' [*Proshlo dva goda*].

In 1938 the Sysoevs's returned to British Columbia, settling first in Thrums and later in the Okanagan Valley, working in orchards and on farms. While summers were taken up with hard manual labour, during the winters Sysoev prepared for publication a new version of the *Book of Life* — initiated by Peter P. Verigin (Chistiakov) before his death — to include Doukhobor psalms, prayers and leaders' speeches, as well as poetry. Verigin was to have been editor-in-chief, delegating Sysoev to edit the poetry and John G. Bondoreff to edit the speeches.

The leader's untimely death interrupted the project, but Sysoev continued to collect new material, and in 1945 he approached the Doukhobor Youth Organisation with a publication proposal. When the Youth Organisation refused, Sysoev decided to proceed on his own. By 1954 he had completed preparations on a projected first volume consisting of religious songs and hymns; a second volume would contain Doukhobor psalms, while a third would comprise a collection of popular songs. Unfortunately, however, his most cherished dream was not realised: the *Book of Life* did not appear in print during his lifetime.[9]

A final turning-point came in 1957, when the Sysoevs moved to Grand Forks. Already retired and not needing to seek outside work, Ivan devoted the last ten years of his life here to his poetry, exploring primarily religious themes, contemplating such eternal questions as the purpose of life and the nature of man's role on this earth. Ultimately, he came to the conclusion that without a belief in Christ, life loses purpose and becomes meaningless — a sentiment revealed in the poems 'I call upon you' [*K tebe vzyvaiu*], 'O Lord, accept my prayer' [*Gospod', primi moe molenie*] and 'I like to contemplate' [*Liubliu sozertsat'*].

As the poet grew older, he became more convinced that people were not living rightly, but had exchanged the high ideals of brotherhood and love for personal gain and the satisfaction of material needs. His primary target was the Doukhobors who, in his opinion, had forgotten the teachings of their forefathers and were no longer concerned about their spiritual life. 'Christ is no longer a relative of the Doukhobors,' he wrote in a bitter message to *V.D. Filippoff*, 'they are worshippers of the dollar and luxury.'

This sharp criticism of his brethren, however, did not further the poet's popularity among all Doukhobor factions. Sysoev's biting, polemical lyrics repelled many Doukhobors and near the end of his life he felt alienated and alone among his people — a feeling expressed in such poems as 'No one came to my anniversary' [*Nikto v godovshchinu*], 'The song is sung' [*Davno stikhov*] and 'Hear ye this' [*Poslushai vot*]. He continued to write until his dying day, considering it his sacred duty to speak the truth, so that sooner or later people might heed his call. His last poems, written in hospital in Trail, express a similar concern about the fate of the Doukhobors and their children, about mankind in general. In peace and no longer bitter, the Doukhobor poet passed away 13 April 1967, and was laid to rest in the Doukhobor cemetery at Grand Forks.

Considering himself first and foremost a Doukhobor poet, Sysoev devoted his life-work to the history of his people and their struggle for Christian ideals. He traced the beginnings of Doukhoborism back to the time of Christ, whence the Doukhobors took their principle 'Thou shalt not kill', and their belief in the universal love and brotherhood of man. As true followers of Christ, the Doukhobors had to walk a thorny road, subject to much hardship and suffering.

> In your struggle for freedom, your hearts filled with love,
> You had fallen with dignity, honour,
> Forward, ever forward the dawn beckoned you on,
> But alas, a battle you entered uneven,
> Amidst turmoil and strife, amidst evil and hate,
> You taught only love, understanding;
> You feared neither foe, nor hardships to face;
> You travelled the pathway of suffering.[10]

The burning of arms and the refusal to do military service were, in the poet's opinion, the shining examples of Doukhobor heroism. He speaks with pride of those exiled to Caucasus villages and those sentenced to eighteen years in Siberia. Such were the true Christian martyrs, he indicates in his poems 'In the struggle for freedom' and 'Along the Vladimir road' [*Po vladimirskoi*], but he also acknowledges the hardship of all the Doukhobors of the 1890s who had to part with their homeland and set off on the long journey. He depicts the Doukhobor exodus of 1899 in 'My beginnings' — intended as a prologue to an historical poem commemorating the fiftieth anniversary of the Doukhobors' arrival in Canada.[11]

The sufferings of the Doukhobors, according to Sysoev, did not stop even in Canada. In 'No one knows', the poet gives an account of the Canadian authorities' pressure on the Doukhobors to swear an oath of allegiance, and of the subsequent repossession of Doukhobor lands on the prairies, their resettlement in British Columbia and the organisation of the Doukhobor community under the leadership of Peter V. ('the Lordly') Verigin. Another poem dealing with the same period is 'Hear ye this', in which the poet speaks of the self-sacrificing toil of the members of the former Community, the internal difficulties, the government pressures and the economic collapse of the CCUB.[12] The poem is addressed to Anna Markova, who did not arrive in Canada until 1960 and so did not personally experience life in the commune.[13] It betrays a rather pessimistic mood, focusing on some of the negative aspects of communal life, but later concludes that a communal system based on Christian principles is the most suitable way of life for the Doukhobors.

In spite of his sympathetic attitude toward the Sons-ofFreedom cause, Sysoev avoids focusing in his poems on internal schims among the Doukhobors. An exception is 'The Freedomites' march westward' [*Pokhod svobodnikov na zapad*], describing in detail the march of 1962 — their departure from Krestova village where they burnt their homes, their camping in Hope, the final march to Vancouver, and their eventual incarceration in a specially built prison at Agassiz. Especially notable is the parallel drawn between the marching Sons of Freedom and the rapidly flowing Coquihalla River, which empties into the mighty Fraser, illustrating the desire to free one's self from stagnation and joining one's energy with still mightier forces. But just as the waters of the Coquihalla, upon reaching their destination, are quickly subdued by the more powerful Fraser, the energetic thrust of the Freedomites is crushed without achieving any positive results:

> The cherished dreams of Coquihalla
> Ignited her with fighting spirit,
> And carried her toward the Fraser,
> As if on wings of ecstasy.

> She strived toward her sacred goal
> Dreaming: 'When I'll reach his mighty streams,
> I shall disrupt his peaceful sleep
> With stormy cyclone of my currents.'
>
> But all her dreams were meant to vanish
> When flowing into Fraser's stream,
> She was subdued by the mighty river,
> Accepting peace as a way of life.

Written in iambic tetrameter, rich in bright imagery and vivid similes, 'The Freedomite's march westward' is one of the poet's best creations. In scope and depth it can be compared only with 'The Legend of my forefathers' [*Predanie o moikh predkakh*], which shows the poet's genealogy, and with the poems 'Then and now' [*Togda i teper'*] and 'Who is a Dou-khobor?' [*Dukhoborets tot*], which deal with Doukhobor ideals. In the latter two poems Sysoev writes about how the Doukhobors strive to serve only God, to love their neighbour and refuse to serve in wars. The principle 'Thou shalt not kill', is, in the poet's opinion, the most important tenet in Doukhobor philosophy, and he skilfully uses poetic imagery to proclaim pacifist ideas. 'People are brothers, not spiteful foes', he writes in 'The Doukhobor Marseillaise' [*Marsel'eza Dukhobortsev*], and makes an appeal to the world to beat swords into ploughs and melt down guns for ploughshares. On the basis of a popular revolutionary song, Sysoev created a hymn glorifying toil and peaceful life. Similarly, in his 'In Harmony with faith in God' [*Druzhno s nadezhdoi*] he replaces revolutionary ideology with Christian beliefs:

> Bravely with faith in our Maker
> Chains of oppression we'll break.
> And to the world we'll show the way,
> Evil, with love, we'll overcome!
>
> In struggle so righteous we'll vanquish
> That age-old oppression forever!
> And so this earth we shall raise up
> The quiet, peaceful banner of Christ.[14]

*   *   *

Doukhobor history and Doukhobor ideals are the central themes permeating Sysoev's mature poetry, along with the parallel theme of Christian faith and religion. As the years go by, he reflects more often upon the eternal question of how to be a true Christian, how best to serve God and one's brethren.

While the religious theme predominates in Sysoev's mature lyrics, his early works are devoted almost without exception to the description of Nature. Among the earliest are short landscape sketches which reproduce his impressions from Nature in detail:

> The night has passed. Around us lingers
> The fragrance of the flower blooms.
> The boundless steppe, so lush and verdant,
> A meadow freshness does exude.
>
> Sparkling in the morning lightning,
> Dewdrops play in myriad hue.
> Birds are chirping, and above us
> Stretch the heavens, deep and blue.

While the time of year is not indicated, one senses that it is springtime, the poet's favourite season. His many poems devoted to spring are also the most joyful and cheerful, departing from a purely external description of Nature in favour of communicating emotions aroused in people by events of the outside world. Thus, in his poem 'Christ has risen' [*Khristos voskres*] he portrays Easter as the time of Nature's awakening — and the simultaneous awakening of man's consciousness, of his spiritual strength:

> With spring may people's hearts rejoice,
> May hatred perish and fear be overcome.
> And a voice from Heaven will then be heard:
> Christ has arisen! Christ has arisen!

In Sysoev's mature poetry Nature exists as living testimony to the Almighty God who created all things on earth, from majestic mountains to minute insects. Contemplation of Nature always leads the poet to think of God, of His greatness and mercy.

Beginning with the 1920s, the religious theme occupies an exclusive place in Sysoev's writings. The poet considers it his task to sing praise to the Creator and to His Son, who descended to the earth as mankind's Saviour. The image of Christ is compared to the ship's captain who helps people reach the shores of salvation. In the poems 'The Ship whirls on' [*Mchitsia korabl'*], 'Rages and moans the boundless sea' [*Bushuet i stonet bezbrezhnoe more*] a man's life is viewed as a stormy sea onto which a small ship is cast. Only through Christ's help can people be saved from destruction:

> On this ship Christ Himself is captain and pilot.

> He is trustworthy, brave and looks after all.
> He bypasses reefs in nights dark and stormy,
> And guides his good ship to safe, divine shores.

Man's struggle with the forces of Nature — a metaphor for his struggle to overcome evil — co-exists in Sysoev's poetry with the portrayal of the face-to-face battle between Christians and their adversaries. The poems 'We stand victorious' [*My s pobedoi*], 'Listen, ye fighters' [*Slushaite, bortsy*] and 'The Christian battle' [*Khristianskoe srazhenie*] introduce a series of metaphors likening a spiritual battle to a military confrontation. 'Put on the armour of truth, the shield of faith, the helmet of salvation',[15] Sysoev writes in 'Listen ye fighters', insisting that Christ's followers must struggle for their ideals and that Christ Himself will help in their spiritual battle.

Such a military metaphor for a 'spiritual battle' may seem odd coming from the lips of a Doukhobor poet who rejects all types of violence in the name of love and brotherhood. He seems to be influenced here by the long Christian tradition of glorifying the struggle for Christ. In following this tradition, he constructs many of his religious poems on the contrast between light and darkness, with light representing everything that is associated with God and faith, while darkness symbolises evil and ignorance:

> Without Christ we'll get to nowhere.
> The night is dark with many paths.
> Without a light, we all shall perish.
> The light is Christ — our heaven — God.

The choice of the right path depends ultimately on the people themselves, and in the end everyone will have to answer for their own actions individually. 'The time of God's harvest is coming', warns the poem 'If we are Christian fighters' [*Esli my bortsy Khristovy*]:

> The day of sowing is now passing,
> The night of reaping is at hand.
> God's own harvest now is nearing,
> Soon our Lord Himself shall come.
>
> He will gather what He sowed
> From the ones that brought forth grain.
> But the straw with disappointment
> Shall be burned by Christ the Lord.

The image of the harvest is one of the few images Sysoev took directly from the Bible. As a Doukhobor, he did not consider the Bible divine, and generally avoided biblical themes and motifs.

The most distinctive artistic quality of Sysoev's poetry is its melodic character (this applies equally to those verses which the poet set to music and to those not conceived as songs). It is seen first of all in the consistent use of the syllabo-tonic metre in various lengths and the avoidance of deviation from the basic rhythm. Sysoev uses his favourite metre, the iamb, for most of his religious poems — most frequently iambic tetrameter, less so pentameter or trimeter. He also employs trochaic tetrameter, especially when depicting Nature. In three-foot metres he prefers the amphibrach, using it in intimate poetry to convey his meditations and reflections.

The majority of his poems are divided into four-verse stanzas with alternating masculine and feminine rhythms, although he occasionally introduces six-line stanzas with the rhyme *aabccb* or *aabbcc*. Sysoev's rhymes are almost always exact; in his earlier verses he adheres to strict grammatical rhyme, while in his later work he sometimes resorts to assonance or inexact rhymes.

The musical quality of Sysoev's lyrics is accentuated by frequent repetitions of separate words and whole phrases. Sometimes the beginnings of individual lines or stanzas are similar, sometimes the ending is repeated. In the poem 'In Victory' [*S pobedoi*], for example, each stanza begins with the words 'we are victorious', which intensifies the victory-asserting tone of this poem. Similarly, in 'Christ has risen', the repetition of the title words at the end of each stanza expresses the joy of all Nature at the resurrection of Christ.

As a whole, Sysoev's poetry is characterised by an almost total absence of metaphors and similes. The only metaphoric poems are his early ones, in which Nature is endowed with human characteristics and feelings, and a few later poems inspired by established literary traditions; here he willingly resorts to literary clichés, such as 'to break up the chains of violence', 'to plant the seeds of love', or 'to forge out happiness and freedom'.

The majority of his poems, however, introduce simple and concrete images with frequent reference to visible objects or scenes. While his early writings tend to concentrate on communicating visual and auditory impressions, his mature poetry portrays emotion. Even here, however, he builds his images on concrete details, astounding the reader with their simplicity and straightforwardness.

Most remarkable is the fact that with the aid of concrete and realistic objects Sysoev created highly spiritual poetry. Far from contradicting the deep religious direction of his writings, the concretising of poetic images actually enhances it in some measure.

*Reprinted (with minor editing and additions) from the journal *Canadian Ethnic Studies* (vol 12, n° 1, 1980).

[1] For a more detailed discussion of this turbulent period of Doukhobor history see: P. Biryukov, *Dukhobortsy: Sbornik statei, vospominanii, pisem i drugikh materialov* (Moscow, 1908); V.A. Sukhorev, *Dokumenty po istorii Dukhobortsev i kratkoe izlozhenie ikh veroispovedaniia* (North Kildonan, Man., 1944); P.N. Maloff, *Doukhobortsy, ikh istoriia, zhizn' i bor'ba* (Winnipeg, 1948); C. Woodcock and I. Avakumovic, *The Doukhobors* (Toronto, 1968).

[2] Lev Tolstoy's involvement in the Doukhobor migration is discussed in: V. Bonch-Bruevich (ed.), *Pis'ma dukhoborcheskogo rukovoditelia P. V. Verigina* (Christchurch, U.K., 1901); J.W. Bienstock, *Tolstoï et les doukhobors : faits historiques réunis et traduits du russe* (Paris, 1902); N. & J. Kolesnikoff, 'Leo Tolstoy and the Doukhobors', in *Canadian contributions to the VIII International Congress of Slavists* (Ottawa, 1978), pp. 37–44.

[3] Except for a few poems that appeared in the Doukhobor publication *Iskra* and the Russian émigré newspaper *Rassvet*, much of Sysoev's poetry remains unpublished. The material used here was obtained from the poet's widow Agafya Sysoev. A privately photocopied and prefaced collection of Sysoev's works appears in *Stikhotvoreniia* [Poetic Works] (Richmond, B.C., 1975, 415 pp.), together with a brief biography written by Nick N. Kalmakoff. Many of these poems have been put to music and appear in USCC's *Sbornik*.

[4] *Zhivotnaia kniga* [*The Book of Life*] is a collection of Doukhobor psalms and hymns collected by V.D. Bonch-Bruevich in Canada and published in St-Petersburg in 1909. The title of the collection refers to the Doukhobor concept of the whole body of oral religious literature as a 'living book', in contrast to 'dead' written or printed texts, unanimated by human emotion and speech. The book was reprinted in 1954 by the Union of Doukhobors of Canada.

[5] *Zolotye kolos'ia* (St-Petersburg, 1897).

[6] *Pushkin*, Aleksandr Sergeevich (1799–1837) — most beloved of all Russian poets, considered the 'father of Russian literature'; *Lermontov*, Mikhail Iur'evich (1814–41) — Russia's second most beloved poet, known esp. for his elegiac poem on Pushkin's tragic death (both poets were killed in duels); *Nadson*, Semen Iakovlevich (1862–87) — lyric poet of the late 19th century; *Kol'tsov*, Aleksei Vasil'evich (1809–42) — early 19th-cent. nature poet —*ed.*

[7] For more information on Peter V. ('the Lordly') Verigin see: Woodcock and Avakumovic, *The Doukhobors*, pp. 181–207. (Note that the Russian word translated 'Lordly' is *Gospodnii*, meaning 'belonging to the Lord' — *ed.*)

[8] For more information on Peter P. (Chistiakov) Verigin see: Woodcock and Avakumovic, pp. 284–307. (The name *Chistiakov* is derived from the Russian verb *chistit'*, meaning 'to cleanse' — *ed.*)

[9]A collection following this pattern was finally published in 1978 — *Sbornik dukhoborcheskikh psalmov, stikhov i pesen,* edited by Peter Legebokoff and Anna Markova (Grand Forks, 1978). The collection includes material written by Sysoev and duly attributed.

[10]The English translations prepared for this article by Doukhobor writer Eli A. Popoff, are intended to convey the ideas and images of Sysoev's poetry, even if the rhyme and rhythmic patterns of the original are not always reproduced.

[11]'My beginnings' was never finished, although Sysoev continued to write about the Doukhobors' history in such poems as 'No one knows', 'Our Forefathers' [*Nashi predki*] and 'The Fateful years have gone by' [*Davno proshli*].

[12]The Christian Community of Universal Brotherhood (CCUB), officially incorporated as a limited company in 1917, lasted until 1938. For more details see Woodcock and Avakumovic, pp. 225–60.

[13]Anna Markova emigrated to Canada from the Soviet Union to join her son, John J. Verigin, Honorary Chairman of the Union of Spiritual Communities of Christ (the official organisation of the Orthodox Doukhobors). She died in September 1978.

[14]This hymn paraphrases the popular revolutionary song 'Bravely comrades marching in step' [*Smelo tovarishchi v nogu*].

[15]Cf. Ephesians 6:13–17 — *ed.*

Part II

Traditions preserved

Doukhobors in Canadian agriculture

Fred Petroff

Historical background

With their experience in growing grain and raising cattle, horses and sheep in Russia, it is no surprise that many Doukhobor migrants to Canada — and their children — became farmers (raising grain, livestock and poultry), veterinarians, agronomists, horticulturalists, professors and scientists. This paper is a tribute to some of the Doukhobor men and women who have made a contribution to Canadian agriculture.

In Russia, the *mir* (or village commune) system, along with the *Sirot-skii dom*[1] administrative structure, provided models for the division of labour and the management of the Doukhobors' domestic resources. This co-operative model was transplanted to Canada in 1899, when 7,500 Doukhobor dissidents arrived on the Canadian prairies and settled in three blocks of land in Assiniboia (now part of Saskatchewan). Without a knowledge of English or Canadian institutions, with very limited resources and an absent leader (*Peter V. Verigin,* then still in exile in Siberia, did not arrive in Canada until December 1902), the Doukhobors immediately realised that some sort of communal or co-operative arrangement was necessary for their initial survival in a new land.

An early survey carried out in 1899 revealed the following limited resources available (Bonch-Bruevich, 1901):

	South Colony	North Colony	Sask. Colony	
	Cyprus exile D'rs	Kars/Elizavetpol	Wet Mtn Region	
Kars Doukhobors				
1 horse per	67.7	22.6	27.9	14.6
1 ox per	58.4	66.1	51.7	23.4
1 cow per	73.6	47.8	58.1	20.4
1 wagon per	105.8	60.4	n/a	30.0
1 plough per	130.2	61.7	107.3	36.1

With resourcefulness and self-sufficiency their first cultivation was with human labour, either by spade or by human beings pulling a plough. By 1903, with the help of oxen, horses and farm machinery, the

131

Assiniboia colonies (North, South and Good Spirit Lake) produced 67,663 bushels of wheat, 78,648 bushels of oats, 39,715 bushels of barley and 5,454 bushels of flax — all used by the villagers themselves. Money to buy supplies was earned by men working on outside jobs or through deficit financing.

Fig. 1. *Harvesting flax by Community Doukhobors in Saskatchewan. c. 1902.*

By 1906 the Doukhobors had become prosperous sellers of grain: in addition to supplying their own and their livestock's needs for both summer and winter, that year they sold 150,000 bushels of wheat and 100,000 bushels of oats. They owned more than 6,000 head of cattle (some pure-bred), more than 1,300 head of horses (again, some pure-bred) and 344 sheep. Furthermore, starting in 1902 the Doukhobors were among the first pioneering settlers to make extensive use of advanced farm technology (in the early 1900s this meant using steam power and machinery), as is evidenced by photographs from the period.

A local doctor and provincial politician, Dr T.A. Patrick, commented in his Reminiscences: 'the Doukhobors were like oases in the desert of other people' (Houston & Houston, 1980). Their farm villages with their carpenters, blacksmiths, harness- and shoe-makers (along with other craftspeople) provided services for the inhabitants that individual home-steaders could not provide for themselves and their families. The community system, offering an ordered division of labour and contributions toward a common coffer, did seem an idyllic arrangement. The advantages, however, were in time outweighed by the Doukhobors' lack of education and their uncertain land-tenure agreements with various levels of government, resulting in the disintegration of some sixty-one prairie farm villages and their entire communal organisation.

Fig. 2. *Harvesting scene of Community Doukhobors in Saskatchewan. c. 1915.*

In 1905 the new Minister of the Interior, Frank Oliver, disregarding the 'letters of understanding' on the Doukhobors' land-tenure rights drawn up by his predecessor, Clifford Sifton, decided that the 'Mennonite clause' (drawn up in 1878 to accomodate new Mennonite immigrants) would no longer apply to Doukhobor applicants. As a result, more than 1,600 homesteads covering 258,880 acres [= 104,769 ha], registered by the Doukhobors in 1903–05, were confiscated by the government in 1907 and made available to the general public.

Between 1908 and 1913, some five thousand Community Doukhobors were obliged to seek new lands further west, which they found in the Boundary and Kootenay Districts of British Columbia. By 1922 the Community owned 21,600 acres [8,742 ha] of improved and virgin lands — along with 71,600 acres [28,977 ha] of improved land still in operation on the prairies. Their dedicated effort and abundance of collective labour enabled them to progress at such a rate as to win them special

133

commendation from William Blakemore in his 1912 Royal Commission report on the Doukhobors in B.C.

However, the pioneer conditions in which the new migrants found themselves meant a return to subsistence-level living. The permanent dwellings evenutally constructed took the form of seventy-four two-storey communal units known as 'hundreds' (or 'families'), built to accomodate a maximum of a hundred people, each surrounded by a hundred acres [= about 40 ha] of land. Over the next few years seventy thousand fruit trees were planted, along with vineyards, vegetable gardens and some cereal crops. Fruit and berry harvests were so successful that processing plants were set up at Nelson and Brilliant to produce the well-known 'K.C. Brand Jam'; in 1922 sixty carloads of this popular product were sold well in advance of production.

Following the death of their leader Peter V. Verigin in 1924, the Community's financial affairs deteriorated rapidly. One problem was a series of arson attacks on Doukhobor property, but the major difficulty was mounting debt. A loan of $350,000 from National Trust imposed a mortgage on all lands, buildings and even the jam plant in Brilliant — up to now virtually mortgage-free, and within a few years the debt-load reached more than a million dollars. Over the next decade the new leader, *Peter P. (Chistiakov[2]) Verigin* managed to pay off about 60% of this debt along with more than a half million dollars in interest and $300,000 in taxes. At the same time he invested several hundred thousand dollars in new land and buildings. He was unable, however, to pay off a remaining $360,000, which resulted in the foreclosure, by National Trust and Sun Life Assurance Co. in 1938, on assets worth between five and six million dollars in Saskatchewan, Alberta and British Columbia.

While prairie Doukhobors were able to buy back their land from the creditors on an individual basis, former Doukhobor lands in British Columbia were sold collectively to the provincial government. The B.C. Land Settlement Board allowed Community members to remain on the property as individual tenants, but without the capital, machinery (along with other moveable assets) or business superstructure necessary to make proper use of the land.

Beginning in 1961 the land was sold back to the Doukhobors, and within two years many properties (except those at Krestova) were in the hands of their former owners. During this period elaborate plans were worked out to return to a communal way of life, based on traditional links with the land), but these failed to reach anything approaching the pre-foreclosure scale. Some Doukhobors managed to practise small-scale market gardening on a few hectares here and there, along with berry-farming and orchard cultivation, but by the 1990s the new Canada/USA FreeTrade Agreement (later the North American Free-Trade Agreement) made even these enterprises unattractive, and most British Columbia Doukhobors today earn their living at outside activities, growing only enough for the needs of their own families. A notable exception is *Nick Abetkoff* in Grand Forks, B.C., who has managed to maintain a fully--integrated, fortyhectare potato farm, selling potato seeds and packaged potatoes through greengrocers and farmers' markets.

Doukhobor agricultural achievements on the prairies

Following the dissolution of the formal Doukhobor Communities in Lundreck and Cowley, Alberta, some members there became successful 'independent'[3] farmers and ranchers. During the decade 1965–75, when the Soviet Union made annual purchases of 200–500 head of cattle from Canada, many Alberta Doukhobors' Herefords were among those selected for shipment. One of the first ranchers to begin selling cattle to Russia was *Pete Holoboff* of Nanton, Alberta. He also acted as a host to the buyers, along with Doukhobor *Peter Samorodin* of Mossleigh, who travelled with the Soviet selectors and in 1967 accompanied the animals to Montréal for embarkation. Some Doukhobor cattle were also sold to Czechoslovakia. These ranchers not only raised high-quality cattle, but also took an active part in the associations promoting good breeds.

But these are the exceptions. In comparison with the 1920s, Doukhobor involvement in Alberta agriculture has all but disappeared. In the current decade some of their former lands have been sold to the government for the Old Man River dam project, which has meant the flooding of some of the original village sites.

Following Frank Oliver's new land-tenure policy in 1907, several hundred Saskatchewan Doukhobors took or affirmed the oath of allegiance to become 'Independent' landholders. The remaining 'Community' Doukhobors were left with 768 homesteads covering almost 123,000 acres [just under 50,000 hectares]. Under considerable pressure for assimilation, the Independents became more secular in their outlook and began to take an active part in Canadian institutions — especially those related to agriculture such as the co-operative movement, local fair boards and councils of 'rural municipalities', where a high degree of formal English-language education would not be a strict requirement.

For example, municipal records of what is now the rural municipality of Coté, Saskatchewan, indicate that as early as 1910 a Mr *Bloudoff* was involved in local government work. Following the establishment of the rural-municipality system in 1913, many Doukhobors participated in the councils of rural municipalities that encompassed their lands. Local records of various Saskatchewan rural municipalities reveal the following Doukhobor names:

Alex Egoroff — Livingston (1915)
P.A. Bloudoff — reeve of St Philips (1922)
J.D. Maloff — Keys (1917)
T.J. Dergousoff — Buchanan (1914)
W.W. Strelioff — Good Lake (1933, 1935)
Koozma Tarasoff — Park (1926–30)
Peter Rebalkin & **John S. Antifaev** — Park (1933–35)

Fig. 3. *Doukhobor flour mill, Verigin, Sask. c. 1922.*

A number of Doukhobors obtained contracts in co-operative grain marketing, a practice which in 1923 and 1924 led to the formation of the Alberta and Saskatchewan Wheat Pools, respectively. In the latter's registers, Doukhobor names appear as early as 1926–27, when *Jacob Dergousoff* of Buchanan was elected as a delegate.

During the 1930s and 1940s the University of Saskatchewan's Extension Department organised beef, dairy, hog and grain clubs to promote improvement in agricultural production and rural leadership. Doukhobor youth participated actively in these clubs and some, like *George Stushnoff* of the Langham district, became leaders in the Canadian branch of the '4-H' movement.

Some Doukhobor farms were selected for the headquarters of stud stations, where government-purchased bulls were introduced to help improve livestock breeds. Individual farmers also ventured out on their own. In 1933 the *W.W. Strelioff* family acquired pure-bred Percheron mares and imported pure-bred stallions from American breeders to run a herd of around sixty head. Their horses won Grand Champion and Reserve Champion ribbons at shows in Regina, Saskatoon, Yorkton and Brandon, as well as a trophy for the best three-year-old Saskatchewan-bred-and-raised stallion colt. The progeny of their herd was used to improve other herds in the surrounding areas.

According to University of Saskatchewan records, the first graduate to receive a B.S.A (Bachelor of Science in Agriculture) from its College of Agriculture was *Paul Mathew Papove* in 1936. Over the next decade many Doukhobors enrolled in both degree and diploma courses. A number of these graduates returned to farming, while some pursued careers in government service, initially in the extension field (although more recently as researchers with PhDs).

A list of Saskatchewan agricultural organisations where Doukhobors hold or have held ranking positions would include: agricultural development and diversification boards; the Western Grains Research Foundation; livestock, oil seed and cereal crop associations; the Saskatchewan Conservation and Development Association and co-operative associations (credit unions, retail co-ops, the Saskatchewan Wheat Pool, seedcleaning plants, etc.).

Doukhobors have also found employment in government and university departments — e.g., crop insurance boards (*John Vanin*), the Soil Survey report (*Richard Stushnoff*), grasslands research (*Wally Vanin*) and soil conservation programmes (*Phylis Kondratoff-Olynick*). *Paul Shukin*, formerly of Buchanan, is a regional manager with the Saskatchewan Rural Service Centres, responsible for sixteen offices and a staff of twenty-seven extension workers.

While few Doukhobors are engaged in private business related to agriculture (other than primary production), a prominent exception is the Senstek manufacturing operation, started in 1974 by *William W. Strelioff,* a university graduate in electrical engineering. It has been notably successful in adapting state-of-the-art microchip technology to the manufacture of electronic weighing equipment, electronic shaft monitors and ultrasonic sound-sensing equipment for height- and depthcontrol on farm equipment. From its Saskatoon plant its products are sold throughout Canada and in several other countries (America, Mexico, Australia, Japan and Belgium).

Despite a wider interest in agriculture, Doukhobor agricultural participation is primarily in cereal, oilseed and livestock production. While the scale of operations is smaller than in former times, one enterprise in the Kamsack (Sask.) region owned by *Paul Strelioff* has grown most impressively — from humble pioneering beginnings to a land-base of 36 sections covering 5,800 acres [2,347 ha]. The operation began to grow by using large-scale equipment (available following World War II) to cultivate registered seed (mainly oats and canola) on virgin lands leased or purchased from the native peoples and the Government of Manitoba. The native peoples also provided some of his long-term employees, staying with him for the entire period of the large-scale operation (1944–75).

Recognising the need for additional alfalfa seed production, *George Strelioff* of Verigin, Sask., established a leaf-cutter bee production business, a secondary enterprise essential for successful pollination and maximum seed set. His bees have been sold mainly to the United States, but sales have also been made to the former Soviet Union, Spain and other European countries. In 1991 he received a '20-year Certificate of Merit' from the Saskatchewan Seed Growers Association for successfully and continuously producing certified alfalfa seed.

While fruit production is not a common industry on the prairies, an interest in horticulture inspired a farmer near Buchanan, *Wasyl Fofonoff,* to discover and propagate a chancemutated seedling that was later recognised as a distinct variety of plum. He worked with the University of Saskatchewan's Department of Horticulture in setting up test-plots of apples, pears, cherries and plums for varietal suitability and commercial possibilities on the prairies. For his efforts he received the Robinson award for high achievement in the field of horticulture.

A number of Doukhobors have taken significant formal education and risen to the forefront of technology in their field. After working for *J.D. Konkin* & Sons — only the second corporate farm to be established in Saskatchewan — *Peter Konkin* became the very first 'mature' student to be accepted at the Ontario Veterinary College at Guelph, and graduated with distinction in 1964. Together with his wife Irene he established a successful veterinary practice and built one of the province's first veterinary hospitals at Yorkton. When some fascinating research in cattle embryo transplants was being conducted at Cambridge University (in England), Peter Konkin was privileged to be one of four Canadians selected to study there under Dr L.E.A. Rowson, the pioneer in the field.

The transplant work Dr Konkin (along with his wife and son) began in Canada upon his return was eventually rewarded with the birth of the first embryo transplant calves in Saskatchewan. It was not long before he sold his practice to devote his whole time to transplant research. He helped refine existing professional techniques to the point where transplants can now be effected with both the donor and the recipient in a standing position, using only local anæsthetics and with a single assistant. Embryos are now routinely frozen and shipped to recipient animals all over the world. As a founding member of the International Embryo Transfer Society, Dr Konkin has travelled to Australia, New Zealand, China, Hong Kong, Germany, Austria, Hungary and the United States of America.

Another Doukhobor who has reached the highest level of academic achievement in the agricultural field is Dr *Cecil Stushnoff*, formerly of Saskatoon. Graduating with distinction in 1963 with a B.S.A degree from the University of Saskatchewan, he went to America, where he earned a Ph.D. at Rutgers University in 1967. He has lectured at both Canadian and American universities and most recently at an American college. From 1981 to 1989 he served as Professor and Head of the Department of Horticultural Science at the University of Saskatchewan, and in 1992 took up duties as Professor of Horticulture and Biochemistry at Colorado State College in Fort Collins, Colorado. He has also been involved in association, extension and other public service activities.

In Saskatchewan Dr Stushnoff worked on breeding small fruits (e.g., blueberries, strawberries) for cold climates, using new methods such as micro-source-cutting for propagation and cryopreservation (freeze--storing) of genetic resources for future use. He pioneered a technique for transferring genetic material from other sources to strawberries to enhance their cold-hardiness and resistance to disease.

Wally Vanin, an extension agrologist in the Kamsack area, established the Parkland Forage Association, resulting in the construction of an alfalfa processing plant at Norquay, Sask., which in 1992 employed forty-two people processing alfalfa grown on 10,000 contracted hectares, yielding total sales of nine million dollars. In 1991 he took a leave of absence to work on the Grazing and Pasture Technology Programme — an area that had earlier received very little attention in Saskatchewan. Wally is now working as an agrologist in the Canora (Sask.) area, where he is promoting better forage and grazing management as a key to higher profits in livestock production.

Fig. 4. *Dr. Cecil Stushnoff (right) , plant breeder, formerly of Saskatoon, Sask.*

A Saskatchwan cattleman who successfully took advantage of modern techniques and technology in livestock management is *Don Horkoff,* who owns the Linden Valley Ranch near Kamsack. Since beginning his operation in 1985, he has exported many of the polled Herefords he has raised for breeding purposes to the United States, to buyers in fifteen different states. Subsequently switching breeds, he and his family now run a breeding herd of seventy polled Charolais cows, implementing in the breeding process several innovative programmes (record of production, bull-testing and ova-transplant technique), all of which earned them the Charolais Breeders-of-the-Year award in 1985. One bull has been exported to England and several animals to America. His wife Audrey has also been active in the Charolais Breeders' Association and on the Board of Directors of the Regina Agrabition.

Even in the earliest years of settlement, the Devil's Lake Annex (an early Doukhobor reserve near Buchanan, Sask.) was not considered to be the most desirable place to farm because of the numerous sloughs that appeared after a spring thaw or a heavy summer rain. These poor drainage conditions remained basically unchanged until the late 1950s,

when local farmers (with help from the province) organised a drainage-and floodcontrol programme in the Tiny-Devil's-Lake area. The first elected board comprised *George Strelioff, Stanley Petroff* and *Nick Strelioff*, while *Fred Petroff* (the present writer) was hired as secretary. Over the next two decades nearly all the poor lands in the area have become fully productive parts of the Buchanan and the Good Lake Conservation & Development Areas, covering more than 80,000 hectares.

Fig. 5. Wally Vanin, Agricultural expert in Saskatchewan.

Since 1957 the writer, hailing from the town of Canora, Saskatchewan, has been involved with drainage and flood programmes and projects in various capacities. He has served first as secretary-treasurer and then as chairman of the Good Lake Conservation & Development Area, secretary-manager of the Saskatchewan Conservation and Development Association and currently as secretary-treasurer of the Buchanan Conservation & Development Area. All these projects have minimised conflict among landowners arising from flooding, at the same time maximising financial returns. Wherever possible, these multi-purpose projects have been designed to maintain wetlands and lake levels and provide water for back-flood irrigation.

Since 1975 *Maurice Cheveldayoff* of Marcelin, Sask., has been involved in forward-looking or futuristic agricultural research. From 1975 to 1991 he served as chairman of the Western Grains Research Foundation, established to initiate, encourage, support and conduct research in both grain production and grain economic and market development, exploring a wider variety of possible uses for grain crops and their by-products. Since 1983 Cheveldayoff has been president of the Western Canada Flax Growers Association, as well as their representative on the board of the Western Grains Research Foundation. At present he is also the manager of Sask-Can Fibre Inc., a Canora-based concern that assembles flax straw under contract with farmers and promotes the use of flax fibre for a variety of uses other than paper.

It should be remembered that agricultural cultivation on the prairies is barely a hundred years old, and many adjustments to old cultural practices and crop types are still in the process of adoption and acceptance. In the early 1900s it was learnt that some soil types are not appropriate for cultivation, and the use of the plough and the double disc actually contributed to the soil drifting and crop failures during the drought of the 1930s. But our forefathers showed their adaptability to adverse situations: when soil-drift prevention was introduced in the 1930s, *Nick Chernoff* and *John Zeebin* were among the first to plant rows of protective shelterbelts across their farms north-east of Verigin, Sask.

Doukhobor farmers also had a hand in coping with the drought of the 1980s, when it was apparent some of the lessons of the 'thirties needed to be re-learnt. *Phylis Kondratoff-Olynick,* for example, took part in a federal-provincial programme called 'Save Our Soil', which encouraged the use of new cultural and technological approaches. As one of a growing number of prairie women taking an active part in the agricultural industry, she has been working through schools and workshops to promote no-till direct seeding, grassing waterways, planting shelterbelts and replacing summer-fallowing with chemicals as a means of weed control.

General observations

By 1926 Canadian census figures revealed a striking similarity in farm size, spending patterns, agricultural methods and products between Saskatchewan Doukhobor settlements in the Kamsack-Canora and Blaine Lake districts and earlier Mennonite settlements in Rosthern, Saskatchewan and the West Reserve in Manitoba. This indicated that the Independent Doukhobors had either reached the Canadian standard of living and production or were moving very rapidly in that direction. It also showed that, far from needing to be dragged kicking and screaming into the mainstream of Canadian society, with a little time they would be able to take full advantage of any opportunity to succeed.

Many of the farms established by Independent Doukhobors in Saskatchewan are still in operation today. Indeed, the majority of Doukhobor farmers earn their entire income from producing grains, pulse crops and oilseeds, others from mixed farming (cow-calf beef operations combined with grain and oilseed production). While Doukhobor farmers have not been involved in dairy, hog or poultry operations on a commercial scale, a few do raise sheep to meet a local demand for lambs.

Education has been a priority among Doukhobor farm families: many sons and daughters have left the farm to enter professions, take advantage of business opportunities or engage in other off-farm employment. The number of Independent Doukhobor farms, after decreasing significantly since 1955, has now stabilised, and the remaining farms are well established. Many farmers have survived thanks to both careful business management and supplemental off-farm income. A number of farms have increased in size to 800 hectares or more, with up to half the land being rented. Modern Doukhobor farmsteads boast well-kept, soundly constructed homes and farm buildings, along with efficient gardens and shelterbelts.

Family partnerships are common in farming enterprises. In some instances, in fact, fourth and fifth generations of Canadian Doukhobors continue to farm lands originally set aside for their immigrant forebears in 1899, still preserving the traditional work ethic and attention to detail. Such traditions are apparent in their sound agronomic and animal husbandry practices which, by efficiently exploiting both old and new technologies, have ensured a high level of productivity along with the conservation of farmland for future generations.

Bibliography[4]

Bonch-Bruevich, Vladimir D. (1901). *Russkie pereselentsy v Kanade: ot"ezd i pervyi god zhizni v Amerike* [Russian settlers in Canada: departure and their first year in America[5]]. St-Petersburg: Narodnoe Khoziastvo, kn. 1.

Dawson, C.A. (1936). 'The Doukhobors'. *Group settlement: Ethnic communities in Western Canada.* Series: Canadian Frontiers of Settlement, vol. 7. Toronto: MacMillan, pp. 1–91.

Government of Canada (1926). Census of the Prairie Provinces. Ottawa: Dominion Bureau of Statistics.

Houston, C.J. and C.S. Houston (1980). *Pioneer of vision: Reminiscences of T.A. Patrick, M.D.* Saskatoon: Western Producer/Prairie Books.

Kootenay Business Journal (1990). Vol. 3, n⁰ 5 (October 1990).

Schmidt, Jeremy (1986). 'Spirit Wrestlers: The Uneasy life of British Columbia Doukhobors'. *Equinox* (Jan/Feb 1986), pp. 60–68.

Tarasoff, Koozma J. (1982). *Plakun trava. The Doukhobors.* Grand Forks, B.C.: MIR Publication Society.

[1]*Sirotskii dom* — the former 'Orphans' Home' in Gorelovka, which became a prayer house and administrative centre for the Caucasus Doukhobors.

[2]The name *Chistiakov* may evoke the Russian verb *chistit'* (to cleanse) — *ed.*

[3]Doukhobors who broke with tradition and took an oath of allegiance to the Canadian monarch (or crossed out the oath clause and 'affirmed the truth') were known as 'Independents', in contrast to the 'Community Doukhobors' who held more strictly to the old ways and refused assimilation — *ed.*

[4]In writing this article I am also indebted to the following people for their kind communications:
- Administrators of Saskatchewan rural municipalities: Coté, Sliding Hills,
  Keys, St Philips, Livingston, Good Lake, Buchanan, Corman Park (Cory)
- Saskatchewan Wheat Pool (Regina, Sask.)
- University of Saskatchewan (Saskatoon, Sask.)
- Dr P. Konkin, Wallace Vanin (Kamsack, Sask.)
- George Strelioff, Don Horkoff (Verigin, Sask.)
- Phylis Kondratoff-Olynick, Irene Sukrat, Wasyl Strelioff Jr. (Canora, Sask.)
- Paul P. Shukin, Bill Strelioff, Richard Stushnoff (Saskatoon, Sask.)
- Dr Cecil Stushnoff (Fort Collins, Colorado, USA)
- Maurice Cheveldayoff (Marcelin, Sask.)
- Nick Abetkoff, Eli A. Popoff, Fred Horkoff (Grand Forks, B.C.)
- Peter P. Verigin (Benito, Man.)
- Michael M. Verigin, Fred P. Maloff, J.J. Semenoff (Cowley, Alta)
- Peter S. Samorodin (Fort McMurray, Alta)
- Mike P. Holoboff (Nanton, Alta)

[5]Russian commentators of the period sometimes used the word *Amerika* to refer to the whole North American continent, including Canada — *ed.*

Doukhobor bread-baking in Saskatoon: a success story

George Stushnoff

Introduction

Bread, salt and water comprise the traditional Slavic and Doukhobor symbols for the basic staff of life, for hospitality, respect and universal humanity on earth. For Doukhobors in the Saskatoon district of Saskatchewan, bread has a special meaning. Since the mid-1950s, every summer during the annual week-long city exhibition, Doukhobor men and women bake bread in brick ovens as their ancestors did during the pioneer era on the Canadian prairies. The bread is then sold in loaves or slices (with or without butter or jam), and sometimes with vegetarian borshch.

So popular has been this undertaking that local Doukhobors have come to rely upon bread-baking as an effective means of funding their organisation (the Doukhobor Society of Saskatoon), as well as supporting community and charitable causes, for example:

- aid to underdeveloped war-torn countries;
- Doukhobor Centenary projects;
- research on heart, cancer, multiple sclerosis and retarded children;
- maintenance of the local Doukhobor Community Home.

While bread-baking is a major effort of the Society, its members (composed of local and area Doukhobors) are also involved in other activities: participating in annual Doukhobor Peace Day celebrations on 29 June, the International Food Fair, annual Folkfests and seasonal bazaars, hosting discussions on the future of the movement and planning for the Doukhobor Centenary. Traditional Russian *a cappella* singing (with some adaptations in English) has continued to be a popular cultural activity of both young and old, along with periodic participation in Sunday prayer meetings, funerals, concerts and other special events.

Preserving the past stimulates action for the present

The celebration of Saskatchewan's Golden Jubilee in 1955 prompted the Saskatoon Doukhobors to organise as a legal entity; official incorporation took place 7 February 1955. A specific incentive was provided by the City of Saskatoon's invitation to provide a unique historical attraction for its first 'Pion-Era' exhibition, namely, baking bread in an outdoor oven built by *Alex Stadnyk* of Choiceland for the Western Development Museum in Saskatoon.

Foreseeing the opportunity of fund-raising for the construction of their Community (Prayer) Home, the Saskatoon Doukhobors commissioned *John K. Tarasoff* to build an additional Doukhobor brick oven for bread-baking. The Saskatchewan Wheat Pool, of which the Doukhobors were long-time supporters, was persuaded to supply free flour on this occasion — a tradition which later continued in exchange for an advertising sign. Local Doukhobors *Koozma K. Tarasoff* and *Alvin Meakin* carted the flour first to the women's houses for mixing[1] and then to the site of the bread-baking.

The four-hundred-dollar profit realised that first year encouraged the members to proceed with the construction of a typical Doukhobor pioneer log-house the following spring. *John Meakin* and *John Papove* helped haul poplar poles from *Pete Androsoff*'s farm north of the city. The house was completely furnished, including a stove, chairs and a table with a full set of dishes — and, of course, its own brick oven for bread--baking. The bedroom even featured a family of mannequins dressed in traditional Doukhobor clothes. Visitors on guided tours could watch demonstrations of wool-carding, weaving and spinning, along with bread-baking. With all the work being done on a volunteer basis, the second year of operation netted a profit of approximately $850.

When the first portable outdoor clay oven accidentally burnt down in 1956, the Doukhobor community built a larger and better three-oven unit, complete with a roofed wooden shelter and an adjoining 'warm room' for kneading the rising dough and setting out the pans. A sales counter was also included. From then on, bread-baking during the Pion-Era exhibition could proceed rain or shine. In 1957 the net profit more than doubled from the previous year, and day-to-day sales during the week-long exhibition were recorded in the Society's minutes for the first time.[2]

Doukhobor women organise

On 13 April 1956 the Doukhobor women of the city held a meeting to form their own auxiliary to the Doukhobor Society of Saskatoon, to raise additional funds for the building and maintenance of their Community

Home. A week later they elected *John Papove* to be the 'man' overseer of the four baking days, while *Mary Shintaruk* and *Mary Sherstobitoff* were chosen as the 'women' overseers. They then organised three working groups of members (headed by *Mary Meakin*, *Mary Tarasoff* and *Nastia Tarasoff*), in which the women would take turns preparing the dough in their own homes and looking after the baking and sales end of the process, while the men were responsible for the preparation of firewood along with the firing and cleaning of the ovens. *Koozma J. Tarasoff Sr* set up a trailer on the Pion-Era grounds where the women portioned out the dough into individual steel bread pans for rising.

Everyone was encouraged to wear white shirts and white aprons. The salesclerk handling the money never touched the food being sold. Some ladies prepared the bread while others served the customers.

Fig. 1. Mixing bread doe by hand and cutting it into pan-sided loaves 1994.This method has been used when bread was first baked in clay ovens at the Pion Era Days in Saskatoon, July 1955. The Saskatoon Doukhobors still rely on intensive labour to bake the bread doe, but now an electric mixer is used.

Ann Kabatoff instructed the women to mix the yeast with lukewarm water to facilitate the rising. During a personal interview she described the operation in her own words as follows:

The year 1955 was the start of our bread-baking project. At first, each one of us had to mix a hundred pounds [= 45 kg] of flour by hand in our own homes. However, in 1956 we mixed the dough at the newly built Prayer Home, while the men took the dough to the grounds where the ladies rolled it out in pans and baked it when ready. We worked till midnight, then stopped til 3 or 4 in the morning and started again. During the first days of the shift we went home to sleep; I spent the night at friends' and was up at 3 next shift.[3] **Tanya Ozeroff** and myself slept in the sod house on board beds. Because the police looked after our safety, we gave them bread in exchange. A few days before Pion-Era many of us gathered and plastered the sod building. My husband **Bill** and myself came from Kinley; we both enjoyed community work as volunteers. Bill used to fire the ovens, while I used to spin wool in the sod house with **Vasunia Demoskoff**. We had fun teaching children and men to spin. Regularly, we had to slice bread, making sure to get a dozen slices out of a loaf. We sold bread at 50 cents a loaf. We brought our own jams, mostly rhubarb or cranberry. I used to bring *pindeer* cheese for our lunches and others brought other tradtional dishes; we all ate in unison, having a great friendly time. People enjoyed warm bread with home-made jam and the *pindeer* cheese I brought was something special. I even brought fresh cream once in a while for coffee. Bill enjoyed the steam engines and often blew the whistles; he had a friend from Kinley who used to run one. I think his name was John Seabrook. We missed only two years when Bill took sick.

While outdoor clay ovens may have been a novelty in 1955, *Olga Serhienko* reports that home-baked bread was still quite common. When the public did not readily respond at first to buying the bread, Olga, who was serving as a cashier, took it upon herself to promote this unique product. In a loud voice, she would call out: 'Doukhobor bread is the tastiest bread. Give it a try, only five cents a slice. The difference in taste comes from the wood-fired clay ovens. Come see how the bread is baked!' And the people came.

The baking proceeded on a daily basis from 8 a.m. to 2.30 the next morning. Crusts were given free of charge to children as a public relations gesture. Americans would come in their motorhomes and buy 40–50 loaves, along with jars of borshch to take back to Florida. Some would return two or three times to get as much as they wanted.

Most of the ingredients for making the bread were donated. The jam was home-made. Flour was donated by the Wheat Pool, along with 75 pounds [34 kg] of butter from local dairies. For lunches, each family would bring some food and share it around a table, picnic style. On the night shift the work group would often break the silence by singing. Local police would come for a midnight snack and would compliment the singers on their beautiful harmony. As a reward for their efforts, volunteer workers received a loaf of bread at the end of their shift. The fruition of all their hard work was seen in the development of the Doukhobor Society of Saskatoon and the construction of their Community and Prayer Home.

Fig. 2. Oven fresh bread by Saskatoon Doukhobors.
(Photo by Koozma J. Tarasoff. 1980).

Basic facts and figures

1954 (October) 'Threshermen's reunion' rehearses volunteers & old machinery in preparation for Saskatchewan's 1955 Golden Jubilee. Western Development Museum curator George Shepherd encourages Doukhobors to preserve their heritage.

1955 (spring)   Under John K. Tarasoff's direction, Doukhobors construct an outdoor bread-baking clay oven to supplement the existing museum oven previously built by Alex Stadnyk of Choiceland.

1955 (4–9 July) First Pion-Era exhibition in Saskatoon celebrating the province's Golden Jubilee.

(4 July, 10 a.m.) First batch of bread from the old clay oven produced by the Doukhobors.

First year of Doukhobor bread-baking, with all goods and services donated; net profit of $400.

1956 (spring)   Doukhobors construct and furnish a pioneer log house with an indoor clay oven.

Doukhobors build their first Community Home (also known as a Prayer Home) at 525 Avenue I South in Saskatoon.

1956 (summer) Second year of Doukhobor bread-baking at PionEra; net profit of $850.

1957 Doukhobors build a new 3-unit clay oven under a wooden-frame shelter.

Third year of bread-baking at Pion-Era; net profit of $1,760.

1960 Bread-baking sale continues; net profit: $1,817.

1961 (January) Decision to raise the Community Home structure and construct a basement underneath.

1961 (April)   Pion-Era board promises up to $5,000 to the Doukhobor Society for relocation expenses to ensure that bread-baking remains a permanent feature.

1961 (July)   Wheat Pool donates 52 100-lb sacks of flour, balance to be paid for in cash and loaves of bread for the Pool staff; net profit of $1,812.

1962 (May)   The Saskatoon Doukhobor Ladies' Society is invited by Mr LeBeau of the board of the Western Development Museum to serve bread and samovar tea to 500 guests at a meeting of the Commonwealth Productivity Council, headed by Prince Philip (a success despite the Prince's absence).

1963 The Western Development Museum requests 75 loaves of bread to host convention delegates of the American Transit Association.

1964 Bread-baking sale continues; net profit: $2,146.

1965 (January) Net surplus declared of $1,970.65. Free bread is distributed to senior-citizen homes and to various businesses for services rendered.

1966 (June)   Decision to pay volunteers honorarium of $1 per hour; net profit reduced to just under $950.
1967   Sale of borshch introduced and volunteer honorarium reconfirmed; net profit of $1,247.48.

1969   Volunteer honorarium raised to $1.25 per hour; net profit of $595.

1971 (June)   200 slices of bread provided for the National Physiotherapy Association banquet at Marquis Hall (Univ. of Saskatchewan).

1971 (July)   Wheat Pool donates 32 100-lb sacks of flour for bread--baking; net profit of $857.

1972 (summer) Decision to abolish volunteer honorarium; net profit of $2,686.

1973 Decision to restore honorarium of $1 per hour, and to raise bread price to 20¢ per slice (+ 5¢ for jam); loaves to sell at 60¢ each, coffee at 15¢; net profit of $2,192.

1974 Honorarium raised to $1.25 per hour plus a loaf of bread per shift; prices raised to 75¢ per loaf, 25¢ a slice (30¢ with jam) and 20¢ for coffee.

1976 Concession fee of $350 paid; net profit: $5,236.

1978 Pion-Era moves from Eleventh Street to the Saskatoon Exhibition Grounds, where Doukhobors build new brick ovens at a cost of $10,000 (with a $7,000 grant from the federal Dept of Secretary of State's Multiculturalism Programmme).

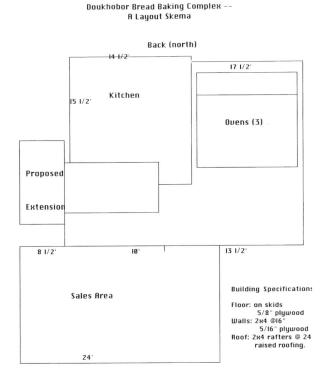

Fig. 3. *A layout schema of the bread baking operations in Saskatoon.*

1980 The Federated Co-op orders 100 loaves of bread for a banquet of 700 people on 11 July.

At Pion-Era loaves sell for $1.50, slices at 50¢ (+ 5¢ each for butter or jam); tea or coffee at 40¢; honey at $2 or $2.50. 200 20-kg sacks of flour donated by Wheat Pool. Total sales: $16,358.

1981 Volunteer honorarium raised to $4/$4.50 per hr; loaves selling at $1.75.

$300 received for bread supplied to Canadian Association of School Administrators conference at the Western Development Museum.

1982 300 loaves of bread supplied to the Doukhobor Pavilion at Saskatoon's Folkfest.

190 loaves of bread ordered by Federated Co-op.

1984 Concession fee of $1,500 paid; net profit: $6,539.

1991 Concession fee: $2,500 paid; net profit: $10,000; Wheat Pool donates 25 20-kg sacks of flour.

1992 (March) Doukhobors led by *Polly Meakin-Tokaryk* cater a full Doukhobor meal to National Dairymen's convention at the Western Development Museum — George Stushnoff is after-dinner speaker and Doukhobors provide choir entertainment (many warm compliments received).

1993 Concession fee: $2,675 paid; bread sales: 10,700 loaves for $37,432; borshch sales: $1,725.

From that meagre start (and Olga Serhienko's strong sales pitch) the popularity of Doukhobor bread has grown steadily from year to year. Daily production-runs from midnight to noon are usually sold out by 6 p.m.; after that customers ask when the next baking will be ready and start queueing up a half-hour ahead of time. An average 90-loaf batch of bread comes out of the ovens every hour and a half. For many queues the quota is one loaf of bread per customer. Permanent exhibition workers (those who travel with it from city to city) purchase their loaves of bread in the morning and use it as their staple diet throughout the day, and on their last day in Saskatoon purchase extra loaves to take with them. Customers are attracted by the first whiff of the fresh-baking aroma; many specifically request 'Doukhobor bread' (although none other is sold).

The increasing popularity of the bread and the favourable publicity it has generated in the media has helped recruit workers for this successful annual project. Despite the often hectic, hot and wearisome conditions, workers enjoy visiting one another and meeting the interesting customers that come to see how it is all done. The smiles on the faces of the curious visitors as they are given tours of the operation help erase the tired and weary looks on those of the workers, and the latter's hearts gladden at the thought of being part a most popular, uniquely Doukhobor event. It is one of those rare moments when one feels a special pride in being a Doukhobor.

The venture has also had some additional fringe benefits for the Doukhobor community. It has kept the people together and attracted many of the younger generation to the Society like no other event in our city's history. As a reliable source of revenue, it has enabled local Doukhobors to maintain and renovate the Community Home as required without increasing membership fees beyond people's means. In a time of recession and scarcity of employment, the $4-per-hour honorarium comes as an added bonus to many of the workers, particularly the youth. And instead of being just a 'local' event, bread-baking brings together Doukhobors from the neighbouring original Doukhobor centres of Langham and Blaine Lake. While Society membership is not required to participate in the bread-baking, many of the workers recruited do eventually become members.

Others are encouraged to help out in the Doukhobor Pavilion during the Saskatoon annual Folkfest, where bread sales are a prominent feature (but no honoraria are paid). For both the volunteers and the general public, the 'Bread and Borshch' concession at the annual Folkfest, combined with Doukhobor concert singing, provides food for the body, education for the mind and beauty for the soul. Within this combination, the fresh aromatic brick-oven bread remains true to its name as the most important ingredient in the 'basic staff of life' — in fact, to life itself.

[1]Beginning in 1956 the mixing was done in the newly constructed Community Home.

[2]Sunday: $33.50 — Monday: $422.90 — Tuesday: $180.90 — Wednesday: $266.06 — Thursday: $318.06 — Friday: $358.62 — Saturday: $250.25. Total sales: $1,830; expenses: $70; net profit: $1,760.

[3]Ann Kabatoff lived in Kinley, about a hundred kilometres distant.

Doukhobor credit unions and co-operatives 1940s–1990s

Peter P. Podovinikoff

Introduction

Although Doukhobors lived communally in Russia as well as during their early years in Canada, it was not until the 1940s that Doukhobors in British Columbia became actively involved in promoting the development of co-operatives and credit unions. In many ways Doukhobors were well equipped through their history and culture to undertake such initiatives. Yet it is that same history that proved to be the undoing of many fine cooperative efforts among them, permeated as it was by their pacifist beliefs and refusal to do military service; the resulting discrimination against them was fed in turn by a general mistrust on the part of officials who did not understand them. In spite of this, however, the Doukhobors' contribution to the development of co-operatives and credit unions at the local, provincial and national level has been substantial and noteworthy.

The Early years

When the Doukhobors first landed in Canada in 1899, some seven thousand strong, they had come from a land where they were persecuted and generally unwanted. Arriving on the Canadian prairies, they re-established their communes — the way of life they knew and understood best. But while in many ways the communes did represent a co-operative effort, they were not co-operatives as we understand them today. Rather, they consisted of groups of families who built villages, developed production facilities and contributed a good part of their earnings to the Doukhobor community. All the communal villages were more or less under the influence of their religious and spiritual leaders.

A schism developed in the mid-1900s when much of the land they had been allowed to register on a communal basis was taken away under a new and stricter interpretation of 'homesteads' by the Canadian government. Many Doukhobors (especially those of the 'Community' persuasion) moved with their leaders to the Kootenay region of British

Columbia, while others who remained in Saskatchewan took individual title to their land and prospered on their own.

The leaders in British Columbia decided that the new communes would be modified and incorporated as limited companies. The most prominent effort in this direction was the incorporation of the *Christian Community of Universal Brotherhood,* Ltd (CCUB), in whose name the Doukhobors undertook vast agricultural projects and became involved in lumbering, sawmills, machine shops, food-processing and other related business activities.

Yet much of this work in many ways reflected a co-operative effort on the part of the entire Doukhobor community. It resulted in a period of development and prosperity lasting from 1910 to the early 1930s. The profits generated by the company were ploughed back into more development. (This is in contrast to the co-operative and credit-union model we know today, where benefits from the collective achievements of a co-operative accrue to individual members.)

In the late 1930s a combination of depressed economic conditions nationwide, poor management and internal fragmentation in the various Doukhobor communities contributed to the collapse of the vast enterprises and ventures undertaken and developed, not only in British Columbia but also in the prairie regions. By 1938, when the organisation was declared officially bankrupt, a glorious period of Doukhobor communal development had come to a sad end.

This did not mean, however, an end to co-operative effort. The war years which followed raised a particular problem for the Doukhobors, who as pacifists declining military service were subjected to considerable discrimination by non-Doukhobors in the communities where they lived. Paradoxically, this adverse experience only served to motivate them to renewed co-operative efforts, particularly among the Orthodox Doukhobors residing in the Kootenays. Their desire to overcome discrimination and the unwillingness of merchants to sell products and services to them during the war years gave rise to the development of genuine co-operative organisations in the mid-1940s.

A personal recollection

My own earliest recollections of Doukhobor co-operative initiatives came through my father in Grand Forks, British Columbia, who was one of the activists in the first co-operative efforts in 1945 and 1946. My father had lived in the communes as a child, but subsequently settled with his family on a small farm east of the community and began farming. The inability to acquire needed goods and services prompted him and others to undertake the first co-operative effort to bring a railway carload of flour and feed, shipped from the Ogilvie Flour Mills in Medicine Hat, Alberta, to a railway siding in Grand Forks; the produce was then purchased by and distributed to Doukhobors who had earlier ordered these supplies.

Only eight years old at the time, I still remember travelling home on a horse-drawn wagon loaded with bags of grain for our chickens, feed for our cattle and flour and cereals for the family. It was only later that I learnt why we were taking home so much — some members of the group had failed to take delivery on their share of the supplies. But through this modest beginning the Doukhobor people of the Grand Forks region were able to show that co-operative effort was indeed not only possible, but also desirable and beneficial to the individuals involved.

These first initiatives led to a campaign to raise the seed capital needed to establish the first retail store facility in Grand Forks in early 1946. Enough money was collected from the founding membership of 400 persons to purchase a building from the city in the downtown area and the Sunshine Valley Cooperative Society was born. There was a need to overcome substantial opposition from both municipal officials and local retail merchants; the latter felt threatened by a loss of business from the many Doukhobors in the area, who had now become prosperous in agricultural and other enterprises.

At the same time, the Kootenay Columbia Co-operative established its own store on the site of the old Doukhobor jam factory in Brilliant (near Castlegar), and this experience with cooperatives led to the creation of viable credit unions in both places. In the 1960s the Slocan Valley Co-operative was formed and continues to prosper to this day, and a small group of Doukhobors established the Grand Forks Milling Co-operative Association to produce untreated flour from grain grown in the valley.

I had the good fortune and opportunity to be employed by the Sunshine Valley Co-operative for eleven years (beginning in 1955), before moving to manage the credit union in Grand Forks for an additional ten years. The common thread of these cooperatives was the desire to work together, building on the experience of the communes, and, more importantly, to take a collective approach to the pressing need to overcome shortages, discrimination and other adversities. This experience has enabled me to spread the Doukhobor and co-operative message provincially, nationally and internationally.

The Sunshine Valley Co-operative Society

The co-op store, a modest effort which generated a great deal of pride, opened for business in September 1946. After only four months of operation, however, tragedy struck. At midnight on 31 December an explosion and fire destroyed the entire store building and its contents. An adherent of the extremist 'Sons of Freedom' sect was later arrested for having set the bomb, although many Doukhobors continue to believe that a wider 'conspiracy' was involved.

This deliberate act of destruction caused such a shock that local Doukhobors gathered for a mass meeting on New Years' Day and immediately resolved to rebuild the facility. Volunteer effort was mobilised. But just as the building was completed and getting ready to re-open for business, the city cancelled their trade licence under pressure from local merchants, who felt that the store was a threat to the safety of the community and would only be destroyed again.

Determined not to give up, the co-op hired a law firm to take the matter to the Supreme Court of British Columbia, which ordered a licence to be issued. This decision, however, was later reversed by the provincial Appeal Court, after an appeal by the city council.

Although tempted at first to re-open the store even without a licence, the co-op members were persuaded to follow the due process of law. Even though their resources had by this time been drained by legal expenses, a renewed and determined effort succeeded in raising additional funds and a Doukhobor lawyer, *Peter G. Makaroff*, QC, of Saskatoon, was engaged to appeal the case to the Supreme Court of Canada. The appeal process was well underway when the council suddenly reversed its decision and granted the licence. But the Doukhobors could not forget the tremendous legal costs they had been subjected to — costs they could ill-afford.

The whole procedure left some harsh feelings between the Doukhobor and non-Doukhobor residents of Grand Forks. The former's acute sense of being unwelcome in the community fostered an even greater determination to succeed in their cooperative venture.

There was also a problem with membership. When the cooperative was re-organised following the fire, the original founders, mainly orthodox Doukhobors, sought to bar from co-op membership anyone associated with the Sons of Freedom (these were not only suspected of destroying the store but were also involved at the time in other acts of violence and civil disobedience). To obviate possible charges of discrimination, coop organisers ruled that those wishing to join the co-op must first become members of the *Union of Spiritual Communities of Christ* (USCC — an organisation representing Orthodox Doukhobors in the province). At the same time, following the principles brought by their forebears from Russia, they prohibited the sale of meat, tobacco and alcoholic beverages in the store.

These restrictions, however, proved to be a significant handicap to the economic viability of the enterprise, since the support of the wider community was needed for survival. The difficulties were partially overcome through the introduction of an incentive programme of patronage rebates, which applied even to non-members who accepted a general invitation to shop at the store.

Non-member patronage (which rose to 60% at its peak) fuelled the rising annual sales volume and ensured the Co-operative's continued prosperity over the next two or three decades. In time it became the city's leading business enterprise and dominated the market in food, dry goods, hardware, petroleum distribution, feed and service stations.

Community pressure to have membership opened to people outside the USCC provoked a debate among the Doukhobors: some encouraged open membership while others vehemently resisted it. In the early 1960s the co-op voted finally voted to remove the membership restriction, but the continued exclusion of meat and tobacco sales deterred many local non-Doukhobors from joining.

In the early 1970s disaster struck once again when the building housing the Co-operative's hardware and feed operations — as well as USCC offices and library — was destroyed by arson. Those responsible were never found. Once again the Co-operative was forced to regroup, substantially curtailing its operations in the one remaining building. A decline had begun which continued through the rest of the decade and into the 1980s. Lack of support among its own creators (the Doukhobors themselves) eventually led to a reluctant foreclosure in 1986 by the Grand Forks District Savings Credit Union (see below). Thus ended a community experiment and business venture that had grown out of hardship and persecution to become a dominant force in the Grand Forks settlement for many years.

The lesson learnt from this experience suggests that it is difficult to maintain a successful retail enterprise while adhering to a narrow interpretation of Doukhobor principles. The ultimate irony was the fact that the Orthodox Doukhobors insisted on excluding meat and tobacco from their own facility, yet as individuals they continued to purchase such products from competing organisations. Had the members at the time been willing to allow the store to become a full retail operation with open membership, I have no doubt it would still be prospering today. This, however, was not to be, and the venture is now relegated to being one more chapter in the troubled history of the Doukhobors in Canada.

The Grand Forks District Savings Credit Union

The founders of the Credit Union incorporated in Grand Forks in 1949 included many of the same people who were instrumental in forming the Sunshine Valley Co-operative, but with the significant difference that membership was open to all who were interested. For a few years it was run out of the Co-operative's offices under the direction of the latter's own manager, but the two organisations separated both physically and administratively in 1955, when the *former* Co-operative manager launched it into a period of aggressive growth and development.

The Credit Union was able to overcome or avoid many of the restrictions that plagued the Co-operative and eventually grew to be the dominant banking facility in the area, largely because the other banks were reluctant to deal with any but the well off.

While the Doukhobor people made up a considerable percentage of the Credit Union's membership, the charter group, as well as the Board of Directors — and the management over the years — included both Doukhobors and non-Doukhobors alike. The organisation provided, in effect, a forum where all residents of the area could work together and develop a mutual understanding that in time spread to the wider community. Its prosperity depended on setting political, religious and ethnic issues aside and focusing on the needs of the areas's individual residents. Today it is still holds pride of place among local financial institutions, attracting some 80% of the population, and has been instrumental in generating overall prosperity in the Grand Forks area.

Other co-operative efforts in British Columbia

As indicated earlier, the *Kootenay Columbia Co-operative Society* opened a retail store in Brilliant, B.C. at approximately the same time as the Sunshine Valley Co-operative. While it did not encounter the same licensing difficulties, it suffered the same fate as its Grand Forks counterpart, again because of resistance from the non-Doukhobor community and an unwillingness (dictated by a strict interpretation of religious principles) to offer full retail service. The store was avoided even by many Doukhobors who wanted such a service, while those who insisted on a strict interpretation of principles were too few to maintain the required support.

The history of the *Brilliant Credit Union,* formed by the members of the Kootenay Columbia Co-operative, paralleled that of the credit union in Grand Forks. With no membership restrictions it became a small but forward-looking credit union providing significant benefits to its members; its leaders were all Doukhobors, but progressive in their thinking. Toward the end of the 1960s the organisation combined with two other unions in Trail and Fruitvale to form the *Kootenay Savings Credit Union,* which continues to be a major financial service facility in the region. Doukhobors still exercise considerable influence as members of its staff and Board of Directors.

The *Slocan Valley Co-operative Society* was formed in the 1960s. As a full-service facility with unrestricted membership, it avoided many of the pitfalls encountered by the groups in Grand Forks and Brilliant and still prospers today, with Doukhobors continuing to play a prominent role in its operation.

Another co-op begun in the 1960s is the *Grand Forks Milling Co-operative Association,* serving the needs of Doukhobor farmers who continue to raise grain and wish to have it processed into quality flour without additives. Though modest in size, it has stood the test of time and is still in successful operation today.

General observations

Participation in the co-operative initiatives described above helped many young Doukhobors make significant contributions to co-operative and credit-union organisations in other communities to which they moved, including taking on leadership roles. I myself have had the good fortune to work at the local, provincial, national and international level in the development of co-operatives and credit unions — including co-operative data-processing and insurance facilities — throughout Canada.

While the Canadian prairies did not see the formation of Doukhobor co-operative organisations as such, many people of Doukhobor origin are active in the major co-operative ventures which dominate the agricultural, consumer and financial sectors there. My comments in this area are minimal in view of the present article's focus on direct Doukhobor involvement in co-operative development, most of which took place in British Columbia.

My own personal experience in the co-operative moment has been positive and most rewarding. My beliefs were formed and significantly influenced by people like my father and his colleagues who overcame tremendous resistance and obstacles to form successful co-operative facilities. It is a tragedy that most of these have now passed from the scene, much as the earlier communal enterprises disappeared during the 1930s.

It is my strong belief that, had the Doukhobor people been able to separate their co-operative enterprises from their religious principles, the outcome would have been different. As a Doukhobor I understand the principle of non-violence, and I cannot fault those who brought this principle to bear on their cooperative enterprises. But I also believe that the co-operative model must supersede race and religion if it is to bring all people together in a democratic way to satisfy their individual needs. This too is a principle which has existed for many years and is still valid today.

Like many aspects of the Doukhobors' history and experience in Canada over the past hundred years, their efforts in forming co-operative organisations have had mixed results. Perhaps the most important thing is that the Doukhobors did try and did succeed. In so doing they not only made a positive contribution to the communties in which they functioned, but they also brought about a lasting change in the dynamics of the relationships between Doukhobor and non-Doukhobor peoples. For this achievement they must forever merit our grateful appreciation.

From photos to video: the USCC Video Club

Steve J. Malloff

Not infrequently among the Doukhobors of British Columbia we find people with vision and the perseverance to overcome almost insurmountable obstacles in following the path of their dreams. One such person was William ('Bill') J. Chiveldave, a millwright by trade, whose hobby was still photography. In 1960, having accumulated countless photographs of Doukhobor weddings, concerts and festivals, Bill foresaw the potential of television while yet in its infancy (in rural B.C.). He electronically recorded Doukhobor programmes and put them on air — that is, he spoke 'from the rooftops' so that others could hear and see.1

With the vision firmly planted in his mind, Bill proceeded to bring it to reality. First, he described the idea to his wife Mabel, who gave the plan her support and later became Bill's devoted helper — carrying, setting up and operating film equipment, logging and storing films and paying the bills. Next, Bill presented the idea to John J. Verigin, Honorary Chairman of the Union of Spiritual Communities of Christ (USCC — the Orthodox or Community Doukhobor organisation), who has given it his enthusiastic endorsement and encouragement right from the start.

Then Bill bought himself a reel-to-reel audio tape recorder, along with an 8mm motion-picture camera and projector. In order to be closer to the centre of Doukhobor events, in 1963 Bill and his family moved from Midway (where he worked) to Grand Forks, B.C., which eventually became the home base of future audiovisual operations among the western Canadian Doukhobors.

With Mabel at his side, Bill used every opportunity over the next twenty years to film a Doukhobor event, no matter how big or how small. He recorded all the annual community USCC banquets, seminars, symposia, talent nights, May Youth Festivals and Declaration Days. He filmed peace manifestations at Suffield, Alberta in 1964, the Dana Radar Base in Saskatchewan in 1965, and across the border in Blaine, Washington, in 1966. He recorded the performances of the Doukhobor choirs at Expo '67 in Montréal and at Expo '74 in Spokane. In 1969 he travelled with Iskra editor Peter Legebokoff to Verigin, Saskatchewan, to film the 70th Jubilee of Doukhobors in Canada. In 1970, along with Sam Horkoff, he recorded the 75th anniversary of the Burning of Arms commemoration held in Castlegar, B.C. Over the next decade he filmed visits to the Kootenays by Prime Minister Pierre Trudeau and Her Majesty Queen Elizabeth II, as well as interviews with Anna Markova and Mark Mealing. Also during this period he captured on film the tragic burnings by arsonists of the Sunshine Valley Co-operative and Sirotskoye in the Grand Forks Valley.2

Bill was often obliged to work under 'less than ideal' circumstances, when he would lack the proper professional equipment or the equipment he had would fail. Many times the lighting would be too low or the sound too resonant. Once in a while his car would break down on the way to or from a production. Especially in his earlier attempts, he sometimes met with objections and unkind remarks from people he was filming who saw his recording as an interference. Naturally, Bill felt frustrated, but he never let these many setbacks deter him.

In the early 1970s, with his children having grown up and left home, Bill began looking for additional volunteers. As one of these volunteers, I made over a thousand slides on Doukhobor history and culture, which I was able to use extensively in my Russian-language and social-studies classes at Grand Forks Secondary School. With our common interest and my background in education, Bill thought I could be very helpful in his work. Alas, I was already taxed with other community projects3 and the workload proved simply too much to offer Bill much in the way of assistance.

Bill Chiveldave was not one just to ask others for help; he himself was always ready to help others. When our Superintendent of Schools in District 12 was quoted in the local paper as saying that 'the Board must go slow in implementing the Russian langauge in the District's elementary schools', Bill wrote a letter to the editor in reply, insisting that 'we already have been waiting 50 years and 50 years is slow enough'. Bill's letter, along with the B.C. Ministry of Education's promise to provide the Board with necessary funding, was a key factor in the Board's decision to introduce Russian language instruction in Grand Forks starting in Grade 2. As chairman of the USCC committee struck for this purpose, I am forever grateful for Bill's assistance.

At this point in the mid-1970s Bill's dream of broadcasting Doukhobor programmes was yet to be realised. While he did show his films to local groups on an 8mm projector, and while he managed to have a clip of the Sunshine Valley Co-operative fire broadcast over KGA Television in Spokane (south of the border), these events fell far short of what he had in mind. In 1977 he discovered that the newly established 'Cable West' company in Trail, B.C. would provide video-cameras and recorders to community groups in exchange for supplying television programmes to their cable system. Bill soon assembled a volunteer production crew after finding a receptive ear in Cable West's programme manager, Ed Chernoff, who gave the new recruits several workshops on the operation of lighting, sound and video equipment. With his crew of more than twenty Doukhobors,4 Bill launched into professional recordings of youth festivals, concerts, guest artists and seminars on video for broadcast over Cable West in Trail and Castlegar. His vision had finally become reality.

The most time-consuming, tedious and least-rewarding task in television production is editing. Travelling to Trail early Saturday mornings or late on weekday evenings in the cold and snow, we would all too often find the needed equipment broken or in use for other productions. We had no choice but to wait for hours and sometimes in vain for our turn — a source of much frustration, which eventually drove us to the only logical solution: purchasing our own equipment. To raise the necessary funds, Bill started the USCC Grand Forks Audio-Visual Club (which soon became known as the USCC Video Club), donated the first hundred dollars to its coffers and challenged other USCC members to follow his example. Soon the Club boasted thirtythree members and had $3,300 to its credit. An evening dinner and variety show organised by a Doukhobor women's group under Laura Verigin netted the Club another $700. These and other donations enabled Bill to purchase a three-quarter-inch VCR/ editor, along with a remote control and TV monitor (together worth some $7,300), which, while not a complete editing suite, did obviate the need for much of the cable company's editing equipment.

Bill Chiveldave's biggest project with the USCC Video Club was the videotaping of the four-day International Doukhobor Intergroup Symposium held in the Brilliant Cultural Centre in June 1982, for the first-ever interdenominational gathering of Doukhobors, Molokans, Mennonites and Quakers. The Symposium comprised a number of sessions featuring presentations by an impressive array of Canadian and foreign scholars along with community leaders,5 who were interviewed for Cable West broadcasts. The videotaping proved a complex operation, involving the setting up of several cameras in different locations and co-ordinating the work of cameramen, video loggers, light operators, sound technicians, camera switchers, interviewers, directors, prducers and editors. Ed Chernoff directed the production and Bill Chiveldave produced it. Fifty one-hour video cassettes were recorded in all.

The Club was naturally saddened by the death of its founder, William ('Bill') J. Chiveldave, on 26 November 1982. However, his perseverance and dedication inspired others to carry on the work he began. After electing a new executive committee,[6] we held regular formal meetings once a month — complete with written agenda and minutes — to hear reports, make decisions and draw up plans. Now our meetings are more frequent but their greater informality makes them more enjoyable.

Fig. 1. Wallace Dergousoff adjusts camera settings.

A list of equipment needs was drawn up and prioritised for order of purchase. It must be remembered that professional video equipment is sophisticated and costly, particularly for a small, volunteer group such as ours. It takes time to learn what products to buy or not to buy and even more time to raise the money to buy them. Hence we feel very fortunate to have been able to purchase some $67,000 worth of equipment over the past ten years — two editing suites, a photoscanner, a high-resolution printer as well as a video toaster for elaborate digital effects. All of which means that we can now record and edit most of our own programmes. Funds have come from a variety of sources including membership fees and fees for services, along with donations and grants from individuals, groups, organisations and government agencies. With new computer technolgoy, the Club is now preparing to purchase a non-linear editing suite.

As in Bill Chiveldave's time, over the past decade we have continued to record the annual USCC Christmas and New Year's programmes, winter Talent Nights, spring Sunday School Festivals, the May Youth Festivals in Brilliant and the August Declaration Days in Grand Forks. 7

Two very important undertakings for our group were the 'Peace through Communication' conference in 1985 and the 1987 Russian-Canadian Heritage Festival and Doukhobor Historical Pageant. The former required 55 hours of recording and the latter 70 hours. The annual USCC Youth Festivals generally involve 12–15 hours of recording, not counting travel, set-up and take-down time. Most of the operation is a tedious job, but one rewarded at the same time by the excitement of working hand in hand with both organisers and participants.

Fig. 2. Bill Chiveldave,Jr. takes his turn in the USCC editing suite

From the creative and educational point of view, our best productions were the Russian radio programmes that my Russianlanguage students from the Grand Forks Secondary School put together (under my direction) during three consecutive summers in 1985–87. Under the auspices of the Federal Student Challenge Programme, each student was responsible, over their ten weeks of summer employment, for producing two 10–15-minute radio programmes per week for airing over the local

CKGF radio station following the daily Russian-language news. Each programme was based on a central theme (nature, friends, peace etc.) and consisted of the student's narration, story and poem readings, interviews with parents and grandparents, songs and music by local, national and foreign Russian-speaking performers and artists. In addition to the radio programmes, the students created on video twenty Russian fairy-tales using popout story-books and dramatic readings. These projects gave valuable artistic and technical experience to a number of Doukhobor young people. For the listening public they helped generate an interest in Russian language and culture.

Fig. 3. Nikita in studio recording Russian radio programs.

Other cable companies have taken an interest in our productions. Beginning in 1982 all of our USCC Youth Festivals along with some other concerts have been aired over Shaw Cable8 in Castlegar, Trail and Nelson and starting in 1990 over County Cable in Grand Forks. These showings have been so well received that viewers still telephone to enquire as to when the next broadcast is going to air. From time to time we show these same programmes to Doukhobor senior citizens' homes and hospital extended-care units in Grand Forks, Castlegar and Nelson, in co-operation with the care-givers, and we often donate copies of our taped programmes to organisers (and participants) of events for recreational and educational purposes. Several times a year we show unedited programmes to the public and special groups in our community centres in return for donations. We have also fulfilled orders for tapes of the Doukhobor Historical Pageant and the Union of Young Doukhobors Anniversary Concert. For the past fifteen years I (along with a few other teachers) have used these programmes in high-school Russian-language classes to make language learning more meaningful to the students. Some of the tapes are available for educational purposes upon request by groups and individuals.

As in the past, the work of the USCC Video Club depends upon the efforts of many volunteers. Video production is a highly technical field and therefore requires a number of skilled personnel — requirements that spare-time enthusiasts can find rather daunting. Most helpful was the 'hands-on' experience provided by Ed Chernoff and Ralph DiSabato of Shaw Cable. Technical books and journals have also been helpful. We have profited from Ed Chernoff's workshops at Selkirk College (in the winter of 1988) and a number of seminars in Vancouver sponsored by Matrix Professional Video Systems, Commercial Electronics, the British Columbia Institute of Technology and The University of British Columbia. We have also learnt through offering workshops of our own, such as the ones Wallace Dergousoff and I recently gave for students and teachers at Grand Forks Secondary School and the USCC Union of Youth Council.

As we look back to the past we can only feel thankful that the work of the USCC Video Club has given western Canadians a deeper understanding of and a greater appreciation for Doukhobor beliefs, history, culture and traditions. The Club's volunteers are grateful for the opportunity it has given them to meet people from various walks of life and from different parts of the world and to share our experiences with each other.

In looking ahead to the Club's future, its current volunteers see many opportunities to learn and to help. There is a continuing need to study the Doukhobor movement and at the same time to learn about other peoples and cultures. Doukhobors need to be informed about the issues and problems facing mankind and to be aware of the technological advances taking place.

Currently (in 1997) the Video Club is studying the feasibility of two projects: (a) the setting up of a low-wattage ethnic radio station in Grand Forks — tentative plans are to have a six-hour broadcast day with hourly local and world news in Russian with Doukhobor singing and Russian music in between; (b) supplying the American Ethnic Broadcast System with weekly Doukhobor cultural programming produced by the USCC Video Club.

Throughout its existence, the mandate of the Video Club has remained the same as when it began years ago: to help preserve the Doukhobor identity in a multicultural Canada by preparing video and computer educational materials that will help pass on to future generations the Russian language and the Doukhobor cultural, social and spiritual values.

Appendix: Special events recorded 1983–97 by the USCC VIdeo Club

1983   Sophia Rotura Concert Shirokov's Evening of Russian Songs

1984   Society Rodina artists Grand Forks Flour Mill Castlegar Doukhobor Village Museum

1985   'Peace through Communication' conference Three 'Lifestyle Planning Committee' seminars 'Peace and Justice' tour in Grand Forks and Castlegar Student Russian radio programmes

1986   USCC Expo '86 Choir in Vancouver Grand Forks Youth Choir at Expo '86 Student Russian radio programmes

1987   Russian-Canadian Heritage Festival in Kamsack (Sask.), Yorkton (Sask.) and Brilliant (B.C.) Doukhobor Historical Pageant Sion Concert Soviet-Canadian Youth HockeyGrand Forks Secondary School—Mount Sentinel Secondary School student tour to the USSR Student Russian radio programmes

1988   Union of Young Doukhobors 20th Anniversary Concert USCC 50th Anniversary Programme Brilliant Choir 30th Anniversary Programme

1989   Dr Nickolai's lecture on alcohol abuse GFSS Court dramatisation Grand Forks International Baseball Tournament

1991   Seven Grand Forks City Council meetings John J. Verigin's 70th birthday celebrations 'Dial-a-law' Russian translations

1992   Grand Forks Secondary School—Mount Sentinel Secondary School student tour to Russia Baturin interview Russian Aid Campaign Sirotskoye concert

1993   Grand Forks ice-skating carnival European tour '93

1994 Hour-long documentary for Heritage Canada: *The Role of Doukhobor women in Canadian society*

1995 Doukhobor choir and drama production *Voices for peace,* commemorating the Centenary of the 1895 Burning of arms in the Caucasus (filmed in multi-camera format)

1996 *Voices within* — a three-hour production by USCC Union of Youth honouring their Russian Doukhobor fore-fathers who refused military service and burned their arms

1997 50th Anniv. of USCC Union of Youth Festivals in B.C. Grand Forks Centenary celebrations in August

[1]Cf. Jesus' command to his disciples in Matth. 10:27: 'What ye hear in the ear, that preach ye upon the housetops' — *ed.*

[2]On the Sunshine Valley Co-operative. cf. Peter Podovinikoff's article in this volume — *ed.*

[3]At this time, with four pre-school children in the family, I was chairman of three local community organisations: the Sunshine Valley Co-operative, the Trustees of the Covert Irrigation District and the USCC Russian School Committee, as well as head of the USCC Committee for implementing Russian-language instruction in elementary schools in School Districts 7, 9 and 12.

[4]The original volunteers were: *Wallace Dergrousoff, Steve Malloff, Walter Hoodikoff, Mabel* and *Bill Chiveldave, Stan Rilkoff, Fred Faminoff, Alec Cheveldave, Joe Cheveldave, Richard Kanigan, Peter Zaytsoff, Lawrence Makortoff, Ken Strellioff, Greg Harasemow, John Postnikoff, Frank* and *Jamie Konken, George Horkoff, Fred Medvedeff* and *K.C. Dergousoff.*

[5]Those interviewed included: *Alexei Ipatov, Gordon Hirabayashi, Ilya V. Tolstoy, Gennadij Andrianow, Peter Elkington, Vasili M. Chuskov, Ethel Dunn, Walter Sawatsky, John Lyons, James Penton, James Stark, Murray Thomson, Charles Franz, Brian Marshall, Frank H. Epp, Edward Soloviov, John J. Verigin, Eli A. Popoff, Mark Mealing, Michael Verigin, Alex Sherstobitoff, Alex Vereschagin, Peter Samoyloff, William N. Papove, Paul J. Semenoff, George Stushnoff, Andrew Konovaloff, Ken Konkin, Frank Vallee, Jim E. Popoff, Nick Nevokshonoff, Koozma J. Tarasoff* and *Don Tarasoff.*

[6]This committee comprised Steve Malloff as chairman, Walter Hoodikoff as secretary, Mabel Chiveldave as treasurer, Wallace Dergousoff as technician and Andy Ozeroff as the Kootenay representative. Two years later Bill Chiveldave Jr was added as vice-chairman. All except Walter Hoodikovv still hold these positions.

[7]A supplementary list of special events recorded from 1983 to 1993 is shown in the Appendix.

[8]Shaw Cable purchased Cable West in 1986.

Doukhobor peace manifestations in Canada

John J. Semenoff

The entire life of Doukhobors in Canada can be thought of as a prolonged manifestation for peace. On the grounds that the human body is a temple fo God, and that human life is sacred — hence the killing of a human cannot be justified under any circumstances whatsoever — they refused to participate in wars or any other forms of killing fellow human beings.

A number of peace manifestations have been held by the Doukhobors over the years:[1]

- 28–29 June 1958: Conference on 'Peace through Non-violence' at the University of British Columbia;

- 5 July 1964: Manifestation for Peace at Suffield, Alberta;

- 8 November 1964: Manifestation for Peace at the gates of the Orcadia Radar Base in Saskatchewan;

- 27 June 1965: peace gathering near the Royal Canadian Air Force Radar Base at Dana, Saskatchewan.

These were all expressions of the Doukhobor spirit longing for a world without war, a world without killing. The Doukhobor spirit was reaching out to the general populace, calling on them to take heed, awaken and free itself from the yoke of war.

---

[1]See Koozma J. Tarasoff, *Plakun Trava: The Doukhobors*. Grand Forks, B.C.: MIR Publication Society, pp. 180–82.

Part III

Learning
and
adapting

Intermarriage:
Changing attitudes and realities

Vera Kanigan

Intermarriage has been viewed by many ethnic, religious and minority groups as a threat to preserving their identity. For the Doukhobors through the past century, the perceived effect of intermarriage has been that the culture, language and religious principles will disappear as people become more integrated and assimilated into Canadian society. My own research and personal observations indicate both positive and negative effects from intermarriage, which in some instances has proved no hindrance to the preservation of language and religious principles. For the most part, Doukhobor young people today continue searching for a common base on which to build their marriage while still incorporating Doukhobor traditions and treasured values.

Many years of active participation in Doukhobor activities have given me ample opportunity for personal observation. However, in order to obtain a broader perspective, a few years ago I submitted an open letter to *Iskra*[1] inviting responses on the subject. A most interesting phenomenon emerged as the responding couples searched to bridge the gaps in their shared life-experiences that resulted from the discrepancies in their backgrounds.

The phenomenon of intermarriage for the Doukhobors includes not only marriage to non-Doukhobors but also between different Doukhobor groups. In the early 1900s the Doukhobors splintered into three religious groupings: (a) the *edinolichniki,* or 'independents', (b) the *obshchinniki,* or 'Community' Doukhobors and (c) the *svobodniki,* or 'Sons of Freedom'.[2] It was not uncommon, for example, for a Community Doukhobor to take a spouse from the Freedomite group. In such cases the discrepancies were not in language or culture but rather in the religious interpretation of basic Doukhobor principles.

Given that marital relationships require a minimal level of communication between the partners, it is not surprising that up to the 1940s there was little intermarriage with non-Doukhobors in British Columbia, since the Community members living there spoke mostly Russian and rarely associated with the Englishspeaking populace. Those who did so were subject to derogatory taunts of *ni-nash* [not one of us], *khamat* [name for another nationality] or *anglik* [English]. The Doukhobors took great pains to guard the purity of their ethnic identity, their beloved traditions and Russian culture, all of which were highly treasured.

It is said that the first Doukhobor leader in Canada, Peter V. Verigin, actually selected partners and encouraged and arranged marriages among some of his followers, and many of these marriages survived until the death of one partner. It should be remembered that couples of that era married for the purpose of building a life together in role divisions established through centuries of tradition: men earned a living while women looked after the household and raised the children, and both had ample time to participate in all the cultural activities of the community. This attitude prevailed at least among the Community Doukhobors even into the 1950s.

Attitudes toward intermarriage also changed slowly. I remember that in the 1950s young women were still expected to take a suitable spouse from within the Doukhobor circle. While some girls (along with a number of boys) were allowed to complete their secondary-school education, women were not expected to seek permanent employment except in the clerical or secretarial fields, or in food and other service industries. Increasing industrial expansion in the Kootenay-Boundary area[3] and the ready availability of jobs in the forest industry meant that the community kept most of its large circle of youth in the immediate vicinity. The 'Union of Youth' formed within the USCC in the 1940s reached its 'golden years' in the 1960s, providing opportunities for young people to meet and fall in love with partners from the same group. However, a growing trend among young Doukhobors to move to the larger cities of the province to acquire a higher education also opened the way for much greater social contact with the non-Doukhobor populace.

In 1971 the Union of Young Doukhobors[4] in Greater Vancouver published the results of a questionnaire on intermarriage in their journal *Mir*. To the 'yes/no' question 'Should a young Doukhobor insist that his spouse of non-Doukhobor background change to his/her ways?' one middle-aged couple from Grand Forks responded: 'Yes. What kind of a Doukhobor is he or she if they think their spouse's outlook is better?', and offered the following 'additional comments':

No one having any Doukhobor worthiness can answer all these questions in anything but a strictly defensive, conservative manner. Any other kind of answers only lead to an undermining of the basis of the society that you stem from.

Younger respondents, those in their twenties (who would be in their late forties or early fifties today) were also mindful of preserving their cultural heritage, witness the following comment:

> Intermarriage will have to be accepted as a social condition. But, if Doukhobor interests lie within the scope of cultural preservation, then we should endeavour to marry someone who possesses a common heritage.

Even today, a number of young people who have married outside the faith feel isolated: they are no longer comfortable about participating in religious or cultural activities in the Kootenay-Boundary Doukhobor community, yet long to contribute in some form.

But not all. Many community members who have intermarried and moved away are still drawn back to the community where they grew up. Family interaction, group projects and activities, philosophical discussions and spiritual gatherings — all serve as a powerful source of warmth and and belonging for young Community Doukhobors. For example, *Helene Jones* (née *Chursinoff*), who married a Welsh husband more than twenty years ago and now lives with her family in Kamloops, still finds herself searching to define her beliefs and to gain the strength to pursue them. While her marriage, she says, has taught her to respect others' beliefs, viewpoints and customs, she misses the sense of belonging to a larger cause she experienced growing up in the Doukhobor community.

As indicated [see indented quotation above], while attitudes toward Doukhobor intermarriage are constantly evolving, many dedicated community members still perceive the ideal mate as someone from the same group who values his/her heritage and is prepared to actively participate in Doukhobor cultural and spiritual activities. In intermarriage one looks for a partner who exemplifies and practises the principles of love, peace, kindness, mutual respect, brotherhood, and a willingness to place the wellbeing of the community over individual needs. Familiarity with the Russian language and culture is also a desirable trait.

In today's 'global village', numerous advances in communications technology and ease of travel has facilitated the growth of cultural exchanges between Canadian Doukhobors and the Russian-speaking peoples of the former Soviet Union. Young Doukhobors have been enrolling for study in that country ever since the 1960s. *Jim Kolesnikoff*, one of the first to take advantage of this opportunity, returned home not only with a post-graduate Russian-language degree from Moscow University, but also with his Polish bride *Nina*, thereby (inadvertently) setting a trend toward intermarriage which continues among young Doukhobors even now, with partners from around the globe. It is not uncommon for Doukhobor family gatherings today to include relatives from places as far away as Moscow, Jyväskylä, Cairo, Tokyo, Queensland, Fairbanks and Florida as well as Toronto, Saskatchewan, Alberta and all parts of British Columbia.

In a 1975 interview with *Mir,*[5] Nina Kolesnikoff offered the following insights into their mixed marital union:

> I think that any marriage to start with is a big challenge. However great the similarities are, there are always points of difference between two people, so it takes a lot of goodwill on the part of both people to adjust and to try to work out a good marriage relationship. When it comes to intermarriage, where people come from different backgrounds, differenct ethnic backgrounds, different religious backgrounds, I think that the difficulties are even greater. First of all, there is the question of accepting the point of view of the other person , understanding it, accepting it, and then possibly trying to get involved in the other person's activities. I think this is very difficult, but if a person makes the decision before getting married, then it helps...

Marisha Perrett (*née Strelaeff*) shares her heartwarming account of life on the 'Gold Coast' of Queensland, Australia, where she and her husband Brian and their family have spent more than twenty years buying and operating convenience stores. They dearly value their visits to the Kootenay area visiting her parents and relatives. Marisha managed to instil Doukhobor values in their children (Shawn and Tanya) by teaching them to recite Doukhobor psalms before they went to sleep at night,[6] and felt proud of her heritage connection when her son was able to recite the Lord's Prayer [*Otche* or *Otche nash*] at his grandfather's funeral in Castlegar.

Bob and Barbie Kalmakoff, a young couple in their late twenties from Shoreacres, B.C., took care to iron the possible wrinkles out of their inter-faith marriage before their actual wedding ceremony, for which they composed their own marriage vows. Barbie sees many similarities between her family's United Church and her husband's Doukhobor faith — both are based on a Christian foundation and the tenet that God is Love, along with family closeness. With five brothers and a sister, Barbie enjoys the warmth of family gatherings and the sharing of lives, and is equally comfortable with Doukhobor traditions. From her frequent references during the interview to *Otche, molenie* [prayer service], *detskii sad* [kindergarten] and *baba* [grandma], one might have taken her for one of the young Doukhobors.

One of the biggest hurdles early in the marriage was role division. Barbie came from a family where both parents worked and whoever arrived home first prepared supper; since she herself intends to return to her nursing career once their first child is born, Bob (who is of a traditional Doukhobor background) must adjust to the role-sharing demands of a modern Canadian family — an extremely desirable quality which has emerged as a result of intermarriage.

In choosing an inter-faith marriage to a spouse in the community, elsewhere in the country or abroad, young people often consider its compatibility with their career goals and a broader understanding of life's concepts.

Fred Samorodin, a Doukhobor currently living on the B.C. Lower Mainland, revealed that after his first marriage to a Soviet citizen failed, he chose to marry someone with whom he shared intellectual and cultural interests rather than according to ethnic origin. He found that exterior differences were far outweighed by significant inner qualities which made them both feel at home. He commented on his second marriage (to *Isabelle*) in an article in the *Vancouver Sun* of 19 October 1991:

> Isabelle is a French-Canadian, born and raised in Montréal, Québec, and living approximately 15 years in British Columbia where she trained and worked as a social worker. Her mother tongue is French and she is fluently bilingual. We were married in a Unitarian Church ceremony in Vancouver. At the time of the marriage I was continuing to uphold the Doukhobor culture through participation, as I have for many years previously, in the UYD [Union of Young Doukhobors]. I continued to seek insights into the Doukhobor faith and the choice of venue for the wedding was influenced by the fact that the tenets of the Unitarian Church have similar liberal interpretations of Christian spirituality that I feel are contained in Doukhobor inspired Christianity. As a 'lapsed Catholic', Isabelle was most comfortable in a Christian wedding ceremony that we helped compose ourselves and which helped reflect a more open understanding of Christian spirituality than that exemplified by the theological rigidity of the Catholic Church.

Fred goes on to note the depth of their shared understanding on questions of life, faith and marriage:

> My beliefs have continued to be inspired by my appreciation of Doukhobor faith that points to an individual relationship with God or a Higher Power without the intercession of a priestly hierarchy. I continue to

struggle with the value I find in ethnic values I was raised with and the spiritual values I was guided towards. I feel the grief arising from the impending loss of some cultural and ethnic uniqueness in Doukhobor society that I, in living away from the centres of Doukhobor population, partially contribute towards. I am searching for the means to better express and share Doukhobor spirituality and certainly acknowledge my origins with pride under all circumstances. The influence my marriage has had on my beliefs is probably that of highlighting the fact that my relationship with my wife does not take away any quality in my relationship with God. In fact, being in this relationship has helped me identify personal issues that draw me nearer to God and other issues that take me away from this spiritual focus.

Both from my research and through personal observation, I have found that, far from abandoning their cultural and heritage through intermarriage, they often seek creative solutions to incorporate them into their daily lives.

Michael and *Leslie Soukochoff* of Prince George are a young couple in their early forties. While Michael's excellent command of Russian gives the impression that he either teaches or has spent several years in a Russian immersion programme, his Russian is entirely self-taught, and by profession he is a physical education teacher. A few years ago he organised an exchange with an Estonian volleyball team. In his leisure time he reads Dostoevsky and Russian magazines, including *Iskra*. Leslie and her Anglican family (formerly of Nelson) are very supportive of Doukhobor principles; she and her husband feel that Doukhobors in the Kootenay area tend to take their lifestyle for granted. While Michael admits to feeling 'guilty' about not participating in the programmes, he has managed to incorporate his beloved heritage into their family's daily life in a number of ways — growing a garden, cooking *vareniki, pirogi* and *borshch*.[7] When their children were eleven and nine and more receptive to the Russian language, Michael conversed with them in Russian and taught them to recite a few psalms. Michael's appreciation of the Doukhobor psalms and their meaning was inculcated during his youth as a member of the Stanley Humphries Doukhobor Youth Choir, organised in the 1970s by *Peter Samoyloff*, a prominent cultural activist in Castlegar, who had a significant influence on Michael's desire to preserve the Doukhobor culture as much as possible in his own life.

Some instances of intermarriage outside Canada involve more than one common denominator. When *Robert Kanigan* (the present writer's son) travelled to Moscow to study the Russian language, he met fellow language student *Marja Liisa Rossi* from Jyväskylä, Finland, whose

Lutheran faith turned out to be not incompatible with Doukhobor Christianity. She has since completed her Master's degree, writing her thesis on the Doukhobor dialect of Russian. Travelling to Jyväskylä for the wedding ceremony, Robert's family shared their Doukhobor culture and history with other wedding guests — a sharing that often comes with inter-faith marriages.

Through intermarriage, Doukhobor principles are in fact being shared with a broad cross-section of people throughout the world. Partners of both faiths are consciously incorporating many desirable changes into their lives to make them healthier and happier. Doukhobor philosophy has enriched many lives, for example, with a broader awareness of environmental, peace and health issues. This is summed up in the comments of Mennonite Frank Epp at a 1982 Intergroup Symposium in Castlegar, referring to his daughter's recent marriage to an English-Canadian:[8]

> When you're talking about losing your young people, you know there is another way of looking at it. And sometimes when we make a little re-thinking in our mind, we lose a lot less young people than we think we lose. When our daughter married outside the Mennonite family, we didn't say we were losing a daughter — we said we were gaining a son. And many of the people you think you have lost, you have really given to the rest of the world. And if I understand Doukhobor philosophy and its universalism, that's really what it's all about. You have not lost your sons and daughters just because they have moved out of the house or out of the community — you have lost them only when they cease to love you and you've lost them only if they take no cherished values into the world. And I have met very few Doukhobor young people out there who've left the Kootenay Valley or Blaine Lake, or Verigin or Kamsack, who've lost their love or their values. But they've gone out into the world and you have given them to the world.

[1] *Iskra* — bilingual (Russian/English) publication of the Union of Spiritual Communities of Christ in Grand Forks, B.C. — *ed.*

[2] The *edinolichniki* [independents] were mainly those who agreed to the federal government's terms to become individual homesteaders on the prairies; most *obshchinniki* ['Community' Doukhobors] moved westward to British Columbia to maintain their communal life-style and religious principles, but were still willing to adapt in some aspects to Canadian ways; while the *svobodniki* ['Sons of Freedom'], insisting on a strict adherence to all aspects of Doukhobor doctrine and communal traditions, defied all government attempts at integration — *ed.* In 1938 the then leader of the Community Doukhobors, **Peter P.**

(**Chistiakov**) **Verigin,** formed the Union of Spiritual Communities of Christ (USCC) as a successor to the Christian Community of Universal Brotherhood (CCUB) founded earlier by **Peter V. ('the Lordly') Verigin**.

[3]An area including the cities of Grand Forks, Castlegar and Nelson, together with the surrounding countryside, comprising the largest concentration of Doukhobors in south-central British Columbia.

[4]Not officially connected to the USCC Union of Youth.

[5]'An interview with Jim and Nina Kolesnikoff'. *Mir* (Grand Forks, B.C.), May 1975, pp. 3–9, 42–45, 48.

[6]Both son and daughter also learnt Christian values when they attended a 'non--denominational country Sunday School'.

[7]*vareniki* — dumplings made with potato, cottage cheese or fruit; *pirogi* — small closed pies or tarts made with meat, vegetables or fruit; *borshch* — a Russian soup made from beets and/or cabbage.

[8]In Koozma J. Tarasoff (ed.), *Symposium proceedings* (International Intergroup Symposium of Doukhobors, Molokans, Mennonites and Quakers, 25–28 June 1982). Castlegar: Symposium Planning Committee, 1983, p. 94.

The Spirit of co-operation in a competitive society

Jim Deacove

Editor's note: It takes a courageous person to stick out his or her neck and go against the grain of society. The Doukhobors did this in 1895 when they destroyed their weapons; and as the *plakun trava*[1] of the day, they dared to choose co-operation instead of conflict as their predominant mode of human interaction when they first settled on the Canadian prairies in 1899. In a capitalistic individualistic environment, this was a courageous move. The author of this paper has been courageous for several decades in developing a unique home-games industry, *Family Pastimes,* based on the co-operative principle. Many banks, many suppliers, many friends and relatives warned him and his wife Ruth that the business would never last with such an outlandish idea.

'Co-operative games? Are you serious? Do not, under any circumstances give up your day-jobs', they cautioned.

But now, twenty-six years later, *Family Pastimes* is solid, dependable and thriving and its developers are very pleased that their thousands of customers have helped prove the naysayers wrong. Today seven people are employed full-time in a farm business with a gross annual turnover of $300,000, some of the games are licensed to companies in Sweden, Germany, Israel and Spain, and there are retailers in places such as America (where 80% of the products are exported), Sweden, New Zealand and the Netherlands. Recently additional interest has been generated in Japan, China and Russia.

These games are the inventions of Doukhobor Jim Deacove. Jim first made a few co-op games for his own family and was encouraged by friends to make more. According to the *Pastimes* catalogue:

'The Deacove family was and is no different from others. Sharing toys, helping mom and dad, being kind to others are values taught in all homes. To find games which help to reinforce such sharing attitudes, however, is very difficult. Thus Jim and Ruth felt they had to create some. The 'hobby' became a small business in their home....

'Slow but steady growth in sales required moving the business into a cottage. With the addition of new games and greater interest by the public, a switch occurred. The family moved into the cottage and the business occupied the two stories of the old farm house. A new workshop was made in 1984 to replace the old barn house destroyed in a terrible fire, October 1983.'

When the Canadian Museum of Civilization launched its Spirit Wrestlers Doukhobor Exhibit (beginning in 1996), Jim took up the challenge of producing a game to honour the centenary of the destruction of weapons by the Doukhobors. He sought inspiration from his grandparents, who told him about the arms burning in Russia in 1895 and how 7,500 Russian Doukhobor dissidents came to Canada in 1899 and co-operated in living, working and singing together.

Ploughshares, as the game is called, addresses the issue of peace and war, with a search for a fresh alternative paradigm to the overfed military 'sacred cow'. According to the game's instructions,

It will be an adventure filled with danger and great rewards. To fulfil our task, we must be gentle as a dove and wise as a serpent. This is a game of collaboration, learning and discussion; a game full of exciting strategy, with each of us making an important contribution.

Ploughshares is Jim's seventieth game, a tribute to his ancestors from Eastern Europe. He continues to revise, upgrade, and reprint earlier games as he gets feedback from his customers by mail and in workshops at schools.

In preparing for one of these workshops, Jim speaks of the philosophy and practice of co-operation, teamwork and shared decision-making — qualities that made possible the survival of his Doukhobor and Polish grandparents and those ancestors who came to Canada to build a new society — as well as bonding, support and playfulness; openness, trust and safety; self worth and personal power; and well-being.

Co-operative games: the beginning

I am always asked, 'How did you get started making co-operative games?' I answer by remembering out loud…

I am in our back yard on the porch watching the neighbourhood kids playing some games. Like most families, my wife Ruth and I have been teaching our two little girls[2] such values as sharing their toys, helping Mum and Dad, being kind to pets. We have been discovering that more and more energy is needed to maintain these values in our home. As we sit and watch the children at play, some rather heady insights come to mind.

The 'kids' gather round and talk over what game they want to play next. They listen for each other's weaknesses, exploiting them for their own advantage. What I am witnessing is a change from consensus to confrontation.

I begin to wonder what would happen if the nature of their decision-making process were transferred into the game situation itself.

Fig. 1. Jim and Ruth Deacove, proprietors of Family Pastimes Co-opetative Games.

A little later when the kids are again deciding on a game, I shout out to them that I know a new game they might like to try. I make up the fine points as I talk to them. 'It's something like *Hide and seek*, but I call it *Lost and found*.'

I go on to describe how I will start the game by covering my eyes at the Home Post and count to a hundred by fives.

Everyone is to hide so no one else can see them. We will pretend that everyone is lost and I am coming to rescue you. When I find someone we join hands, rush back and both touch the post, which is the Rescue Station. Then the two of us will go out and each try to find someone and bring them back to the post. This goes on until we have just one person left to find. When this person is rescued, since they are the best at hiding, they get to start the next game.

I finish counting to a hundred and wander out, keeping my eyes open. I find a little girl first. With great delight, big person and little person join hands and hippity-hop to the Rescue Station. Already I feel that something tremendous is about to burst open within me. I'm joyously discovering something here. The child looks at me, eyes free of fearing that this big person is going to wipe her out of the game. The delight on her face is teaching me a lesson which marks my soul deeply.

'I'm not very good at finding people', she confides shyly at the post. 'Can I come with you?' I agree to her suggestion. It's a friendly, flexible game, so we change the rules right there. Soon three of us are running to the post. Then I venture out alone again and the little girl and her friend go off as a pair of rescuers.

The game is nearing an end, but we cannot find one nine-year-old boy. We gather at the post — an impressive search party — and compare theories. 'Have we looked by Riley's garage? Lots of good spots to hide there.' We devise other plans but don't find the boy. Then someone says, 'Hey, we've been looking everywhere but up.' We immediately spread out and look up. Sure enough, the rascal is up a tree, enjoying the spectacle of us scurrying around. A big cheer goes up when we find him. We carry him on our shoulders to the post. He is given the honour of starting the next game.

Later, on the porch, I reflect further on the game we have just played. I know that this is a turning-point in my life. I can't look back now.

The laughter of the kids. The collective good will. No one is eliminated from the game. Even the youngest is playing and making a contribution right to the end. The nature and quality of the relationships of the participants feeels healthy, feels very right. No 'It' pitted against the rest of the group. What a name we assign to that person who does the chasing — *It!*

I realise what has been bothering me about the game we recently bought for our two girls. The game always puts them in conflict with each other. The point of the game is to beat one another and because the older one has the advantage of experience and co-ordination (among other things), she usually wins. The younger one either has to be coaxed to go on playing or, worse, she cheats in order to 'get even' with her big sister! Then the big sister doesn't want to play anymore. 'Christa always cheats!' is the complaint.

I also reflect on situations outside the family. I teach Sunday School in our local church. We have our lesson from the Bible and we discuss finding non-violent ways to solve problems. We explore the meaning of compassion, sharing, affection and so on. Then I set up the recreation programme and the kids pound and push each other something awful. What a contrast here!

They often drift through the class lesson listlessly, but have great vitality for the games. I now see how my recreation programme is not reinforcing my lessons on living. Let's be honest: the recreation programme is undermining my lessons.

I reflect on my high-school teaching as well. Many more things come together. Competition is an effective tool for classroom management, for realising various academic goals. This is the devilish attraction of the competitive technique: you get those quick, short-term results. To take the co-operative route which tries to nurture action through understanding is 'messy' and takes too much time. I can get my daughter to clean up her room by setting up comparison/ competition images with her neat friend, Amanda. Tanya will clean up under that kind of pressure. But will she understand what cleanliness, punctuality and so on are about if I continue doing that to her? I no longer think so.

Co-operative games: development

That day some twenty-six years ago on my back porch shook up my perspectives for good. I challenged myself to begin the adventure of doing things differently in the family, the neighbourhood, the church and my school-teaching. I had set myself many goals in those areas of endeavour, but now I was challenging myself to realise them by *co-operative* rather than *competitive* means.

For our family it meant going to toy and game stores and asking the salespeople about games that stressed sharing and helping each other. 'We want a good family game.'

I remember well the first store owner laughing aloud, then seeing that we were not laughing with him, he gave serious consideration to our request. We were soon flabbergasted. He could not find a solitary thing in the entire store.

We were forced to change the rules of many of the games we had at home — *Scrabble,* for example: instead of keeping individual scores, we kept a family score. Just that simple rule change created subtle shifts in the dynamics of the game.

Some examples: we allowed free use of the dictionary by all, and helping each other to spell words. Far from hiding behind our tokens, we not only exposed them, we even traded them. Finally, instead of using my cunning to maximise my own score with the treasured letters X, Q, Z, etc., burying them so no one else could use them, I now found I could still use these letters ingeniously and at the same time create opportunities for others to use them.

I can honestly say that I feel a thousand times better using my mind to assist and share rather than as a weapon. Why? The reason is simple.

Our initial impulse to play a game is social — that is, we bring out a game because we want to do something together. So how ironic it is that in most games we spend so much energy and effort trying to bankrupt someone, destroy their armies, or in other words try to get rid of the very people we just invited over to play with us. If we can play a game that *develops,* rather than *defeats* that social impulse, then everyone feels better for it.

In addition to altering existing games, I began to cook up my own. The old cliché that 'necessity is the mother of invention' proved true in my case: since I could not find any co-operative games, I simply began inventing them.

Once my mind began seeing the possibilities, I found myself creating original games for birthday parties and 'Play Days' at school, or co-op games as Christmas gifts, and it was not long before friends suggested that I start selling them. Ruth and I ran a few advertisements and were encouraged by the response. Slow but steady growth in sales made us move the little business, which we called *Family Pastimes,* from our own living room into a 'prefab' cottage. We literally had a 'cottage industry'.

The several hundred games I have invented over the years fall roughly into three categories: (1) Co-op-type games and activities such as *Lost and found,* which I have written up in several manuals; (2) 'Parlour'-type games in board, card and block format; (3) Large wooden table-action games — the co-operative answer to Table Hockey, Soccer, etc.

Co-operative games: distinctiveness

What makes a co-operative game different? My working definition of a co-operative game is simple. I never have people being against people in any of my games. I have to make this clear because I am often asked at conferences and workshops whether I would not consider such and such a sport an example of co-operative effort. I acknowledge that a group may co-operate among its members, but often with the purpose of obliterating the opposing group. The goal cannot be separated from the means by which it is achieved. We could point out, by extension, that even fighting a war requires a kind of co-operation. The ultimate game for altogether too many people!

I have noticed some magazine reviews refer to various gangland crime games and certain adventure fantasy games as 'co-operative'. In each case, what the reviewer is describing is the opportunity the game offers for some players to combine efforts for a brief time in order to destroy another player, which is not my idea of a co-operative game. Very simply, in a cooperative game, people play together and not against each other.

To this day we still make a full range of co-operative games by hand in small quantities. We sell mostly by mail through a colour catalogue as well as through a variety of stores.[3] Also there are a growing number of people who willingly distribute our games from their homes and churches.

Initially, I hoped my idea would eventually be adopted by some of the big game companies (I was perfectly happy in my teaching position and had no intentions of becoming a full-time inventor and manufacturer). I was keenly disappointed by repeated rejection from the giants of the game industry. My approach was extremely naïve. I walked into company presidents' offices expecting to talk about the worthwhile game concepts I had developed and tested, but I quickly learned that they had other priorities. I became quite cynical about the brutally competitive toy and game industry when I saw that behind the façade of cute and cuddly stuff for kids were hardnosed business-men and -women. Very few of them were cute or cuddly themselves. Hence my own introduction to the business of producing co-operative games.

Co-operative workshop: *Musical chairs*

I recall another workshop for a church group. I like the format — children are invited to join in. The adults are well educated and sophisticated. From the chit-chat beforehand I realise that they are also not convinced. It is a challenge to spend a couple of hours with people who are sceptical about co-op games. I decide to play a typical 'little kid's' game with them.

'Grown-ups, please be little children with me for the next while and begin to re-experience what a child feels in playing the games we offer them.'

The first game we play is the first game I ever remember playing myself as a child. My Grade One teacher introduced it to our class of children who came mainly from farming families. Since they lived far apart, the kids did not know each other and were apprehensive about starting school. The teacher attempted to 'socialise' us and help us feel at home by using games, one of which was *Musical chairs*. Being a shy child and not tuned in to the cultural roles required to play the game successfully, I was bewildered by the rush and push for a chair when the music stopped. Eliminated early from the game, I felt puzzled and embarrassed when told that I was 'out' and had to take away a chair with me. Of course, the more we played, the better I got at elbowing my way to a chair. A prime example of quick cultural conditioning!

I wonder what will happen in the workshop now as we start playing the same game. The game itself speaks louder than words ever could. One little boy in the group, four or five years old, is eager to play. The music stops: people push and take places, then look around to see who the first casualty is. Some adults audibly moan upon seeing that the little boy is 'out'. He is crushed and flees to his mum's arms. After that some people are polite or do not try very hard, and are soon eliminated, but later confide that they feel uncomfortable being forced into an aggressive role of having to push others around. Children who drop out of the game early say much the same thing. Finally, we have a big group of spectators watching the last two participants go for the big win.

I know that the adults can see how even though the game may begin as a socialisation process, it quickly defeats this very objective as players get eliminated and must sit around watching.

I talk a bit about how I felt in Grade One when I was made to leave the game early. I try to make plain to adults and children alike why the games I make up today are different.

Then I introduce *Co-operative musical chairs* and bring the players back again with the same furniture.

'People are now going to be more important than the chairs,' I announce, 'so the only rule-change is that after each round we take away a chair, but we keep all the people. It's up to the imagination of the group to figure out how to make a place for everyone.' I can still vividly see the laughter as the people hug each other, sit on each other's laps and succeed in all getting on one chair at the end. The little boy is on the shoulders of an adult. He is having a fine time.

The game uses the same hardware, the same music and the same people. But with the change in the structure of the game the roles the people play change too. People relax after a few rounds when they suddenly realise: 'Hey, I don't have to rush and push because I am guaranteed a spot.'

People afterwards remark on how good they feel using their strength to hug instead of push. Children make the same observation over and over.

Other co-operative games

The workshop then moves into a sampling of various table games. Groups of people gather round different games I have set out. *Harvest time* is a board game for families with children aged 3 to 7 years of age. People enjoy being neighbours helping each other bring in the harvest before winter comes — a very real-life situation. I often look to real life for my game themes. Cooperative games are rooted in reality.

If *Harvest time* were competitive, players would each be trying to get a garden harvested before anyone else. If an opponent were getting too close to winning, others would have to send some disaster into that garden to slow him or her down. That is reality? Yet that is exactly how most competitive games are set up and instruct us to behave accordingly.

I also set up *Housebuilders* for children 5 to 8 years of age — a game inspired by my working with friends to build our home. *Mountaineering* (ages 7 to 12) is based on an experience I once had mountain-climbing in the Rockies with several friends. We were tied to one another at times. The last person we wanted or needed was some clown racing ahead trying to be 'King (or Queen) of the Mountain'.

Other co-operative board games which have proved popular include *Community* (9 to adult), where people work together to make a community or build a stable economy in their town, *Space future* (10 to adult) whose players engage in the adventure of completing a common mission in space, and *Earth game* (10 to adult), in which ' world leaders' develop strategies to solve the many problems on 'Spaceship Earth'.

Co-operative *Puzzle game*

We have time for one more game. I select the *Puzzle game* as it brings the entire group together again for a big co-operative effort.

A tiny six-year-old girl named Cindy comes to the front of the church auditorium where I stand holding out a paper bag. She and several other children reach into the bag and each take out one piece of a puzzle. Rather it is three puzzles, whose pieces are all mixed together. Cindy must find out which puzzle her piece belongs to.

She goes around to all three tables where people are working on the puzzles. 'Does this piece belong here?' she asks a teenaged boy at the last table. He eagerly examines the new piece and pops it into place.

Cindy smiles triumphantly before returning for another puzzle piece. She prefers selecting the puzzle pieces, while others enjoy fitting the pieces together. The adults in the group seem more interested in solving the cartoon mysteries printed on the puzzles. But because she's playing a co-operative game, Cindy's contribution is as valuable as anyone else's.

Finally, the children go off after the play session to their study groups and the adults remain with me for a concluding questionand-answer session. The questions are direct and challenging. Some are surprising to me, coming from a church group; I realise that I have brought with me some mistaken assumptions about adults who belong to churches.

Co-operative games: questions and answers

Q. Don't you think that co-operative games and the cooperative philosophy will tend toward mediocrity, toward making everyone the same, while competitive approaches bring out individuality, qualities of leadership, etc.?

A. On the contrary. The games I make and the games we have just played allow for the gifted to do their very best and for those less able to make their best contribution too. Each is valued. Those with leadership qualities quite naturally emerge and contribute. What pleases me is that these leaders had to use their abilities in a responsible way that showed caring for others. They were not asked to dominate, exploit weaknesses for selfaggrandisement, manipulate and then defend themselves from others trying to take over and get rid of them. It's a deeper challenge to the gifted to work with people in a co-operative way.

You see, some people like to think that co-operative games are for losers only. Indeed, while a co-operative game does allow for the 'loser' to express ability without fear of elimination, it also serves the winner, whose character might otherwise suffer from constant winning at the expense of others. I see no harm in the quick-minded learning to be patient with the slow.

Finally, one of the best features about our games is that most are fun for adults and children to play together. The trouble with many competitive games of strategy is that parents deliberately play poorly in order to make the game fair and interesting for children. When competition between individuals is removed, skilful players are able to make sincere efforts to win, because their efforts help all the players, while competition forces the more skilled to be mediocre in their efforts in such situations.

Q. I need competition to better myself, to learn new things, to pursue excellence in what I do. Otherwise where is the incentive to get ahead?

A. There seems to be a lot of concern here about 'getting ahead'... What is wrong, if I may ask (a bit facetiously), with the head you now have? Perhaps we spend too much time pursuing an ideal we are not and not enough time enjoying and realising what we already are. We strive to be this someone else whom we are constantly comparing ourselves to. If you look at it closely you'll see that this comparison is the very root of competition. For me, competition kills the pursuit of excellence. Let me offer some examples.

When I have friends over for a meal, I go to a lot of trouble to provide a superb meal, the best I can cook. If someone comes early, I get him or her involved in making the meal. We are tasting, slicing, adding this and that until the meal shapes up 'just right'. Getting things 'just right' is what we naturally do. You see it in children when, say, their blocks fall down. They try again. They want it to be right. Now in making this meal what has been my incentive? I am doing it for its own joy. What is operating here is affection, simple affection for what I am doing. To introduce competition would be extraneous and unnecessary. It's only necessary when there is no affection. Really, I don't need the 'Galloping Gourmet' or some famous chef in the next room whipping together a better meal than mine to drive me to do better.

Or let's take dancing. My wife and I are dancing and there are a lot of other couples on the dance floor as well. We are both getting into the rhythm of the music and of each other. We try some neat steps and greatly enjoy what we are doing. Suddenly there is a spotlight focused on us and a voice over the P.A. announces that a dancing contest is on and the spotlight will move from couple to couple with the judges declaring a winner of incredible prizes. Personally, this would ruin the occasion for me. I don't need the competitive element to make me dance better.

I am reminded of the time when our two girls were in Grades One and Two. They loved to sing in the little kids' school choir and to do simple folk dancing in groups. Every year there was a 'Music Festival', or so it was called. A festival is a time for people to get together and celebrate, but, alas, this festival turned out to be a contest. A number of trophies donated by local merchants were awarded to the best choir and the best folk-dancing group. The Killarney School down the road won both trophies. This happened the next year as well.

Coming home from this second festival, our older girl said she didn't want to take singing or folk dancing any more. 'Why?' I asked, a bit stunned.

'Because Killarney always wins the trophies. They are better than we are and they'll always win,' was her solemn answer. You see what had happened to her love of singing and dancing? We adults with our structuring of winners and losers, trophies and hoopla, had corrupted it. It happens slowly but thoroughly, until you get to be my age and like me do not want to do very much unless prodded and pulled by the carrots of reward and punishment. Reward and punishment are central to competitive patterns of behaviour.

Q. Still, don't co-operative games tend to shelter, even coddle children?

A. I am providing a supportive play experience, it's true, but not a fail-safe shelter. I don't protect children from not making it to the summit of the mountain or completing the space voyage. Our games are designed to offer realistic challenges. It is entirely possible for people to fail in our games. Of course, the way failure arises and is faced differs from that in a competitive endeavour. But the risk of failure is present.

In addition, I should point out that the cultural habit of competing and confronting adversaries runs deep. Some players end up fighting the game itself, even when it's a co-operative game. We suggest that people will get better results learning how to get along with Time, with Winter, with Gravity, with Mountains and so on rather than fighting them.

Q. What I'm worried about is that children are going to take their place in a competitive society and it's a tough, even brutal, society. Don't we do them a disservice if we commit them to the kind of philosophy and environment that you are suggesting? They should be given the tools and skills to make their way in a competitive society. They have to be prepared to live in the reality of today.

A. First, let us not underestimate the amount of sharing and caring that takes place daily in our families, neighborhoods and societies... If we didn't have at least 50% co-operation, we wouldn't have much of a society at all. So, people can find a place in society to live and work and be friendly, sharing human beings. I think we adults have to be active in creating more such places for our young.

Secondly, it is an open question for me as to which is the best way to prepare children for that dog-eat-dog society you describe. I'll say more about that.

Thirdly, I think that at some point you have to decide what kind of society you want to see achieved. I've had a glimpse of compassion, sharing and caring and it feels a whole lot better to me than confrontation, violence, greed, etc. The danger in saying that society is brutal and then following that with the notion of preparing our children for it is that we accept the status quo and go on perpetuating it. I refuse to accept that way of living. I've seen and you have also seen that there is a better way for people to live and work and play together on this planet. And when this sense of caring gets firmly established within you, you have to act out from that source. You can't help it. But also you see what happens when the caring isn't there!

Your relationships — at all levels and of all kinds — begin to change in the glow of caring. As a teacher I simply couldn't go on doing the same old things as before. I had no new formulas, but the insight and intelligence newly uncovered began to work out better ways to teach and relate to the students in my care.

Life began unfolding differently in my family as well. The skills and values we taught our children just had to be different. First it meant moving out of the city into a rural area. It eventually led to home--schooling and then a small parent-run school. We gave our energy to this kind of non-competitive environment for ourselves as adults and for the kids.

Now I admit that we were operating on faith about this, because at some point the kids would have to go to the local high school and then take their places as citizens in this 'brutal society' you speak of. But Ruth and I had to find out if it was possible for people to live in a different way, personally. If so, perhaps it is possible for society at large.

When our girls went to high school, they began not without tears. They were inwardly prepared for all the competition for marks they knew would be there, but they were not as well prepared for the competition for popularity and peer approval. We worked through this and other traumas as a family. Our girls are friendly people and diligent students, curious and wanting to learn. Over a period of time they came to be liked and also to be enjoyed by their teachers for being good students.

The girls have survived and thrived without being trained to compete, strive and do all those things we think will better equip children to deal with a tough society. And they were not so insecure, fearful and anxious as many of their peers were.

I think the key reason is that our girls did not have a big emotional investment in winning and losing. Winning and losing were not tied in with their sense of self-worth. When they failed a test, they looked it over to see what went wrong. They didn't feel somehow diminished as a person by not succeeding at something. But they did try to do their best — to 'get it right'. They gained a self-confidence, flexibility, resilience that has served them well as members of adult society. I am pleased with their growth and the intelligent adaptability they show in a competitive environment. I want them to be 'good citizens' in the special sense of 'goodness' we have been talking about.

Q. Our family plays a lot of games and we get pretty enthusiastic about them. I'm wondering if it will be hard for us to play a co-operative game. It sounds like we would have a lot of re-educating to do.

A. Some re-orientation will have to take place. You won't have to view each other as enemies anymore, for one thing. Your enjoyment of games will take you a long way as an incentive to play a co-op game. I think that the enthusiasm we have for games is a social impulse to do something enjoyable together. If that is your basic motivation, then you will adjust to a cooperative game quickly. However, if your enthusisam and enjoyment have developed further than that and depend on gaining satisfaction from wiping out the other person, then you'll have a tough time at first. You'll be disoriented. You keep wanting to attack and keep waiting to be attacked and it never happens. Someone else gets in trouble and you can help out by sharing your carefully amassed fortune, or else if you get in trouble and someone else extends a helping hand, you may get confused. It's a sad comment on our culture. But there it is. We see it every day writ large on the front pages of our newspapers. The fruits of a competitive way of life!

Conclusion

Let me sum up this article. Games are used in various settings and for various reasons — socialisation, entertainment, academic learning and character-building,to name a few. Whatever your objective, I invite you to try realising it by co-operative means. Parents and teachers attempting to teach children to share, to be kind to living things and to help others are often troubled by games and recreational programmes which undermine these values. Co-operative games provide the opportunity to experience sharing and caring behaviour. I believe we simply do not yet have enough such experiences.

[1]*Plakun trava* — a water plant that stretches against the current. It was used as a metaphor by the Doukhobors to characterise themselves as a people who dared to challenge unpopular ideas such as conflict, militarism and war.

[2]Tanya, born in 1967, is currently living on Saltspring Island, British Columbia ,

working in a toy store as well as doing art therapy with street kids. She is also studying piano and hopes to use this skill in teaching children. Christa, born in 1968, owned a bookstore in West Vancouver; in 1996 she and her husband Hugh moved back to join the family in Perth, Ontario, and both are now closely connected with *Family Pastimes*. Both Tanya and Christa were brought up in a co-operative atmosphere; they received their primary education at home from their parents and later made a successful transition to high school, where they excelled in their studies. Tanya went on to obtain Art and Art Therapy degrees, while Christa took a degree in business administration — *ed*.

[3]This catalogue is available at no charge from: Family Pastimes, RR#4, Perth, Ontario, Canada K7H 3C6.

An experiment in public participation

Peter J. Popoff

As a member of the Doukhobor Society of Canada, I initiated a series of (now 68) monthly research symposia, organised in Western Canada by the Joint Doukhobor Research Committee beginning in November 1974. Up to four hundred people would come out regularly to these meetings held in alternate districts, speaking out on the origins of the Doukhobor movement, the first ten years in Canada, the period of the Community Doukhobors' migration to British Columbia (1908–13), the deaths of the first two leaders in Canada, *Peter V. ('the Lordly') Verigin* in 1924 and *Peter P. (Chistiakov) Verigin* in 1939, and offering a critical look at the present situation, whereby Doukhobor principles seem to have been transmitted so poorly to our younger generation.

At each symposium all those who were interested in speaking were invited to share their views on the topic of the day. This was followed by an opportunity to elucidate the theme more clearly through a 'question period' — first with members of the Joint Doukhobor Research Committee and subsequently with members of the audience. Overall, it was a unique adventure in self-learning and shared learning.

We did not pretend to know all the answers. But we believed that with the power of discussion and God's help we would be able to find the right answers to the questions confronting us, according to the maxim: 'Reasoning is the highest virtue...'.

Having lived for generations with spiritual leaders who nourished their audiences with inspirational discourses, we were aware that many Doukhobors had developed the habit of taking in the message in a manner dictated by the hearts of each individual listener, seldom reflecting on the possibility of a misinterpertation of the text. The immediate effect was a pleasant one, giving peace to each and healing balm to life's ailments. An unfortunate consequence was that listeners were not always aware of the speaker's ultimate goal in his discourse, and discrepancies in interpretation sometimes led to divisions among the people. We have reason to believe that Peter P. Verigin was endeavouring to correct this situation when he exhorted his followers to meet, discuss and reason with one another so as to arrive at a correct understanding of Doukhobor principles and to identify the right path one should take in life. This was the rationale behind the symposia.

There is much value in people coming together to discuss a theme of common interest. It is an example of direct learning in action, like attending an educational seminar. A proper analysis of the worth of this project will require an examination, digestion, classification and report of the findings based on the multitude of tape-recordings and summary transcripts which constitute the record of this ambitious project. It is hoped that this can be done before the end of the century.[1]

[1]See: Eli A. Popoff (compiler and translator). *Summarized report. Joint Doukhobor Research Committee. Symposium meetings 1974–1982.* Castlegar: Selkirk College, 1997. Reviewed by Koozma J. Tarasoff in *Iskar* (Grand Forks), issue of 25 June 1997, pp. 32–33.

Bridge-building across Cold-War boundaries

Paul J. Seminoff

Over forty years have passed since **William A. Soukoreff** of Grand Forks, B.C., made his historic trip to the USSR in 1954, at a time when it was difficult to correspond and travel across EastWest boundaries. Much has changed since then, not only in what was once the Soviet Union but also within the Doukhobor community itself.

However, one ideal that has remained steadfast among the Doukhobors for all this time is their passionate commitment to peace, regardless of where they live. Their dedication and perseverance were always in the forefront, even though not officially recognised until 1989, when **John J. Verigin,** representing the Doukhobors, was awarded the 'Order of Friendship of Peoples' by then Soviet leader Mikhail S. Gorbachev.

Doukhobors have always had a tremendous respect and love for the homeland of their forebears. What was happening in the USSR (whether it was perceived as good or bad) also had its effect on the Doukhobor community, who shared in the joy or sorrow, respectively, of their compatriots in Soviet Russia.

The various cultural exchanges that have occurred since William Soukoreff's visit have brought innumerable benefits not only to the members of the USCC1 but to Doukhobors as a whole. The exchanges which helped build bridges of understanding, friendship and mutual respect have continued even after the breakup of the Soviet Union. The USCC is grateful to the Rodina Society in Russia for all the assistance that they have provided over the years with tourism, cultural activities, educational opportunities for students and more.

In the summer of 1984 John J. Verigin, **Paul J. Seminoff** and other members of the USCC Peace Committee met with two Conservative Members of Parliament: Bob Brisco and (former Prime Minister) Joe Clark. Some of the parliamentarians' comments during their presentation at this meeting are worth quoting here:

> The Doukhobor religious and moral ethic is based on 'toil and peaceful life'. This ethic has been demonstrated throughout their history but was never more apparent than their present efforts in the cause of world peace and their significant involvement in and contribution to the peace movement.

Further, by reason of their ethnic origin, they have an understanding of the culture, customs and social and political fabric of Russia.

This understanding has been strengthened by frequent visits to Russia by members of the Doukhobor community. These visits have often led to cultural exchanges with people from Russia, in a spirit of good will.

In consideration of the above, more than any other ethnic group in Canadian society, they are uniquely suited for the role of 'Ambassadors of Peace'.

[1]Union of Spiritual Communities of Christ — the formal organisation of the Community Doukhobors, centred in British Columbia.

Part IV

Stories remembered

The Circle journey

Vi Plotnikoff

'Write about what you know. Write about your Doukhobor roots.' So stated my creative writing instructor at Selkirk College in Castlegar. I didn't agree.

To be Doukhobor was to hide your background, not flaunt it. To be Doukhobor was to be proud of your ancestors, customs, beliefs, yet at the same time to feel defensive or embarrassed about them.

To be Doukhobor was to be a young adult working in Vancouver yet concealing your roots — the same roots you were so proud of when you stood on the stage of the cultural centre, singing the hymns and psalms your parents, and your grandparents before them, had sung.

To be Doukhobor was to be competitive. You had to prove you were the best. Being 'as good as' was not enough. And to be Doukhobor was to have mixed, confused feelings. For how could one be defensive and proud at the same time?

I had always believed in the simple Doukhobor philosophy, based on peace and the commandment 'love thy neighbour'. Yet I let the insecure child within me dictate the actions of the adult. And then one day I realised my attitude was changing. I wanted to tell the world about being Doukhobor through my writing, and I wanted to do it in an entertaining and positive way, so people would read my work, and understand.

Fig. 1. Vi Plotnikoff.

I decided that fictional short stories would be my medium. Fiction, because I could let my imagination go, but I would employ authentic Doukhobor culture, beliefs and customs in my work — even food, which is the backbone of every culture.

I began giving my characters Russian names, putting them into Doukhobor settings, having my central character feel the joy and pain of being a young Doukhobor girl emerging into womanhood — experiencing prejudices, being prejudiced herself — all the while threading customs and culture throughout my stories.

A 'circle journey' is how I refer to my evolution from secure child to insecure child and teenager, to defensive young adult, to confident adult with a story to tell and being secure as a Doukhobor once again. However, this circle journey took many years to complete and was not without pain.

'*Olia... Olechka...*' *Baba*'s voice...[1] my first memory. 'We're moving far, far away. To British Columbia.'

I put down the little can of water I had been drowning my watermelon plant with, thinking hard. Why were we moving when it was so beautiful here in Saskatchewan? I looked at the red geraniums around the farmhouse, the golden wheat ripening in the fields, the geese and turkeys around the pond. I didn't want to leave.

The farm in Saskatchewan... in Linden Valley, halfway between Verigin and Kamsack, where my parents and grandparents grew wheat for the Doukhobor community, where *Deda*'s Indian friends came to dig potatoes in exchange for winter wood, bringing their dark-eyed babies into the big farm kitchen.

'Pete's our friend', they said, presenting grandfather with hand-made gifts.

Sundays we went to visit my Kootnekoff grandparents in the big community house near the grain elevators in Verigin. If it were winter, I would be smothered under a *tulup* [sheepskin coat], as the runners of the sleigh squeaked on the blue-white snow, the horse's breath almost turning to ice.

Summer Sundays I would play on the porch of the Doukhobor *Dom* [community home] at Verigin, the lacey metalwork lending a delicate air to the white building. There was always a multitude of people and wonderful mass singing. And then there were the letters read by lamplight from relatives in far-off British Columbia and sometimes a box of apples. I had my beloved horse, Sivka. I was secure and happy.

My father left to work in British Columbia and to build our log house in the mountains. We were dismantling the farm... packing. 'Sivka... is she coming?' I enquired. 'She is ill, *Dochka*.' 'We can take her in a big box', I ventured.

We were leaving the community farm to join the Doukhobors in B.C.

I didn't mind… all my grandparents and cousins were moving too.

The long train journey to Grand Forks. My mother, sister, cousin… myself. The isolated ranch… the house with its freshly peeled logs, lush meadows to roam barefoot… a creek to wade in, where *krapiva* [stinging nettles] grew in the green coolness… delicious when Mama cooked it. We were again secure… except when the serious voice of the CBC announcer boomed over the static of the tiny battery radio… war news. Neighbours walked a mile every day to listen to the news on our radio. Papa rode his bicycle eight miles [= 13 km] into town, teaching Russian School during the week, staying with my Kootnekoff grandparents, returning weekends. Mama looked after the cows and horses, warning us not to go into the woods, to watch out for rattlesnakes, wolves and bears. At night, we fell asleep to the yodelling of coyotes. We were never afraid.

Then we stayed in town so I could start school. We children had playmates… most had one parent… a mother. Their fathers were overseas, fighting. I was glad my father didn't go to war. I knew war was evil and we didn't believe in killing anyone, not even the enemy. At school we all wore Junior Red Cross pins and raised money for the Red Cross war effort. A war which seemed very far away.

Shortly after I started Grade One, the teacher, red-faced, announced: 'Class, the war is over. You are dismissed for today…' I was mainly excited about the free merry-go-round rides in the schoolyard that afternoon.

'Your children are black…' said Mrs Baker, the English lady across the road. We had moved into our own house on the edge of town, complete with a cow, and a garden encircled by tall sunflower plants. Mr and Mrs Baker were from England. Mr Baker lost an arm in the First World War. They both adored the Royal Family, whose solemn faces looked down on the Bakers from every wall of their tiny, incredibly untidy, rose-covered cottage.

Mama looked at her dandelion-headed gaggle of daughters — all five of us — pretending innocence.

'Whatever do you mean, Mrs Baker? Look at their white hair and skin. See how blue their eyes are…'

'Mrs Makaeff, you know what I mean. They're Doukhobor, not British… not whites, like us.'

When we played under the big trees, I always gave myself an English name. English was better.

'You Russian kids…' our Grade Three teacher said. 'Leave your sunflower seeds at home. They're hard to sweep up on the wooden floors.'

I scrunched low in my seat, ignoring the *angliki* [the English] with their ringlets and short dresses and hid my scuffed sturdy shoes. I hated my braids. I had never brought sunflower seeds to school.

'You Russian kids...' said our Grade Six teacher, a young male straight out of Vancouver. 'If you speak Russian in the school or the playground, you'll get strapped.' This time I stared back defiantly. I never spoke Russian at school, even though my father taught Russian School and Sunday School and we spent every weekend at choir practice, learning hymns and psalms.

'Speak Russian at home,' my father said. 'No English.'

Papa taught both schools in the plain wooden building across the bridge, where we sat at long tables and painfully wrote out the unfamiliar letters of the Russian alphabet. There was a stage where we practised plays and songs in Russian. When we were older, we attended an *otdel* (or local cultural group), learning hymns, participating in or mostly listening to discussions, and preparing programmes for the big *sobranie* [gathering] at the cultural centre. Most of my friends attended, and we would walk home together in the cold winter nights, dodging snowballs from the always pesky boys.

Once a year it was our turn to host my father's choir. My mother baked cakes all week, made mounds of sandwiches from bought bread (an unheard-of treat), and pots of coffee. The ladies of the choir served the singers in the tiny living room, and after eating, we children would go to bed, listen drowsily to the harmonies drifting up the stairs. By this time my father's song 'Life is worth living' was sung by many of the choirs, and I was very proud.

Another important date on the Doukhobor calendar was Declaration Day, when we would get our once-a-year new dresses. Mother packed a huge lunch to eat on the shady lawns of the white *Dom*, bringing lots of food, because no family ate alone; there were always guests and lonesome bachelors or widowed people to invite. Watermelon, hard--boiled eggs, fruit tarts, cucumbers and maybe, just maybe, the first tomatoes of the season, along with big jars of *otvar* [fruit compote] to drink.

Then I was a teenager, and the most exciting weekend of the year was the Youth Festival. By this time I was on the Youth Board of *Iskra*,[2] president of our *otdel*, and youth delegate to various conventions, making speeches in Russian and singing at the Festival.

My secure Doukhobor life ran parallel to my school life — never meeting, yet not too far apart. I lived in two worlds — school, where Russian was an embarrassment, and my Doukhobor life, where the *angliki* were looked down upon because they couldn't cook like us and didn't eat well, and were too thin as a result (a fact much envied by some). In school I was very active in drama, participating in drama festivals and working on the school paper. It seemed as if I had to prove myself, and when I was on stage, I felt I was as good as anyone.

My best friends were the Japanese kids whose families had been relocated from the West Coast during the war. They too didn't quite fit in.

When we began dating, my girlfriends and I didn't volunteer details about our background as we danced with out-of-town boys in the big pavilion at Christina Lake. And we had nothing to do with the Sons of Freedom kids, nor they with us, even though we sometimes dated the boys, which was considered as bad as dating an *anglik* by our parents.

Then I left the security of home for Vancouver and became part of the unidentified mass of white, English-speaking Canadians with no particular ethnic background. I was a stenographer with the Canadian National Railway, and never volunteered anything about my roots.

'You're from Doukhobor country,' I heard over and over and read a thousand injustices into that phrase. And felt terrible guilt for not speaking up. But in Vancouver there were Chinese and East Indian and Native people who stood out more than I.

When I married a good Doukhobor boy and had children, I became a typical Canadian mum. Hockey, baseball, swim club. But I also taught them psalms, the Russian language, and as a Sunday School teacher I wrote my own bilingual lessons. However, I was still defensive and angry, because of the roadblocks and violence in the Kootenays at that time. I felt singled out whenever we were asked our names, told to 'pull over' by the police, then questioned.

My husband Serge and I were among the founding members of the Doukhobor Cultural Association, and during the heady 'seventies we were young and idealistic and out to change the world. The peace movement was the most important thing in our lives, and my husband wrote songs and performed them at concerts and peace marches. In Saskatchewan we celebrated seventy years of Doukhobor life in Canada, and we were euphoric. My most memorable moment came during the big parade in Kamsack as my father's choir walked by, singing, carrying banners underneath the rainy skies, and I cried as I watched.

A year and a half later, just before Christmas, my father died in an industrial accident. Sure-footed, unafraid of heights... how could this have happened to him? Active in the Doukhobor community, a writer, singer, mentor... my children's *deda*. My mother — stricken with multiple sclerosis, widowed — was still young. My father's song seemed ironic.

Then, in the early 1980s, I signed up for creative writing classes at Selkirk College, and it was there that I was advised to write about my culture. I rejected the idea at first, not feeling confident in myself at the time.

What changed my mind? Why did I go on to write about myself and about being a Doukhobor? Was it the memory of my father? My mother's pride in her roots? Or a writer friend saying she was envious of my rich cultural background?

Possibly a little of each. However, when I finally looked back, beyond myself and my insecurities, and I realised the enormous strength of my ancestors and their beliefs... I felt very humble and very proud.

And I knew I had finally completed my 'circle journey'.

[1]*Baba* = Grandma; *Deda* = Grandpa; *Dochka* = Daughter.

[2]*Iskra* — bilingual (Russian/English) publication of the Union of Spiritual Communities of Christ in Grand Forks, B.C. — *ed.*

A True story about
a pioneer Doukhobor babushka

Eli A. Popoff

A mere wisp of a woman. Barely over five feet tall.[1] Slight of build, but wiry and tenacious as only a true peasant of the Russian steppes could be. This apparently 'slight' peasant woman embodied not only the strength and the fortitude of our glorified pioneers, who settled and developed the 'wild' Canadian West, but time and again she manifested the deeper inherent traits of humankind, which were eventually to make her a legend in her time.

This particular experience occurred in the years 1909–10. The *Popov* family, comprising father *Aleksei Ivanovich,* mother *Ekaterina Timofeevna* (*'Katiusha'*) and their four-year old son *Nikolai,* were living in a small log cabin on their homestead near Blaine Lake, Saskatchewan. This was the smaller Doukhobor settlement, referred to as the Northern Prince Albert Colony, situated about 80 miles [= 130 km] west of Prince Albert. Out of the 7,500 souls who had arrived in Canada on four shiploads, from the port of Batum on the Black Sea, the larger part of the group had settled in the Yorkton-Thunder Hill area, north-east of Regina.

As part of a predominantly younger group of Doukhobors who had been sentenced to an eighteen-year exile in the Yakutsk area of Siberia for refusing to do military service, Aleksei and Katiusha Popov did not arrive in Canada until 1905, the year they were granted early release by a Manifesto of Liberation issued by the reigning Tsar Nicholas II to celebrate the birth of a royal son. Thus they emigrated directly from Siberia, sailing from the Latvian port of Libava (renamed Liepäja in 1917). After a brief stop in Liverpool, the British ship *Southwark* landed them at Québec city on 9 September 1905.

Katiusha Popova[2] often talked of this momentous voyage. She had been given away in marriage by her mother when she was barely fifteen years old; exile did not afford young women much of a selection. Her father *Timofei Ivanovich* was a religious exile from Perm Province; his wife *Anna ('Annushka')* had followed him to Yakutsk from their home base in Sverdlovsk, only to have him taken away once more. Re-arrested in Yakutsk and charged with the more serious crime of sedition against the church and the state, he was sent to the most distant northern reaches of

Siberia, where his family was not permitted to follow. Annushka was left with five small children to support, with no family or friends to help. Forced to give up her youngest son Sasha for adoption, she began living with a Doukhobor bachelor, whom she eventually married, and soon afterward gave her eldest daughter Katiusha in marriage to her new husband's chum, one Aleksei Ivanovich Popov — thereby keeping her three middle sons in her new, 'blended' family.

All this had taken place in 1905. Here was Katiusha Popova, a teen--aged bride already pregnant, coming across the ocean to the promised new land, in the hot, not too comfortable secondclass cabins of the *Southwark*. She always said in recalling the trip that it was 'most re-markable' that at five months pregnant she did not suffer from sea--sickness. Her most poignant memories were always of looking back to the homeland she left behind, her happy early childhood with her parents and grandparents in Russia, including the difficult but unifying times with her brothers and mother in Siberia. Above all, she had left behind her father whom she had loved so dearly — back there, some-where, in that newly developing harsh expanse of Siberia.

*   *   *

The arrival of the Popovs and some one hundred and fifty other Siberian exiles in the Canadian Doukhobor settlements was a heart-warming occasion. Families were reunited after being apart for a decade or so. Most exiles had relatives who had arrived six years earlier, and even those that didn't were welcomed and integrated into the communes that had sprung up in the new land.

Aleksei Ivanovich and Katiusha were warmly accepted by the Popovs already in Canada: Aleksei's parents *Vania* and *Onia*, a younger brother *Ivan* and sister *Nastia* (both still unmarried), and an elder brother *Nikola*, who was the acknowledged head of the family, with his wife *Mavrunia*.

In a very short time Katiusha came to love her mother-in-law, her *Starushka*[3] Onia. A devout soul, she was always puttering around at something, never raising her voice at anyone. She was often occupied in pacifying Nikola's two children. Her counsel to her children, especially her two youngest, her level tone of voice, her remarkable memory, her practical approach to things and her insight into the very finest points of Doukhobor faith, always had a profound effect. Katiusha especially marvelled at how the mother handled her temperamental daughter Nastia (who was the same age as Katiusha), along with maintaining harmony in the entire household.

*Fig.1 Babushka Siminishcheva with her husband Ivan Simeonovich Popov.
The latter who was 6 feet 4 inches tall is sitting, while his wife at 5 feet is standing.
Photo taken c. 1920 when Babushka was about 70 years old.*

The first year of life in the Blaine Lake village of Pazirayevka proved a real haven for Katiusha. Her *Starushka*, ever thoughtful of her, taught her to cook according to all the accepted Doukhobor standards, but did it so imperceptibly that Katiusha never felt she was being 'instructed'. Instead, Onia constantly praised her daughter-in-law's knowledge, style and abilities that she had learnt from her own mother. Katiusha's expertise in this and other household tasks (throughout her life she was an outstanding cook, gardener and housekeeper) thus became enriched by the blending of two distinct cultural backgrounds — from two totally different environmental spheres within Russia's vast two-continent empire.

In December of that year her *Starushka* helped bring into the world her first-born, *Nikolai*, and then proceeded to teach Katiusha how to care for the baby. Katiusha felt her mother-in-law did everything so capably and naturally, never reacting to any mishap and never fearing for the future, even though Katiusha herself sometimes doubted that they would manage to survive the winter on the meagre supplies available. Onia would always declare:

We must have faith that God will provide that which is essential for our well-being. We must only, always, be careful that we are not wasteful and over-indulgent ourselves...

While Onia had never learnt to read or write, she never missed reciting — evenings, mornings and at mealtimes — the many Doukhobor prayers (called *psalms*) and hymns she had learnt by heart as a child. She would teach these, along with their melodies, to her grandchildren, making sure any neighbour child who happened to be around had an opportunity to hear them too. For Katiusha, her *Starushka* was an angelic presence sent into her life to establish an equilibrium after her unsettled and emotionally unstable childhood.

*   *   *

However, this 'haven' of Katiusha's was not to last. In the year following the Popov family decided that the Prince Albert Doukhobor colony at Blaine Lake was not evolving in line with their inner concepts of the true Doukhobor faith. About half of the two hundred or so Blaine Lake families were contemplating the decision to accede to the government's demand of an oath of allegiance to the Crown and abandon the communal form of living in favour of individual homesteads. The Popovs, along with the majority of their fellow-villagers, decided to move to the southern colony at Yorkton, where the vast majority were determined to continue their communal way of life and refuse to take the oath.

As far as Katiusha was concerned, her *Starushka's* word was not to be questioned. Onia had put it simply and straightforwardly:

We refused allegiance to the Tsar of Russia, because allegiance required military service, which we could not and would not perform. How can we now swear allegiance to the Tsar in England, when this will require us to perform military service here? We were promised that we would be allowed our religious freedom here inCanada, and that is why we came here. We ought to toil peacefully on the land, and live our own way... There is no way that we will go back on our principles, because we have made our Trust with God, that we will follow these principles — no matter what sacrifices this would require. God will punish us if we do not keep our Trust...

The organising and carrying out of the trek by covered wagon from Blaine Lake to the Yorkton/Thunder Hill area took a good part of the summer. The domestic animals were led and herded. Their belongings were transported on the wagons, along with the women and children, while most of the men-folk made the 320kilometre trek on foot. At their destination the trekkers were welcomed with open arms by none other than the leader himself, Peter Vasilevich Verigin, along with other Community Doukhobors, and were subsequently absorbed into the Dou-khobor villages surrounding the prairie railway station named Verigin.

Katiusha took to the communal way of living right from the start, which she later remembered with fondness as being the true Christian way of life. No doubt this impression was at least partly due to the example of her *Starushka* — who, according to Doukhobor custom, would now be called *Babushka* (Grandmother) by all the children of the village. (Specifically, she would be referred to as *Babushka Siminishcheva*[4] to dis-tinguishing her from the many others in the village bearing the Popov name.) Babushka Siminishcheva helped shield her daughter-in-law from the rough edges encountered in merging into an already functioning communal system, reminding her neighbours that Katiusha was not only an orphan but was only seventeen years old and a breast-feeding mother.

However, things were turning out quite differently for her husband, Aleksei Ivanovich. A full-fledged working man of thirty years of age, in excellent health, he had mastered his knowledge of grain-growing and cattle- and sheep-raising back in the Caucasus; his evolutionary ex-perience of close co-operation with fellow-Doukhobors for survival in Siberia had made him (and the others) very frugal, self-dependent and more democratically inclined than the majority of the Yorkton colony whose lives had been less harsh.

As time went by, Aleksei Ivanovich was finding it more and more dif-ficult to fit in with the existing Yorkton communal structure — he became dissatisfied with the many instances of the waste of labour, the lack of individual initiative for innovation, not to mention the continual bowing down to local village elders whose consciousness had not evolved, as had his, through harsh experiences. Eventually he decided he could no longer accept what he saw as an overly restrictive status quo, and despite his family's pleadings decided to take his wife and son back to Blaine Lake, where he felt he had a better chance of working with the more independently minded Doukhobors.

Thus in the autumn of 1908 Aleksei Ivanovich Popov drove back to his former colony with a small team of two horses. Katiusha and Nikolai came later, travelling by train as far as Rosthern (some fifty kilometres from Blaine Lake), where Aleksei met them with the wagon.

His expectations were not disappointed. The three of them were able to stay with his second cousins, *Fiodor* and *Aliosha Popov*, near their old village of Pazirayevka. These cousins lived side by side with two more distant relatives, *Nikola* and *Fedia Tikhonov*, who had been childhood chums. Before winter set in they were able to plant a vegetable garden, put up enough hay for the horses and a cow they had managed to purchase (along with chickens, which were eventually moved into the barn when it got too cold for them outside to lay eggs), and build a small log cabin and a log barn on a neighbouring homestead.

In spite of the cold weather and heavy snow, the winter turned out to be not a difficult one to endure. Their new log cabin was snug and warm. They had enough flour, their garden yielded enough cabbage, potatoes, beets, onions and cabbage, the cow and chickens supplied them with milk and eggs. They had frequent visits with their neighbours, the Tikhonovs and the Popovs. Katiusha rejoiced that Nikolai was an exceptionally strong and healthy child, and that her husband could spend most of the time at home, except for his occasional expeditions to an area some thirty kilometres north to fetch logs (both for firewood and for expansion of their cabin). These trips usually entailed a two- or three-day journey, and he would often stay overnight with local Indians and Métis, who were friendly to the Doukhobors. Their dwellings, however, were far more flimsy and less coldresistant than his log cabin at home.

The spring and summer proved more challenging. Aleksei found the land-breaking work extremely strenuous both on himself and his two horses, in spite of generous help from the neighbours. Not being able to afford a team of oxen (which many Doukhobor farmers were still using), he came up with the idea of training the cow to pull alongside the horses — a strange sight Katiusha would describe to her children and grandchildren for many years to come.

Their labour proved fruitful, for the harvest was very good that year. But all the extra work of stooking both her own and the neighbours's sheaves (partly in repayment for all the help they had received from them) took its toll on Katiusha's health: she discovered she had developed a serious hernia in her abdomen.

Adding to her anxiety was the anticipation of a long winter alone with young Nikolai. To acquire some urgently needed income, Aleksei had accepted a job at a sawmill in Prince Albert, which had been unexpectedly postponed from the autumn to the winter. Conscious of their desperate need, Katiusha played down the seriousness of her physical difficulty and urged him to take the work, saying she would be all right.

But that winter of 1909–10 proved to be less than 'all right' for Katiusha, obliged to spend long and dreary (sometimes stormy, always cold) winter nights alone with a son who was not yet five years old. A month after her husband's departure she realised she was pregnant again. Their only daily contact amid the white wasteland was with their farm animals. Aleksei had arranged for one of the Tikhonovs to look in on them every ten days or so, and each time Katiusha spotted Fedia or the eldest boy Simeon coming across the field she felt a sense of rejuvenation at the thought that here were people coming to her place to show that she was still included in their sphere of life.

In spite of her loneliness and occasional despondency, she was still satisfied that she had managed to keep her household (including the horses, cow and chickens) going normally through the winter. Spring was approaching however, which meant she would have to be planting the garden again, and do extra work in the fields, as her husband would not be returning from the sawmill until late spring.

She was also feeling the baby growing inside her, which she estimated would be due for delivery in late summer. Despite all her care about her diet and lifting heavy objects, her hernia seemed to be worsening. With all the spring chores ahead of her, how many times she thought of her *Starushka*, Babushka Siminishcheva, and the 'haven' she had felt when they had lived together. How she longed to have her with her again, right here in her little log cabin! She had to remind herself that even if she wrote her to come, it could be months before the message reached her, and how would Onia ever get to her in the midst of winter storms, when even getting to one's neighbours was such a challenge!

Still, as spring was beginning to break, Katiusha wept into her pillow every night, praying that by some miracle her *Starushka* would come to her in her hour of need.

Then one evening, in the latter part of April, Katiusha was preparing to go to bed, after finishing her outside chores and tucking Nikolai in for the night. She was startled to hear a light knock on the door, as if the caller did not have the strength to knock briskly. She was somewhat taken aback, since Fedia had come to see her only a few days ago, and the Tikhonovs came more rarely now that spring was breaking. Opening the door cautiously, Katiusha was utterly amazed by what she saw: there stood Babushka Siminishcheva, with a small packsack on her back. Even though she looked a bit haggard, she still had that sparkle in her eyes and that never-waning smile on her face.

Nikolai jumped out of bed at once and came running to the door.

Amidst tears, hugs and kisses, Katiusha kept asking her *Starushka:* 'How did you know I needed you so much? How did you guess I was all alone, and terribly needed your help?..'

At last Babushka took her daughter-in-law by the shoulders, and looking devoutly and wistfully into her eyes, exclaimed: 'But, my dear Katiusha, I heard you calling for me, and so I came as soon as I could!'

How this wisp of a woman, barely five feet tall, traversed more than three hundred kilometres of wilderness over obscure trails she had covered only once before in her life, in early spring weather that, to say the least, was not conducive to spending nights on the road, is a matter of conjecture. She declined to talk about it at any length, saying only: 'I knew I had to go through with this journey. So I kept going, and kept going, and here I am!'

Fig. 2   The Alexei J. and Katyoosha Popov family taken about 1915 in the old homestead near Blaine Lake, Saskatchewan. Left to right: Nick, Annie, Leonard, and Grandmother (Babushka S) with Alex J. and Katherine Popoff. Babushka Siminischeva dropped in before moving to British Columbia.

Perhaps it is not too far-fetched to suppose that here was a soul that, in addition to being intuitive enough to 'hear' a call for help across great distances, also had the ability to make use of those mythical 'seven--league boots' of Russian fairy tales to transport herself to the place she was needed. Given the distances and the difficult circumstances in-volved, it would be safe to assume that a logical, rational person would not have dared to attempt what Babushka Siminishcheva accomplished so matter-of-factly and so humbly.

But there is more to this true story than simply a proof that boundless stamina is available to the human soul when dedication requires it. Its real lesson is the realisation of the need to recognise, in honouring the fortitude and perseverance of our pioneer grandparents, along with their many worthy accomplishments, the significant evolution of their 'inner soul' to a level where it was able to conquer any frontier, including geographical distance. A soul capable, in times of dire stress, regardless of distance or circumstance, to 'hear' and 'do', and then to say as Babushka Siminishcheva did, 'But, my dear Katiusha, I heard you calling, and so I came...'

[1]Five feet = 152 cm.

[2]*Popova* — in Russian, the variant of the surname used by the female members of the family.

[3]*Starushka* — a Russian word referring to an older woman, but used among the Doukhobors as an endearing term for an older female family member — in this case, Katiusha's mother-in-law.

[4]*Siminishcheva* — from the name *Simion,* designating the original patriarch of her particular branch of the family.

Grandmother Berikoff: a special gift

Natalie Voykin

On the evening of 12 February 1965 the nurse at the Vancouver General Hospital greeted us with unexpected news: grandmother had died! Disbelief, grief, flashed through me like a bolt of lightning. How could it be? Just hours before my beloved grandmother was very much alive, smiling and talking. I wanted to see her at once. I ran into her room. My grandmother lay there, quiet and peaceful. I gathered her in my arms and held her close to my heart. Her body was still warm, but limp.

I wept. Slowly I released her. Her two braids of hair fell loose by her shoulders. Her long white gown made her look like an angel.

Grandmother *Dunia Berikoff* was just a year and a half old when her father fled the harsh persecution at the hands of both Church and State in the Russian homeland for the principles the family and their community stood for. Believing that life is a sacred gift of God abiding in all people, the Doukhobors considered it wrong to destroy life and hence wrong to bear arms, and consequently were subjected to severe punishment and incarceration. Whole families were sent into exile. In other cases children and parents were separated. Communities were disrupted. Conditions of life were made impossible. At this point, Count Lev Nikolaevich Tolstoy stepped in and helped organise and finance the exodus to Canada.

Shortly after her mother's death, in 1899 little Dunia boarded the *S.S. Lake Huron* in Batum along with her father *Misha Chernenkoff* and hundreds of other Doukhobors driven into exile for their faith. A month later they arrived in Halifax and almost immediately headed west to the Canadian prairies — their new home. For all who came, it was to be a strange and challenging experience.

Finding it a particular challenge coping with his infant daughter in this new environment, Misha Chernenkoff soon married a young Doukhobor girl who became Dunia's stepmother, thereby adding yet another complexity to the life of the growing child. Dunia found the needed warmth and love from her *Aunt Malasha*, who looked after her little needs and made her feel welcome at this stage of her life. Dunia remained ever grateful to this aunt for her tenderness and caring, and for the beneficial influence she exercised on both her outward and inner (spiritual) development.

Her family being of peasant background, no formal schooling was included in Dunia's upbringing in the settlement of Aaron (on the Saskatchewan-Manitoba border). Life's experiences were her teachers. Life's events were marked by the seasons; Dunia's birthday, for example, was associated with the harvest season.

In her late teens Dunia fell in love, but as her intended was not a *verushchii* (i.e., not a believer of the Doukhobor faith), her father disapproved. She married Koozma Berikoff, a handsome, charismatic, sports-loving lad. Though of Doukhobor upbringing, Koozma indulged in meat-eating and social drinking, both foreign to Dunia, who adhered to the strict Doukhobor tradition of refusing to eat animal flesh. Obliged to accomodate her husband's habits, she was especially bothered by having to prepare meat (in particular, chicken) at harvest time to feed the men from the surrounding community who came to help take in the crop.

By this time the newly-weds had established their home on a 160acre [65-hectare] farm[1] with few conveniences, and begun raising a family. Two days before the New Year of 1912, their first-born, *Florence (Fenia)* arrived. Three years later came a son, *Alex,* followed by two more daughters — *Mabel (Nastia)* and *Harriet (Grunia).* She engaged in the routine duties of farm and family, but always had an inner feeling in her heart telling her there was more to life than her isolated experience on the prairies.

After several years misfortune befell the family. One evening, upon bringing full pails of milk down to the cellar from the barn, Koozma accidentally hit his head with severe force against a low beam spanning the cellar entrance. The local doctors could do very little about the serious headaches, sore eyes and other disorders which followed. Relatives managed to raise enough money to send Koozma (then 40) to the Mayo Clinic in Rochester (USA), and while the operation there was successful, he died of a hæmorrhage when he attempted to get out of bed some time later (because of nursing staff shortages he had been left unattended at the time).

The tragic death of her husband brought Dunia untold hardships. With four children ranging in age from three to sixteen and with no knowledge of English, and no government social programmes yet in existence, she was obliged to depend mostly upon her own resources and limited help from relatives, along with the power of God for protection and guidance.

The Doukhobors' first leader in Canada, *Peter V. ('the Lordly'[2]) Verigin,* had worked with his people in their efforts to bring about the realisation of God's 'universal spirit of oneness' — the building of a heaven on earth. The Doukhobor people lived, toiled and prayed for this goal, evndeavouring to share their lands, resources and talents in harmony with the natural environment, with themselves and the world around them. But this 'new social order' was perceived as a significant threat by certain elements of the established Canadian society who believed in 'every one for himself'. In 1924 Verigin was killed by an explosion near Farron in the high Kootenay Mountains, while travelling by train from Brilliant to Grand Forks.[3]

Now a leaderless flock in a still new and unfriendly environment, the Canadian Doukhobors sent a delegation to Verigin's son, then living in Russia — *Peter P. Verigin,* who had adopted the pseudonym *Chistiakov* ('the Cleanser') and was informally known as *Petushka* — to come and help restore order to the Christian Community of Universal Brotherhood (CCUB) established by his father.[4] Arriving in 1927, he fascinated his new Canadian followers with his stamina and dynamic spirit; the wisdom expressed in his charismatic voice drew the attention of Doukhobors from all sections of the community.

He held a special fascination for Grandmother Dunia's eldest daughter Florence, in whom she had instilled a strong belief in God and in Doukhobor principles. She would ask friends and neighbours to take her with them when they went to hear him speak. His dynamic personality not only inspired her own spirituality, but eventually took the whole family in a whole new direction, to the zealot 'Sons of Freedom' movement.

In 1930 Dunia gained further inspiration through a visit from her half-brother, *Alex Chernenkoff* (then living in British Columbia), who told her and her family about the spiritual stirrings going on among young people in Doukhobor communities throughout Canada. She did her best to live out her sense of spiritual awareness as she and her children coped with life on the farm.

When Verigin was arrested in 1932 and sent to prison in Prince Albert, Dunia and Florence took part in successive protests, even to the point of disrobing on the highway, to call attention to the injustice directed at their leader. They themselves were arrested and held for a time in a women's prison at North Battleford. While the younger children were initially taken to foster homes, they were eventually allowed to be cared for by relatives until the family was reunited.

For some time Dunia had been cherishing the idea of the communal way of life adopted by Community Doukhobors in British Columbia, and following her prison experience, she was led — by her faith and the dictates of her heart — to leave her farm (unsold) in Saskatchewan and take her family and possessions out west, settling in the village of Krestova, B.C., just a few doors away from her half-brother.

By this time Florence had married a young Saskatchewan farmer, *Joseph Podovinikoff*, a Doukhobor who fervently shared her aspirations and ideals and her family's conviction in the rightness of communal living. He (along with other family members) persuaded his father to sell their prairie homestead and follow the Berikoffs to the B.C. interior, settling in Slocan Park.

Dunia's son Alex married a beautiful, kind and thoughtful young woman named *Natasha*, who was exceptionally talented as a handcraft artist and dearly loved by all who knew her. One day, when Natasha was seven months pregnant, she and her brother died after eating some contaminated processed food brought from town.

A day or two later Florence was in the process of giving birth to her first baby, attended by an elderly Doukhobor midwife and her mother-in-law *Nastia*. After many hours of labour, a baby girl finally arrived — lifeless, not breathing. But Nastia, who had brought up seven children of her own, was so elated at the new baby girl that she refused to give up. Wrapping the baby up, she cuddled it close to her heart and began walking to and fro in the living room, all the time breathing into the baby's mouth. All at once she heard a cry — the baby was alive!

They named her *Natasha* after Florence's sister-in-law, whom they had just laid to rest in Krestova. Florence had also been enchanted with the spirited character of Natasha portrayed in Tolstoy's epic novel *War and peace*.

Both *Babushkas* — Dunia (Berikoff) and Nastia (Podovinikoff) — had a significant influence on my life. I spent a great deal of time in my early years with my much-beloved Grandmother Podovinikoff, who lived close by and took care of us children while our parents were busy clearing land or weeding or picking strawberries to earn money for the next winter's supply of groceries and warm clothing.

But I felt a special love for Grandmother Berikoff, who, living eight kilometres away up the mountain in Krestova, visited us as often as she possibly could. When I was older, I would stay at her house for a week or so. An extraordinary person (in my eyes), she always kept her modest home in perfect order and cleanliness; its atmosphere was always warm, homey and nurturing. I always remember the feeling of security, strength and beauty evoked by her presence.

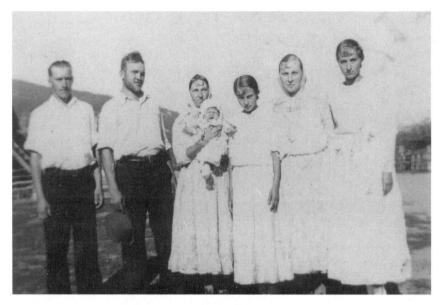

Fig. 1. Dunia Berikoff's family, Krestova, BC, l937.
Left to right: "Uncle Alex; my father Joseph; grandmother Dunia, hold me,
Natalie, 2-months old; Aunt Harriet; my mother Florence and Aunt Nellie."

One particularly vivid memory is of standing by Grandmother Berikoff's side as she opened the lid of a large shortening can to inspect the precious garden seeds she had gathered the previous autumn — each variety wrapped in white cotton bundles — to determine what needed to be planted in early spring. I remember the mysterious, invigorating, aroma that came from this special seed collection — a heavenly whiff of gentle potency unlike any other I had experienced. When spring came, once she had worked the soil in her garden patch into neat, straight rows, Grandmother Dunia would drop the seeds into them ever so gently, all the while affirming out loud: *na priezzhago i na prikhozhago* — signifying that the food to be produced from this seed by Mother Earth was not only for her and her family but also to share with strangers who might come riding or walking by. Grandmother was a prime example of Doukhobor kindness and loving hospitality.

In line with Doukhobor custom, the first question my grandmother would ask was whether the visitor was hungry; somehow there was always food to share. And, I must add, she was a wonderful cook — resourceful in converting simple and modest means into imaginative and successful creations. Very handy with her knitting needles, she sewed all her own clothes, always in the neatest fashion; she was unable to read patterns, but her socks, mittens and slippers were expertly executed, many times with intricate designs.

Her petite physical stature belied her formidable capabilities. I remember from my visits that her days never ended without reciting the psalm she taught me:

> My guardian angel, do guard and protect my soul, strengthen my heart and also all my thoughts. Grant me, O Lord, Thy protection for the sleep of the coming night, peace for the physical body, salvation for the soul and for the mouth to utter prayer. Glory be to God.

These were the words I was invariably put to bed with. This was the time, too, to talk about the day's events, before Grandmother sent me off to sleep by gently stroking my back. It was 'heaven'! And one of the first duties in the morning was to wash my face and hands. Grandmother told me to always start the day by saying: *Gospodi blagoslovi* (roughly translated: 'Lord, may thy blessings abide').

The death of Peter P. Verigin in 1939 left the B.C. Doukhobor community (including Krestova) in a rather unsettled state. In searching for answers amid the many different interpretations which surfaced, some in the village could not hold back their feelings of extreme frustration at the injustices and misundertandings they perceived on the part of the government. But Grandmother Berikoff did not take part in this radical trend.

Her life underwent a radical change, however, when she was introduced to a certain *Michael Verigin* (a distant relative and close associate of Peter P. Verigin) who had moved from the Verigin district in Saskatchewan toVancouver with his wife and son to operate a rooming house and work in the labour force on the side.

Peter P. (Chistiakov) Verigin had at one point told Michael that 'the Father wanted to see him', although Michael did not understand what that meant at the time. Several weeks after the leader's death, Michael happened to be walking down a street in Vancouver when he felt a tap on his shoulder. Turning around, he saw his late friend standing beside him, and heard his voice say: 'The time is now. Come, the Father is ready to see you.' Boarding a train at the station, the two men sped away 'swiftly upward' to a place where 'the Father met with Michael', instructing him to come back to earth and deliver a message to the Doukhobor people.

Some listeners utterly discredited his message, while others accepted it, at least in their own way. The message essentially urged all Doukhobors to

Stop thinking, doing and living in unconstructive ways. Begin to organise yourselves in communities where all can live in the spirit of communal brotherhood, working for peace and harmony. Share and learn to overcome greed, selfishness, jealousy and mistrust.

A particular part of the message was directed toward the 'Sons of Freedom':

Enough burning and jails for you. When one of you goes to jail there are ten people who must work to support you. You come and work together in the community where everything is held in common, where one person works and that goes to support ten people, the women, the children, the elders and the indigent.

Michael appealed to Doukhobors to help him launch the 'New Spiritual Community of Christ', to share his vision of a cooperative social and economic order of security based on the traditional teaching of 'toil and a peaceful life'. Time and again he tried to convince those who would obtain 'migration through jails' that the real migration was inner transformation, a change of heart from one of negativity and destruction to one of holy, peaceful construction.

Another conspicuous part of this multifaceted 'message' was the requirement to abolish bonds of ownership in marriage. *Women must be freed from male domination.* Grandmother Berikoff came forth as one of a group of six women and six men to launch this new order, under the name 'Elders of the Spiritual Community of Christ'.[5]

The new order, however, met with a mixed reception from the larger Doukhobor community. Some accepted the idea of communal living based on non-possessiveness — in respect not only to material possessions but also to the private family unit — while others felt threatened by the concept. The core group of twelve people Michael established at Krestova was soon disrupted by an extremist segment and forced to move to a homestead formerly occupied by one of his followers.[6]

The communal kitchen, bath-house and store (supplied with staples bought wholesale) was supplemented by a school, where one young mother taught basic reading and writing skills in both English and Russian, along with lessons in Doukhobor culture. The extremists, however, seeing the store and school as violating the sacredness of their fundamental beliefs, attacked again: a large group came out from Krestova, threw out the school furnishings and set the buildings ablaze. Once more homeless, Michael and his Elders were offered temporary accomodation by a sympathetic family[7] living in nearby Robson.

Even though I as a ten-year-old had not yet attended any school, my parents (Florence and Joseph) were indeed concerned about their children's education. After yet another attack by the Krestova group, Michael resolved to relocate further afield, away from trouble. He asked my father to accompany him on an exploratory trip to Vancouver Island, where a suitable location was quickly found, purchased and occupied (thanks to the former owners' willingness to move out immediately following the sale).

The new community established near the village of Hilliers toward the end of June 1946 (shortly after an earthquake in the area) immediately began to draw attention from far and wide. My parents readily accepted their invitation to young families with children to come and help construct the Community, arriving there lock, stock and barrel in 1947. A large kitchen, sleeping quarters, storeroom, prayer-hall, school, steamhouse and gardens all had to be set up and put in place. It was in this school that I received my first formal education, through a curriculum organised by the community itself in both Russian and English.

Grandmother Berikoff was one of the women actively participating in this new experience, drawing upon her expertise in household affairs, involving herself in finances, organising cooking groups, laundry, gardening and other duties. Her contribution to the stability and order of the community was recognised by Michael and the other Elders, many of whom came to her for advice and direction.

Unfortunately, the distance from the mainland did not ensure peace. This time the extremists not only destroyed property (worth thousands of dollars) but fabricated accusations which landed both Michael and my father (his secretary) in jail, charging that his vision of fulfilling certain prophecies in the Doukhobor psalms was nothing but a personal fantasy.

Michael died soon after being released from prison; he and other elders who had passed away from old age were buried in a special Community cemetery at Hilliers. The remainder, about four years after the experiment began, moved back to the B.C. interior, but did not lose sight of Michael's original ideology. They spent about a year at Gilpin, near Grand Forks, but feeling isolated from the main body of the Doukhobor community in the Kootenays (where they still considered their roots to be), they accepted an invitation to occupy a communal property in Krestova. Once more they constructed a place to live and work, and once more they settled down to practise their faith.

I remember Grandmother telling me one spring in the mid1950s how the Elders had decided to renew their appeal to the Doukhobor community to join the new order and build a true brotherhood of selfless sharing. Grandmother Berikoff was even sent door-to-door along the dusty streets of Krestova to spread the message of love she carried in her heart. But none of the Elders' efforts (Grandmother's included) met with any positive response.

Fig. 2. *Grandmother Berikoff in her later years.*

Now a married woman with two children, living some thirty kilometres away in Castlegar, I still kept in close touch with Grandmother Berikoff, whom I loved immensely. It was a matter of some amazement to me that she always knew when I needed her most, even though she had no telephone. She would show up at my doorstep with a basket of fresh strawberries, or a package of knitted socks, slippers or mittens to help meet whatever might be the need. When the babies were sick, she was there to help, like a guardian angel. As a young and inexperienced gardner, I watched as she virtually produced magic during her short summer visits to our home with her simple but effective handling of soil and plants. 'Do this', she would advise, and, sure enough, the weak shoots would quickly develop into strong, shiny, productive plants.

Grandmother was a never-ending source of interesting conversation for me and my family. Her philosophy and knowledge fuelled my insatiable thirst for ideas, my wonder at the underlying factors that motivated her quest and worked such a powerful and meaningful influence on her character. The oneness of the life we shared and her indestructible faith in God left a deep imprint on my heart. Her stamina and the natural intelligence that guided her filled me with unbounded love and respect. Our tea-time sharings — another experience of heaven — were especially memorable. She would explain the many psalms she knew by heart on a spiritual level, and we would talk about their hidden symbolic meaning and source — this was an entirely natural unfoldment in our relationship.

Grandmother Berikoff applied her belief in God to practical everyday life. For example, when my babies were restless and unable to sleep peacefully, she had healing remedies which worked. After helping me bathe my new-born (the air and water temperature had to be warm and comfortable!) she would hold the baby in one hand and pour a pitcher of lukewarm water over her for a rinse, then wrap the baby in a warm towel, all the while affirming: *kak s gusochki vody vsia skorb' i khodor'ba* (roughly: 'like water off a goose, all negativity is washed clean and gone'). In Grandmother's presence I had the feeling that all was well with my world.

In the autumn of 1962, when I was eight months pregnant with our third child, the outbreak of Freedomite unrest in the Kootenays reached its peak. With local prisons unable to accomodate all the sect members charged with acts of terrorism, the authorities had constructed a special fireproof prison for them at Agassiz. Many supporters of the Freedomite cause began a trek to Agassiz to draw attention to what they saw as a great injustice against the Doukhobor people.

At Grandmother's urging, my husband and I, who similarly felt our people were being misunderstood and unfairly treated, decided to join the protest. We sold our home, stored furniture at my in-laws, and followed the trek — living in tents, sharing rides, finances and moral support. The march took us through Castlegar, Grand Forks and on through Princeton, where in late September we stopped to camp in Bromley Park. Feeling the onset of labour, I (together with my husband) headed for the nearest hospital. When stopped by an RCMP roadblock along the way, I told them they could deliver the baby themselves if that was their choice. We were given immediate clearance! Our beautiful daughter Katya was born in Princeton on 26 September 1962.

I felt surrounded by love and care: the wonderful doctor who delivered the baby, a sympathetic Princeton family[8] who took us into their home after my release from hospital, and, above all, my mother, who was a guardian angel to me during this time. My father had little time to attend to his own family, involved as he was with the many relationship problems among the trekkers, the authorities, the press and the representatives of the towns and villages through which we marched. Grandmother, too, needed all the energy she could muster to organise and keep order among the group of Elders, by this time all of senior years.

One incident in particular left an indelible imprint on my heart. By late autumn we had reached the town of Hope, where we were obliged to stop. Many local people offered shelter to the crowd of people descending upon this small town. On one rainy day Grandmother and I sat face to face on some apple boxes in a small station house; between us was a bundle about one metre square wrapped in dark blue cloth and neatly tied in a knot on top, containing all her earthly possessions. As we sat there, just the two of us, not knowing where we were going or where it would all end, I felt a sense of tremendous love and respect for her, of sharing in some mysterious way in her deep faith, of the whole world being on our side.

Upon finally arriving (weeks later) at the Agassiz Mountain site, the families set up their *palatki* [tents] in a neat row alongside the road leading to the prison. The local garbage dump, surprisingly, yielded several old stoves still in usable condition, which after some cleaning and fixing provided warmth and a place to cook. It was amusing to see chimneys made out of recycled juice tins. Even a small steam bath-house was erected from scrap timber and served for both baths and laundry. Plastic was bought to provide a shield from the rain and wind.

While the authorities indeed had their hands full (they had no choice but to allow events to unfold), they were pleased to find their concerns over sanitation problems and adverse incidents unjustified, noting only cleanliness and tidiness in and around the tent dwellings, and the snow-white laundry hung out to dry.

Grandmother Berikoff and her group of Elders occupied the first tent down the lane from us. They held together as a small unit of ten people, living according to their traditional communal order, uncomplainingly making the best of a difficult situation.

When I think back on this period, it all seems like an adventurous dream. It was indeed a learning experience of togetherness, one of fulfilment and revelation — my husband and our three children (five-year-

-old *Daniel*, three-year-old *Tamara* and three-month-old *Katya*), and Grandmother Dunia by my side, for advice.

Fig. 3. Bill and Natalie Voykin with grandchildren. 1990.

After several months my husband, children and I moved on to Vancouver, where Grandmother would often come to visit us, sharing a ride with friends from the camp who had occasion to make a trip to the 'Big City'. For me it was a special time of sharing her company.

Now and again during these visits she would complain about chest pains. She was seventy-five years old. She was examined several times by a doctor, who eventually asked her to go to hospital for further observation. She obliged reluctantly, commenting that any of the elders who ended up there 'did not make it back'. While I naturally rejected this suggestion, it did leave me with a sense of fear and dread. The third day there, during our visit she shared with us a dream she had had, one she could not explain:

A most beautiful young woman appeared and stood at the foot of my bed. She just looked at me and said nothing.

Grandmother also mentioned the clothes she had prepared for herself in case 'something did happen' to her — a white homespun linen skirt and blouse, hand-made slippers and a fine white woollen shawl with tiny pink rosebuds. They were part of the bundle she had carried throughout the trek.

As I sat by her bedside, Grandmother wanted to go over a psalm, one that dealt with the meaning of life, God and the 'Universal Laws of Being and Knowing'. 'I do want to be prepared', she said, 'when I go to meet the Great One.'

The following evening the 'beautiful young woman' took the hand of my beloved Grandmother and led her to meet 'the Great One'. I held her warm body close to my heart and sobbed. My teacher, guide and angel had finished her earthly journey. I realised I had to go on alone without the benefit of her wisdom, strength and unshakeable faith upon which I had relied so heavily. Now it is my turn, for now my own seven grandchildren turn to me for spiritual support.

I am convinced that Grandmother Dunia Berikoff was a special gift to me from God, and perhaps to others, too, who now have the opportunity to read and share this account of a rare and most precious angel who came to earth to fulfil her mission of unselfish love.

Grandmother Berikoff was laid to rest in the cemetery next to the Agassiz encampment, alongside twenty others who had shared in the trek. May their souls rest in the blessedness of the Heavenly Peace they earned and so richly deserve!

Appendix: A Doukhobor Psalm[9]

The bridegroom Christ did project His celestial voice from His mouth of purity... The grace of the Living God does speak unto us: Harken unto Me ye the Virgin-brides of the bridegroom; harken unto Me ye youths, the vicars of Christ; harken unto Me ye the Elders, heralds of the King — do accept from Me the gifts of eternal salvation... And I in turn shall give unto you crowns, those of redemtpion from the second death. Come unto Me ye the beloved, do follow (the path) of My holy ones. Sit not with the vain man, look up toward the righteous one, turn your eyes away from that which is temporal, judge not the innocent, but judge ye each his own sins within himself — what will then be a righteous judgement from you — a love that is not hypocritical. By such means your souls shall be delivered from eternal suffering.

God be praised!

[1]This consititued a 'quarter-section' — the minimum land-area required for subsistence.

[2]The Russian term is *Gospodnii*, meaning 'belonging to the Lord' — *ed.*

[3]Eight other passengers died in the same explosion, including a young lady companion (Doukhobor *Maria Strilioff*), and Conservative Member of the B.C. Legislative Assembly John McKie.

[4]This organisation was spread throughout British Columbia, Saskatchewan and Alberta.

[5]A branch of the 'Sons of Freedom' movement — *ed.* The title 'Elder' is from a Doukhobor psalm (see Appendix) referring to 'Elders, heralds of the King'.

[6]*K. Nazaroff.*

[7]The *Maloff-Makhortoffs.*

[8]The Gabors.

[9]Translated by Joseph Podovinikoff from the original Russian text; published in *Sbornik dukhoborcheskikh psalmov, stikhov i pesen* [Anthology of Doukhobor psalms, hymns and songs]. Grand Forks: USCC, 1978, p. 99.

Doukhobors of Alberta — an insider's view

Michael Verigin

'Land of opportunity! Western Canada is another name for Opportunity!' read one of the posters urging Europeans to come to Canada in the late 1800s. '160 acres of farm land free. There's room for 50,000,000 people. A magnificent heritage for our children!'

Many Europeans attracted by this promotion came to Western Canada, where they accepted the offer of homestead land and became model farmers. The Doukhobors came in 1899, but in June 1907 clashed with the authorities over the 'oath of allegiance' clause — a requirement of the 'free land' arrangement, in preparation for becoming Canadian citizens. Those Doukhobors who refused to comply were deprived (collectively) of 256,000 acres [= approx. 104,000 ha] of choice farmland,[1] which they had already cleared and improved, valued at $11,000,000. However, a communally owned piece of property at Verigin, Saskatchewan, complete with brick factory, flour mill and horse ranch, managed to be preserved as the central headquarters of the Christian Community of Universal Brotherhood (CCUB).

Forced to seek land elsewhere, the majority of 'Community Doukhobors' moved west to the interior of British Columbia, where they by-passed the oath requirement by purchasing land privately. By 1912 some four thousand Doukhobor were living in B.C.; many more arrived over the next two years. Grain and horses were brought out — initially from Saskatchewan, a journey of more than 1,600 km by rail. It was soon realised, however, that the $300 transportation cost involved could be reduced by two-thirds if the shipments originated in the foothills of the Rockies in Alberta.[2]

First Doukhobor building in Alberta: 1915

Thus in July 1915 the Community Doukhobors purchased four sections of land (a total of 1036 ha) belonging to the former Terrill Ranch in the Cowley-Lundbreck area of south-western Alberta. The site — approximately 50 km from either the B.C. or the American border and only 500 km from the Doukhobor centre at Brilliant, B.C. — included a large two-storey prefabricated house (from the T. Eaton Co. in Winnipeg) erected in 1895, a 42-hp Gaars-Scott steam engine and a wooden 107-cm Case threshing machine.3 The new settlement was named Bogatoi Rodnik [Bountiful Spring] or simply Bogataia for the abundant waters gushing out of the local springs.

My grandfather, *Simeon Ivanovich Verigin*, who was living in Brilliant at the time, was asked by the leader of the Community Doukhobors *Peter V. ('the Lordly') Verigin* to select a group needed to construct the new settlement and go to Alberta. The fourteen men that came in the summer of 1915 included carpenters, steam engineers and a blacksmith.[4] They immediately began breaking land and cutting the abundant hay in the meadows. Two men,[5] each using two teams of horses and working five hours with each team, were able to harvest twenty-four stacks of hay by autumn. Steam-engines, oxen and horses were used to break the virgin prairie sod. One double-bottomed plough could be pulled by either four oxen or seven horses (three hitched in front and four behind), and a single ten-bottomed plough could be pulled by a steam engine. The first year alone, more than 120 hectares of land were broken.

Simultaneously, another group of Doukhobor men from B.C. began construction on a 60,000-bushel [= two-million-litre] capacity grain elevator at Lundbreck, the nearest town and railway point . In a letter dated 8 October 1915 at Brilliant, we read that a second carload of lumber had been shipped that day with a third to follow, while 75,000 board feet [= 177 cubic metres] of two-by-fours would be purchased in Alberta.

A letter written from Lundbreck by Peter V. Verigin 24 November 1915 to one of his followers at Brilliant reads in part:[6]

> We arrived in Alberta safely, praise be to the Lord, and here everything is fine. The elevator is completed. Grandfather Verigin with his family left this morning for Bogatoi Rodnik. This is how I named our farm that we have bought from Terrill.
>
> I will wait here until Fred Sookochoff comes for me. They did not know that we were coming. When we arrived by train in Lundbreck, there was a very strong cold wind blowing. I told Grandfather Verigin to roll up his collar. 'This is not British Columbia for you', I said.

Another one of his letters written 29 November 1915 reads:

> Have spent some time at Bogatoi Rodnik and now will be on my way to Sasakatchewan. Went with Paul Potapoff to Cowley. This is 5 miles from Lundbreck. In Cowley there is a bank and Michael Kazakoff will have to

transfer money here to buy grain in Lundbreck for us in B.C. The elevator is completed and ready to receive grain. With God's help, everything is coming along very well, praise be to the Lord.

Fig. 1. Peter V .Verigin, spiritual leader of the Community Doukhobors on the left with his friend and companion Anastasia Golubova. Taken in 1924. After Peter Verigin's death, Anastasia became the spiritual leader of the Lordly Christian Community of Universal Brotherhood near Shouldice, Alberta.

From Yorkton, Sask., Peter V. Verigin wrote to Simeon Verigin 10 December 1915 that on that day they had shipped two carloads of horses and one carload of calves to the men in Lundbreck.

In the late autumn all the workmen returned to B.C. except the Verigins, the Sookochoffs and Zibins, whose families came to join them.

The kind of welcome received by the Doukhobors in Alberta in 1915 (in comparison to their first visit almost three decades earlier) may be surmised from a letter by a prominent Cowley area rancher, Frederick William Godsal, published in the 3 December 1915 issue of the *Pincher Creek Echo*:

As some of the Doukhobors have come to live in the district, and I find that they are much misunderstood by many of the people, and by those

236

who would greet them as fellow Christians if they knew the truth about them, kindly allow me space while I do my duty to my neighbours... I have no fear that the Doukhobors will hurt Canada or the district; but I do fear, and have reason for it already, that Canadian methods will hurt the Doukhobors.

Further development: 1916–24

Early in the spring of the following year Peter V. Verigin ordered 500 bushels [= 18,200 litres] of wheat and oats from Verigin, Sask., for seeding in the Alberta colony and on 27 March the men began returning from British Columbia. That year additional land was bought south of Lundbreck — along with the Riley Ranch and part of the Godsal ranch near Cowley. The following year an additional 1,300 hectares of the latter estate was purchased, including an elaborate modern house. Mr Godsal became a close friend of the Doukhobors and travelled with Peter V. Verigin on his visits to the Saskatchewan and British Columbia communities.7

In November 1916 a new, 80,000-bushel [three-million-litre] capacity elevator was completed in Cowley,[8] receiving wheat, oats, barley and flax, which were being grown in abundance.[9] Spring seeding usually commenced in mid-April and fall seeding for winter wheat in mid-August. Up to half a dozen binders were used in the harvest. Women did most of the stooking. At threshing time it took twelve teams of horses with wagons to haul the bundles and two men on each rack, on either side of the conveyor, to pitch them into the threshing machine. Up to 103,000 bushels [= 3,750 litres] of grain a year were threshed by the CCUB in Alberta.

While waiting for permanent housing, some of the men lived in tents, others in a large two-storey building they had purchased on the main street of Cowley. For most of the thirteen Doukhobor settlements eventually established in the area houses were hauled in from Cowley or from nearby farms,[10] while *Bogatoi Rodnik* and the Godsal ranch came with existing houses. In the summer of 1917 construction began on a new house and barn at *Bogatoi Rodnik,* where a team of carpenters headed by *Alex Cheveldaoff* constructed a copy of the Doukhobor communal homes in B.C. The 'Blue House' (it was painted a light blue and had a red roof) — square, two storeys high with an attic, 13 metres distant from the original yellow ranch house — was ready for occupancy in October of the same year.

Not far away another group of twenty men built a red 26-metre-long barn with a green roof. The main part of the barn contained sixteen two--horse stalls, while lean-tos on either side housed the community's stallions. A year later a similar barn was built some five kilometres away near the Castle River.[11] As it was set against a hill and a road could be built on the same level as the hayloft to make the hay-storing process easier. The lean-to housed five families temporarily pending completion of more permanent dwellings. Barns were also built at the Faminoff settlement south of Lundbreck and at the former Godsal ranch (renamed the *Bozhiya* village).[12]

Settlements frequently took their names from the principal families who founded or occupied them. Several villages were named by Peter V. Verigin, including *Bogatoi Rodnik, Bozhiya Milost'* [God's Grace] and *Gradavaya Dolina* [Hail Valley]. One settlement, Sedjwick Place, was jokingly referred to as *Sibir'* [Siberia] because of its isolated location amid the foothills of the Rockies. Its residents included the *Vishloff, Shkuratoff* and *Sookochoff* families, as well as my maternal grandfather, *Harry Elitch Konkin,* his brother *George* and other members of his family. In addition to renting 450 hectares of land (one and three-quarter sections), Community members were also allowed to pasture their cattle and horses during the summer months on neighbouring government reserve land.

By 1924 (the year of Peter V. Verigin's assassination) the CCUB of Alberta owned or rented almost 5,460 hectares. The three hundred or so Doukhobors comprising the thirteen villages[13] held communal prayers every Sunday at a Community Meeting House in Cowley; their cemetery was located just south of Lundbreck. In addition to the two elevators mentioned earlier, the community also constructed a modern flour mill capable of turning out one hundred barrels per day. The Community owned more than 300 horses, including some pedigreed mares and ten purebred Percheron stallions (one of which, named *Dorogoi* [Priceless] was purchased for $5,000) and a large herd of cattle with eight purebred shorthorn bulls.[14]

Work and income

Income for each family varied according to the number of its able-bodied workers and the total village income for the year. In our own family, for example, with only one worker (my father), in 1934 we received:

15 January, worker	Mike S. Verigin	$100.00
17 December, worker	Mike S. Verigin	$113.00
	Mike S. Verigin	$53.00
	Annie H. Verigin	$53.00
	Michael M. Verigin	$26.50
	Nick M. Verigin	$26.50

As in the early years of their settlement in Saskatchewan, so too in Alberta a number of Doukhobor men left their villages from time to time to supplement their income by working for non-Doukhobor farmers and ranchers. In 1915 a small group of Doukhobors earned $85 per month working on Raymond Knight's sheep ranch. From March to December 1916 a group of thirty B.C. Doukhobors (headed by *Paul Planidin*) worked for James D. McGregor on his large land holdings in south-western Alberta, as they had earlier on his Glencarnock Stock Farm near Brandon, Manitoba, where he raised prize Aberdeen Angus cattle, Suffolk sheep and Benshire pigs.[15] And the following year a few Alberta Doukhobors were paid $65 per month plus board to break sod with a steam engine for a Mr Cook near Pincher Creek.

Leadership and land changes

While the Doukhobors in Alberta were generally left in relative peace, not all their neighbours were favourable to their presence, especially following the return of the Canadian soldiers from the First World War, in which the Doukhobors had naturally refused to serve because of their religious convictions. An article appearing in the *Pincher Creek Echo* of 4 April 1919 under the headline 'Government asked to buy Doukhobor land' reads in part:

> We do not wish the Doukhobor Community to remain in Cowley. It is up to the Dominion Government to buy their land for settlement by returned soldiers. The Doukhobors do not make desirable settlers, and they do not become citizens. A resolution to this effect was carried at the meeting of the Council at the Municipal District of Livingstone No.70 at Cowley.

From 1918 to 1924 Peter V. Verigin rented land for the CCUB from James McGregor — approximately 800 hectares in a solid block of three sections near the Bow River in the Queenstown area, bordering a native reservation — for a new settlement which he appropriately named *Kra-*

sivaya Dolina [Beautiful Valley]. The first settlers, Paul Planidin and his sons, were joined by John *Kooznetsoff* and his sons, the *Koochins*, the *Osachoffs* and the *Fofonoffs*. Since there was no rail service nearby, grain had to be hauled by wagon 24 kilometres to Cluny, which was also the nearest post office. In 1923 the Planidin families moved to Kylemore, Sask., but returned to the McGregor farm in Alberta two years later to rent it privately and eventually to purchase it.

After Peter V. Verigin's death in a train explosion in 1924, *Anastasia Fedorovna Golobova* (or Anastasia Lord's[16] as she was more commonly known) was recognised by several hundred Doukhobors as his successor. She had been his close companion for twenty-two years and was a respected lady of the Community. The majority of the Community, however, proclaimed as leader Verigin's son, *Peter Petrovich (Chistiakov) Verigin*, who was still living in Russia and did not come to Canada until 1927.

Fig. 2. Part of the village of Anastasia's colony near Shouldice, Alberta. Nov. 9, 1928.

The year before Chistiakov's arrival, Anastasia Lord's removed from Brilliant with more than a hundred and sixty of her followers and settled on about 450 hectares of land near Shouldice, Alberta (in the Arrowood area). They constructed a village on a model found in Russia and in the Doukhobor settlements in Saskatchewan — including a school, a large horsebarn, a blacksmith's shop and granaries. The following year the

Canadian Pacific Railway constructed a railway siding near the village, complete with a large water tank whereon the name *Anastasia* was painted in big letters.[17] A Community Prayer Home was built in 1929.

While the settlement was indeed popularly referred to as 'Anastasia's Village', it was more properly known as the 'Lord's Settlement' or the 'Lordly Christian Community of Universal Brotherhood'. Anastasia continued to live on at the village site until her death in November 1965; she was buried in the Lord's Settlement Cemetry along with her lifetime companion Fedosia Loukianovna Verigin, who passed away sixteen years later. Two brothers and one sister of Peter V. Verigin were also laid to rest in this cemetery.

Demise of the CCUB

The village's main occupation was grain-growing, and some income was earned by selling garden produce. The good harvests of the first three years were followed by the poor crops of the 1930s, when many of the men had to work outside the commune to supplement their income. The Depression and especially the exodus that followed — when many of its members took advantage of new opportunities for successful independent farming — severely affected the Community. By the mid-1940s the communal way of life among Alberta Doukhobors had all but disappeared. In fact, even in the late 1920s independent Doukhobor families had begun moving into the area from B.C. and Saskatchewan and it was not long before their numbers equalled those of the Community members.

During the 1930s the Community's debts continued to mount, until in 1938 its insurance-and trust-company creditors decided toforeclose on its assets (valued at twelve million dollars for all properties in Western Canada). In British Columbia the provincial government took over trusteeship of the land, forcing those living on it to become tenants, while in Alberta and Saskatchewan the land was offered for sale back to the Doukhobors; any land not purchased by them would be put on the open market.[18]

By the end of 1938 about 200 Community members remained in the Cowley-Lundbreck area of Alberta, three families in our village of *Bozhiya Milost'*.[19] On 15 December my father received the following letter from the National Trust Company in Edmonton:

Re: CCUB of Alberta Limited

We have now received the necessary authority from the Court to dispose of the assets of the above company at a figure not less than the valuations filed with the Court. We have also the necessary authority to sell to you under one arrangement the lands and chattels. It will be necessary for you to pay one-tenth of this amount on the execution of the agreement, and the balance to be spread over a term of nine years, with interest at 6%, payable on the 1st of November in each year, and the interest will start from the 1st of January, 1939.

We would appreciate you letting us know immediately as to whether you accept this proposition, as it is our intention to put the properties on the market if you are not intending to purchase same.

My father was one of the Community Doukhobors that chose to remain in Alberta by purchasing 289 acres [= 117 ha] of former CCUB land near the Castle River and farming it on an individual basis.[20] Since it was necessary to first build a house and a barn (the site included no buildings), we did not actually remove there until the late autumn of 1940. Payment for the 'lands and chattels'[21] was to be made on a yearly crop-share basis, a full one-third share of the crops to be delivered to the Cowley elevators during harvest time.

In 1942, after the communal lands were dispersed, the Alberta government passed the Land Sales Prohibition Act, forbidding the sale of lands to 'Hutterites and enemy aliens'. In 1944 the word 'aliens' was replaced by 'Doukhobors'; Doukhobors were also excluded in the Communal Property Act which succeeded the former legislation in 1947 (it was rescinded in 1972).

With the demise of the Christian Community of Universal Brotherhood, all Doukhobors in the Cowley-Lundbreck area, along with many others from across the Western provinces, joined a newly formed successor organisation, the Union of Spiritual Communities of Christ (USCC), with headquarters at Brilliant, B.C. The Cowley-Lundbreck branch became known as 'Kavkaz No 33'.

Sunday meetings continued to be held, but not every weekend as before, since the local Community Home had been sold by the receiver for the trust company and dismantled, forcing people to gather in private homes. Construction on a new Community Home began in 1953; it was eventually registered (in August 1955) under the provincial Religious Societies Land Act under the title 'United Doukhobors of Alberta, Cowley-Lundbreck'.

Recent events in Alberta Doukhobor history

The following are some of the highlights of the Doukhobor experience in the Cowley-Lundbreck area of south-western Alberta over the past three decades or so:

1964 (summer) On 4 July Doukhobors and Quakers from all over Western Canada gathered at the Community home for the annual Doukhobor celebration of the burning of firearms in the Caucasus in 1895 (29 June by the old calendar). The following morning some four hundred people journeyed 320 km to the government military laboratory at Suffield (Alberta) to protest against the development of chemical, biological and radiological weapons as well as the stockpiling of nerve gases and germ weapons. A second demonstration at the same base took place in May 1970.

1969 (spring)   Organisation of the United Doukhobor Choir of Alberta, with members from Calgary, Lethbridge, Mossleigh, Pincher Creek and Cowley, with the aim of participating in the celebration of the 70th anniversary of the arrival of the Doukhobors in Canada, held 6–7 July in Verigin (Saskatchewan).

1974 (11 August) Unveiling of an Historical Site sign just west of Cowley, dedicated to the Doukhobor settlers who came to the CowleyLundbreck area in 1915 and to Shouldice in 1926. The unveiling was the occasion for a large gathering in the Community Home; local village mayors were in attendance, along with the Alberta Minister of Culture, Youth and Recreation (Horst A. Schmid). The following summer, again at a large gathering, the original sign was replaced by two new ones on opposite sides of the highway, with text in both English and Russian. It was replaced by a new sign in June 1995 (see below).

1984 (August) On the provincial Heritage Day, a new street in Cowley was named 'Kavkaz View' in honour of the Doukhobors.

1987 (July) Many Alberta Doukhobors attended the unveiling of life-size statues of Lev Tolstoy in both Verigin (Saskatchewan) and Brilliant (B.C.). The famous writer had openly supported the Doukhobors during their persecution in Russia and had provided generous financial assistance for their emigration to Canada.

1988 (29 October) Unveiling of a marker at the Lord's Settlement Cemetery, dedicated to the settlers who had founded the village.

Fig. 3. Heritage site sign, one mile west of Cowley, Alberta on No. 3 Highway. Erected in July 1975 by the Honourable Horst A. Schmidt, Alberta Minister of Culture, Youth and Recreation.

1990 (8 July)   Unveiling of a plaque on the Verigin Barn and Bath House at the Pincher Creek Museum, with many municipal and provincial government officials in attendance. The buildings had been moved from their original site to Pincher Creek prior to the flooding of the river valleys by the newly-built Three Rivers Dam.

1992 (11 October)   A third Centenary Planning meeting was held at the Community Home in Lundbreck to plan the 1995 observance of the 100th anniversary of the burning of firearms. Delegates and guests came from the Western provinces and Ottawa.

1995 (summer)   Celebration of the Centenary of the Burning of Arms in the Caucasus (29 June 1895 by the old Russian calendar). The centenary was also marked by the unveiling of a new Historical Site sign to replace the earlier one (see 1974 above), attended by government officials and representatives of the Hutterite movement; the Centennial Doukhobor choir performed at the ceremony. In addition, a Doukhobor exhibit was organised in Lethbridge under the title 'Toil and peaceful life'.

Fig. 4. Michael M. Verigin, Doukhobor activist, Cowley, Alberta.

In retrospect

In 1911, according to the census of Canada, there were only 45 Dou-khobors in the province of Alberta. By 1951 the official count had grown to 822, but dropped by 1991 to some 200. The actual number of Alberta Doukhobors today, however, is many times that figure (it is estimated that more than 1,600 Doukhobors live in Calgary alone). But very few have remained in their original rural settlements; over the years Doukhobor children came to stay longer in school, and since 1960 many of them have gone on to university and acquired urban, 'white-collar' jobs which have taken them away from their parents' and grandparents' farms.

It is not unusual today to meet people of Doukhobor background in almost any town or city in the province. And in addition to exploring still-standing ruins of some of the former villages, Alberta residents and visitors have the opportunity to become acquainted with Doukhobor history through several museum exhibits.

In 1979 a permanent exhibit of thirteen of the world's major religions (entitled *Spiritual life — Sacred ritual*) was opened at the Provincial Museum and Archives in Edmonton. Thanks to the museum staff, especially Folk Life Curator David J. Goa, one of the religious groups represented right from the start was the Doukhobors.

Another exhibit was put together by Dorothy Burnham for the same museum in 1988, this one devoted to the textiles and tools of the Doukhobors. *Unlike the lilies* was the first thorough examination of the rich textile tradition that was once acknowledged as the equal of the best on the North American continent. Its centrepiece display featured a large rug with unusual plant and animal designs (including camels), hand-made by Anatasia Golubova.

Many years have now come and gone, and very few of the people who first came to Alberta in the early part of the century are still living. The Russian language and traditional clothing once common in the Cowley, Lundbreck and Shouldice areas have now given way to modern English--Canadian language and dress.

Like their cousins in British Columbia and Saskatchewan, Alberta Doukhobors have witnessed many changes over the years — in their own culture and lifestyle as well as in the larger society around them. However, they, like Doukhobors everywhere, continue even today to abide by their motto 'Toil and peaceful life'. With their unique communal lifestyle and religious and cultural traditions, the Doukhobors of Alberta have made an immeasurable contribution to the multifaceted heritage of their province and their country.

[1]Carl Tracie in his book *'Toil and peaceful life: Doukhobor village settlement in Saskatchewan 1899–1918* (Regina: Canadian Plains Research Centre, 1966, p. 109) contends that this estimate is in error because the allotment (after the 1907 takeover) given by the government to the Doukhobors was fifteen acres per person rather than per family. Hence the average cultivated acreage lost that year 'was no more than 25,000 acres [= approx. 10,000 ha] and, quite likely, considerably less'. Nonetheless, the loss of *uncultivated* acreage remained well over 300,000 acres [= appx. 121,000 ha]. Dr Tracie concludes (p. 210): 'No matter what the actual figure was, it represented to the Doukhobors a huge loss in the investment of capital and labour; of more fundamental importance, it represented broken promises and rekindled long-held fears of governments which could not be trusted'. — *ed.*

[2]Doukhobors had come to Alberta several times before — once, shortly after their arrival in Canada to purchase a large herd of horses, and again in 1907 in their quest for new land. In the fall of 1909, a hundred Doukhobors came to work on the construction of the Lake McGregor Dam near Milo, Alberta, to earn money for the Community. In 1911, forty-five Doukhobors worked for a British-financed farming company (Canadian Wheatland) near Suffield, Alberta, breaking prairie sod with oxen pulling single-bottomed ploughs.

[3]Within a year several additional machines were acquired: two smaller (25-hp) engines for pulling ploughs, and a Holt gasoline engine driven with a steering wheel, on caterpillar tracks.

[4]The group included my grandfather's son *William Verigin,* his father-in-law *Steve Kalmakoff,* his two brothers-in-law *Fred Sookochoff* and *William Zibin* and the latter's son *John Zibin,* along with *Peter* and *Simeon Kabatoff, William Maloff, Jakob Evashin, John Bojay* and others. John Zibin's wife *Martha* and Fred Sookochoff's wife *Tania* served as cooks.

[5]William Verigin and John Bojay.

[6]This and the following letter were translated from the Russian by Michael Verigin.

[7]The Doukhobors were granted title to the Godsal land in 1930.

[8]The *Pincher Creek Echo* of 29 September 1916 compared the structure to 'a New York skyscraper, towering over the Village'.

[9]Approximately 40 hectares of flax were sown at Bogatoi Rodnik, along with about 325 hectares of wheat; as much as 25,000 bushels of barley were threshed in a single year.

[10]Lean-tos were sometimes added to afford additional living space.

[11]Built by *Timothy Ogloff,* this barn measured 25 by 11 metres; a 4.5-metre-wide lean-to was attached to one side.

[12]The latter barn, measuring 15 by 10 metres, was constructed by Nick Zibin and his team from B.C. cedar; the exterior was covered with red shiplap, with the top two-thirds overlaid with shingles.

[13]*Bogatoi Rodnik* was the largest village, with about fifty inhabitants.

[14]By law, all horses and cattle had to be branded. The Community's brand was the first letter in the Russian word for *Doukhobor* — D — and was known as 'the Doukhobor D'. Horses were branded on the right hip, cattle on the right side of the neck.

[15]Other Doukhobors had worked with him earlier on the construction of the Lake McGregor Dam (cf. note 1 above), where he was an engineer.

[16]*Lord's* — a variant of *Lordly,* translated from *Gospodnia,* meaning 'belonging to the Lord'; this adjective was also used in reference to Peter V. Verigin—*ed.*

[17]The water was brought through a wooden pipe from a bountiful spring just south of the village. While the tank itself served the needs of the CPR steam engines, seven outlets from the pipe provided water to the village.

[18]The Community was unsuccessful in its application for protection under the federal Farmers-Creditors Arrangement Act.

[19]*George G. Maloff, Fred F. Sookochoff, Mike S. Verigin* (my father) and their respective families.

[20]As for the other two families, the Maloffs remained at the village site while the Sookochoffs decided to remove to British Columbia.

[21]The 'chattels' that came with the land were listed as follows: 1 black mare, age 18 — 1 black mare, age 9 — 1 black saddle-horse, age 8 — 1 red-and-white shorthorn cow, age 9 — 1 red-and-white shorthorn cow, age 8 — 1 old Massey--Harris binder — 1 gang plow — 1 McCormick wagon — 1 disc.

Part V

Through others' eyes

The Doukhobors of Georgia: traditional food & farming*

Nadezhda Grigulevich

My field work among the Dukhoboria or Doukhobors of Georgia1 showed that these people, like that of the famed Caucasus octogenerians, have preserved their traditional food and farming practices almost intact. As a member of an interdiscplinary study team I went to the high mountain region of Georgia, where I found these long-time settlers who had come here from the Molochnye Vody [Milky Waters] region of the Crimæa in the early 1840s.

Fig. 1. Doukhobor women in the village of Gorelovka, Bogdanovskii Raion, Georgia, 1988, wearing traditional costumes.

Upon entering the town of Bogdanovka at the end of May, 1988, we saw Doukhobor women walking in the streets, dressed for the *Troitsa* [Whitsunday] holiday in flowery skirts, white kerchiefs and small caps.[2] We then continued our journey to the former capital of *Dukhoboria*, the village of Gorelovka, which impressed us immediately. The main street was lined with old houses covered with turf roofs, which sprouted grass and dandelions. Middle-aged Doukhobors were just returning from their holiday prayers.

During our month-long stay in Georgia, our team had time to visit the neighbouring Doukhobor villages of Orlovka and Spasovka, as well as Tambovka and Rodionovka, more remotely situated on the shore of Lake Paravani, high in the mountains. In this summer of 1988 these villagers were still fairly happy, not yet affected by the later mass migrations to central Russia, which regrettably continue even today.[3] These beautifully maintained Russian villages gave us an indication of the high standard of prosperity characteristic of the Doukhobor people of this region.

Russian Doukhobor peasants readily took advantage of the opportunity to establish their own settlements in the Caucasus at the beginning of the past century. Undaunted by the great distances, untamed landscape and severe climate of their new mountain homeland and unperturbed by their new ethnic environment, they stoically endured the difficult journey and the early, most difficult years of life in the Caucasus.

Realising that raising their traditional agricultural crops under their new conditions would be too expensive and inefficient, they turned to cattle-breeding, yet still preserving their traditional culture as much as possible, especially in regard to food. For this they needed to seek out suitable sites in the high mountains to grow potatoes and wheat, and employ hardy varieties of seeds. Not far from Gorelovka they discovered a hill (which they dubbed *Kartoshkin kurgan* [Potato Mound]) with outcroppings of volcanic rock, which served as a natural fertilizer. The surrounding grasslands also abounded in rich wild plants.

Farming in the 1920s and early 1930s

A typical Doukhobor farm of this period would include five or six horses, four cows and a few dozen sheep. Such farmers in the 1930s would have been considered excessively prosperous and classified as kulaks.[4] In many cases this classification was simply a pretext for repression against dissidents, which the Doukhobor people undoubtedly appeared to be in the eyes of the new régime.

In 1931 many Doukhobor families were dispossessed and banished to Central Asia. Those who returned to Gorelovka some two years later were arrested a second time as political offenders and sent back across the Caspian Sea to be imprisoned near Aktiubinsk in Kazakhstan. Some returned home again, but this time their incarceration in a prison closer to home was followed by an early release.

While forced collectivisation did not really begin among the Doukhobors until 1937, their greater prosperity before this event meant their subsequent suffering was especially severe. There is hardly a single family in which someone was not killed or exiled.

Vasilii Petrovich Chiveldeev told of his father's family, which before the Revolution of 1917 kept a virtually self-sufficient farm, including six cows, a number of horses, fifty sheep and twentyfive hens. They had horse-drawn mowers and rakes which his father had become acquainted with after his capture by the Germans in the First World War and which he subsequently introduced into the village. The first mowers were made by the American McCormick firm; eventually Soviet-made machines became available.

Grain was threshed with stone rollers and separated using Astrakhan hand-winnowers. Barley and wheat were ground with water-mills. Crops included barley, oats, wheat, rye, flax and saffron. Dye was purchased in Tiflis[5] for fabrics woven from flax, which were subsequently sold to the Armenians.

Farming in the 1930s–1950s

Beets, carrots, cabbages and radishes were grown on the collective farms (known as *kolkhozy*). For the winter, bulls weighing 300 kilograms — and sometimes sheep — were slaughtered and salted away in tubs. The 'Potato Mound', however, was no longer cultivated after collectivisation.

Kuz'ma Aleksandrovich Balabanov recounted that before the war his farm boasted ten cows, two hundred sheep and six horses. It is now reduced to five sheep and ten pigs, which are fed with buttermilk from the cheese factory where he works. They kill one pig for the winter and give the remainder to the State. While they do not keep cows because of a lack of fodder, they do eat meat every day.

The severe climactic conditions in the Caucasus prevented the Doukhobors from growing the majority of their usual crops, forcing them to obtain them through purchase or barter for the high-quality cheeses they produced. The barter took place with neighbours with whom the Doukhobors had managed to establish friendly relations — local Caucasus populations (Georgians, Armenians and Azerbaidzhanis) as well as

German Mennonites and Molokans, who had been relocated along with the Doukhobors from Molochnye Vody more than a century ago.

The Mennonites, who lived in Kolonka (Balnisi) and Molotov (Tsalka), made vans of somewhat better quality than the Doukhobors', which the latter could acquire in exchange for horses. The Doukhobors also purchased wine, watermelons, grapes and dried fruit from the Mennonites.

Flour and pastry dishes

While the Doukhobors were obliged to become cattle-breeders in order to survive in the Caucasus, they remained vegetarian farmers at heart. They continued to bake bread — as many as four or five loaves a day — in the traditional way, with barley flour (sometimes mixed with wheat flour), adding grated potato for softness, especially in wartime when food supplies were scarce. White bread was normally reserved for holidays. For leaven they would use a piece of dough left over from the previous kneading. Frying pans would be greased with sheep- or bull-lard. According to some of the older residents, the bread produced today is less flavourful than in earlier times.

When hops arrived from Kakhetiia, they were dried, then doused with boiling water and allowed to settle before straining. The little leaves were thrown away. Bought yeast and flour were added to give the consistency of a liquid paste; the mixture was then set aside to ferment for three to five days. With the addition of more flour, a thick dough was kneaded into a high-quality home-made yeast which, after drying, could be stored for four or five months. Like their Molokan neighbours, Doukhobors retained many recipes for old Russian peasant dishes from the 19th century based on malt or malt flour.

In making *zatirka* (or *bryzgushka*) — a dish prepared only in summer — flour is ground with water and eggs, and dried a little in a frying pan. After boiling, butter is added. A variant is to combine barley flour with onion, potato and sometimes curds.

Salamata is made in the Doukhobor manner by dissolving roasted flour with hot water and bringing to a boil, adding butter when done. A jelly-like dessert known as *kisel'* which used to be cooked with flour, is often prepared today from pre-processed products (such as frozen or dried fruits or berries).

The most time-tested dishes are those prepared from whole grains. For funerals and memorial feasts Doukhobor women cook a meatless dish called *kut'ia* from whole grains of wheat, sweetened with honey, in an earthenware pot; after it is ready they add butter and sugar. One very elderly woman recalled that once upon a time, *kut'ia* was a daily dish. Wheat gruel boiled for a long time also serves as a basis for *kulesh.*

The celebrated Doukhobor festive noodle dish *lapshá* is cooked as follows: four or five eggs, a glass of water and salt are kneaded with flour into a thick dough. The puff is rolled out, dried and cut into very narrow strips. It can then be used to make *lapshevnik,* in which noodles are fried on slow heat in the oven, until a distinct aroma is discernible. After dousing with salted boiling water it is fried in butter in a frying pan.

Fig. 2. Making a large crepe (blinetz) in village of Gorelovka, Georgia, 1888.

Pirogi (small closed pies) are made with liver, jam, grated carrot, or baked apples (among other ingredients), wrapped in dough. *Pirozhki* (smaller than *pirogi*) include fillings with curds, potatoes or beans. They are baked in an oven (formerly the huge Russian *pech'*). *Kalachi* are a kind of fancy bread made from yeast, eggs, sugar, sour cream and flour. Other popular Doukhobor dishes are *bliny* (pancakes) and *blintsy* (flat pancakes made from very thin batter). Other dishes made with flour are *oladi* (a kind of thick pancake made with sour milk), *pel'meni* (meat dumplings), *vareniki* (curd or fruit dumplings) and *khvorost* (pastry sticks). *Khachapuri* (a cheese-bread) and *khinkali* (dumplings) were adopted from local peoples of the Caucasus.

Kasha (porridge) is cooked from pearl-barley. *Sorochinskaia krupa* was a kind of rice gruel — a rather rare and expensive product prepared during the more important holidays.

Soups and drinks

A variety of soups are prepared. *Tiuria* is a summer soup made from bread, dried crusts, sugar and either water, milk or *kvas* [see below]. *Gerkules* is an everyday soup made from oatmeal or oatmeal porridge. *Okroshka* is a cold vegetable soup made with potatoes, onion, greens, cucumbers, eggs, horseradish and sour cream, although sometimes it consisted simply of horseradish, sour cream and water. *Pokhlevka* is a bread-based soup formerly prepared from nettles. *Borshch* is a beet soup prepared from *svinushki* (flat-capped mushrooms), pickled in summer. Savory is sometimes added as a seasoning to soups, and may be used for making tea. Tea can also be brewed using mint, raspberry or sweetbrier.

Among fermented drinks, *kvas* is a nut-flavoured beer, prepared from dried barley crusts. In olden days it was made by pouring boiling water on flour, adding sour dough upon cooling and leaving the mixture to ferment. *Kvas* was also poured over jellied beef or mutton. Other home-brewed alcohol was distilled using malt (or sometimes sugar) and a dough which underwent excessive fermentation.

In the past, alcohol was consumed only during holidays — usually either wine bought from the Germans or vodka from the Armenians. Following World War II, the distillation of breadbased vodka became a common practice: thick dough was kneaded and left to ferment for two to three weeks. Buns baked from this dough would be thrown into a large wooden tub filled with warm water, with the addition of an appropriate amount of cultivated malt. After sufficient fermentation, the mixture would be ready for distilling.

Vegetables and fruits

Some vegetables, such as turnips and radishes, were eaten raw with sour cream; carrots and beets were also eaten raw, although beets might be steamed whole in the oven. Radishes might be eaten with salt, *kvas* and *mazun* (the Doukhobor name for *matsoni*, a Georgian yoghurt).

Grated carrots and cabbage would be fermented in a tub; the process might be aided by adding a slice of bread wrapped in a cabbage leaf. Cucumbers were a relative latecomer to the Doukhobors' diet; they are pickled in tubs with pepper and garlic. *Baklazhany* (aubergine, or egg-plant) were also adopted only recently, from the Armenians. Bulgarian peppers stuffed with meat, rice and carrots are served at weddings, funerals and memorial feasts.

Many vegetables were prepared for winter storage, including cabbage, cucumbers, tomatoes, aubergine and *svinushki*. The latter, a variety of mushroom, were believed to possess certain healing properties. While the Armenians usually boiled and then salted the *svinushki* stems, the Doukhobors tended to salt them whole. Most cabbages would be salted, although some were left fresh. Salting used to be done in barrels, with beets and grated carrots added. Today, however, the Doukhobors prefer to use glass jars, which improves preservation and prevents mould growth. Salt continues to be added periodically to prevent the cabbage from becoming soft.

A variety of marinades are made from tomatoes, garlic, carrots, apples, Bulgarian pepper and beet leaves.

Oil pressed out of hemp or flax was added to salads or used for frying, and in the autumn children used to eat raw hemp seeds. However, hemp has not been sown for the last few decades.

Many fruits were adopted from local peoples, such as cherries, apples, pears, plums, nuts, grapes, watermelons, prunes and apricots, all grown, along with sea-buckthorn, by Azerbaidzhanis living at Akhaltsikhe. These were bought by the Doukhobors or bartered for *chichel* (stringy cheese). Wild strawberries, stone raspberries, mountain cranberries and bilberries were gathered on the *Sinii kurgan* ['Blue Mound']. Rowanberries [*riabina*] are used to make jam, juices and wine, as are some other fruits.

A boiled fruit dish called *solodukha* (called *kulaga* by the Molokans) is prepared as follows: whole wheat flour [*razmol*] is placed into a cast-iron kettle full of boiling water with prunes, dried apricots, other dried fruit and sugar, and put into the oven. After two or three hours the paste takes on a dark-brown colour and a dense consistency, and the resulting mixture is considered to be a very wholesome and nutritious food for children and the elderly, particularly in wintertime, when there is a shortage of vitamins. Sometimes *solodukha* is prepared from ground sprouted barley doused with boiling water. Again, dried fruit is added.

Dairy foods and drinks

The Doukhobors' table is rich and diverse in dairy products. Especially noteworthy is their tasty, fragrant butter, and Caucasus-style cheeses. The water of the mountain rivers is crystal clear and pure, and, like the air, is free from environmental pollution.6 In the past, butter was such a plentiful commodity that it was melted and stored in cast-iron pots for the winter.

Children are given fresh milk to drink; two or three buckets a day may be delivered by a single cow. In days gone by, fresh milk would be poured into a jug and stored temporarily in a cellar, later to be mixed with bread for the evening meal. Sour clotted milk, derived from unboiled milk, would be used for baking puffs, in combination with eggs, salt and soda.

Boiled milk, on the other hand, was used in the preparation of *mazun* (i.e., the Georgian yoghurt *matsoni*), where buttermilk is added to bread. While it is sometimes given to cattle, Doukhobor elders indicated that *mazun* once stood in great esteem among the people, even more than *kisel'*.

The dry remains from *mazun* were wrung out into linen sacks and frozen for winter, when a little piece of such 'preserved milk' would be defrosted and diluted with water for drinking. In times of 'short supply', this meant people were able to conserve milk for a long time. Sometimes in the summer, however, they would simply dilute the dry remains of the milk with water, add salt and drink it during working hours — a drink very similar to the Azerbaidzhanis' *airan*.

Another kind of yoghurt is *riazhenka*, produced by letting milk bake in a *pech'* (Russian oven) — either in cast-iron kettles or in *makhortochki* (earthenware pots with handles) — for twenty-four hours, and then leaving it to cool and set.

Cream is made by passing milk through a separator, after which it may be used in turn to produce butter; in one experiment, 3.5 kg of butter was obtained from six litres of milk. While butter is frequently added to food, it is not produced in sufficient quantities to be sold. Cream would be eaten with pancakes, and was also used to make sour cream.

Cheese curds would be used to make *vareniki, pirozhki* or *syrniki* (cheesecakes), to which a quantity of eggs was added. Cheese was made using the specially treated stomach of a calf, sheep or suckling-pig. A piece of the stomach might be added to the buttermilk in the production of *mazun*.

In the production of *chichel*, an Armenian cheese-dish, head cheese was added to fresh milk in a large wooden tub, followed by a fermented substance and boiling water; the resulting clotted mixture would be poured into linen sacks, left in metal pots for buttermilk separation, and preserved in salted water.

Meat dishes

The Doukhobors were so successful in their new occupation as cattle-breeders that they soon became wholesale suppliers of small cattle and thoroughbred horses. On some Doukhobor farms before the Revolution, flocks of sheep numbered thousands of heads. The abundance of cattle on private farms together with the harsh climate and the influence of their Caucasus neighbours on their cuisine led to a significant increase in the use of meat and meat products in the Doukhobors' daily diet.

Doukhobors have kept geese, ducks and hens for many years. In the past, geese and ducks would be salted and stored for the winter.

Sheep and beef liver are used in making soup, while goose and chicken giblets are used for stuffing *pirozhki*. Two major meat dishes are *tefteli* (meatballs) and *rulet*. The latter dish formerly consisted of collared beef combined with eggs, rolled up in raw, thin meat and fried in a frying pan in the *pech'*, although now it tends to be prepared in a way similar to *khinkali* (dumplings). Beef and mutton preserves continue to be made and eaten year round.

A soup known as *ukha* was a popular dish made from fish, with the addition of wheat, rice, bay-leaf, black pepper and savory. Fish abounded in the mountain rivers: carp, trout, whitefish, chub, barbel and *khromulia* (related to the carp). Whitefish, a tasty and high-quality catch, was used to prepare smoked fish. Most fish dishes (except for roach) were jellied.

Salt and sugar

Rock salt was heavily used even as late as ten years ago — in the preparation of salt cabbage, among other things. The salt would be crumbled, washed, dried and ground in a hollowed-out wooden log. One Doukhobor felt that this product was superior to the more finely ground, iodine-treated salt used today, procured from Tatar merchants travelling by camel. Bread and salt are a traditional symbol of Doukhobor (and Russian) hospitality.

Sugar is used in glasses of tea (usually two or three teaspoonfuls at a time); it is also added to jam, marmalade and compotes as they are being prepared for the winter. Before the war it used to be purchased in solid chunks, and then chipped. Because of an earlier shortage of sugar for feeding bees, the bees stopped producing honey, which was previously plentiful.

The festive table

The Doukhobors' table is most abundant and varied during holidays. In addition to their own special days (such as Frol — the patron saint of Gorelovka), Doukhobors also celebrate such traditional holidays as Christmas, Shrovetide, Easter and Whitsunday. Some days (such as Christmas and New Year's) are celebrated twice — according to both the old- and new-style calendars.[7]

Christmas dishes include *kalachi* or *kalachiki* (festive bread), *pirogi* with potatoes and curds, *oladi* (pancakes) with *iurashka* (buttermilk left after butter production), *kotlety* (fried meat patties), *golubtsy* (stuffed cabbage rolls), as well as chicken and chicken soup.

New Year torchlight processions might be followed by *vareniki* (dumplings with cheese curds), *pel'meni* (boiled meat dumplings), *kotlety*, *golubtsy* and chicken soup.

For *Kreshchenie* [Epiphany] 6 January (new style: 19 January), cold snacks are served along with salads, sauerkraut, beans, boiled beets, meat with vegetable oil and market-bought apples.

During *Maslenitsa* (Shrovetide) in February pancakes are the main item on the menu, along with *kotlety, golubtsy,* salads, jellied meat, chicken, *borshch* and *lapshá*. Some families still observe an old custom of feeding the first pancakes to the household pets.

Soroki on 9 March (new style: 22 March) heralds the advent of spring; the holiday is celebrated with *zhavoronki* (skylark-shaped pastry buns). In some families they are given as food to the cattle.

Easter is the most important feast-day of the year for Eastern Christians, and all work on this day is strictly prohibited. Celebrations involve the baking of *pasochki* (Easter cakes) and the painting of eggs, which are then brought to the *Sirotskii dom*[8] in Gorelovka, as well as to the cemetery.

Omlettes are traditional for *Zhzheny,* the second Sunday after Easter, while on *Troitsa* (Whitsunday), celebrated on the seventh Sunday after Easter, the table is set with fresh cucumbers, market-bought tomatoes, jellied chicken, boiled meat, salads and *vinegret* (a vegetable salad with oil-and-vinegar dressing). Doukhobor women bake *kalachiki* and *pishki* (buns), along with cakes and pastries. A tradition derived from other Caucasus people is that of baking and sometimes boiling lamb.

Gorelovka has its own patron saint's feast, the day of Frol, which usually falls toward the end of August — a day on which people are committed to doing good deeds. The table is set with a variety of fruits (tomatoes, watermelons, strawberries, apples and grapes) as well as jellied meat, fried chicken and *kartoshnik* (potato first boiled, then mashed, and, after eggs are added, baked).

Funeral and memorial feasts

According to custom, for funeral suppers Doukhobors prepare *kut'ia* (a meatless wheat-grain dish, though sometimes made with rice and currants). In winter, a *vinegret* made of peas, salted tomatoes and cucumbers, is more common. Beans, vegetable greens, onion and parsley are stewed. *Borshch* is made from a meat stock with potatoes, cabbage and beets, but without the customary carrots. Other funeral feast dishes are *lapshevnik* (a baked noodle cake), baked chicken (rubbed with salt and pepper, and stuffed with nuts), jellied meat and *zakuski* (hors-d'œuvres).

The day following the funeral Doukhobors feast on cheese with greens, *lapshá* and meat with potatoes, but no *zakuski*.

For the memorial feast held six weeks later, cold *zakuski* are served, along with *borshch*, *lapshá*, meat with potatoes, jellied meat (beef, mutton or fowl but never pork), sweet rice with currants. Compote usually replaces tea; lemonade, wine and vodka are also served (although the custom of drinking alcohol on such occasions began only about thirty years ago).

Another memorial feast is held a year later, for which goats and sheep are slaughtered.

Daily meals

Breakfast used to consist generally of *pirozhki* and *blinchiki*, although now it may include the larger *bliny*, possibly with hemp-seed oil. For mid-day dinner (the most substantial meal of the day) the Doukhobors would eat *borshch*, meat and potatoes with gravy (or milk) and onions, meat stock with noodles, *kartoshnik* (baked potato cake), sweet breads, pies and compote. Supper would comprise boiled eggs, sheep cheese, home-made butter, raspberry tea, *zveroboi* (St John's wort) and wild marjoram.

Tea is taken several times a day. A two-kilogram loaf of bread would be consumed by a family of four in a day. Bread is often purchased in stores during the summer, but home-baked in winter-time to avoid travel. Flour-based products tend to be consumed more in winter than in summer. During harvest times *zatirka* or *bryzguhka* might be prepared and taken out to the harvesters. Milk-cows yield about 15–16 litres of milk per day in the summer, but only a couple of litres per day during the winter.

Over the period of a year, one family might consume 60–75 kilograms of flour, 100–150 kg of meat and lard, 80–120 kg of fresh cabbage and 500 kg of potatoes. One 300-kg bull calf, for example, was divided between two families.

'Borrowed' dishes and the 'modernisation' of cuisine

As mentioned before, the Doukhobors often formed close relationships with the local peoples of the Caucasus; this accelerated their acclimatisation to their new home and led to some noteworthy cross-cultural influences in the field of nutrition. Dishes adopted by the Doukhobors include *lobio* (beans), *chakhokhbili* (chicken with tomatoes)[9], and *khinkali* (dumplings). Beet-leaves braised with nuts were taken specifically from Georgian cuisine, while a wide range of dishes was borrowed from the Armenians: fried liver with greens wrapped in *lavash* (Armenian bread), *liulia-kebab, plov* (rice) and *khalva* (a paste of nuts, sugar and oil), as well as yoghurt-like foods such as *mazun/matsoni, airan* and *abur* (Armenian buttermilk).

A number of Doukhobor dishes were in turn adopted by local populations, especially *lapshá, pirogi* and, of course, their bread. In mixed Doukhobor-Armenian families food from both traditions is to be found — popular Doukhobor dishes here are *borshch, vareniki, kartoshnik* and *ukha*, as well as *pirogi* with sunflower oil.

Local ecological conditions

The Doukhobors were skilled in mastering the ecology of the land wherever they lived. They quickly learnt what crops could be most effectively planted in each settlement. They knew, for example, that grain crops did best in Bogdanovka, possibly because of the lower altitude.

The Doukhobors in the past used only organic fertilisers (ashes and manure), although today some inorganic fertilisers are also in use, causing soil pollution and retarding crop production.

In sum, it should be noted that the Doukhobor people, who long ago were forced to emigrate from the Crimæa to this relatively inhospitable mountain country (where even in the summer the temperature rarely rises above 15°), have not only been able to survive in these harsh conditions, but also managed to prove the incredible strength of their spiritual power, their courage and their proud allegiance to their ideals.

[*]Based on a translation from Russian provided by the Translation Bureau, Department of Secretary of State, Canada.

[10]This article is devoted to the traditional food habits of the Doukhobor people of Georgia (Gruziia), and is based on field data gathered by the author during expeditions organised by the ethnic ecology sector of the Russian Academy of Sciences' Institute of Ethnology and Anthropology. The expedition conducted its research in May–June 1988 under the direction of Dr A.N. Iamskov. The results of the multiyear research project are presented in: *Russkie starozhili Azerbaidzhana* [Russian octogenerians of Azerbaidzhan], 2 vols. (Moscow, 1990) and *Dukhobortsy i molokane v Zakavkaze* [Doukhobors and Molokans in the Transcaucasus] (Moscow, Russian Academy of Sciences, 1992).

[11]For an historical overview of Doukhobor traditional costumes, see: Svetlana A. Inikova, 'Peculiarities of the costumes of the Caucasus Doukhobors' in: *Dukhobortsy i molokane v Zakavkaze*, pp. 89–105.

[12]For more information on the problem of migration of the Russian population of the Caucasus, see: A.N. Iamskov, 'Differences in the professional composition of ethnic groups and migration' in: *Russkie starozhili Azerbaidzhana*, pp. 51–61; A.N. Iamskov, 'Ethnic differences in the social-professional composition of the rural Russian and aboriginal populations of the Transcaucasus' in: *Dukhobortsy i molokane v Zakavkaze*, pp. 144–61; O.D. Komarova, 'Contemporary population migrations from the Russian villages of the Transcaucasus', *ibid.*, pp. 105–44.

[13]*kulak* — a Soviet term for a peasant working for personal profit.

[14]*Tiflis* — capital of Georgia, renamed Tbilisi in 1936.

[15]It should be noted, however, that the water around Gorelovka is somewhat deficient in iodine and minerals — a deficiency which may be associated with certain diseases prevalent there.

[16]The 'old-style' calendar is the Julian calendar adopted in the time of Julius Cæsar, and is still in use by the Russian Orthodox Church. The 'new-style', or Gregorian, calendar, introduced in the West by Pope Gregory XIII in 1582, was not officially proclaimed in Russia until after the 1917 Revolution. In the 20th century the old calendar has remained 13 days behind the new — *ed.*

[17]*Sirotskii dom* — the former 'Orphans' Home' in Gorelovka which became a prayer house and administrative centre for the Caucasus Doukhobors.

[18]The Doukhobors were actually introduced to the tomato only in the 1930s, after some of their people returned from the deportation camps of Central Asia.

Wasyl Ivanovich Zubenkoff: Doukhobor folk artist

Jim Shockey

Discovering great works of Western Canadian ethnocentric folk art has been my all-consuming goal for more than a decade now. The pleasure I experience when I first lay eyes on a newly discovered work of art can be likened only to that which comes from the finding of sunken treasure. Though searching through a barn on the prairies is by no means as perilous an adventure as walking the ocean bottom, there is no mistaking the reality of the romance and the passion.

The next barn, the next farm — or perhaps the next underwater cavern. There is no difference. Always you think: 'maybe, just maybe' the treasure of your dreams is right there around the corner waiting to be discovered. But of course it seldom is.

I believe that, over a period of time filled with endless disappointment, every treasure hunter comes to feel a spiritual bond with the people who lived with the treasure originally. The treasure hunter comes to love the hunt, one may say, more than the finding of the treasure. For it is during the hunt that knowledge is shared, a kind of kindred knowledge where the treasure hunter becomes acquainted with the life of the original owner. He knows the fear and feels the fury of the storm as he places himself beside the helmsman battling the wind. The treasure hunter will know the currents as well as does the helmsman; he will know the reefs and the dangers. He will know the boat and its limitations as well as any captain. In his mind the treasure hunter will live the scene a thousand times, imagining the actions of the helmsman, the captain and the crew. Then, when in his mind the ship and the treasure have been swallowed by the seas for the thousandth time, he will start his search where he believes they went down. Sometimes indeed there is treasure — but there is always the hunt.

Do not misunderstand me: the treasure is important. While the treasure hunter and those in the past may share a kindred knowledge and a spiritual bond, the gulf of time, often centuries wide, is insurmountable. The treasure then becomes the only common material link to the lives of those in the past. The problem with both sunken treasure and great folk art is that, once found, they can often only serve as a blurry window to the days gone by. As a treasure hunter, one is compelled to search further than the piece itself — to find the story behind the treasure — to grasp at the meaning of the piece. Occasionally, with enough study and research the hazy veil of time will clear slightly to reveal the barest hint of what lies in the past. More rarely still, the finder may come across solid documented provenance for the treasure, sweeping the veil away for a much clearer vision.

But then, perhaps once in a career, the window opens: a special treasure is found which offers answers that can never be found in a library. The treasure itself tells more than the provenance can because the piece reveals the true nature of the maker and his time. Most importantly the treasure confirms the knowledge gained during the hunt. When such a treasure is found, it is usually art and the maker is an artist. Such an artist is *Wasyl Ivanovich Zubenkoff*. Through his work he has provided us with an open window to the past and an insight into the turmoil he lived through, both as a Doukhobor and with the Doukhobors.

Wasyl's life is very much the inside story of the Doukhobors from the day he was born in Russia in 1863 to the day he died in Canada in 1933, but it is also the story of *immigration* — and its patron-saint, *assimilation*. It is the story of upheaval and homesickness. It is the story of the lost generation always found between any new land and any old. And it is important to remember that his life represents only one of thousands who lived as he did and shared similar experiences. Not only Doukhobors but all those who emigrate for whatever reason must live with a sense of doubt as they exist from day to day with one foot in the past and one in the future. To understand the treasures made by these immigrants one must become a treasure hunter one's self, even if just for a moment — one must feel as they felt in the past and live with their fears and doubts.

At the age of fourteen Wasyl was chosen to be one of the personal guards of *Lukeria Kalmykova*. This greatest of Doukhobor leaders picked only twenty men from all her subjects to be trained in the ways of the *Kazakí* [Cossacks]. These men, who accompanied her wherever she went, were reputed to be the best singers and the best riders in the community, and, according to her wishes, were given the time to practise their individual talents. Wasyl, who cut a fine figure in his Cossack uniform practised his art, a talent for which he undoubtedly was renowned and in great demand.

Lukeria Kalmykova presided over the Doukhobors' 'Golden Age'. In the Caucasus one may still find the cave where she held secret meetings with the most influential Doukhobors. Over the entrance to the cave may be seen a relief depicting a flowing vine with tulips, carved in granite — the signature work of Wasyl Zubenkoff.

Following Lukeria's death in 1886, however, the Doukhobor world Wasyl knew began to crumble. The 'Cossack' guard was disbanded and Wasyl's new duties as a carpenter left him no time for art. The new leader, *Peter V. ('the Lordly'[1]) Verigin* introduced different ways; he urged a 'return to tradition'; he spoke of 'morality and peace'. Wasyl must have been torn between Verigin's pacifism and his own Cossack training. What might have gone through his head at the Burning of Arms in 1895, as the Tsar's own Cossack horsemen descended on the helpless Doukhobors? He would have been among the handful who were trained to fight back and yet ordered not to. I wonder whether or not he actually did.

Then there was the exile and the death, within a year, of more than a thousand Doukhobors. Wasyl was there among them, along with his wife and four children. No doubt they survived thanks to his own resourcefulness. But did he ever compromise his leader's demands — for the sake of his family? Did he ever think back to his former life as a privileged guard and artist as he struggled to feed his children? One will never know the answer, but surely he must have lived with doubt.

During that first winter of 1899 in emigration, while everyone was waiting for the Canadian winter to soften, Wasyl made a trunk. He dated it, and inscribed it (in Cyrillic) with the name of his loving wife Dora. For a brief period he returned to his art. He painted a swirling circle of opposing vines and tulips, joined together by a ring. When I asked my wife whether she saw any significance in the design (without telling her anything about the trunk), she said it reminded her of a man and a woman together, bound by marriage and protecting four children from the world outside the circle.

Along with other Doukhobors, Wasyl and his family spent the next few years establishing their right to the new land. Working again as a carpenter, he had no free time for art. The villages were bustling with a hope and desire for permanent settlement free from yet another threat of relocation, but it was not to be. A new official interpretation of homesteading rules forced the Doukhobors to vacate many of their lands on the prairies and seek a new home further west. I wonder whether this evoked in Wasyl's mind memories of earlier times. Did he recognise the insidious cancer of assimilation as it seeped into the everyday life of the Doukhobors?

In 1907, an artist once more, Wasyl Zubenkoff designed a mirror frame for his wife and his growing daughters Maria and Malasha. It was to be his best work. I wonder whether the artist had any inkling of the people who would stand before that frame over the years to come. Did he understand the significance of creating a frame for the only mirror in the village, to which Doukhobor women would come from miles around to look into its forbidden reflection? Given the fact that mirrors were prohibited by the leader, was this act a subtle statement of some of his followers' growing discontent?

Fig. 1. This stunning Wasyl Zubenkoff mirror frame speaks for itself.
It features a superb carving of traditional elements from the Old Country — Russian
eagles and the crown Inlaid marguetry surrounds the mirror,
coupled with painted multi-coloured tulips and vines on the sides
along with the finishing touch. 1907.

Is it possible that the twin eagles of the Russian crest crowning the mirror could be seen as a tribute to his years as a fighting 'Cossack' guardsman? And could the depiction of ladies in western garb, busily sewing, be pointing a symbolic finger at the quiet assimilation which was busy, even in 1907, undermining traditional Doukhobor morality? Was this the artist's (perhaps unwitting) attempt to offer an insight into the hidden turmoil and conflicting ideals the Canadian Doukhobors had to contend with in the first decade of the twentieth century?

I do not know the answer. Perhaps the frame is just an interesting piece of good folk art that happens to lend itself to interpretation.

I would like to believe otherwise. Whatever the answer, in 1918 Wasyl left the Doukhobor community to buy his own land, which he farmed with his son Alex. It was during those years that he produced the last two of his works that I have been able to trace. The table and cupboard he made both testify to a craftsman in his twilight years and to diminishing skills. The artistry is still there, however, along with the vines and tulips.

Fig. 2. Another view of the same.

In 1927, with failing eyesight, Wasyl rejoined the Doukhobor community, donating his half of the farm to the new leader, *Peter P. (Chistiakov[2]) Verigin*. Six years later he died. While I shall never meet Wasyl in person, I feel it is possible, through his work, to know him.

Fortunately, Wasyl also left descendants to provide provenance. One advantage of treasure hunting on dry land (as opposed to the ocean bottom) is that it is possible to meet the descendants of the original makers and owners. In this case I had the privilege of meeting Wasyl's grandson, who led me to the last remaining member of the artist's immediate family, his daughter Mabel.[3] Between the two of them, they succeeeded in preserving Wasyl's art in pristine condition for more than a half-century.

Mabel, who lives in Drumheller, Alberta, helped fill in the story of her artist-father. She remarked that he could not understand people who did not like colour.

'Each post on our fence was painted a different colour', she told me. 'Even my mother's milk-stool was painted. The painted table sat in the middle of our log house with a cloth over it. Only on very special occasions was the cloth lifted.'

'My father would sit on a bench over there,' she added, pointing across her townhouse living room, 'and he would carve picture frames for people.'

In tears she described her father's never-ending anguish at leaving Russia, and his own tears sometimes brought on simply by looking at the intricately carved harness-rings he had made for his horse while still one of Lukeria Kalmykova's guards. He was a hero then, Mabel told me. He felt betrayed by his leader, Peter V. ('the Lordly') Verigin, when the Doukhobors were deprived of their lands in Saskatchewan. Even during the nine years when he voluntarily left the Community, he still considered himself a Doukhobor.

'His last years were bad', she admitted. 'My father gave everything to the community. He was an old man without sight and yet he was expected to work with the younger men. He deserved better.'

I am grateful to know that at least nine of this great man's works have been found, and that he will, even if belatedly, receive the recognition he deserves. For through his work he has helped us understand what it means to be a Doukhobor.

He was one of thousands of his community, but by showing us his own doubt so clearly, he makes us appreciate the others as well. After seeing his work, one can no longer merely glance at a piece of Doukhobor (or any pioneer) furniture without thinking not only of its maker, but also of its subsequent owners, of the many hands that touched that piece over the years, of the love and sorrow in the home or homes that it shared.

Through his work, Wasyl Ivanovich Zubenkoff has confirmed something most treasure hunters already know: that it is during the hunt itself that the real treasure is most often found — the knowledge of and insight into a lost way of life.

Appendix

The following letter, dated 29 June 1993, was written by Wasyl's grandson *Alex Zubenkoff* to *Koozma J. Tarasoff* in Ottawa:

In reply to your letter about my grandfather, **Wasil Zubenkoff**. First of all, his family. He was born in Russia in 1863 and was married to **Dunia** [= **Dora**] **Rezansoff**. They had eight children. Two boys died in infancy. One 6-year-old girl was trying to stay warm by an open fire when her clothes caught on fire and [she] died shortly after. The oldest daughter **Masha** married **Wasyl Potapoff** and they had a store in Verigin, Saskatchewan. Son **Wasyl** married **Nastia Markin** and farmed in the Verigin district, then moved to Skiff, Alberta. Daughter **Malasha** married **Alex Ogloff,** farmed in the Verigin district, then moved to Grand Forks, B.C. Son **Alex**, my dad, married **Florence Storgeoff**; they farmed in the Verigin district, then moved to Coté, Saskatchewan, and continued farming. Daughter **Mabel** married **Alex Bokoff** who worked in a mine in East Coulee, Alberta, then lived in Drumheller where Mabel is still residing.

While my grandfather still lived in Russia, he was one of the Cossacks serving Lukeria Kalmykova. He also built wagon boxes and was very famous for painting flowers on them. There is a big picture of him in uniform at the National Doukhobor Heritage Village Museum in Verigin, and one picture that I have sent to Grand Forks of all the Cossacks that served Lukeria.

You are asking if we have any furniture that was built by grandfather, well we have none. As far as Wasyl's craftsmanship, if you could only see a mirror and a frame that he has built, it will give you an idea of his work. On top of the frame are two eagle heads carved in wood and painted. Also there is a very narrow strip inlaid with small pieces. This alone will give you an idea of his hand work. Mr. **Shockey** has this mirror as he got it from me…

---

[1]The Russian term is *Gospodnii,* meaning 'belonging to the Lord' — *ed.*

[2]The name *Chistiakov* is related to the Russian verb *chistit'* (to cleanse) — *ed.*

[3]Additional information about Wasyl Zubenkoff's family is given in the appendix at the end of this article — *ed.*

The Oral tradition of
the Dzhavakhetiia Doukhobors*

Serafima Nikitina

She was the eldest keeper of the tradition, and her funeral ceremony justly reflected her status. She lay there at the front, in a corner, under ceremonial towels in a coffin fashioned by the most skilled Doukhobor craftsmen: the area of the coffin under her chest, over which her hands were folded, holding an embroidered handkerchief, had been cut at a wider angle so that she could rest more comfortably. The coffin had been made exactly according to her measurements, as if more dead bodies were shortly to be expected in the house. She lay dressed in two night-gowns, according to her own request (what if it suddenly became chilly 'over there'!), along with a padded jacket embroidered in bright rosy shades over the nightgowns. From the waist down she was covered in a curtain of multi-coloured stripes; her hand-made leather boots with their *medochki* [coppercovered heels] were also decorated with embroidery, while on her head was a woollen kerchief with tassels. Women dressed in fancy clothes kept coming up to the coffin, while men in satin-embroidered jackets had seated themselves on the benches and begun to recite psalms:

> The confession of the Doukhobors is meant to serve and to worship our God-Spirit. We are committed to the course of salvation and do not recognise anything that is superficial, we reject and do not know any symbols of faith...
> Let us come together, brothers, and meditate in one unified monastic apostolic church. Let us, brothers, create an angelic joy. The church is protected when the evening settles in and the church is consecrated when midnight falls, while at the break of day the church seeks justice from our God...

They recited the lines by heart, in a particular manner, alternating between high and low pitches evenly, as though the psalms were drifting on the waves.

Forty men were sitting there, and forty different psalms had been recited, and now the singing began. A newcomer could not help but feel mesmerised by this type of singing. It moves at a slow pace, with an unusually lengthy phrase for each syllable, and it comes in waves which keep growing higher and higher before falling abruptly. Almost every sound seems suspended in the air individually, and this produces the effect of an elevated soaring into eternity.

At one point, totally unexpectedly, an entirely different sound broke into the solemn singing of the psalm: the cry of a daughter wailing over her dead mother, a typical mourning in the style of ancience Rus'. In a thin and tense voice choked with sobs, though nevertheless clearly enunciating the melody, the young woman lamented over her dear 'nanny', calling for her by name. The most striking feature, however, was the fact that the estranged and almost 'cosmic' singing merged with the earthly elements of the wailing to produce an absolutely natural and organic effect.

An audiotape recorded a few years earlier was then played, on which the deceased was heard reciting 'The Dream of the Virgin Mary', the most popular of the Russian apocrypha. The Doukhobors consider such a recitation a vital element in remembering the dead.

After the final good-byes and terrestrial bows, the men placed the coffin on two long poles fastened with ropes and carried it to the cemetery, singing all the way. They sang on the way back as well.

> The sun is setting, the evening glow is on the wane,
> God's slave is approaching her end…

Upon returning from the cemetery the men announced: 'We have passed on our warmest regards' — signifying that during the digging of the grave, those still alive had the opportunity to pass on their 'warmest regards' to their dead ancestors, after which the grave would be ready to accept the most recently deceased.

This was the beginning (in 1985) of my acquaintance with the Doukhobors residing in Dzhavakhetiia (formerly known as the Bogdanovka region) — a mountain plateau in southern Georgia near the border point where Georgia meets both Turkey and Armenia. By then I had already accumulated many years of experience in field research on the rites of the Russian Old Believers [*Starovertsy*]. Already my eyes had becomed used to the dark-coloured sarafans, while my ears had grown accustomed to the stark unison of the ancient Russian melodies and the old liturgical utterances of the Church Slavonic and canonical texts.

Here in Dzhavakhetiia, however, I was witnessing a funeral which featured bright and festive ceremonial clothing. I listened to psalms with just a gentle touch of Church Slavonic in their texts — sometimes revealingly clear in their thought, at other times dark and mysterious.

Most certainly, this was a type of singing which knew no parallels. It was one I came to hear over and over again during my two-week stay in the Wet Mountains (as Dzhavakhetiia is also known).

This field trip was unlike any of my previous ones, which had all proceeded according to a plan and revolved around a questionnaire, both worked out in advance. This time, however, I was utterly smitten with the Doukhobor culture. What I should be listening to, what I should be looking at, as well as how I should proceed — all this was dictated by the events themselves. These events, which followed precipitously one after the other, turned out to be rites, texts and singing which originated within the depths of the Doukhobor culture — funerals, for example, or ceremonies held to see new recruits off to their military service. And despite the narrow time-frame between the events, I was able, nonetheless, to catch a glimpse into the expanses of the folkloric nature of the nonritual lyrics, the exorcisms, the historic legends and traditions of the Doukhobors, and to gain an appreciation of the incredible dimensions of their collective oral and musical memory.

It is well known that the Doukhobors perceive themselves to be a distinct ethnic group.

'We Doukhobors are a special people', the villagers of Efremovka told me. 'We represent a mixture: there are Russians, Ukrainians, Cossacks, Mordvinians and even gypsies among us.' Many claimed their origins to be in the Tambov region of central Russia. However, now that a significant number of them have already moved to western Russia (most notably to the Tula Oblast), the ethnic counterargument of 'Doukhobors being Russians' is gradually losing ground.

During my stay among the Doukhobors and my transcribing of a number of texts they recited, I had the impression that their world outlook (along with all its manifestations) constituted a unique, consciously elaborated mode of thinking — a blend, in fact, of the richest Russian fokloric traditions drawn from a number of local cultures (especially those of Southern Russia and the Cossacks). This link, which brings various forms of oral culture together, became, in effect, the focus of my study.

Comparison with Molokans and Old Believers

The fate and culture of the Doukhobors has a great deal in common with that of two other Russian denominational groups: the *Molokans*, who are close to the Doukhobors in their religious beliefs, and the *Old*

Believers, who share a similar fate, if not a confessional viewpoint. All three groups have gone through periods of persecution and discrimination, resulting in frequent migrations, sometimes taking them far away from their homelands into a foreign ethnic, linguistic and denominational environment. The self-awareness of all three groups may be characterised by a strong 'we-versus-they' mentality.

All three cultures made a conscious effort to develop an opposition to the established church and the governing social institutions, taking upon itself responsibility for organising and maintaining its own institutions, especially as regards education. Special care was taken to ensure proper teaching of the basic denominational tenets, along with the proper interpretation of elements of the popular culture intruding from external sources (church parochial schools, activities of the priests, printed editions of Christian books). Cultural self-reliance, which used the 'we--versus-they' frame of reference to deepen and intensify a sense of group identity, was expressed in fostering a collective understanding of the created texts through the promotion of group-wide hermeneutics (Scriptural interpretations), adapting religious texts to the denomination's prescribed world outlook and contrasting them with opposing views, emphasising the concept of *our* [*nash*] — e.g., '*our* beliefs', '*our* rites', '*our* singing' and '*our* language'.

Denominational cultures generally feature three types of traditional texts: (a) texts of religious dogma; (b) more 'secular', folkloric texts; (c) transitional texts, which link the previous two types together, interpreting religious texts according to modes of thinking and styles of language. In the Doukhobor vocal culture, these are represented respectively by (a) psalms, (b) numerous traditional folkloric genres and (c) verses or 'hymns'[1].

In any denominational culture traditional folklore is directly influenced by the regulative function of religious teaching, which determines when, where and how the folkloric presentation will be performed, and by whom; it reduces or transforms the texts of the entire folkloric genre. The means, directions and extent of such determination and transformation depend upon the specifics of the particular denominational culture, especially the nature and strength of individual points of (religious) doctrine.

Two important characteristics of Doukhobor culture

The Doukhobor culture differs from that of the Molokans and Old Believers in two important respects: (1) except for a few phrases and psalms pertaining to Doukhobor commandments,[2] virtually no use is made of original Biblical texts; (2) the texts have been (and still are today) almost exclusively oral rather than written.

These two fundamental attributes determine a range of significant characteristics of Doukhobor culture — for example, a smaller stylistic gap (than in other denominational cultures) between the religious psalms and their folkloric correspondents. An illustration may be seen in studying the so-called *Book of Life of the Doukhobors* [*Zhivotnaia kniga Doukhobortsev*].

It is important to realise that in refusing to worship the Holy Scriptures, the Doukhobors took it upon themselves to create a religious teaching centred around 'God-Man'. In rejecting such concepts as holiness, church ritual and fasting, they in effect took away a large part of Christian symbolism and placed it inside the human being. Unwilling to recognise any 'outward appearance', the Doukhobors turned away from Orthodoxy while continuing to consider themselves Christians. In so doing, they displaced the content of the Bible texts in favour of their own interpretation of Christian symbols, introducing a hermeneutics expressed in the language of the people, folkloric motifs and entire texts drawn from common Russian traditions as well as other Russian religious movements.

The study of the *Book of Life* is indeed a difficult undertaking. From a philologist's point of view such a study must include an examination of the sources from which the psalm texts are drawn, a semantic analysis of their entire content with a description of the most typical semantic structures, including an identification of both links between texts and any inconsistencies discovered in comparing different parts thereof. The study should also include a semantic analysis of the concepts examined, as well as a description of the style pertinent to each text, in which the play of language resulting from sound correlation would merit particular attention. Here I can touch only briefly upon some of the questions associated first of all with the sources, and secondly with the semantic structure involved in the question-and-answer psalms of the Doukhobors.

In regard to the sources, credit is most certainly due Vladimir Dmitrievich Bonch-Bruevich for his tremendous work in collecting materials for and publishing the *Book of Life of the Doukhobors*.[3] In it he identified the biblical sources for many of the Doukhobor texts. Here I shall focus on a few comparisons with the verses of the Old Believers.[4] For example, the text of the Doukhobor Psalm n⁰ 267 — 'We ourselves do not know and people shall not tell us how to live and survive in this world' — is very close to a verse of the Pomortsy sect of the Old Believers[5] which reads: 'I myself do not know how to live in this world.'

The content of Doukhobor Psalm n⁰ 345 — 'Onward to the Jordan Waters' — is shared not only by the Old Believers but also by the Molokans. The theme of escaping from evil and the world of the anti-Christ permeates a great many verses of the Old Believers as well as a number of Doukhobor psalms, e.g. Psalm n⁰ 190 — 'The Evil anti-Christ was born in the year 1008'; Psalm n⁰ 129 — 'The Years are passing throughout the entire world'; Psalm n⁰ 140 — 'Those who will cherish God's touch'; Psalm n⁰ 143 — 'We will shed our tears'. The latter psalm is almost an exact copy of a Beguny[6] verse which reads: 'There is no escape for my slaves either in the mountains, the caves or the remote deserts'.

One of the most frequently sung psalms (n⁰ 158 — 'Look at yourself at the approach of death, perishable man') is in fact a verse written by Stefan Iavorskii (1658–1722), a distinguished Orthodox writer. It is also popular among the Old Believers, who are quite unaware of the opposing views of its author. While its specific provenance remains unclarified, it is possible that this song, along with other verses, found its way to the Doukhobors through the Old Believers.

The most significant text borrowed by the Doukhobors from common Russian sources is undoubtedly Psalm n⁰ 89 — 'Tsar David Aseevich' [see Appendix A], which is still being read and until quite recently sung. It is in fact a variant of a well-known poem about the Book of the Dove; its text is analogous to a text found in Varentsov's collection of Russian spiritual verses[7] — one written down, though not in full, in the village of Verkhotishanka (in Voronezh Province) in the first half of the 19th century.

The complete version of the poem can be divided into three parts: (1) the story of how a huge book which no one could read fell onto Mount Favorsk; (2) the story of Tsar David Oseevich, who relates the contents of the book (describing the arrangement of the Universe and its hierarchy and history) in the form of questions and answers; (3) the story of the conflict between *Krivda* and *Pravda* [Falsehood and Truth] in the Universe. Only the second part remains in the Doukhobor psalm, its questionand-answer format corresponding to the structure of other Doukhobor psalms, which are similarly permeated with the idea of the unity of man, God and the Universe. Both its form and content facilitated its acceptance by the Doukhobors, along with its 'organic' incorporation into their *Book of Life*.

While this psalm speaks about the Universe being created from the Divine flesh,[8] another psalm of similar apocryphal origin (Psalm n⁰ 43 —

'The Meeting of the three holy figures') addresses the issue of the unity of Man and the Universe. In response to the question: 'How many parts does Man consist of?', the answer reads:

> The flesh takes its origin from the earth, the bones from the rock, the veins from the roots, the blood from the water, the hair from the grass, and the eyes from the dew, while the soul is the image of God.

These two psalms, in my opinion, most vividly reflect the Doukhobor way of thinking, in their illustration of such universal concepts as cosmism and pantheism, as well as in the catechism and question-and-answer format. Both have analogous structures and sources in the general folk culture of the Russian people. This format, however, is characteristic of the majority of Doukhobor texts.

The Doukhobors claim that some of the sixty odd questionand-answer psalms[9] (out of a total of some 360) originated in the questions the Doukhobors put before the Synod of the Russian Orthodox Church at the beginning of the 19th century. Upon examining the questions raised, we find that the majority refer to concepts, rather than to situations, and the corresponding answers collectively represent a semantic description of such important Doukhobor concepts as *soul, the cross, fasting, hell, church, wisdom, singing* etc., and of course the fundamental notion of *Spirit Wrestler* [i.e. *Doukhobor*], which is repeatedly clarified throughout the psalms (e.g., 'We serve God with our soul... we fight with our spiritual sword').

Many Doukhobor cultural traditions embody important Christian concepts, interpreted in terms of a teaching which refuses to recognise superficial Christian symbols. While the forty or so questions dealing with *church* seem, at first glance, to relate mainly to physical structure (walls, windows, gates, location, presence of a throne, functions and purposes of different parts of the church), the answers given provide in effect a description highlighting more the purely spiritual aspects of the concept of *church*.

The format of the questions reminds one of a socio-psychological questionnaire, or alternatively a thesaurus outlining the semantic ties among related words in a language. Yu.M. Lotman's study[10] suggests an appropriate division of the questions into those referring to the *structure* of the universe (i.e., *statics*) and those dealing with its *operation* (i.e., *dynamics*). The study bears examination not only by a religious philosopher but also by a specialist in linguistics.

The other major characteristic of Doukhobor culture, as indicated above, is the *oral tradition* of passing on texts (either religious or secular, some of which may have existed initially in written form) from one generation to another over the past two centuries. 'Jesus did not spread out books before him, but affirmed the word by heart', says one of the Doukhobor psalms, while another exhorts: 'Write it in your hearts and proclaim it with your mouths'. In fact, the conscious juxtaposition of 'written' versus 'oral' (as stated by Lotman[11]) serves to determine the type of culture as a whole. Oral culture is distinguished by prediction and prophecy, which permeate Doukhobor texts, especially the didactic psalms.

One function of the oral tradition is to protect the teachings from the threat of external corruption posed (say the Doukhobors) by written sources, by keeping them within the boundaries of the group. Plato describes the advantages of oral teaching as follows:[12]

> During the process of acquiring knowledge it is written in the soul of the disciple, is capable of protecting itself, is able to speak with whomever it chooses and knows how to keep silent.

The function of protection is also fulfilled by the muscial language of the psalms — a language so complex that only those who are part of the culture can fully master it. The unusual length of the syllables, the many inserts between them and the wide range of alternating vowels render the verbal text virtually incomprehensible to the uninitiated — a crucial factor during times of persecution. Hence the conclusion that Doukhobor singing is analogous to coded professional languages. While the need for protection no longer exists, the particular form created therefor remains as a powerful æsthetic influence on Doukhobor culture.

Nevertheless, the oral tradition was partially undermined by an external event around the turn of the century — namely, the publication in 1909 of Bonch-Bruevich's *Book of Life of the Doukhobors* [*Zhivotnaia kniga Dukhobortsev*], which eventually found its way into Doukhobor homes and provided oral memory with a degree of support.[13] In addition, Doukhobor psalms have been written down in numerous notebooks, either from memory (in case one's memory should subsequently fail) or copied from 'Bon-Bruevich' or another notebook. The existence of the *Book of Life* makes it difficult to establish just how the texts of the oral tradition have changed over the years since its publication.

During Sunday services and ceremonies, however, the oral tradition still prevails; nothing is looked up in 'Bon-Bruevich', which remains at home as a handbook. Collective memory of their psalms, which are still considered common property to be shared by all, is still a predominant feature in Doukhobor communities. The most active members may know more than a hundred psalms by heart, but not all three hundred and sixty. In fact, according to one former Gorelovka resident,[14] only about half of the 143 psalms in one particular sequence are in current use in the Bogdanovka region.

It should also be remembered that there are psalms beyond those accounted for in the *Book of Life* and thus the range of psalms recited or sung by the Doukhobors today has yet to be fully documented.

It is interesting to compare reliance on the printed word among the three denominational groups mentioned earlier. In order to keep his religious culture alive, the Old Believer is obliged to carry a trunk of books with him at each migration. The Molokan will be satisfied simply with a Bible, while the Doukhobor, relying on the collective memory of his group, seems to need no literature at all. Hence a weakening of collective cohesiveness resulting from geographical dispersion can be particularly damaging for the Doukhobors and intensify the threat of a potential loss of their culture.

Another group of texts included in Bonch-Bruevich's *Book of Life* are the verses (or 'hymns') of a transitional nature, combining stylistic elements from both psalms and secular folk songs. They are in effect poems on religious and moral themes, a unique poetic interpretation of the main ideas embodied in the psalms. In contrast to the psalms themselves, only a few stanzas of which are actually sung while the rest are recited, the verses are more lyrical and are sung in their entirety. Hundreds of them are still in use by Doukhobors today.

Some verses, in fact, are hardly distinguishable from psalms,[15] while others are very close to secular ballads. One of the old recruiting songs — 'A Young lad was taken from a large household into a regiment' — is called a verse by some who sing it, inasmuch as the sufferings of the 'young lad' from beatings and whippings can be equated with sufferings endured for one's religious convictions. The song ends with these words:

> To interrogation they took him;
> Being at an interrogation is hell,
> Being among the *loyal* is good.

Like the psalms, Doukhobor verses include many 'spiritual' poems still in use today — e.g. the 'Two Lazars', 'Joseph the Wonderful', 'The Tsar is marching into the desert', and 'The Holy Virgin kept walking and walking'. A number of these poems are common to other denominational groups; for example, 'Ah, you doves' (about the parting of the soul from the body) used for weddings and funerals is also popular with the

Molokans, while another wedding verse — 'The Young man walked and passed by' — is actually taken from an Old-Believers poem about a monk. And, like folkloric works, the verses are known in a multitude of versions.

It may be seen, then, that the Doukhobor culture presents a fairly smooth transition from religious texts to secular folklore. One may also note the influence of religious teachings on secular repertoire, for example, in the erstwhile ban[16] on musical instruments (as with the Molokans) and on any songs involving dancing or other physical movement; another effect is seen in the structure of wedding rites and the repertoire of permissible wedding texts. The various types of texts were united by their common oral expression, which facilitated the preservation of traditional folklore by stimulating the development and enhancement of collective memory.

The Doukhobor folk ballad

One genre which has been rather underrepresented of late in general Russian culture but is still flourishing in the Doukhobor environment is that of the *folk ballad,* usually associated (in both style and content) with southern Russia. Over the course of a two-week visit with the Doukhobors in 1985 I was able to make more than forty transcripts of 18 ballad themes, a number of which have been popular throughout Russia itself — including, for example, 'A Young girl was washing on a steep bank' (telling the story of a husband who tormented his wife to death), the Cossack ballad 'An Argument between the Eagle and the Horse' and the south-Russian ballads 'My brother is being conscripted' and 'Our prince has gone away'.

A particularly notable find was the ballad 'Tsar David and his daughter Alena',[17] a version of a similarly named ballad dating from the first half of the 19th century in Orenburg Province, originally published in Bessonov's collection of spiritual poems[18] and later in a collection of ballads. It may be said that the Doukhobor text, an epic tale of the tragic fate of Alena, married off to her own brother, is in no way artistically inferior to the earlier version.

Pantheism, cosmism and 'folk Christianity'

Another example of the smooth transition from psalms to traditional folkloric genres can be seen in the apocryphal 'Dream of the Virgin Mary', as well as in the texts of prayers. A number of prayers parallel the psalms and include well-known Christian prayers such as the Lord's Prayer [*Otche nash*], customarily recited before supper. Other prayers are in the nature of exorcisms, which, in contrast to church ideology, Doukhoborism does not necessarily deem an expression to be avoided, provided the intent is to help rather than harm the individual. In fact, the protection of man is a universal element permeating both their psalms and prayers. In preparing for travel, for example, the Doukhobors often recite the following prayer:

> God's slave is getting ready to set out on a journey, on the road, and he is protected by the sky and the earth, by the moon in heaven, by the red sun, by the bright moon and by the multitude of stars.

While in prayers like this the Doukhobors appear to be drawing heavily upon the magical language of general Russian folklore, it should be noted that they take care to extract only those texts capable of most vividly describing the unity between man and nature. Even in reference to preparations for going to a purely social institution such as a court of law, they evoke a wide range of both living and inanimate entities in seeking protection from injustice:

> Please, God, give your blessings to my heart. Please, God, give your blessings to the hearts of the lions; with the eyes of the eagle I look away, with the strength of a bear I shall fight back. As smoothly as the feather glides over the water, so smooth should it be for God's slave before the court. Amen, Amen, Amen.

Religious sentiment, however, is counterbalanced among the Doukhobors (as in many segments of the Russian population at large) by a strong conviction in the influence of cosmic powers, expressed in superstition and a belief in omens. Certain building and agricultural activities are associated positively or negatively with phases of the moon, for example:

- in construction, foundations are to be laid during a full moon;
- brick manure [*kiziak*] should not be cut during a new moon or it will produce worms;
- cattle are best slaughtered during a full moon, so that the bones will be filled with meat and the taste will be better;
- wedding ceremonies should not be held when the full moon begins to wane or the marriage will not be happy and possibly be childless.

Thus it is seen how the most diverse Doukhobor texts are permeated by both pantheism and cosmism. The eschatalogical orientation of many of the dogmatic psalms in which excerpts from St John's Revelation were set to music can also be seen in Doukhobors' statements on the end-of--the-world superstition; the latter are not unlike the eschatalogical premonitions and mysteries of the Old Believers and other sects (electrical wires linked to tales of an iron spider web wrapped around the earth, airplanes associated with myths of iron birds flying above the skies, and so forth).

However, certain discrepancies may be observed between Doukhobor ideology and Doukhobor people's actual perceptions of theological concepts. Some of the latter actually have more in common with the Russian Orthodox roots from which Doukhoborism originally sprang — perceptions usually classified as 'folk Orthodoxy', although when the Doukhobors and Molokans are included, the term might well be broadened to 'folk Christianity'. For example, while a Doukhobor psalm describes hell simply as 'people who do not know light and in whom evil spirits dwell', one woman who had heard the psalm many times offered a description suggesting much more the Orthodox view of hell as a specific location where sinners receive their punishment: 'Hell? Do you know how they are going to fry you for the sins you have committed!'

General observations

In conclusion, I should like to emphasise that this study is only the beginning of a proper investigation into the oral Doukhobor culture. Several important steps lie ahead: (a) compiling an index of the psalms functional in various local cultures (including the Doukhobors of Dzhavakhetiia and their Tula relatives, those in the Rostov area and those who reside in Canada); (b) describing as fully as possible the contemporary folkloric repertoire of the Doukhobors; (c) undertaking an exhaustive study of Doukhobor dialects. These steps are essential if we are to learn how a marginal denominational culture manages to survive the many obstacles historical circumstances have placed in its way. It is the task of the philologist to show how the traditional system of values which constitutes the spiritual basis of the culture is being reproduced or transformed in the widest possible range of texts, be they collective or individual, traditional or contemporary.

Appendix: A:
Doukhobor Psalm 'Tsar David Oseevich'[19]

I will tell you from my ancient memory,
I have the Book of Doves,
The width of the book is three cubits,
The height of the book is six cubits.
On it is written the words:
The wide world comes from the heart of our Lord:
The red sun from His face;
The bright moon from His eyes;
The parts of the stars are from his word;
Mount Zion is here because
Our Lord God blessed us to live on it;
The ocean-sea is here because
It embraced the entire wide world;
The whale-fish is here because
The entire world rests on it;
Plakun trava is here because
It floats against the current of the water;
The fearful owl-bird is here because
It sits on the sea, on the Ocean;
It lays its eggs in the sea, it rears its
children from the sea;
The cypress tree is here because
Jesus Christ Himself was crucified on it.

Appendix B:
Doukhobor verse 'There once lived two brothers'[21]

There once lived two brothers:
The elder was a rich man,
And the younger was a poor man.
The poor man was the beggar Lazarus.

Lazarus once went to his brother:
'My brother, my brother, you a rich man,
Create a good deed for me, my brother, on this earth,
Bread or salt to feed the soul.'

That rich man came out onto a new porch,
The rich man cried out in a loud voice:
'What kind of new brother are you to me?
I have never had such brothers from birth.
I have brothers such as I.'
They drink and eat sweetly and walk tall,
They wear velvet and satin on their shouldres,
They sail the sea in boats,
While your brothers are table dogs.

Appendix C:
Doukhobor song 'How they took our brother'[22]

How they took our brother to be a soldier;
There was no one to weep profusely over him;
There were just he and three sisters in the family.
The three sisters felt sorry for him.
The first sister led out the horse,
The second sister brought the saddle,
The third sister came out with the brother.
She came out with the brother and lamented:
'O, brother, our brother, you are all we have,
You are all we have, have pity on us.'

'O, my sister, how foolish you are!
Go you to the River Danube,
Take some sand from the water's edge
And sprinkle the sand over the stones,
And get up earlier and water them more often,
And when that sand begins to sprout,
Then your brother will come home.'

[*]Based on a translation from Russian provided by the Translation Bureau, Department of Secretary of State, Canada.

[23]The term *hymns* is used among the Doukhobors in Canada.

[24]These are an almost literal repetition of corresponding Bible verses.

[25]See V.D. Bonch-Bruevich's materials on the history and study of Russian sectarianism and the schism. *Zhivotnaia kniga Doukhbortsev* [The Book of Life of the Doukhobors], 3rd ed. Winnipeg, 1954.

[26]In both cases the texts I transcribed in the course of my field-trips are still part of current living tradition.

[27]*Pomortsy* (lit. 'coastal dwellers') — a sect which emerged in Karelia (near what is now the Gulf of Finland) at the end of the 17th-century; the sect at first rejected marriage and prayer for the tsar; some of its members later came to accept marriage and formed a new subgroup.

[28]*Beguny* (lit. 'Runners') — a sect dating from the latter part of the 18th century whose members were encouraged to 'run' away rather than perform military service or other state obligations.

[29]V. Varentsov, *A Collection of Russian spiritual verses*. 1960, pp. 16–17.

[30]Note especially the lines: 'The wide world comes from the heart of our Lord, the red sun from His face, and the bright moon from His eyes'.

[31]It should be noted that this format is also present, even if implicitly, in a number of the so-called 'dogmatic' psalms.

[32]See Yu.M. Lotman, *On the metalanguage of typological descriptions of culture: Works on systems of symbols*. 1969.

[33]See Yu.M. Lotman, *A few thoughts on the typology of culture: the Languages of culture and the problems of transference*. Moscow, 1987.

[34]Plato, *Collected works*. Moscow, 1970, vol. 2, p. 218.

[35]During my first visit to Gorelovka a woman who was reciting one the psalms for me suddenly stopped and said: 'I've forgotten the line. Let me go look it up in Bon-Bruevich' [a common Doukhobor pronunciation of *Bonch-Bruevich*].

[36]The informant, V.M. Gololobov, currently residing in the village of Arkhangel'sk in the Tula Oblast (south of Moscow), proceeded to name the people who knew this or that psalm, for example, 'This is Petrunina's psalm, this one is Sarrin's', and so forth.

[37]This is sometimes noted by the performers themselves, for example, in the verse 'A Man of convictions'.

[38]No longer in effect.

[39]In 1985 I transcribed this particular ballad twice: once as recited by Polina Grigor'evna Terekhova of Orlovka, and then by a group in the village of Efremovka. An excerpt from another ballad performed by Terekhova was included in the two-record album *Poiut Dukhobortsy Dzhavakhetii* [Doukhobors of Dzhavakhetiia sing], which I prepared for the 150th anniversary (in 1991) of the migration of the Doukhobors to the Caucasus. Unfortunately it was not released until two years later (by a joint Russian-American venture known as Aprelevka Sound Inc. — #C30 30693 009), and that largely due to the heroic efforts of Doukhobor activists, especially Aleksei Kinakin, president of the Religious Organisation of the United Doukhobors of Russia. The full text of the ballad with musical notation was recently published in the journal *The Living Past*.

[40]See P. Bessonov, *The Migrating cripples*. 1961–63.

[41]Transcribed by S.E. Nikitina in May 1985 in the village of Spasovka (in the Bogdanovka region of Georgia); performed by Melaniia Fedorovna Trokhimenkova (76, illiterate) and Evdokiia Andreevna Miroshnikova (80, semi-literate). They sang four stanzas, then the entire psalm was recited by Evdokiia Miroshnikova.

[42]*Plakun trava* — an ancient grass that could float against the water current. It is the grass that Jesus of Nazareth is said to have grown and which he used metaphorically to describe his true followers (notation by musicologist N. Danchenkova).

[43]Transcribed by S.E. Nikitina in May 1985 in the village of Orlovka (Bogdanovka region); performed by Polina Grigor'evna Terekhova (53, blind since age 3) and Praskov'ia Nikolaevna Kalmykova (75). They sang three stanzas and then Polina Terekhova recited. Genre identified by N. Danchenkova.

[44]Transcribed by S.E. Nikitina in May 1985 in the village of Spasovka; performed by Melaniia Fedorovna Trokhimenkova and Evdokiia Andreevna Miroshnikova. They sang all except the last five lines and then Melaniia Trokhimenkova recited. Genre identified by N. Danchenkova.

One island — two worlds

Arnie Weeks

Editor's Note: The family described in this paper has been the object of abuse from various sects and others who do not agree with its philosophy or lifestyle. As a condition of allowing their lives to be written about, the family has inisisted that their surname not be used or their current location revealed. The story gives some insight into the workings of an isolated zealot community in British Columbia in the late 1940s and 1950s.

Introduction

I was born on Vancouver Island in the City of Nanaimo (B.C.) in 1941. While my parents were also Canadian-born, my ancestors had originally come from Cornwall and Yorkshire (England) to work in the British Columbia coal mines. I grew up in a rather stern working-class world (some would call it Victorian), but events happened during my childhood that would introduce me to quite another world — that of the Doukhobors — a world which subconsciously influenced my whole career and adult life and helped make me the man that I am today.

My first vivid memories of my home on Vancouver Island date from the autumn of 1945 when long lines of marching soldiers, trucks and tanks came up my street. My father had taken me to the front verandah of our home and put me on his shoulders so I could watch the victorious Canadian army returning to its Nanaimo base from Europe and the Pacific at the end of the Second World War. Residents celebrated with fireworks and shotgun blasts into the air and many noisy parties. It took several weeks for the city to return to normal.

My first introduction to the Doukhobors

It was during this period of excitement that my father, Jack Weeks, received an urgent telephone call from his Uncle Edward (I also called him 'Uncle Ed'), who was then living in a cabin somewhere near Errington on the Parksville–Alberni highway. Equipped with two shotguns and two pockets of shells, my father and I set out in the direction of Edward's cabin, stopping along the way to pick up my Uncle Gordon. It turned out that some rowdy people had surrounded a nearby cabin and were threatening to set it ablaze with a family inside. The men's angry shouts and the women's screams sent shivers through my entire body and I grabbed hold of my father's leg for security.

As far as I can recall, the B.C. Provincial Police were supposed to patrol the area but were not present. The extremely angry mob, many of them drunk, were accusing the family in the cabin of being traitors to Canada because their sons had refused to go off and fight in the Second World War. They pelted the cabin with rocks, broke their windows and yelled: 'Burn them out!'. In the years to come, the *Svobodniki* [Sons of Freedom] who lived nearby would be accused of burning their own homes, but obviously they had models to follow.[1]

Uncle Ed told me to stay with my father while he approached the family's cabin with a shotgun. He stood in the doorway, faced the mob and fired into the air. He loaded two more shells and pointed his gun at the crowd. They dispersed, knowing his reputation as a serious and experienced woodsman, but not before Uncle gave them a lecture, explaining that this family's religious beliefs did not permit them to fight and that they were good, decent, hardworking people who should be left alone as they had caused no harm to anyone. When it began to rain heavily, everyone left the area. While I did not get to meet the family in the cabin at that time, I sensed why Uncle Edward was protecting them. Despite a violent temper, he was essentially a peaceful man, well acquainted with his Bible. While he lived alone unmarried and never held a job for more than a few months at at time, he was somehow respected.

Later in life I was to learn that my own family had emigrated to Canada because their ancestors had been persecuted for their ancient Cornish-Celtic Catholic faith. The only crime of these *recusants,* as they were called, was that they refused to renounce the Pope and convert to the Church of England.

My first meeting with a Doukhobor family

It was only two years later, in the fall of 1947, that I was to learn who the people in the cabin were and what they were really like. My father and I were visiting my Uncle Ed on the forested slopes of Mount Arrowsmith and I was learning to fish for trout. My father was hunting deer in a small meadow when suddenly a shot rang out and a buck fell to the ground.

Within minutes a little blonde, blue-eyed girl appeared, carrying a white rabbit in her arms. Her hair was done up in a long braid; she wore a white blouse, a blue dress with a white daisy print, partly covered by a white apron, and a white kerchief on her head. She was barefoot, but her father who soon arrived was wearing felt boots which he called *sapozhki*.

I introduced myself to the little girl but she did not understand English very well and spoke another language. Her father introduced her as *Katia* and himself as *Semyon*. He was visibly upset at the death of the deer because his daughter had been feeding it for years as a pet.

An argument broke out between my father and Semyon over the deer and my father struck Semyon across the face. Instead of striking back, Semyon turned his other cheek and asked my father to hit him again. At this point my Uncle Edward stepped in and offered to find another deer for the little girl (which he soon did).

Taking the dead deer back to Nanaimo, my father cut it up for venison dinners. He boasted how he had killed a fine buck and even mounted the antlers on the garage as a souvenir. When my parents died years later (in 1980), I burnt the antlers. My father's gun collection, left to my son, was eventually destroyed as well.

The following summer, when I had completed my first year in school and was on holiday at my Uncle Edward's, he took me to the family's cabin. There I learnt that Katia did not attend school but was being taught by her father to speak, read and write in Russian. Her older brother *Petia* (Peter) was helping her with English. I also met her mother *Anna* and *Grandmother Sonia*. *Grandfather Andrei* was quite old and spent most of his time in the garden. As he grew older and could no longer leave his bed, the entire family gladly cared for him. I was amazed by this love for older people — such a sharp contrast to the way much of my world treats its senior citizens. He would always ask me to tell him of my recent doings and I would obligingly sit by his bedside, hold his hand and tell him what had happened in my life since our last meeting.

One day in the spring of 1949 my father and mother took me to see Uncle Edward, whom we eventually found at Semyon's cabin, recovering from an illness brought on by drinking bad liquor (Uncle Edward used to make his own whisky or buy it from a local hermit). Under Anna's care — which included steam-baths in the *bania* [a Russian sauna][2] and gallons of tea made with herbs Anna had collected in the forest — my uncle's health greatly improved.

The *bania* was located directly behind the cabin, which Semyon called an *izba*. Beside it was a woodshed and a stable for goats and horses. A short distance away was a smaller cabin, or *izbushka* [little hut], their original dwelling they had built in the winter of 1924,[3] but which now served as a temporary refuge for the *stranniki* — the religious wanderers who frequently visited their home. Many of their visitors, in fact, were holy men who wandered from one person's home to another, always finding a welcome. They were carrying on a centuries-old tradition from tsarist Russia, where pilgrims would wander from one holy place to the next, visiting shrines of saints, relics and icons, all in the quest for salvation.[4]

Grandmother Sonia told me that their home on Vancouver Island resembled the type of *izba* their ancestors had lived in around the *Zatatarskoe boloto* [Zatatar Marsh] in Siberia, where the great-grandparents had come from. The only difference was that the Canadian variant had two rooms whereas in Siberia they had had to make do with only one.

The central feature of the *izba* was the *pech'* [stove/oven], a large structure covered with wooden boards, on which the family slept in their *odeialki* [eiderdown quilts]. Around the walls were some wooden benches. In the middle of the floor stood a large wooden table surrounded by small three-legged stools. I was told this was a Tatar idea borrowed originally from China; the stools had the advantage of not rocking back and forth if one leg were short (as would a four-legged chair).

The table rested on a well-worn grey rug, which in turn covered a trap door leading to a cellar for storing foodstuffs. One corner of the house was left vacant. Clothes were hung along one wall. Their woollen coats were made with loops and wooden pegs held on with knots. Their *rubashki* [shirts] were tied by string made from old flour sacks.

In one corner were hung twelve black-and-white *kartinki* [pictures], depicting (in clockwise order) the early years of the family's ancestors before the *raskol* [schism] in the Russian Orthodox Church (one of the events leading to the founding of the Doukhobor sect). Years later I would learn that in Russian Orthodox homes this was the corner reserved for the icon, symbolising the religious messages of the Bible.

One day in 1952 my Uncle Ed telephoned my father in Nanaimo from a small sawmill in the bush where Semyon worked part-time[5]. Semyon was upset that local officials accompanied by police with dogs were searching for his son and daughter because they had not been to public school for months. In fact, Uncle Ed had hidden both children in an old barn, where he was looking after them. The children were never discovered, even by the police dogs, because my uncle had had them cross and walk up and down a local creek so many times that the dogs could not pick up their scent. Uncle Ed was an outstanding woodsman and could live in the bush all alone for months, as he frequently did when he went to the west coast of the Island to prospect for gold in the many creeks there.

Even though the children were being taught to speak, read and write English in their *izba,* the concept of home schooling accepted in many provinces today was not accepted then. When I asked why his family had rejected the public school system I was told that, by tradition, the Doukhobors did not trust the established churches and government who justified killing other people in time of war. The Doukhobors believed it was a sin to kill another person since God resided in all persons and creatures. They perceived the secular teachings of our schools as being in conflict with this belief.

Katia would celebrate the arrival of spring by picking a bouquet of curly lilies. She gathered strawberries from the neighbouring field to make home-made jam, which Russians often use in tea in place of sugar. Jam was also made from the gooseberry plants that grew behind the cabin, and wild huckleberries grew on rotten tree stumps — a legacy of the logging industry of many years before. In summer Katia and I would pick plums and apples from old abandoned orchards from which she and her mother would make plum jam and apple sauce.

I also remember accompanying the family to Englishman's River to harvest licorice root. Sacks of the entire plant were gathered, and the extracted essence of the root was used in making candy and home medicines. The family did not have a well; they simply carried wooden buckets of water from the crystal clear stream next to their cabin. And while there were many animals around the cabin, these people were vegetarians.

I was invited to stay for supper on many occasions. A loaf of home--made black bread sat on the table with a small wooden bowl full of salt on top of it.[6] Katia's mother baked fresh bread almost daily in a special oven behind the cabin. After prayers, each person would break the bread and put a pinch of salt on it, eat warm vegetable borshch with sour cream, and drink lots of hot tea. The two main food dressings were sour cream and garlic.

It appears to me that the garlic served them well as a fine preventative medicine (even though to this day I cannot endure its smell). But through the many years that I knew the family closely, I never once saw any of the sick with the common cold or any other malady.

My first lesson in Doukhobor history

After supper Anna would bring me a stool and place it in the corner where the twelve *kartinki* were hung. Starting with the first picture, she would begin telling me the early history of her people, and continued picture by picture (or, as it turned out in retrospect, chapter by chapter). Through the summers which followed I learnt a great deal about the family and their history from the *kartinki*. Each summer Sonia, Semyon or Anna would recount two or three chapters of their history based on these pictures. The following year I would recite for hours what I had learnt, until I could tell their whole story almost entirely from memory. These kind and simple people who befriended me taught me a great deal, and many of their lessons sank into my subconsciousness without my realising it. The preparation of this article is my way of honouring them for the values they taught me.

In the summers of 1953–55 Anna's son Peter began to teach me how to play the balalaika, along with some simple Russian folk songs.

It was during the summer of 1955 that Grandfather Andrei passed away in the home he had built with his own bare hands. The family obeyed his wishes and did not let him die in the unfamiliar surroundings of a hospital. Before the burial his widow, following an old superstition, turned a mirror to face the wall. Semyon thought it was a silly custom, but Anna settled the argument by simply putting a cloth over the mirror. Semyon explained the ancient superstition, dating from pre-Christianity times in Old Russia, which held that a dying person's soul could take a living person's reflection with it, and thus another person might die shortly afterward. After Grandfather's burial, the cloth was removed from the mirror.

Five years later Katia visited me on the University of British Columbia campus; she was on her way to the Kootenays to visit her fiancé, a young man named Sasha. She mentioned her brother Peter was going to Paraguay to seek out a spiritual leader there and search for long-lost relatives. When I asked about the rest of her family on the Island, she told me that her Grandmother Sonia had just passed away. Her mother Anna had heard a dog howl the night before.

The next day I decided to pay a visit to the family. I took the ferry to Nanaimo, borrowed my father's car and drove to the cabin, which, much to my surprise, was still being lit by candles; there was no electrical hook-up (although they had acquired a battery radio). The same mirror was covered by a cloth.

People had come from as far away as the B.C. interior to view Grandmother's body and mourn her passing. Her casket was then removed and buried behind the cabin with her gooseberries. Her son Peter bade farewell. Anna and a small choir of five or six girls sang religious songs and a lament. After the burial service Anna swept the house, opening all the windows and doors until sunset. Forty days later a prayer session was held for the grandmother — an old Russian Orthodox custom (it appears that not everything was discarded from the old faith when they became fundamentalists).

During that same forty-day period, however, the family was visited by police and government officials who objected to their custom of private burials. My parents and uncles contributed money toward the family's legal expenses. I do not recall the outcome. I only know that shortly afterward an old hermit from Englishman's River helped the family abandon the cabin and move closer to Parksville.

The Family's history and religious beliefs

The ancestral family had originally settled as runaway serfs in Prokovskoe Selo (a village on the Tura River in Western Siberia) in the late 16th century, after the Cossack Yermak had opened up the land. For several centuries their ancestors lived near the *Zatatarskoe boloto,* a land of marshes and old pine trees — a refuge for the so-called *neschastnye* [lit. 'unfortunates'], i.e., people hiding from the law.

According to other sources I have read, this area was also famous for ancient pagan remnants such as *kolduny* [wizards] and *khvostiteli* ['broomstick travellers']. Once when I made fun of such beliefs, Katia chided me by reminding me that my world celebrated a pagan custom of its own (called *Hallowe'en*) with lit pumpkins and images of witches riding broomsticks.

Semyon took pains to point out that his ancestors in Siberia were 'free men' — not like the relatives they had left behind in Old Russia who were still serfs, bound to the land. In Siberia their land was controlled by the community and allocated to individual farmers by the community *duma,* or council of elders. There were no fences separating the farmers' allotments, only a fence around the communal pasture itself. The village consisted of long rows of unpainted log houses with the cracks or chinks stuffed with straw, moss, clay or dung. This was essentially the same kind of communal living the family practised later as Doukhobors in Canada.

Community life among the Doukhobors was regulated according to the 'saints' days', religious festivals and seasons of the year. One of the traditions observed by the family occurred at the end of June: they would tie a bundle of straw (*yarilo*) together on a board, set it alight and let it float down the stream. This was not so much a religious custom, I was told by Semyon and Peter, as a sign of respect for their ancestors; the *yarilo* symbolised the closeness of man to agriculture and the coming harvest.

In the 17th century their ancestors were among those classified as *ikonobortsy* [icon wrestlers] because they did not believe in the Russian Orthodox practice of icon worship. The group arose initially out of a larger movement known as the *Staroobriadtsy*, or 'Old Believers', who refused to accept the changes to the Old Church Slavonic Bible and liturgy imposed by the then Orthodox Patriarch Nikon.[7] Yet another reform rejected by the 'Old Believers' was making the sign of the cross with three fingers instead of two.

The resulting *raskol* [schism] in the church ushered in a long period of persecution and tragic deaths of millions of simple people. Thousands fled to Siberia where they either kept the 'Old Believer' traditions or formed new sects that relied on fundamentalism and rejected ritual. Among the latter were the groups that came to be known as *Bozhie liudi* [lit. 'God's people'], the *Molokane*, the *Baptisty* and the *Dukhobortsy*.

Grandmother Sonia explained that the name *Dukhobortsy* (literally, 'Spirit-wrestlers') symbolised this people's constant struggle to maintain a spiritual way of life, in harmony with a God-created universe. According to one of the sect leaders, Danila Philippov,[8] whose teachings served as an inspiration to the family, the faithful could not rely on icons or liturgy or the biblical translations and interpretations of the Orthodox clergy; God and salvation were to be found only through listening to the divine voice within the heart of the individual believer. The church and state were seen as equally corrupt and virtually indivisible. Further, the Doukhobors were strong believers in pacifism: since all creatures were a part of God, no one should kill another living creature. This belief in particular made them targets of harassment, beatings and other acts of violence (a trend which still prevailed, as we have seen, among the Doukhobors of Vancouver Island after the Second World War).

In the early 1800s, in an effort to physically separate them from Orthodox Russians, the Doukhobors and other sects were relocated from their ancestral homes to the Crimæa, to an area known as *Molochnye vody* [Milky Waters]. In the 1840s it was decided to remove them even further afield, this time to the Caucasus, where they were settled in areas such as Kars, Elizavetpol and Tiflis (in Georgia) and were able to practise their communal lifestyle more or less independently for about fifty years.

Toward the end of the century a man named *Peter V. Verigin* (known as 'the Lordly'[9]) became the Doukhobor leader. Like his predecessor, *Lukeria Kalmykova*, he stressed the need to live like the early Christians, who held all wealth and property in common. (Were the Doukhobors the first Russian 'communists'?). When the government required them to accept firearms to defend imperial Russia against the rebellious Tatars, the Doukhobors responded by burning their rifles in defiance. The Russian Cossacks in turn unleashed a terrible revenge against the sect (not unlike the later pogroms against the Jews) and reduced their members to extreme poverty.

At this point help came to the Doukhobors from a variety of sources: the Quakers, Prince Petr Kropotkin, and Count Lev Tolstoy, who used the earnings from his novel *Resurrection* to help the Doukhobors find new homes in Canada. By 1899, thousands of them had begun to settle in Saskatchewan, where the Canadian government set land aside for them and granted them exemption from military service.

Peter V. Verigin joined his followers in Canada in December 1902, after his release from exile. He died tragically in a train explosion in the B.C. interior in 1924. Many Doukhobors blamed his death on splinter groups, but no one was ever arrested. It was a disagreement with his followers that brought Andrei and Sonia and their family to Vancouver Island that same year.[10] Moreover, they found the Island wilderness to be conducive to experiencing true Christian spirituality, free from pressure from the outside world.

They believed that every living creature was part of a great universe where we are all interconnected through God the Creator. Such a belief has recently found an echo in physicists' discoveries that all the elements present in our bodies come from stars which evolved as supernova — millions, if not billions of years ago. It appears these simple people possessed knowledge far in advance of their time.

While they did not approve of alcoholic drinks and often spoke of the suffering and poverty it had caused in old Russia, it could be argued that the raspberry juice they prepared in summer did develop a 'fizz' and was mildly alcoholic. However, I do not believe the family was even aware of this minor inconsistency. (My aunt Annie once told me she was opposed to liquor but drank wines made from local berries — wines I later discovered to contain at least 11% alcohol.) Even though Uncle Edward was a heavy drinker, Semyon's family still accepted him; Semyon's son Peter jokingly confessed: 'God loves drunks, fools and gypsies!'

As an outsider to the Doukhobor faith, I perceived their generous hospitality as a significant feature of their lives, second only to their pacifism, respect for all creation and a simple lifestyle in tune with God and the universe.

Only once did I witness an incident where visitors were asked to leave. One day while a group of three *stranniki* (holy wanderers) were at the family table, the oldest of the group took a spoonful of soup from his wooden bowl and blessed it; after taking a sip from it, he passed it to the other visitors around the table in what I understood as a form of communion. The family, however, did not participate, and Semyon asked the men to leave, calling them 'holy fools'.

Once every three months (at the beginning of a season) the parents would go to Hilliers, the nearest village, to shop at Goslin's Store. The children would play with other children from the Stockade built by the local *Svobodniki* ('Sons of Freedom'). The parents, however, would not speak to the *Svobodniki* adults; the atmosphere seemed to be one of quiet, polite hostility.

In retrospect

In 1988 I visited Vancouver Island and attempted to reestablish contact with the family. I managed to locate Peter, who was afraid to talk to me at first. But once I explained that I had left the government service because of a deep personal mistrust of the system and my own failing health, he welcomed me with a bear hug and tears flowed down my cheeks.

In 1992 I went back to Peter's home and asked him if I could write about his family. He agreed on the condition that I respect their privacy and not use their surname. He told me that many of the old animosities had not yet been extinguished, and that they were still experiencing problems with various sects and individuals.

That same year I discovered an interesting echo of the Doukhobor approach to life in a series of tapes by an American psychologist, Dr Wayne Dyer, entitled: *The Universe within you — your secret source of strength*. According to Dr Dyer, if you learn the secret strength within yourself, you can deal with everyone and everything. Such self--knowledge leads to true freedom and success, which is not measured by money or possessions but by the satisfaction derived from living life every day. While I had not stayed with the family since 1959, I am still hearing truths similar to these taught by my Doukhobor friends in the 1990s — truths I had lost sight of in the hustle and bustle of the money-oriented, materialistic world I have lived in for so many years.

Writing about my experiences with the Doukhobors has given me an opportunity to rediscover a lifestyle and values that I deeply admire. Henry David Thoreau once said: 'It takes two to speak the truth — one to speak and another to hear.' Somewhere along the road of life I stopped listening.

My Uncle Ed once said that 'when you begin to feel that you know everything' — that is the first sign that you have a lot to learn. Perhaps all those who live and work in my world will learn some new lessons, like the ones I have been rediscovering from my childhood on one Island — but two different worlds.

[1]It also seems ironic that several centuries earlier the Old Believers of ancient Russia had locked themselves in their wooden churches and set them ablaze so that they all perished.

[2]The men would go to the *bania* first and sit there for at least an hour completely naked, laughing and singing songs. They would hit each other's backs with cedar boughs, and then go for a swim in the clear, cold creek that ran beside the cabin. Once the men had finished, the women would follow the same routine.

[3]I later learnt that my Uncle Ed had helped them build that first cabin, using only a double-bladed axe, a nine-foot cross-cut saw and wooden pegs for nails. Only logs from windfalls were used, since the family did not believe in cutting down living trees unless absolute necessary.

[4]The *stranniki* could tell stories for hours on end about how relatives and friends were faring in faraway places (such as the Kootenays or Paraguay). They seemed to have phenomenal memories, memorising huge sections of the Old and New Testaments; I never noticed them carrying notes or money

[5]I had met him before at this sawmill and was amazed that he never took his gloves off. When I asked him about that one day as we were driving home, he said that he had to touch large pieces of metal (such as handles, rollers and saws), and metal to him was 'a tool of the devil').

[6]A traditional Russian symbol of hospitality — *ed.*

[7]To prevent tampering with the ancient religious texts, many of the original *ikonobortsy* began to memorise and recite by heart large sections of the New Testament — a tradition which the Doukhobors of Vancouver Island were still tenaciously following some three hundred years later.

[8]*Danila Philippov* — a peasant from Kostroma and an army deserter, who believed that that there was no barrier between the human and the divine so that man could become literally The Lord Incarnate.

[9]The Russian term is *Gospodnii,* meaning 'belonging to the Lord' — *ed.*

[10]In 1958, quite by chance, I met an old man in front of the Rod and Gun Hotel in Parksville, who asked me for a ride to the ferry wharf in Nanaimo. When I mentioned visiting my Doukhobor friends during our conversation along the way, he claimed to know the family. As a boy living near Hilliers he had heard a rumour that the family had been accused of offering shelter to an individual accused of complicity in Peter V. Verigin's death. There had ensued an endless debate among the community over whether the Good Samaritan principle outweighed that of loyalty to one's leader; when the debate failed to be resolved, the family separated themselves from the rest of the community.

Doukhobor psalms and their auditory function*

Kenneth Peacock

The study of sectarian folk music of European origin raises some problems not usually encountered in secular folk-music research. Most of the folk cultures we study exist within the established framework of state-approved religious institutions. We do not ordinarily conduct ersearch on the music and liturgy of the established churches, but confine our attention to those comparatively few religious items of folk origin. However, the strong religious orientations of some sectarian cultures compels us to change our emphasis: we find ourselves dealing primarily with religious materials, while the secular aspects of the research (though still important in some aspects) are of a secondary nature. Since very little research has been done on the music and oral literature of the Doukhobors, it might be useful to examine very briefly their early historical background.

The Doukhobors were originally a Russian peasant sect whose fundamentalist Christian beliefs branded them as heretics in the eyes of the Russian Orthodox Church. The derisive nickname *Dukhobortsy,* or 'Spirit-Wrestlers', was first applied to them by Archbishop Amvrosii in 1785, although the sect as such had been in existence at least a century before that. Indeed, the Doukhobors had inherited many of their beliefs from several proto-Doukhobor sects, some of which had emerged much earlier. Most recent were the *Khlisty,* or 'Self-Lashers' of the mid-seventeenth century and the *Starovery,* or 'believers in the old ways', who were unmercifully persecuted during the reign of Peter the Great from 1672 to 1725. One of the earliest sectarian heresies was recorded in 1471 in the city of Novgorod. The adherents of this so-called 'Isrælite' cult openly professed disbelief in the efficacy of worshipping icons, in the supernatural birth of Christ through the Virgin Mary and in the doctrine of the Trinity of the Godhead. It is remarkable that such heresies, currently under fervent dispute in Western churches, should have emerged in Russia at least five hundred years ago. Even more remarkable is the fact that these and other beliefs are almost identical with those of the Bogomil doctrine that originated in Bulgaria in the tenth century and subsequently spread into southern Russia during the eleventh (see Edgerton, 1988 and 1989). The teachings of the Bogomils, in turn, are thought to be derived in part from the Manichean doctrines that emanated from Persia in the third century A.D. (Lavrin, 1929).

The extent to which Doukhoborism has been influenced by these early fundamentalist cults remains to be established. In the case of Bogomil beliefs and practices, the influence appears to be considerable. However, conclusive evidence will depend upon comparative studies between Doukhobor oral literature and the Slavonic texts underlying our knowledge of the Bogomil doctrines. Preliminary examination of the five hundred Doukhobor songs I recorded in the 1970s for the National Museum of Canada indicates a bewildering variety of textual and musical influences, which will be sorted out only after the most assiduous research on various levels.

In the meantime, I have established a few guidelines for the study of this material which I used in my Museum publication (Peacock, 1970). Material of predominantly Doukhobor origin includes psalms as well as early, transitional, contemporary and historical hymns. Non-Doukhobor religious material includes sectarian hymns (borrowed from other Russian sects like the Molokans and New Israelites) and interdenominational hymns (borrowed from Western Protestant groups like the Mennonites). Secular songs are of three types: (1) folk songs absorbed directly from Russian tradition; (2) folk songs learnt from Soviet recordings; (3) a potpourri of literary materials by poets like Lermontov, whose writings, by the way, are popular among the Doukhobors, probably because he also was banished to the Caucasus in the nineteenth century.

Since space does not permit me to discuss any of the categories in detail, I should like to make a few general observations on Doukhobor culture using just one category — the *psalms* — as a kind of auditory probe. The psalms lend themselves particularly well to this technique because they are the oldest corpus of oral literature and music surviving in Doukhobor tradition. As such, they constitute the ideological basis upon which Doukhoborism is founded.

As we have seen, most other folk cultures abide by the behavioural directives laid down by the church and the state. For them, the church is a convenient edifice where, on a weekly basis, one may participate in the dramatised legends of Christianity through priestly intermediaries and where, from time to time, rites of passage are ritualistically consecrated and legally approved. The Doukhobors, like the Bogomil followers before them, rejected this attempt to institutionalise spiritual phenomena — to make the voice of God visible, so to speak, by means of ritualistic devices. Instead, they used auditory techniques to reveal and promulgate spiritual phenomena. The singing of psalms and hymns became a way of life itself — the means by which spiritual revelation informed every aspect of social action. This so-called 'Living Book' of Doukhobor tradition was passed on orally from generation to generation either by recitation or, more usually, by the singing of massed choirs and congregations (Bonch-Bruevich, 1909).

Although occasionally based upon Biblical materials, Doukhobor psalms have no direct relationship to the Psalms of David. They were composed by Doukhobors themselves or inherited from proto-Doukhobor sects. The structural organisation of the psalms is quite archaic. Both the texts and the music are non-metrical, although contrapuntal and harmonic passages sometimes occur at irregular intervals. Individual syllables are extended throughout long configurations of archaic polyphony. I clocked one psalm, 'The Singing of psalms beautifies our souls', and found that it took about ten minutes to sing just eight words, an average of a minute and a quarter per word. Since the complete psalm contains about 180 words of two syllables or more, it must have taken well over three hours to sing it in its entirety. Nowadays only the first few words are sung, the remainder being recited. The continuity of the prose text is further enhanced by the technique of staggered breathing, which ensures a continuous flow of polyphonic sound. Staggered breathing is done quite spontaneously without prior rehearsal, although it is not used for the later, metrically organised hymns.

I must emphasise that traditional Doukhobor choral and part singing, even in its most complex manifestations, is a completely oral phenomenon. Total reliance is placed on the auditory memory and its powers of spontaneous improvisation. No visual aids like hymn books and conductors are used in traditional singing. The Doukhobors do not normally read music. From childhood onward, all sect members absorb the musical and ideological traditions of Doukhoborism through their ears, not their eyes. One's eventual position in the social and musical scheme of things depends upon one's innate spiritual and musical endowments. As in tribal cultures, the possession of a superlative oral memory and singing voice is a great boon to the culture, and carries with it the responsibility of using the talent for the good of all, not as a vehicle for personal aggrandisement.

The significance of psalm singing may be studied on two levels, the auditory and the ideational. Both are inextricably interwoven. I use the word *ideational* to cover the whole spectrum of mental imagery evoked by the text, and *auditory* to refer to the aural process by which this imagery is externalised in the sound continuum. These terms cover much more than the simple designation *words and music*. In psalm singing this auditory gestalt may be regarded as the musical projection of the basic Doukhobor ideal of spiritual communalism through social interdependence. Conversely (and probably more to the point), the social expression of Doukhoborism is the embodiment of ideational and auditory configurations experienced during the act of singing psalms. In any case, the important thing is the use of audio-ideational techniques to elicit and implement revelationary experience. Or, as the Doukhobors put it, much more succinctly in one of their psalms: 'it is through the lips of man that God speaks (from 'What is a Doukhobor?', a psalm attributed to Savelii Kapustin, a Doukhobor prophet and leader of the late eighteenth and early nineteenth centuries).

The above paragraph indicates how difficult it is to rationalise visionary experience induced by audio-ideational techniques. When visual aids like statuary, stained glass, paintings and rituals are used to induce and dramatise visionary experience — as they are in the Orthodox and Catholic Churches — we can study the considerable influence these devices have had on the visual orientation of folk culture intimately associated with these religious institutions.

In many cultures the primacy of the visual sense has produced folk art of remarkable workmanship and beauty. In rejecting the visual apparatus of church ritual, the Doukhobors developed a way of life based largely on aural imagination. Their artifacts must be heard and not seen. The æsthetic poverty of their material culture is more than compensated for by their music and literature, a body of oral materials unique among folk cultures in Canada. Its evolution as an auditory device for evoking and implementing visionary experience need not deter us from exploring its cultural implications, despite the obvious difficulties such research involves.

In conclusion, I would like to make one last observation which should help to remove any mystical bias from the study of audio-ideational techniques as aids to visionary experience. This has nothing to do with textual imagery or aural process. Its significance is purely chemical. In recent years the use of hallucinogenic drugs to induce states of visionary experience has received widespread attention. Less well known is the mild hallucinogenic effect of gaseous carbon dioxide when it is absorbed into the bloodstream. This has been demonstrated in laboratory experiments using three parts carbon dioxide and seven parts oxygen. This optimum concentration can be achieved outside the laboratory only by special breathing techniques. The all-important breathing exercises of yogi cults, for example, are perhaps the best known methods for achieving 'spiritual' euphoria through high concentrations of carbon dioxide in the bloodstream. Also to be considered is the prolonged chanting of Buddhist and Christian monks, the singing and shouting of revivalist sects and the endless incantations intoned by shamans in tribal cultures. These and other aids to visionary experience are described in detail in Aldous Huxley's long essays *Heaven and hell* and *The Doors of perception*. The classic experiments in carbon dioxide intoxication were done by Meduna (Bennett, 1968). It is hardly necessary to point out that none of the cultists who experience CO_2 narcosis, with the possible exception of some of the sophisticated yogi, are aware of the simple chemical basis of the experience.

Fig. 1 Ladies Doukhobor Choir at the Annual Doukhobor Youth Festival, Brilliant, British Columbia, May 19, 1995.

We must infer, therefore, that the singing of Doukhobor psalms and hymns over prolonged periods of time may produce euphoria caused by carbon dioxide intoxication. The text, with its religious content, is merely the channel through which the feeling of euphoria is expressed. Thus, we are left free to examine the text as a linguistic receptacle of visionary data, the validity of which need not concern us because we have already considered the chemical basis of visionary experience. For its part, the music serves as an auditory vehicle which continuously reinforces the visionary experience by a process of acoustic feedback so long as the singing continues.

The attempt to study the data of visionary experience on a scientific level is in no way a denigration of Doukhobor beliefs. As I have pointed out above, we are interested in the auditory medium, not the religious message; although this, too, might turn out to be significant. As our techniques mature, we may even have the courage to scrutinise our own religious institutions and may come to the conclusion that the singing of psalms, after all, really does beautify our souls.

Bibliography

Bennett, Peter (1968, January). 'The Narcotic Effects of Air'. *Science Journal* (UK).

Bonch-Bruevich, Vladimir Dmitrevich (1909). *Zhivotnaia Kniga Dukhobortsev* [Book of Life of the Doukhobors]. St-Petersburg.

Edgerton, William (1988). 'The Social influence of Lev Tolstoj in Bulgaria.' Series: Literature, Vol. 2, ed. Jane Gary Harris. Columbus, Ohio: Slavica, pp. 123–38.

Edgerton, William (1989). 'Tolstoi i tolstovtsy [Tolstoy and Tolstoyans]', *Novy mir* (Moscow, March 1990), pp. 266–67.

Huxley, Aldous (1954). *The Doors of perception.*

Huxley, Aldous (1977). *Heaven and hell.*

Lavrin, Janko (1929). 'The Bogomils and Bogomilism'. *Slavonic and East European Review*, nº 8 (December 1929).

Peacock, Kenneth (1970). *Songs of the Doukhobors — an introductory outline.* Folklore Series nº 7: National Museums of Canada Bulletin nº 231. Ottawa: Queen's Printer.

* A revised and updated version of a paper prepared for the Annual Meeting of the American Folklore Society held in Toronto 17–19 November 1967. Used by permission of the Canadian Museum of Civilization.

War in the teaching and life of Russian Doukhobors

Svetlana A. Inikova

A people's oral tradition embraces major events of national importance involving its vital interests, especially *war,* which more than any other phenomenon causes intense reflection on questions of a people's goals and self-identity. This was definitely true of the Russian people, whose numerous songs and legends of war and military history bear testimony to their perception of struggle against an enemy as a struggle for their faith and the Fatherland. War (or the threat thereof) helped consolidate the unity of religious and patriotic feelings. Indeed it may be said that a people's attitude toward defending one's faith and country in time of war is a significant indicator of that people's self-awareness.

It is interesting to compare in this light the attitude toward war manifested by a small group of Russians isolated from their main ethnic body, with their own denominational beliefs — namely, the Doukhobors. This sect came to life at the beginning of the eighteenth century and spread among the serfs of southern Russia and north-eastern Ukraine as well as among the Don Cossacks. Because of its opposition to both the imperial state (including the tsar himself) and the established Russian Orthodox Church (which they saw as posing as an intermediary between man and God), the sect was considered extremely dangerous to the authorities and was subjected to severe repression.

In the early nineteenth century tsar Alexander I, hoping to check the spread of the movement, ordered the grouping together of Doukhobors from various provinces into a territory known as Molochnye Vody (Milky Waters) in Taurida (now the Crimæa) — between German colonists on the one hand and Nogai nomads on the other. But as the growing Russian population expanded into that area, by the 1840s it was decided to relocate the Doukhobors to remote areas of the Caucasus, where many of their descendants still live.

In the Caucasus the Doukhobors quickly managed to regain most of their former prosperity. They maintained many of their Russian linguistic and cultural traditions,[1] along with their own unique religious teachings, which included obedience to the will of religious leaders who frequently portrayed themselves as modern-day incarnations of Christ.

Attitude to war in the late 19th century

United by their past sufferings and their sense of mission as a 'chosen people', the Doukhobors, over a period of time, became aware of themselves as an independent people, in both religious and secular terms — i.e., separate not only from Russian orthodoxy but from the Russian people as well. This sense of isolation was reflected in their social organisation which had some of the trappings of 'statehood' — a central authority, a treasury, a court and even a tiny army. They referred to their society as *Dukhoboriia*, and themselves as tributaries, but not subjects, of the Russian tsar. Not being able to sympathise with the struggle for what they saw as an alien faith and Fatherland, they gradually acquired a negative attitude to war and military service.

This attitude toward war was prominently echoed in the Doukhobors' religious doctrine, expressed in the *psalms.* The psalms, composed orally at different times by different leaders, were mostly free interpretations of the Gospels, although some constituted an original presentation of their teachings in the form of questions and answers. They were transmitted orally[2] from one generation to another since, according to the Doukhobors, the only true word was that which was inspired by God and written in one's heart — cf. the declaration in of one of the psalms: 'Jesus did not spread books, but instructed with the word learnt by heart'.[3]

At the heart of the Doukhobor teachings about war lies the Judæo-Christian commandment 'Thou shalt not kill' (Exodus 20:13): since God is embodied in the memory, intellect and will of every human being, whose body is perceived as the temple of God, an attempt to take a human life is considered tantamount to an attempt on God Himself. Murder and complicity therein were considered to be the gravest of sins.

The Doukhobor opposition to the secular state is based on the notion of homeland not as an earthly location but a state of heaven

> …whence all of us are received and born and all of us are divine. The earth is not the fatherland for us, we are but wanderers on the earth.

The 'fatherland' is the abode of God, but pursuing this line of reasoning, the Doukhobors also recognised as 'fatherland' the residence of their 'Christ' leaders — the so-called *Sirotskii dom* (Orphanage) that had been set up initially for homeless children — thereby further dissassociating themselves from the general Russian 'fatherland'.

An examination of Doukhobor history, however, reveals a more complex motivation underlying their attitude to war. Before their resettlement to the Caucasus, Doukhobors had served in the army, but their service had been marked with a number of cases of desertion and refusal to take arms. Witness the account of one senator, I.V. Lopukhin, who had become intimately acquainted with the Doukhobors before their move to Molochnye Vody:[4]

> ...they take as their duty to defend themselves against enemies but reject any offensive action, even if ordered by superiors; as a result, during the first Turkish war those of them who were with the Vologda regiment under Perekop threw down their arms.

One eyewitness to such incidents remembers that, in refusing to shoot, the Doukhobors would say that 'the law of Moses allows defending one's self but says nothing about one's fatherland'.[5]

Schism, arms-burning and emigration

The Doukhobor movement experienced its 'golden age' under the leadership of Lukeria Vasil'evna Kalmykova; not only was she able to maintain internal unity among the sect members but she managed to prevent the tsarist government from interfering in the Doukhobors' affairs. With her death in 1886, however, a schism arose in the movement: the so-called 'Smaller Party', willing to come to terms with the authorities, recognised Lukeria's brother as the heir of the *Sirotskii dom,* while the 'Large Party', more radical in its anti-establishment teaching, acknowledged Peter V. Verigin's claim to be Lukeria's successor. When the government intervened in support of the Smaller Party's claim to the *Sirotskii dom,* Large Party members took advantage of the occasion to also protest against the government's recent annulment of the Doukhobors' exemption from military service (which had been in effect since 1845), proclaiming their adherence to the original Doukhobor opposition to war and military activities.

This opposition became enshrined in a new postulate of 'rejection of violent resistance to evil' (*nesoprotivlenie zlu nasiliem*), which now included even a rejection of physical self-defence. This spirited resistance intensified even more when compulsory military service was introduced in the Caucasus in 1887. In June 1895 the Doukhobors' non-violent protests culminated in the burning of all firearms owned by Verigin's followers, accompanied by psalm-singing.[6] The local authorities reacted with brutal repression, and the persecution which followed over the next few years eventually led to the bulk of the Large Party emigrating to

Canada.[7] The less-persecuted group elected to remain in the Caucasus.

During these years of conflict Large Party members composed several new psalms emphasising the anti-war theme in their teaching: each learnt by heart the psalm *Oborona khristianskaia* [Christian defence], which included a formulated reponse to the question of military service:

> Because I am a Christian, I wish neither to kill nor to force brethren of mine... Because I believe according to the word of our Lord Jesus Christ that everybody living on the earth is a child of one Father, and is a brother to us.[8]

In another psalm the question 'Why do you not want to serve your emperor?' is answered thus:

> I would have fulfilled the emperor's will but he teaches killing people, which my soul is against.[9]

Other anti-war poems in the form of so-called *stishki* (verses) were composed by Large Party Doukhobors in emigration, and performed as choral songs. Some of these were borrowed from the Baptists and Molokans, while others were based on popular songs or the works of recognised poets. A number of the Canadian Doukhobors' *stishki* later spread back to Verigin's followers still in the Caucasus, though they were never sung by the Smaller Party members.

War songs in the Doukhobor culture

Yet it was not that long ago that the Doukhobors' musical repertoire also included traditional Russian songs glorifying the valour and heroism of past military campaigns — about Alexander I, the struggle against Napoleon, Prince Vorontsov's Caucasus campaign, the battle for Port Arthur — songs which were also popular among the Russian peasantry at large. Eight such songs still remain, but before the emigration there were probably many more.

This may be taken as a sign of the Doukhobors' continuing attachment to their Russian historical and cultural roots, which could not be completely supplanted by the religious ideology of their leaders. It must not be forgotten that prior to their resettlement to Molochnye Vody the Doukhobors had lived mostly among the Russian population, and even today many older sect members can recall which provinces their ancestors had come from. The tradition of oral transmission of historical knowledge (such knowledge being one of the main components of ethnic self-awareness) is thus seen to be independent of the sublimating influence of religious belief.

These military songs were probably brought back to the settlements by Doukhobors returning from army service (from which they were not exempted prior to 1845), some of them even bearing medals of honour for their military deeds. True, in many cases it was simply a compromise to avoid persecution, but even during the exemption period, the Doukhobors on occasion helped the Russian army — as during the Russo-Turkish war of 1878–79 when they conveyed food supplies and ammunition to the front line and cared for wounded soldiers in their villages.[10] But it is worth noting that while Doukhobors accepted some of the popular war songs from outside, they never composed any of their own.

The Soviet period

The overthrow of the tsars by the Bolsheviks in 1917 was taken in stride by the Large Party, which recognised the new Soviet government and in 1918 presented their best horses to the Soviet army. A year later the government granted all pacifist groups an exemption from military service. The Smaller Party, however, refused both to acknowledge the new government and to serve in its armed forces (though some of its members had previously, by individual decision, served in the tsarist army).

During the 1918–21 occupation of a part of Georgia by the Turks, the Doukhobors (of both parties) offered no resistance to the Turkish troops and offered them food and hospitality, even while they were secretly sheltering Armenians in their homes to protect them from the instruments of Turkish genocide. According to one legend, as the Turkish troops were leaving the area, the Turkish general paid his respects to the Doukhobors and remarked that while he had won many victories, such people who respond to evil with kindness could not be defeated.

During the NEP period (1921–28), when strict communist ideology was somewhat relaxed overall, the new Soviet government granted the Doukhobors one more respite from military service, but this was repealed with the advent of Stalinism and the consolidation of Soviet power in the Caucasus. Following a decision taken by a district conference in the Georgian city of Akhalkalaki in 1928 the Doukhobors were once again compelled to serve — this time in the Soviet army. The few cases of resistance (this time from Smaller Party members) was crushed very quickly.

Both through subtle acculturation (exposure to Soviet schools, newspapers and other vehicles of propaganda which had penetrated the local municipalities) and the state's active efforts to destroy the Doukhobors' isolation and the dissident thinking (*inakomyslie*) that accompanied it (during the census of the late 1930s they were not even allowed to identify themselves as Doukhobors), the Russian Doukhobors gradually lost much of their distinctive identity and self-awareness.

The trend has continued. Russian Doukhobors served in the Soviet army in the 'Great Patriotic War' (1941–45) and serve in the post-Soviet Russian army today. The question of rejecting war and defence of the 'fatherland' has all but faded. The religious protesters' modern descendants identify themselves as Russians first; they regard Doukhoborism more as a cultural tradition inherited from their ancestors than as their own spiritual home.

But times are changing once more. Since the collapse of the Soviet system at the end of 1991, there has been a movement on the part of Doukhobors in the now independent Caucasus nations to return to Russia; only a small group of them still remains in the Caucasus.

Conclusion

The Doukhobors' attitude to war reflects two internal levels of consciousness: religious and ethnic Russian. The former, manifest in their teachings and psalms, has long negated certain concepts (such as fatherland and patriotism) inherent in the latter and may be said to have artificially suppressed them. Yet the latter consciousness is still found expressed in their folklore, at least in the singing of Russian patriotic war songs. Hence the Doukhobors' attitude toward war as proclaimed by their teaching has not always coincided with actual practice.

The anti-war actions of the Russian Doukhobors may be seen as a kind of struggle against the state for the interests of the group, since at any specific point in time real attitudes toward war were determined by the current state of relations with the state. Hence the teachings of the Doukhobors on the subject of war may be considered not so much anti--Russian as anti-state in character.

[1]Most Doukhobors were Russian, although the sect embraced a number of Ukrainians, Mordvinians and some other ethnic groups.

[2]Around the turn of the century many of the psalms were recorded by an outside

observer named Vladimir Bonch-Bruevich, who in 1909 published them as a book entitled *Zhivotnaia kniga* (The Book of Life).

[3]Bonch-Bruevich, *Zhivotnaia kniga* (St-Petersburg, 1909), Psalm 14, p. 72.

[4]*Chteniia v Impertaroskom obshchestve istorii i drevnostei rossiiskikh* [Readings at the Imperial society of history and antiquities] (Moscow, 1964), Book IV.

[5]RO GPB, folio 73, delo 236, 1.3. At Molochnye Vody it is said that wealthy Doukhobors frequently paid handsome sums to non-Doukhobors on the recruitment list to be called up in the place of their sons, although this may have been due as much to their interest in larger farmsteads as to religious prohibitions.

[6]This event has since become part of the Doukhobors' oral tradition, itself celebrated in a number of psalms, still popular among Caucasus Doukhobors.

[7]The emigration was made possible thanks mainly to the financial support of writer Lev Tolstoy, who saw in the Doukhobor life-style a practical application of his religious philosophy — *ed.*

[8]Bonch-Bruevich, *Zhivotnaia kniga*, 1909, p. 279.

[9]*Ibid.*, Psalm 59, p. 84.

[10]The Doukhobors' assistance to the war effort may well have gone even further. There is a legend that at one point during the war the Imperial vicegerent in the Caucasus approached Lukeria Kalmykova (who was said to have the gift of prophecy) for advice on how to overcome fierce enemy resistance in the city of Kars. Lukeria assured him that Kars would be 'Russian' by the time the vicegerent returned home — a prophecy which proved true.

Recent and current studies on the Doukhobors at Ottawa universities

John A. Woodsworth

As January 1999 approaches — the Centenary of the first arrival of the Doukhobors in Canada, more and more interest in this remarkable chapter of our nation's history is being expressed not only by Doukhobors themselves, but also by the Canadian public at large — witness the extremely popular Doukhobor exhibit at the Canadian Museum of Civilization organised by *Koozma J. Tarasoff* and Robert B. Klymasz — and the academic community in particular. It is the interest of this latter community that this paper will endeavour to explore.

Tolstoy-Verigin correspondence

My own interest in the Doukhobors began toward the end of 1994, when I was asked by my colleague, Professor Andrew Donskov (a long-time student of Tolstoy) to undertake a translation of the complete correspondence between Lev Nikolaevich Tolstoy and the Doukhobors' spiritual leader at the time, *Petr Vasil'evich Verigin*. The volume was published six months later under Donskov's editorship, with a foreword by Lidia Dmitrievna Gromova-Opul'skaya of the Russian Academy of Sciences in Moscow.[1] Prof. Donskov and I had the honour of introducing this book at a July 1995 conference in Castlegar marking the Centenary of the Burning of Arms in the Caucasus. It traces the development of a remarkable relationship between these two leaders, beginning in 1895, when Tolstoy first heard of the Siberia-exiled Doukhobor leader through a mutual acquaintance, a Tolstoyan named Ivan Mikhailovich Tregubov. The relationship was first conducted across the thousands of kilometres of land between Yasnaya Polyana and Eastern Siberia, and then across the thousands of kilometres of ocean and two continents in the other direction, when Verigin lived among his followers in Saskatchewan and British Columbia, having been given permission to emigrate to Canada in 1902. It ended only with Tolstoy's passing in 1910.

After completing the translation I prepared a paper based on this volume entitled 'Attitude and character transformation as revealed in the correspondence of Tolstoy and Verigin',[2] which was presented in condensed form at the 1995 Centenary conference and subsequently published in full in a special volume of the *Canadian Ethnic Studies* journal (*CES*), under the guest editorship of Koozma J. Tarasoff. This article explores a significant change in Verigin's attitude and character over the period of their correspondence. As a peasant who had risen far above most of his peers in terms of education and linguistic expression, Verigin began the correspondence with a forceful defence of his own concept of what was right and a fierce attack on the whole notion of literacy and book-learning exemplified by Tolstoy. But, at least partly under Tolstoy's gentle influence through their exchange of letters, the Doukhobor leader's forcefulness gradually mellowed into the kind of character more often associated with the Doukhobor movement — by his own admission he became 'kinder of heart'.[3] His transformation in effect echoed Tolstoy's own 'spiritual conversion' some two decades earlier. Yet Verigin still maintained in a degree his original qualities of forthrightness and self-assurance that had attracted Tolstoy to him in the first place, stating in his final letter to his 'mentor':[4]

> I'm starting to believe absolutely that if I could, if I desired, to make the effort to develop within myself an understanding of the value of eternal life and wanted to enter into it, then that too would come to pass. It would happen just like with the mountain Christ speaks of in his parable.

Doukhobor film sources

The same issue of *CES* includes submissions by two other Ottawa scholars. Richard Sokoloski, professor of Polish and Russian in the University of Ottawa's Department of Modern Languages and Literatures (a department he currently chairs), conducted a survey of eleven documentary films on the Doukhobors, ten of them produced between 1978 and 1992 (the other dating from 1949) — in English and/or Russian. His report on this survey, entitled 'Images of the Doukhobors: a record of film sources',[5] provides a brief critical analysis of all eleven films, ranging from an early primitive effort undertaken in 1949 by the Doukhobor Society of Northeastern Saskatchewan with the bilingual title *Ternistyi put'* / *Thorny road* to Kristina Kristova and Koozma Tarasoff's 'work-in-progress' *Interviews with Doukhobors,* begun in 1992.

Sokoloski takes note of the high level of scholarship evident in works such as Larry Ewashen and Koozma Tarasoff's *In Search of Utopia: The Doukhobors* (1978) and the two-part CBC documentary on the Doukhobors produced the same year by Gordon Babineau, the 'warm biographical look' at Doukhobor musicologist *Nick Kalmakoff* in Larry Ewashen's *The Last Hurrah* (1990), the objectivity of Tamara Lisitsian's *Vstrechi s dukhobortsami Kanady* [Meetings with Canadian Doukhobors] made in post-*glasnost'* Russia (1991), as well as the historical significance of Soviet TV journalist Aleksei Mel'nikov's eightminute piece *Russkie dukhobortsy Kanady* [The Russian Doukhobors of Canada] (1986), aired several times on national Soviet television during the last years of that decade.

The author of the article points to 'a common theme in all Russian films on the subject, the Doukhobors' attachment and nostalgia for their first homeland', and concludes the following:[6]

> All of the films described above are as much a testimony to the endurance of the Doukhobors in Canada as they are to a process of renewal with which all movements periodically must contend. ... Ultimately, the varied images of the Doukhobors that emerge from these films reveal, in some measure, a timeless sense of introspection and an affinity for oral dialogue that implicitly binds the movement to both past and present, word and deed, thought and belief.

Memos from Caucasus governors

In his article in the 'Doukhobor' issue of *CES*, entitled 'On the Doukhobors: from Imperial Russian Archival files',[7] Andrew Donskov, also of the Department of Modern Languages and Literatures at the University of Ottawa, presented three archival documents dealing with the persecution of Doukhobors by Imperial Russian authorities in the Caucasus in the 1890s, along with his annotations. The primary focus is on a memo dated 13 July 1897 from Prince Grigorii Sergeevich Golitsyn, who in 1896 succeeded Sergei Aleksandrovich Sheremetev as Governor of the Caucasus, entitled 'On the current status of the Caucasus Doukhobor movement and on the measures taken by the governor of the Caucasus to check the harmful anti-government influence among the followers of this sect'.[8] It outlines Golitsyn's view of the Doukhobors' attitude to the authorities, land and patriotism, observed discrepancies between Doukhobor teachings and the practice of some members of the sect, the radical nature of the Kars Doukhobors and their espousal of anarchy, and a list of proposed severe measures to deal with the alleged threat posed by the more radical Doukhobors.[9]

The extensive annotations provided by Donskov lead to the inclusion of two additional documents:

(a) a résumé by Tiflis Governor Prince Shervashidze of his own lengthy memo of 4 October 1895 to Sheremetev headed: 'On the Criminal brotherhood of sectarian Doukhobors, whose aim is insubordination to the higher authorities'[10] — contrasting the essentially Christian character of the true Doukhobor teachings with the 'broadest possible cosmopolitanism' of the Tolstoyans, and warning of the dangers of the 'dark masses' of the Russian peasantry being influenced against military service and paying taxes;

(b) another letter from Prince Golitsyn, this one dated 24 April 1898 and directed to the then Minister of External Affairs Count Mikhail Nikitich Murav'ev[11] — dismissing as unrealistic a proposal by Prince Èsper Èsperovich Ukhtomskii to send the Doukhobors to Mongolia to establish a more solid Russian presence among the local population.

According to Donskov, the accounts contained in the three documents present 'another stark page' in the history of the Russian government's injustices and persecutions in respect to minority groups. He continues:[12]

> They also bear witness to the Doukhobors' love of honest labour, their ability to weather the harsh climate, their courage to persevere in their beliefs and to die, if need be, in their struggle for freedom from what they regarded as unjust interference in their lives on the part of the Russian government.

Lev Tolstoy and the Doukhobors

Donskov concludes his 1995 CES article with the hope that the publication of this newly available material will encourage scholars in different fields 'to make full use of the archival depositories of the Russian Federation, so that future publications on the history of this movement may rest on a more complete documentation'.13 For much of this past decade, world-recognised Tolstoy scholar Andrew Donskov has been doing just that, as part of an ongoing long-term project he has undertaken in collaboration with two scholars from the Russian Academy of Sciences (Lidia Dmitrievna Gromova-Opul'skaya in Moscow and Galina Galagan in St Petersburg) to produce a twovolume edition called The Unity of people in L. N. Tolstoy's works.

Volume I (to consist of approximately 600 pages) will examine three aspects of Tolstoy's view of unity: from the standpoint of (a) the individual, (b) society and (c) 'the law of violence and the law of love' —

a teaching Tolstoy espoused in his later years after his so-called 'spiritual crisis' and renewal of a spiritual outlook on life. Of course the latter theme is also significant in looking at Tolstoy's relationship with the Doukhobors, whom the great writer more than once described as a living embodiment of his spiritual ideals, especially in their approach to issues of land ownership, communal living, rejection of church ritual and dogma along with military service to the state. Indeed, certain texts relating to the Doukhobor movement are to be included in Volume II, along with correspondence, police reports and draft variants of some of his philosophical manuscripts.

In February 1996 Prof. Donskov and I co-organised a conference at the University of Ottawa on the theme of 'Lev Tolstoy and the concept of brotherhood' which drew prominent Tolstoy scholars from all over Canada and America, with keynote speakers from the Russian Academy of Sciences.[14] A special feature of this conference was an 'Open Forum' (to which not just scholars but members of the Ottawa community were invited), on the topic 'Tolstoy at the threshold of the twenty-first century', exploring the relevance of Tolstoy's ideas on brotherhood (which he shared to a great extent with the Doukhobors) to the generations of mankind to come. At the closing banquet, the featured speaker was well-known Doukhobor writer and filmmaker (and curator of the Doukhobor Museum at Castlegar) *Larry Ewashen*, who spoke about the continuing impact of Tolstoy's legacy on the Canadian Doukhobors today. The entire proceedings of the conference, including Ewashen's banquet speech, were published in the late spring of 1996, under the joint editorship of Prof. Donskov and myself.[15]

In addition to the Tolstoy–Verigin correspondence, Donskov has also published, in the Doukhobor magazine *Iskra*, several other letters concerning the Doukhobors: (a) 'An unpublished letter from V. Tchertkov's file', *Iskra*, n⁰ 1808 (1995): 6–12, 47–52; (b) 'Peter V. Verigin to E. Popov and I. Konkin to L.N. Tolstoy: two unpublished letters', *Iskra*, n⁰ 1817 (1996): 40–46 and n⁰ 1818 (1996): 29–34; (c) 'Neopublikovannoe pis'mo I. M. Sergeeva k L. N. Tolstomu', *Iskra*, n⁰ 1823 (1996): 10–12, 34–39.[16]

Still in the planning stages is a projected volume on the whole subject of Tolstoy and the whole Doukhobor movement — examining the moral and ethical underpinnings of their mutual attraction, his financing of their emigration to Canada through the proceeds from his novel *Voskresenie* [Resurrection], and the activities of many of the Tolstoyans (as his followers were known) in accompanying the Doukhobors to Canada and assisting them in settling in their new homeland.

Sergei Tolstoy and the Doukhobors

At the moment, Andrew Donskov and I are involved in preparing for publication an historic volume entitled *Sergej Tolstoy and the Doukhobors: a journey to Canada*. Following Donskov's editorial introduction and a biographical sketch of Sergei L'vovich Tolstoy (eldest son of Lev Nikolaevich Tolstoy) written by Tatiana Grigor'evna Nikiforova of the State Tolstoy Museum in Moscow, the book is divided into the following sections:

1. Sergei Tolstoy's diaries of his journey from Batoum to the Canadian prairies (accompanying the second boatload of Doukhobors) and his experiences in Canada helping the Doukhobors settle in their new home; his original text and my English translation appear on facing pages.

2. Four hitherto unpublished letters written by Sergei Tolstoy from abroad (again, printed in Russian with English translation) — one to his father, one to his mother and two to his sister Tatiana.[17] A fifth letter was written in English to Professor James Mavor at the University of Toronto, who had been asked by Prince Petr Kropotkin to assist with the Doukhobors' emigration, passing along an invitation to visit his father at Yasnaya Polyana.

3. Twenty unpublished letters written (in English) to Sergei Tolstoy between 1898 and 1902 by three people involved in the emigration: James Mavor, Herbert P. Archer (a member of the Purleigh Tolstoy colony in Essex, England) and Canadian immigration commissioner William F. McCreary.

4. Fifteen letters written to Sergei Tolstoy between 1899 and 1911 by two Doukhobor brothers, *Savelii* and *Nikolai Khudiakoff*. Savelii arrived in Canada with the 1899 emigration and knew Sergei Tolstoy personally (in fact, he was greatly disappointed when the latter was obliged to go home to Russia, never to return); his letters describe the farming activities of the Doukhobors on the prairies, their joy at receiving a much-desired shipment of Russian books from Yasnaya Polyana, and the breakaway dissident movement of radical Doukhobors who let loose their cattle and began a long trek, only to be herded back by the authorities. His brother Nikolai, on the other hand, was still in exile in Yakutsk Province in Siberia, from which he was released only in 1903, when he wrote to Sergei from Elizavetpol', asking for his help in securing official permission to emigrate. His only letter after that was written from Nelson, B.C. in December 1911, in what evidently proved an

unsuccessful attempt to re-establish correspondence (no further letters between the two are extant).

The original text of the diaries and Russian-language correspondence was initially prepared by Tatiana Nikiforova, while Andrew Donskov provided the annotations to the correspondence written in English. An appendix to the book contains six letters written by friends and officials involved in the emigration to each other, along with additional materials pertaining to the emigration process.

Student research on the Doukhobors

The Doukhobors and their historic emigration to Canada have attracted the attention of at least two university students in Ottawa in the past few years. In the autumn of 1997 Karine Hopper, a fourth-year Russian student at the University of Ottawa, wrote a paper for Prof. Donskov's Tolstoy course on 'Tolstoy, the Doukhobors and the rejection of materialism',[18] which focuses in part on the Tolstoy–Verigin correspondence mentioned above.[19] On the basis of this and other sources she notes a number of commonalities between the writer and the sect in respect to their distrust of both governmental and ecclesiastical hierarchies and the importance of seeking the spiritual world more than the material. But she also explains Verigin's apparent emphasis on daily human needs during their initial years in Canada:[20]

> Verigin understands human nature. His people will not be happy if they do not have food or shelter, and these needs must be taken care of before they begin to focus on spiritual, and intangible, issues. … It can be said that letting the community's children go hungry and cold would be equivalent to not doing one's Christian duty.

Hopper sees the Doukhobors' practical approach, finding 'a way to balance material self-sufficiency and spiritual concerns', as a contributing factor to their success; this is achieved, she notes, by looking at financial success 'as another way to serve God, and see[ing] that same success as extending from that same faith in God and individual determinism'; she goes on to speculate on how such a solution could be 'a perfect cure of the ills of modern society'.[21]

In 1996 Carleton University student Jennifer Anderson wrote her M.A. thesis on the topic 'Three men and a cause: Lev Tolstoy, James Mavor, Peter Kropotkin and the Doukhobor Migration to Canada, 1899';[22] she

subsequently defended the thesis to earn a Masters' degree in Central/
East European and Russian-Area Studies. Her paper examines the role
each of the three men played (and how these roles interrelated) in assisting the Doukhobors in their emigration — a role that gave each the
opportunity to put their own philosophical and societal theories 'to the
test': Tolstoy the Christian anarchist, Kropotkin the anarcho-communist
and Mavor the advocate of communalism.[23] She sums up her principal
theme as follows:[24]

> These men were drawn to the Doukhobors by what they perceived to be
> unique, and in some cases, revolutionary, principles and practices. Tolstoy
> wholeheartedly supported the Doukhobors in their resistance to Ortho-
> doxy, and their pacifist ideals based on Christian morality. Mavor was
> fascinated by economic aspects of the Doukhobor lifestyle, which featured
> communal social arrangements, and Kropotkin was intrigued by their
> politically anarchistic tenets. Delighted to find living examples of their
> own theoretical investigations, the efforts of these three men to secure a
> home in which the Doukhobors could live more congruently with their
> traditions, benefitted everyone.

After analysing in turn each of the three men's contributions to the
Doukhobor cause and its interrelationship with the others' roles,
Anderson points to the success of the Canadian Doukhobors today as
testimony to the effectiveness of their combined efforts. She sees a
modern echo of the uniting of their diverse talents by a common goal in
the fact that, today, 'a study of [the Doukhobor] movement ... cuts across
the boundaries of time, nations, and academic disciplines to tell an old
story from a new perspective', adding that 'for Russians, Canadians and
Doukhobors it is a tale worth recounting'.[25]

Russian archival documents on the Doukhobors

Another institution at in Ottawa that has taken a considerable interest
in the Doukhobors is Carleton University's Centre for Research on Canadian-Russian Relations (CRCR), headed by director Larry Black. Over
the past few years Dr Black and his assistant George Bolotenko (second-
ed from the National Archives of Canada) have managed to secure
photocopies of a vast array of documents on the Doukhobors contained
in several archival sources as well as translation and publication rights to
a good many of them (primarily those from the State Archive of the
Russian Federation, more commonly known by its Russian acronym:
GARF).

In the summer of 1996 I was appointed an External Researcher for CRCR with the task of preparing an annotated catalogue of some 1,667 pages of documents acquired to date — some of them in barely legible handwriting, others exquisitely copied by professional scribes (*pisari*), the remainder typed or printed. The catalogue has already been republished by CRCR in a second, revised edition (in May 1997) under the title: *The Doukhobors: 1895–1943. Annotated, cross-referenced and summarised.*[26] The volume includes an appendix containing more detailed summaries of several of the longer documents and a complete index of names. It is also available in electronic format, with built-in codes for rapid computer searching by name, date, alternate date, file number or leaf number.

These documents, most of them written between 1895 and 1906 (one of them dated as late as 1943), were originally taken from the files of the Russian Department of Police under the Tsarist régime. They include:

- reports by government officials in the Caucasus on the current activities of the Doukhobors (including their famous burning of arms at Bogdanovka in June 1895), as well as on the activities of Tolstoyans endeavouring to help the Doukhobors;

- directives from the Minister of Internal Affairs and the Department of Police in Moscow to officials and operatives stationed in areas of the country inhabited by Doukhobors and Tolstoyans, regarding surveillance or direct action to be undertaken;

- letters written by Doukhobors and Tolstoyans to each other both before and after the emigration (including one written by Petr Vasil'evich Verigin), all intercepted by secret police agents;

- Russian and foreign newspaper accounts by and about Lev Nikolaevich Tolstoy in respect to the Doukhobor movement;

- reports from various Russian newspapers of the Doukhobors' emigration to and settlement in Canada, including a series of detailed articles appearing in *Russkie vedomosti* written by a Tolstoyan nurse Vera Mikhailovna Velichkina, who accompanied the fourth boatload in May 1899, as well as a polemic carried on in several papers (including *Novoe vremia*) over the attempts of one P.A. Tverskoi (believed to be a pseudonym for P.A. Dementiev) to persuade the Doukhobors to move from Canada to America;[27]

- letters from Imperial Russian (and later Soviet) diplomatic representatives in Canada on the Canadian Doukhobors, especially on the role of Petr Vasil'evich Verigin and his proposals to hire additional railway construction workers from Russia;[28]

- a number of documents from 1918 and 1923 concerning the prospect of resettling the Canadian Doukhobors in Soviet Russia.

Some of the more significant documents in the first category above deserve special mention:

- #1895-10-04b: 'Copy of confidential report of the Governor of Tiflis, Prince Shervashidze, to His High Excellency, Chief of Civil Affairs in the Caucasus Adjutant-General S.A. Sheremetev, dated 4 October 1895' (56 pp.) — an extensive outline of Doukhobor history — mostly as seen through official eyes but also including a nine-page analysis by Second-Party Doukhobor leader Aleksei Vorob'ev of the sect's beliefs and what led to the split and to the confrontation with authorities in Bogdanovka, with the recommendation that the Fasters be exiled either outside the country or to some area of the Russian empire with a completely foreign population (see Woodsworth 1997:A6, D1–2).
- #1895-11-29d: 'Excerpt from a copy of a report by the Division Commander of the First Uman cavalry regiment [Esaul Praga] to the Commander of the same regiment, dated 1 August 1895' (19 pp.) — a look at the events in Bogdanovka from the Cossack commander's point of view (see Woodsworth 1997:A17, D3).
- #1896-02-09b: 'Report of Major-General Surovtsov and Colonel Greben-shchikov, Tiflis, to the Chief of Civil Affairs in the Caucasus [Adjutant-General Sheremetev]. 15 Dec. 1895' (43 pp.) — a report on an official investigation into allegations that Cmdr Praga had overstepped his authority in dealing with the Doukhobors at Bogdanovka. Among the investigators' conclusions (as summarised in the catalogue):[29]

  [The] Cossack commander Esaul Praga, left without adequate military supervision, is guilty of wanton disregard of established rules in his treatment of the Doukhobors; rape incidents represent a sad blemish on military honour and indicate a complete lack of discipline and internal order, for which not only squadron commanders but also regimental authorities must bear responsibility...

- #1897-07-13b: 'Report by Chief of Civil Affairs in the Caucasus Senator Adjutant-Gen. Prince [Grigorij] Golitsyn: "On the current situation of the Caucasus Doukhobors and on the measures adopted by the Chief's Office to stop the harmful anti-government movement among the followers of this sect". 13 Jul. 1897' (98 pp.) — an outline of Golitsyn's view of the history and current situation of the Doukhobors in the Caucasus upon taking up his current post, with recommendations for the future (see Woodsworth 1997:A52, D5–6).[30]

- #1900-3VA'a–n: A series of fourteen letters (22 pages in all), dated between January 1900 and March 1901 revealing the touching story of a schoolmistress (and wife of a Titular Councillor) named Ekaterina Dmitrievna Vagner, who, having requested to be assigned to work among either the Doukhobors or the Molokans, ended up in the Doukhobor village of Slavianka.[31] Evidently a Tolstoyan, Vagner felt a special attraction to the Doukhobors and their way of life, making friends with local Doukhobor activists and offering to do reading and writing for Doukhobor wives. Following a period of covert surveillance by the authorities, she was dismissed from her post in November 1900, although there is an indication that she was subsequently permitted to take a teaching position 'in areas where there are no sectarians' (see Woodsworth 1997:B62–64).

I might add that I have now been given the task of translating a selection of these documents (between 200 and 300 pages) for publication in English by CRCR. It is hoped that this volume will be available by the end of 1998.

Tolstoyans and the Doukhobors

Before concluding this survey I might mention one more research project that is still in the formative stages. In May 1998 I am planning to go to Saskatoon, Vancouver and Victoria to undertake research in the Public Archives of Saskatchewan and British Columbia, as well as in the University of British Columbia Library, on the role of the so-called 'Tolstoyans' in helping the Doukhobors emigrate and settle in their new land. In particular, I wish to study the history of Leopold Antonovich Sulerzhitzky, Sergei L'vovich Tolstoy, Vladimir Dmitrievich Bonch--Bruevich and Aleksandr Mikhailovich Bodianskii, who accompanied the various boatloads of Doukhobors to Canada in 1899. I have been asked to present a paper on my findings at a Tolstoy conference at Yasnaya Polyana in September 1998.

Conclusion

I think it is evident from the above survey that scholarly interest in the history of the Doukhobor movement, the Doukhobors' emigration to

Canada and their contribution to Canadian society is alive and well in the Ottawa academic community, at both the city's two major universities. I might mention, too, that the study of the Doukhobors is one of the first priorities of a brand new Slavic Research Group, which is in the process of being set up at the University of Ottawa. We can look forward to a number of publications resulting from its activity, as well as from that of CRCR at Carleton — certainly over the next year or so as the Doukhobors celebrate the centenary of their arrival in Canada and a hundred years of their own history in the context of Canadian society.

References

Anderson, Jennifer (1996). 'Three men and a cause: Lev Tolstoy, James Mavor, Peter Kropotkin and the Doukhobor migration to Canada, 1899'. Unpublished M.A. thesis, Carleton University.

Donskov, Andrew, ed. (1995a). *Leo Tolstoy—Peter Verigin: Correspondence*. With an introduction by Lidia Gromova-Opul'skaya. Translated from the Russian by John Woodsworth. Ottawa: Legas.

Donskov, Andrew (1995b). 'On the Doukhobors: from Imperial Russian Archival files'. *Canadian Ethnic Studies*, vol. 27, n⁰ 3: 252–61.

Donskov, Andrew, ed. (1996). 'The Burning of arms 1895 and its consequences'. *Novyi zhurnal* (New York), n⁰ 197: 272–87.

Donskov, Andrew, and John Woodsworth, eds. (1996). *Lev Tolstoy and the concept of brotherhood*. Proceedings of a conference held at the University of Ottawa, 22–24 February 1996. Ottawa: Legas.

Hopper, Karine (1997). 'Tolstoy, the Doukhobors and the rejection of materialism'. Unpublished course paper for SLV 4901A, University of Ottawa.

Sokoloski, Richard (1995). 'Images of the Doukhobors: a record of film sources'. *Canadian Ethnic Studies*, vol. 27, n⁰ 3: 281–88.

Woodsworth, John (1995). 'Attitude and character transformation as revealed in the correspondence of Tolstoy and Verigin'. *Canadian Ethnic Studies,* vol. 27, n⁰ 3: 245–51.

Woodsworth, John (1997). *The Doukhobors: 1895–1943. Annotated, crossreferenced and summarised*. Russian Archival Documents on Canada: Catalogue N⁰ 2. 2nd ed. (revised). Ottawa: Carleton University, Centre for Research on Canadian-Russian Relations.

[1]See Donskov 1995a.

[2]See Woodsworth 1995.

[3]Donskov 1995:88 (Letter nº 32).

[4]Donskov 1995:99 (Letter nº 38).

[5]See Sokoloski 1995.

[6]Sokoloski 1995:286, 287.

[7]See Donskov 1995b. Like Woodsworth (1995), this article is also based on a paper given at the 1995 Centenary celebrations in Castlegar.

[8]State Archives of the Russian Federation (GARF), Collection 102, Inventory 93, Case No 1053, Part I.

[9]See Donskov 1995b:254–56. Another perspective on this remarkable event is presented in Donskov's article in *Novyi zhurnal* (New York) on 'The Burning of arms 1895 and its consequences' — see Donskov 1996.

[10]GARF, Col. 102, Inv. 192, Case No 163. See Donskov 1995b:257–58 (Note 5).

[11]GARF Col. 102, Inv. 26, Case No 12, Pt I. See Donskov 1995b:259–60 (Note 15).

[12]Donskov 1995:253.

[13]Donskov 1995b:253.

[14]Dr Lidia Dmitrievna Gromova-Opul'skaya and Dr Galina Galagan. I was privileged to serve as their interpreter during the conference and to translate their keynote addresses into English for publication.

[15]See Donskov & Woodsworth 1996.

[16]It might also be interesting to note that in 1996 Donskov also published two volumes of Tolstoy's correspondence with nonDoukhobor sectarians (M.P. Novikov and T.M. Bondarev) and is currently editing for publication the writer's correspondence with Fedor Zheltov, a Molokan.

[17]The last of these was written on the RMS *Umbria* en route home.

[18]See Hopper 1997.

[19]See Donskov 1995a.

[20]Hopper 1997:10.

[21]Hopper 1997:11, 12.

[22]See Anderson 1996.

[23]See Anderson 1996:ii (Abstract).

[24]Anderson 1996:19–20.

[25]Anderson 1996:110.

[26]See Woodsworth 1997.

[27]See Woodsworth 1997:B6–B14. One of Tverskoi's critics was none other than Moscow Art Theatre actor and Tolstoyan Leopold Antonovich Sulerzhitsky, who accompanied the first and third boatloads of Doukhobors to Canada. Writ-

ing in the 1 July 1900 issue of *Severnyi Kur'er* (document #1900-1SK-c, described in Woodsworth 1997:B13), Sulerzhitsky affirmed that the Doukhobors knew exactly what they were doing when they chose Canada rather than the United States as their preferred destination, and that Tverskoi's claims of the Doukhobors' farming difficulties on the Canadian prairies were greatly exaggerated.

[28]See the summary of document #1906-12-09c in Woodsworth 1997:C6. The president of the Grand Trunk Pacific Railway was so impressed with the quality of the Doukhobors' work on the construction of the new railway line that he asked Verigin to speak to Russian consular authorities about bringing over more Russian workers for this project.

[29]Woodsworth 1997:D4 (see also p. A21).

[30]This document is also described in Donskov 1995b (for more information, see 'Memos from Caucasus governors' above).

[31]Two of the letters were written by Vagner herself, intercepted by a secret agent. The remainder were memos among officials in Moscow and the Caucasus.

Part VI

Stretching
the
future

Multiculturalism and the rise of a new spirit[1]

Koozma J. Tarasoff

Introduction

Dean Wood, Vice-president Academic of Keyano College in Fort McMurray (B.C.), wrote in a personal essay (Wood, 1994:29):

> ...Multiculturalism is central to the common good of Canadians. We will not uphold the core values of our heritage and contemporary society unless we actively seek the mutual respect, cross-cultural communications and acceptance of diversity which are the essence of multiculturalism....

The Doukhobors make up some 30,000 of Canada's population; they are citizens of Canada and are part of that multicultural mix Dean Wood wrote about. In this paper I would like to show how the Doukhobors fit in with — or are different from — other groups in Canada's mosaic. I would especially like to point out those critical fault lines where the multicultural fabric of Canadian society has been tested to the limit and where understanding and mutual respect are key ingredients that ensure legitimate citizenship.

1. Doukhobors and the Old State

In Tsarist Russia, the Doukhobors arose as a dissident group challenging the authority of the church and state. As heretics they were perceived as dangerous to the dominant society. When both the state and the church failed to exterminate them, in 1802 Tsar Alexander I brought them together for the first time into one central area — the *Molochnye Vody* (Milky Waters) region of the Crimea. Living in village communes, they prospered for several decades as a state within a state. Exiled to Transcaucasia in the 1840s, the pacifist Doukhobors were forced to survive amidst the marauding mountain peoples they called 'Tatars'. When their soldiers-in-training threw down their firearms on Easter Day 1895, followed by the mass demonstration of weapon-burning in June, a great many Doukhobors (at least one-third their number) became subject to persecution. A few years later 7,500 Doukhobors fled to Canada as a 'persecuted minority'.

Those who stayed behind in Russia faced the new forces of the

revolution and communism. Because they possessed collective attributes, they were at first respected and granted exemption from military
service in 1919. The policy would not last long, however, for by the 1930s,
Stalin's *pogrom* against the so-called *kulaks*[2] included the arrest and
deportation to Siberia of many hardworking Doukhobors. The Doukhobors' reaction to these persecutions is typical of their overall spirit and
attitude to life, as illustrated in the following examples:

- In the village of Orlovka, in the Bogdanovka District of the Caucasus,
  some forty Doukhobors were exiled to Siberia, but only seven were
  known to have survived (Tarasoff, 1991:73). One of those who survived
  twelve years in exile was a family man who had several more sheep
  than the limit of two dictated by Stalin. In an attempt to save his own
  skin the man's nephew had pointed a finger at his uncle. When the
  uncle returned years later to the same village, the nephew was still
  there. The man had no hard feelings towards his kin and even lent him
  some money when asked to do so. 'Why did you do it?' asked another
  relative. 'Because I felt it was the right thing to do', the uncle replied.
- Another case is that of **Anna Petrovna Markova** (born 1902) who spent
  fifteen years in Siberian exile. When she came to Canada in 1960 to join
  her son, **John J. Verigin**, she expressed no anger toward her motherland
  for persecuting her. In her own words (Markova, 1974:8):

  I felt no hard feelings toward those who were directly responsible for my
  misfortunes; I departed with a clear and tranquil conscience, as before
  God, likewise before the people.

In Canada the Doukhobor emigrants found a liberal capitalist state
based on a British model, where the ruling class (nearly all of British
heritage) tended to relegate all immigrants to the castelike category of
'foreign workers'. Promises of free land, exemption from military service
and non-interference in education were not always fulfilled to the Doukhobors' expectations. In fact history was to reveal significantly differing
expectations on each side. Stephen Leacock's inelegant assessment of
several groups of immigrants, (including Doukhobors) revealed the
temper of the day (1937:161):

  The government could hardly eliminate these 'undigested and undiges-
  table' lumps in the ethnic stew of the Canadian West, but it could make
  certain that no special advantages were given them.

2. Doukhobors participate in Canada

The majority of Canadian officials, along with the mainstream Anglo-Saxon population, would ask the question: 'Will these people assimilate to Canada?'

The Doukhobors chose another path, saying: 'We support integration, not assimilation'. Inspired by the world-renowned writer and philosopher Lev Tolstoy as well as their own tradition of non-violence, they saw themselves as bearers of a global citizenship. 'Love is the central beacon of their life's path', they said. The commandment 'Thou shalt not kill' was taken to heart.

Upon arriving at the immigration halls in Winnipeg, the new migrants shared their culture with Canadians. They made wooden ladles and gave them to passers-by in gratitude to Canada for accepting them as new pioneers and giving them hope of becoming *bona-fide* citizens. The hospitality inherent in their cultural history helped them make friends in Canada — an auspicious start to their new life in this 'land of opportunity'.

3. Accommodation to modern society

Not all Doukhobors have accomodated to their new surroundings in the same way however. Of the 30,000 Doukhobors in Canada, the majority are known as *Independents*. Generally the least organised, they have adapted more quickly to modern times, rejecting inherited charismatic leadership in favour of the tradition of collective leadership, while still preserving their inner integrity.

The *Community Doukhobors*, today known as the Union of Spiritual Communities of Christ (USCC) under Honorary Chariman *John J. Verigin Sr*, clung to the spiritual charismatic leadership of *Peter V. Verigin*, the leader who was finally released from exile in Siberia in 1902 and permitted to join the Doukhobors in Canada. While this group is the most organised and the wealthiest in terms of corporate property, their official paid membership is less than 2,000. They consider themselves the 'real' Doukhobors, in contrast to the Independents, who are seen as having 'sold out' to the government.

Even more radical is a fringe *zealot* group known as the 'Sons of Freedom' (or alternatively as Freedomites, Wanderers, Pilgrims or Sons of God), considered untrustworthy (if not outright criminals) by other Doukhobors. The zealots see themselves as the true followers of God's laws, the 'bell ringers' of society, and seek to return to the earlier traditions of a more simple life, free from both horses and machines. In terms of numbers the group is practically negligible, though still observable on the Western Canadian landscape.

Finding difficulty in understanding these peculiar Russian immigrants and their behaviour, the Canadian public revealed an often hidden intolerance of diversity by calling for rational, legalistic regulations to enforce assimilation, appealing to the 'the rule of law' to compel conformity to its own historical models.

The media contributed to the over-reaction by exploiting the actions of the zealots and tarring all Doukhobors with the brush of sensationalism. In time, the zealots saw an opportunity to use this publicity for their own interests — at the expense of the movement as a whole. The vast majority of Doukhobors felt deeply hurt at being branded nudists and criminals by misidentifiction with the zealots.

4. Canadian Multiculturalism Policy (1971) and Act (1988)

The 1971 Multicultural Policy and the 1988 Multiculturalism Act aimed to reflect tolerance of diversity in Canada by going beyond two official languages and cultures. The Doukhobors considered this new trend of cultural maturity beneficial not only for them but for all Canadian citizens of whatever ethnic background. Most Doukhobors are proud to be Canadians and are also proud of their Russian heritage. They think of themselves as bridge-builders — a synthesis between liberal individual rights and collective community rights. Hence they embraced multiculturalism as the way of the future.

Yet it is a fact that core values in a multicultural society (a 'social family', so to speak) may sometimes be in conflict: *'fault lines'* appear — certain issues on which people from opposite sides of the cross-cultural axis do not see eye to eye. Mutual respect and acceptance is needed for the family to stay together. Several fault lines can be identified: military service, land ownership, the oathof-allegiance clause, public school education, heritage language and culture, as well as the cooperative ethic and communal structure. Let us examine these 'fault lines', or crisis points, each of which may offer new insights into relations between the Doukhobors and their fellow Canadians of other backgrounds.

4.1 Military service and the oath of allegiance

Military service and the oath of allegiance to a ruling monarch was as offensive to Doukhobors in Canada as it had been in Tsarist Russia. They are internationalists and cosmopolitans at heart — people who refuse to think of themselves as defined by geographical location, ancestry, citizenship or language, although in practice, some compromise is required for survival in a multicultural setting — a balance of continuity and change which will ensure a stable group cohesion.

The Doukhobors' long pacifist tradition directly conflicts with the more prevalent beliefs that might is right, that conflicts are best resolved through military force, and that military service is a pragmatic means of promoting 'manhood'.

In 1932 the Royal Canadian Legion petitioned the federal government to prohibit all Doukhobors from becoming registered owners of any property outside the areas already set aside for their use (Lanthier and Wong, 1996).

In both world wars, more than 95 percent of eligible Doukhobor men in Canada refused to join the military. They were jailed, did alternative work on roads or in the bush, made donations to the Red Cross,[3] or somehow managed to otherwise ignore the whole rotten disease of war. Distinguished lawyer and civil libertarian *Peter G. Makaroff* 'turned the other cheek' in a Municipal Council chamber in Saskatoon (and was slapped in the face by an alderman) when he supported CCF leader J. S. Woodsworth's lone call in Parliament for Canada not to participate in World War II.[4]

Later during the Cold War period the Doukhobors were subjected to discrimination as a 'Russian collective group' and therefore a potentially 'subversive presence' in Canada. A number of Doukhobors reported hiding in their own communities from the critical eyes of the authorities. Many, sceptical of politics and the whole political process, ceased to vote in elections altogether.[5]

For the past fifty years Canadian Doukhobors have been actively working with other peace groups in holding peace and disarmament demonstrations — opposing the atomic bomb, the cruise missile, the Distant Early Warning Line, biological and radiological weapons, and military training in schools and universities. A committed pacifist, Peter Makaroff actively participated in and promoted these peace events in the 1960s. Before he died in 1970, he established an annual World Federalist Peace Prize of $500, open to any student or faculty member in any

Canadian university, 'for the best annual essay relating to world peace through world law' (Robertson/ Stromberg, 1996:5).

To this day, Doukhobors maintain a deep aversion to war and violence. To them (as to many others) the dropping of atomic bombs on Hiroshima and Nagasaki in 1945 was an uncivilised act that threatened our planet. In 1997 they proclaimed Canadian Minister of Foreign Affairs Lloyd Axworthy a courageous hero for spearheading an international campaign to ban land mines around the world.

The Doukhobors' opposition to war, fully shared by writer Lev Tolstoy, and their conviction that non-violence is the only rational way of the future — is a deep-rooted value that flies in the face of the so-called 'military-industrial complex'. To them the overall deterioration of health and social programmes is directly tied to the armed services' addiction to expensive and uncivilised military solutions. For pacifist activists such as the Doukhobors, the right way to live is something to be taught by example, while the state-sanctioned slaughter of fellow human beings is the very antithesis of love and universal brotherhood.

4.2 Land ownership

On this point Doukhobors fully shared the view of Tolstoy and other philosophers, as well as Canadian native peoples: land is a divine gift to be used by humanity but not to be bought or sold. The old Russian *mir* or commune system had embraced land as a common resource to be used by those working on it.

When the Doukhobors arrived in Canada they (like the Mennonites before them) were allowed to settle in hamlets and work land in common around the villages. But with an rapid influx of new settlers and a new electorate, the government soon changed its policy and restricted the 'free' allotment of one quarter-section (160 acres = 65 ha) to individual homesteaders who would agree to cultivate only their own land and to swear an oath of allegiance to the Crown.

Some Doukhobors reluctantly accepted the former provision but were able to take advantage of a legal provision the government had earlier offered earlier Mennonite settlers in Manitoba: they were allowed to cross out the oath-of-allegiance clause on their application in favour of simply 'affirming the truth' before the presiding official. These were the *Independent* Doukhobors, who were the first to allow their children to be educated in the Canadian system, and hence the first to gain entry into the professions, as early as their second decade in their new land.

Other Doukhobors were too steeped in their earlier habits of the mir system to give up communal ownership. Organised as the Christian Community of Universal Brotherhood (CCUB) under the leadership of Peter V. Verigin, in 1907–08 these *Communal Doukhobors* gave up millions of dollars' worth of property on the Canadian prairies to trek hundreds of kilometres westward to British Columbia. Here they could purchase land privately and avoid the restrictions of the Homestead Act, including the oath-of-allegiance question. In 1938, however, the CCUB's six--million-dollar collective enterprise fell prey to the general Depression and, when the provincial government withdrew their support, came to an abrupt end. For more than twenty years its members were forced to live as squatters on their own land. Eventually, in 1961, the land was sold back to them, notwithstanding their earlier objection to private ownership.

Some Community Doukhobors, however, refused to accept this new arrangement, fearing it would only lead total assimilation and the loss of inner integrity.[6] Opposed to materialism and to accomodation with any political structure, they identified with the breakaway *zealot* 'Sons of Freedom' group, deciding to live in a wilderness community they called the 'New Settlement'[7] — in effect, a self-proclaimed 'state within a state' — and refusing to pay either federal or provincial taxes. Some zealots went from village to village trying to recruit support for their ideas. Others even turned to nudity and violence to promulgate their ideas, first burning the canvas of a grain-harvesting binder and later setting fire to the residence of a community leader. Several bombings and burnings followed erratically, often without the specific culprits being identified. The vast majority of Doukhobors, however, by nature a peaceful lot, saw this behaviour as uncivilised, and a threat to their selfimage and cultural prosperity.

It was not until the 1990s that a humanities student at the University of Victoria, a non-Doukhobor by the name of Charles Ball, recognising some legitimacy in the zealots' wishes to lead their own way of life, took it upon himself to act as an intermediary between them and the government. Through his efforts a Memorandum of Understanding was drawn up in 1995 between the New Settlement and the B.C. Government, whereby zealots were allowed to continue their collective lifestyle and perform community service (such as road construction) in lieu of taxes. Their communal land was to be held in trust by a society (under Ball's chairmanship) known as the Reformed Sons of Freedom Communal

Doukhobors. Their numbers, however, are dwindling, as many zealots have opted to pay taxes for government services, and with exposure to new technologies, television, computers and education (Tarasoff & Kristova, 1995:83), even some of the younger members have decided to leave the hold-out group and integrate themselves into the larger Canadian society.[8]

4.3 Public education, registration of births, marriages and deaths

In Saskatchewan, Independent Doukhobors saw education as the way to adapt to the new land. As the first lawyer of nonAnglo-Saxon origin to graduate from the University of Saskatchewan in 1918, Peter G. Makaroff set an example for many Independent Doukhobors who became professional doctors, engineers, nurses and educators, as well as agronomists. These people went through local school boards with little difficulty because Saskatchewan allowed ethnic minorities (including Doukhobors) to have a voice on local school boards. Problem areas such as military training were generally dealt with sensitively.

Doukhobors faced a different situation in British Columbia, where local school boards were selected by the ministry of education in Victoria, often excluding local minority representation. Utterly confounded by the Doukhobors' opposition to saluting the flag, doing military exercises, learning the value of patriotism, not to mention regularly attending public school, registering for births, marriages and deaths, the government of the day chose to enforce conformity through legislation: in 1914 it created the *Community Regulations Act,* which had the effect of punishing the whole Community for infractions of the act on the part of individual members.

In September 1915 a temporary compromise was reached when the B.C. attorney-general promised a delegation of Doukhobors that no military training would be forced upon their children and that they would be excused from religious exercises in the public schools. However, following World War II, these accords were put under strain as the government, under pressure to find lands for returning soldiers, attempted to take communal lands away from the Doukhobors. Some parents responded by taking their children out of school.

A new school inspector by the name of E.G. Daniels took countermeasures in the form of fines (Janzen, 1990:130): in April 1923 fines of $50 each were levied on six parents. When they were slow in paying, the B.C. government seized CCUB property, including a large truck that was used for farm work, which was not returned until the Community paid the fine. When all nine schools that the Doukhobors had built for their children were burnt to the ground, possibly by some radical members (a very small minority), the government again used its Community Regulations Act to blame the Community rather than go after the individual culprits — a policy it continued to follow for many more years to come. This in spite of public declarations by Verigin and other Community leaders that the Community as a whole had nothing to do with the burnings and that many of their children were still attending school.

4.4 Heritage language and culture

One hundred years after leaving their homeland, one of the Doukhobors' prominent concerns is how the Russian language, the linguistic expression of their heritage for over three centuries, will survive in the next century. Some fear that if it is not maintained the Doukhobor movement itself will die. Parents have sent their children to both day and evening Russian classes (day classes have been held in the Grand Forks and Castlegar districts since 1975 under a federal Multiculturalism programme). Young Doukhobors have been encouraged to travel to Russia and enrol in Russian universities (an opportunity that over the past three decades has been taken advantage of by more than 150 Canadian Doukhobors with the assistance of the Russian *Rodina* Society).

Some see a more radical solution still, namely, making a permanent move back to Russia. According to one USCC member *Mary Shukin* of Nelson, B.C. (Tarasoff & Kristova, 1995:57),

> We are losing our traditions here. We used to have many more singers before. Young people now speak English in school. They intermarry. We want them to speak Russian at home... In Nelson we went to a neighbour's place; they said: 'Our dog eats meat, but does not speak Russian'. Many speak of migrating back to Russia because it was prophesied by Lukeria Kalmykova that a small group would return... I fear that we will lose the Russian language. If we lose Russian, we will lose our Doukhoborism. Already Saskatchewan Doukhobors have translated some psalms into English. You can't do that!

Along with the Russian language, a prominent part of the culture, at least of the Community Doukhobors, is *a cappella* singing, which is intimately connected to their beliefs, attitudes and way of life. By illustration, choir leader and singer *Bill Kootnekoff* says (Tarasoff & Kristova, 1995:70):

> In our organisation [USCC], we do not accept [written] music. We believe that would harm our live singing. We strive to remember by heart — so that our voices would remain harmonious. That is why we do not need music. Our singing is live; it comes from the heart.... We strive for harmony.

4.5 Co-operative ethic and communal structure

The Doukhobor co-operative ethic and communal structure is designed to provide equality and access to the goods and services of a normally functioning society. Unlike the profitoriented free enterprise system, where the emphasis is on making money rather than redistributing it to others, profit plays a role in the co-operative, but not at the expense of its members or of society at large.

Through their incorporated Christian Community of Universal Brotherhood (CCUB), the communal Doukhobors initiated a wide array of business ventures, including agricultural projects, lumbering, sawmill operations, brick factories, machine shops, food processing and retail stores.[9] The rapid growth of these enterprises attested to the significant communal profits that could be quickly derived from cooperative ventures. Under pressure from neighbours, however, who saw such enterprises as a threat to their own livelihood, politicians sought measures to curb the growth of this trend, including abolishing Doukhobors' rights to own communal land (see *4.2* above).

The Bolshevik Revolution of 1917 gave the Canadian government a ready excuse to deport certain Slavs, Finns and Jews they considered potential communist troublemakers (McLaren, 1995:113). As a communal Russian-speaking group, the Doukhobors came under particular suspicion and surveillance almost as soon as they arrived in Canada (see also *4.1* above). From 1919 to 1926 further Doukhobor immigration was barred under Canadian law. In 1933 there was an unsuccessful attempt to deport their current leader *Peter P. Verigin* (see McLaren, 1995).

However, over the years the co-operative principle underlying the Doukhobor philosophy has managed to leave its mark on at least some private enterprise ventures. A prime example is the home industry of co-operative games developed by *Jim Deacove* in 1971 which promotes the co-operative spirit not only in its product but in the very nature of its business operation.[10] It is a hopeful sign that co-operation, rather than competition, will yet become the guiding principle of business in the twenty-first century.

5. Liberal democracy and multiculturalism

Law professor John McLaren has noted that for most of this century, social and legal policy toward communal groups within the fabric of Canadian social policy has been 'notable for its lack of imagination and accommodation and for its propensity to force conformity and assimilation in a crude and capricious manner' (McLaren, 1995:110). We have already seen this with the communal land confiscation of 1907, the Community Regulations Act of 1914 which held the Community collectively liable for its individual members' actions, and the B.C. government's complete withdrawal of support for communal enterprises in 1938.

Multiculturalism is a form of pluralism in society. A healthy liberal society needs a good dose of cultural interaction and blending in order for its citizens to learn to tolerate diversity. It needs to learn that different styles of life do not normally harm society, but contribute to its creativity, development and renewal. Lessons from groups such as Doukhobors, Hutterites, Mennonites and Quakers help benefit and enrich the nation as a whole.

Anthropologists have shown that a healthy dynamic society requires both *continuity* (based on custom and tradition) and *change* (adaptability). When small islands of peoples are not involved in the normal societal process of development, solitudes tend to arise, often resulting in inter--group discrimination and disorder.

Journalist *Bill Koreluik* has noticed a positive societal change in Saskatchewan (Tarasoff & Kristova, 1995:107). He contrasts the negative attitudes toward the radical Doukhobor 'Freedomites' (extended, by ignorance, to the Doukhobors as a whole) portrayed in a 1908 issue of the *Kamsack Times*, for example, with the near-universal acceptance of the group by Canadian society today: many years of peaceful inter-group contact, co-existence and integration have erased virtually all trace of the old mistrust and hostility.

Another example comes from the Castlegar district of British Columbia. *Tammy Verigin* talks about the process of acceptance and belongng (Tarasoff & Kristova, 1995:52):

> When I was growing up in Castlegar, it was a hard time being a Doukhobor. I remember when I used to go to Sunday School on Sunday. If we

saw any of our friends, we used to hide. We had to hide our *platoks* [kerchiefs]. We were afraid our friends would see us... I loved what happened when we got to the *Dom* [Community Home]. But I didn't want my friends to see me in a *platok*... Everything my parents taught me... I didn't really go away from it self-consciously. But I did when I moved away to Vancouver. I found the more people asked me about it and I explained about it, the more I realised the kind of lifestyle I lead is very much a Doukhobor lifestyle. I became more and more proud of it as I got older. When I came back to the Kootenay area, I became involved in Mum and Dad's Doukhobor Heritage Retreat project. I find that whenever there is a Doukhobor event, not only myself but my partner is very interested in the Doukhobor faith. He comes along. I just become more and more involved and proud of my past too.

6. The Rise of the 'New Spirit'

For the past decade Professor John Friesen has taught a course on multiculturalism — including the Doukhobors — at the University of Calgary. He recalls visiting Doukhobors in their B.C. community of Brilliant during his childhood days in nearby Trail. At the 1995 Doukhobor Centenary of the Burning of Arms, he stated (Tarasoff & Kristova, 1995:35):

> My own roots are deep. My grandfather was a Mennonite lay preacher...
> I am very pleased that the image of the Doukhobors in literature is really
> being promoted in a more public way...as many Doukhobors are rising
> up from the inside... They really tell the story from inside, from the heart.

He then added that an adaptability to change is required to ensure continuity (*ibid.*):

> Ask not what the USCC or the Canadian Doukhobor Society can do for
> you, but what you can do as an individual. What will be the spark to keep
> *Toil and Peaceful Life* and love of brotherhood going as individuals to
> commune together, to go forth and carry the message individually? My
> students hear this. They are amazed that such people could exist.

One recent changes affecting Doukhobor society has been the computer revolution, especially the Internet. Doukhobors have been included not only in the Canadian Museum of Civilization's displays but also in its website, with a whole web page on the Doukhobors complete with images and sounds.[11] Some Doukhobors have set up their own home pages, — for example the *Doukhobor Home Page*[12] and the *Canadian Doukhobor Society Gateway Website.*[13]

The 1995 Arms-Burning Centenary released a new spirit of involvement. As part of the celebrations, a Centennial Choir of 65 participants
from all the Doukhobor groups toured the country before going abroad
to New York and Russia. When *Jeanette Derksen* was asked why she
joined the *Voices for Peace* choir tour, she replied (Tarasoff & Kristova,
1995:54):

> To awaken mankind. We are all singing the same songs, only in different
> languages. It's my hope and my dream that we will be part of humanity
> making the turn and creating a more peaceful and better world in which
> to live.

Another choir member, *Alex Kalesnikoff*, has been active in
reviving the Doukhobor movement in Calgary. He also took a personal
interest in sponsoring a number of Russian Doukhobor visitors to
Canada. He says that not only can we preserve our tradition, culture,
language and identity, we can even enhance it (Tarasoff & Kristova,
1995:54):

> Many of us are in the business world. I think we should get more polit-
> ically involved because we will then have that inner voice within gov-
> ernment — and I think it does play a part as with the Native people.

Orator *Norm Rebin* echoed the call for political involvement in society
both as individuals and as a collective body (Tarasoff & Kristova,
1995:47):

> By being part of the game, we can introduce legislation...options and
> alternatives. This is an age of co-venture, co-working, men working with
> women, a child working with father, son and father working on a business
> together, mother and granddaughter owning a business together. If they
> can co-venture, surely we can now take the message out and coventure
> with all the groups that have a common belief with us.

Max Zbitnoff of California created a T-shirt in honour of the arms-
burning centenary. His brother and two sisters joined the celebrations in
Castlegar and they promise to do the same for the 1999 Centenary of the
Doukhobor emigration to Canada. Max's father, who was born in
Canada, become a prominent doctor with an interest in genealogy
and photography.

For three months in 1995 Russian artist *Volodia Gubanov* from the
Doukhobor community of Bogdanovka in the Caucasus, was a guest of
the Canadian Doukhobors. The several dozen portraits he executed in
Canada are a first step toward creating a large collage portraying

Doukhobors of the world. He describes his dream as follows (Tarasoff & Kristova, 1995:63):

> I would like to [establish] a Russian Doukhobor Centre in Verigin, Saskatchewan. Also in Moscow and Tula [near Tolstoy's Yasnaya Polyana] I see a need for a Doukhobor Centre — a place to stay, a place to learn the Russian language... I see a place where some rebirth could take place.

For the 1995 Centenary, Volodia painted a philosophical scene of the arms burning and used it to illustrate a calendar which he made for the occasion.

Summary and conclusion

Canadian Doukhobors are part of a world body which has survived for more than three centuries under tsarism, communism and capitalism. In the process of survival they have had to compromise in order to share and promote their central message of love and universal brotherhood. Most of these compromises have touched one of several 'fault lines' or crisis points: military service, land ownership, public school education, heritage language & culture and the co-operative communal ethic.

> Multiculturalism and changing times have given Doukhobors a new opportunity to express themselves and be counted. The 1995 and 1999 Centenaries have provided the occasion for new interests and creative energies to appear. Recognition by institutions such as the Canadian Museum of Civilization has made them feel at home in their adopted country, while Heritage Canada has helped them understand themselves by funding some of their efforts. Peter Gzowski's interview on the Doukhobors in January 1996[14] was an example of a genuine attempt on the part of the media to discover the Doukhobors on the occasion of the arms-burning Centenary. The publication of celebratory books and journals (Tarasoff and Klymasz, 1995; *Canadian Ethnic Studies*, 1995) has provided an additional opportunity to spread the Doukhobor spirit to the public at large. Still another important sign of societal accommodation was the University of Victoria's selection of a Doukhobor as their 1997 Lansdowne lecturer (see footnote 1 above). This new spirit of recognition and participation indeed bodes well for the future of the Doukhobors and their unique role in the Canadian multicultural fabric.

References

Doukhobor Home Page (1996/ed. Ryan Androsoff). Internet address: http://www
.dlcwest.com/~r.androsoff/index.htm

Canadian Ethnic Studies (1995). Special Issue: From Russia With Love: The Doukhobors. Comp./ed. Koozma J. Tarasoff. Calgary, Alberta, vol. 27, n°. 3, 1995, 303 pp.

Canadian Museum of Civilization (1997). The Doukhobors: Spirit Wrestlers. Cdn Mus. of Civilization Web Page. Internet address: http://www.cmcc.muse.digital.ca/membrs/traditio/doukhobors/dou01eng.html

Deacove, Jim (1997). Family Pastimes: Catalogue of Co-operative Games. Created by Jim Deacove. Perth, Ont.

CDS Gateway Website (1997/ed. Larry Ewashen). Internet address: http://www.kootenay.net/~cds/news.htm

Janzen, William (1990). The experience of Mennonite, Hutterite and Doukhobor communities in Canada. Toronto: University of Toronto Press.

McLaren, John (1995). 'Wrestling Spirits: the strange case of Peter Verigin II'. Canadian Ethnic Studies, vol. 27, n° 3, 1995: 95–130.

Lanthier, Mario and Lloyd L. Wong (1996). Chapter V, 'The Doukhobors: 1930s –1950s', in Ethnic agricultural labour in the Okanagan Valley: 1880s to 1960s.

Leacock, Stephen (1937). My Memory of the West. New York: Hale, Cushman & Flint.

Markova, Anna Petrovna (1974). 'An Interview with Anna Petrovna Markova'. Mir (Grand Forks, B.C.), vol. l, n° 7–10, Feb. 1974.

Robertson/Stromberg (1996). 'Peter G. Makaroff, K. C. 1894–1970' (Firm History). Robertson Stromberg Web Page. Internet address: http://www.robertsonstromberg.com/makaroff.htm

Tarasoff, Koozma J. (1982). Plakun Trava: The Doukhobors. Grand Forks, B.C.: Mir Publications Society.

Tarasoff, Koozma J. (1991). Notes on the Doukhobor expedition to the USSR (Aug. 1991), unpublished.

Tarasoff, Koozma J. and Robert B. Klymasz (eds.) (1995). Spirit Wrestlers: Centennial Papers in Honour of Canada's Doukhobor Heritage. Ottawa: Canadian Museum of Civilization.

Tarasoff, Koozma J. and Kristina Kristova (1995). Photo Shot Log on the Doukhobors (undertaken as part of the 1995 Burning of Arms Centenary, May–Aug 1995), unpublished.

Wood, Dean (1994). 'Multiculturalism toward the year 2000'. Multicultural Education Journal (Edmonton, Alta.), vol. 12, n° 2 (Autumn 1994): 21–29.

[1]This is a revised and updated version of the third of Koozma J. Tarasoff's three Lansdowne lectures on the Doukhobors at the University of Victoria, Victoria, British Columbia, 20-22 October 1997. The first two were entitled: 'Spirit Wrestlers: Early Canadian Pioneers' and 'Doukhobors at the Threshold of the Millenium'.

[2]*kulak* — a member of a wealthier peasant-class accused of exploiting other peasants for their own gain.

[3]In mid-November 1943 a delegation of both Independent and Community Doukhobors met with officials in Ottawa to discuss exemption from military service. In an effort to recognise the Doukhobors' historical claims while still assuring the public that this group was making 'a contribution to the welfare of Canada' (Janzen, 1990:235) and not detracting from the general war effort, the government offered exemption from military service on the condition that the Doukhobors either (a) accept employment in one of the alternative work-camps at a rate of $15 per month or (b) stay on their farms or in their current jobs and make monthly donations to the Red Cross. William Janzen (244) further notes: 'In summary, then, the social climate, the contribution of the conscientious objectors through the alternative-service program, the government's commitment to honour the historic promises of exemption, the persistent lobbying by leaders of these groups, and the flexibility of the political system all help to explain why, despite numerous problems, these groups [the Doukhobors, Mennonites, Hutterites etc.] were permitted to enjoy a relatively broad freedom during the Second World War.'

[4]Makaroff was known for his determined efforts on behalf of labour and persecuted minorities during the Great Depression. Born in Kars, Russia, he came to Canada with the 1899 migration, settling on the banks of the North Saskatchewan River north-east of Saskatoon. Educated first by the Quakers in Philadelphia, he then attended Rosthern Academy and later the University of Saskatchewan, where he obtained a B.A. in 1915 and a Bachelor of Laws in 1918. He became the first Doukhobor in the world to receive a university degree and enter a profession. A close friend and kindred spirit to pacifist J. S. Woodsworth, founder of the social-democratic Co-operative Commonwealth Federation (CCF), he stood for the CCF twice: first in the Saskatchewan provincial election of 1934 in the riding of Shellbrook and later in the Rosthern riding in the 1940 federal election (Stromberg Web Page, 1996: 5).

[5]The USCC in its Declaration states that its members are above party politics and therefore should abstain from voting; in reality, however, most members have voted in recent elections.

[6]This was the view held by zealot *Mike Chernenkoff,* who sees himself and his fellow zealots as revolutionaries: 'They are an advance party with the role of accomplishing a mission for the Doukhobors... to prevent the assimilation of the core ideas', who cannot compromise in purchasing land or paying taxes (Tarasoff & Kristova, 1995:77–78).

[7]Formed in 1972, the 'New Settlement' (Russian: *Novaia Poselka*) was located in an

idyllic wilderness setting near the village of Krestova, between Nelson and Castlegar.

[8]Mike Chernenkoff himself now uses a computer (operated on batteries, since the community still does not accept electrification), as does his self-educated Krestova neighbour *Steve Lapshinoff*, who is now publishing Doukhobor historical materials from his home base.

[9]On this point see *Peter Podovinikoff*'s paper in this volume.

[10]See Jim Deacove's paper in this volume for a description.

[11]http://www.cmcc.muse.digital.ca/membrs/traditio/doukhobors/dou01eng. html — the *Canadian Museum of Civilization/Doukhobor Website*, a site complete with a visual walking tour of the CMC Doukhobor exhibit and sound clips of their singing. This was the first full web site on the Doukhobors and was designed to complement the museum's Spirit Wrestlers/Doukhobor exhibit which opened in January 1996.

[12]http://www.dlcwest.com/~r.androsoff/index.htm — the *Doukhobor Home Page*, organised by *Ryan Androsoff* of Saskatoon and supported by several groups and individuals: the Union of Spiritual Communities of Christ, the Doukhobor Cultural Society of Sasakatchewan, the Saskatoon Doukhobor Society and Jon-Lee Kootnekoff. It gives links to other Doukhobor websites.

[13]http://www.kootenay.net/~cds/news.htm — *The CDS Gateway Website*, produced in British Columbia as a co-operative by the Canadian Doukhobor Society as an independent voice of Doukhobor thinking, currently edited by *Larry Ewashen*. Its webmaster *John J. Semenoff* regularly updates the extensive site and provides links not only to other Doukhobor sites but also to sites on Tolstoy, the Quakers, Mennonites and Molokans, United Nations and various peace organisations.

[14]Peter Gzowski on *Morningside* (CBC Radio One): interview with Koozma Tarasoff and John Woodsworth, 12 January 1996.

Doukhobor youth: the yeast of the new leadership loaf

Norman K. Rebin

When asked to contribute to Koozma Tarasoff's tome of essays on the Doukhobors, I was uncertain. One part of me said: 'What a privilege to join the crew of this new Doukhobor voyage!', while the other (perhaps saner) side of me argued: 'What a drag! Who really cares if this voyage takes place except die-hard Doukhobor voyeurs of our controversial, colourful and charismatic clan? Do you really want to write this essay only for them?'

Yet, in sane analysis, there is always the germ of salvation. I decided that, in doing this piece, I would be writing neither for the anointed — or the appointed — friends of Doukhoborism, but for all those who have yet to immerse themselves in the waters of our faith. I would write to, for, and about, the youth of our movement — those sprouting from the seeds of Doukhobor parentage, as well as those whose seed-base is philosophical, rather than biological.

In Doukhoborism there is, I believe, a calling which is both cleansing and challenging — a calling which should appeal to youth everywhere. For in this age of pollution — both external and internal — Doukhoborism offers a viable, do-able option: to live in peace and harmony both with our ecology and with our planetary brothers and sisters. To embrace that option, however, Doukhobor youth, by birth or by choice, will need to be audacious, articulate, adaptable and active. Call it the 'A-factor' of Doukhobor survival — the yeast by which the new loaf of Doukhobor leadership will rise.

I have always believed in being audacious, being daring! If I had not been daring, I would not, now, be enjoying my current (and original) English-Scottish wife, my avocation of oratory, my political status among my peers, my incredible global network of friends, my one-of-a-kind residence, retreat and refuge, or, for that matter, my life. Most importantly, I would not be in a position to enjoy, for half a century now, the harmony and balance of Doukhborism that, as a minority of one, I have carried with me to the many places where I have studied, lived, travelled and worked throughout the world.

Let me summarise the reasons behind these statements. I grew up in

Blaine Lake, Saskatchewan, on a 'mixed'1 farm where my neighbours were primarily Doukhobors of Russian descent, with some Ukrainians, English and French Canadians thrown in for good measure. From earliest memory I attended services conducted in Russian, visited Russian-speaking grandparents and other relatives, and complemented my one-room country school education in English with Russian language studies under the tutelage of a refined and well-educated aristocrat by the name of Mrs Fedoroff.

At that time, being a Doukhobor also very much meant being Russian; socialising and procreation were basically restricted to the 'clan'. In fact, I was raised believing that the 'other side' (i.e., anyone who was not a Doukhobor) was 'okay', but different enough not to be completely trusted. Some groups were definitely of the 'suspicious' variety: the Anglo-Saxons, for example, who were seen as both dominant and domineering; and the Ukrainians, who, in spite of being fellow Slavs, made their borshch blood-red with beets, instead of orange-ish with cabbage and tomato as 'we' did, obviously a bizarre, perhaps even barbaric, culinary practice!

I 'rode' a pony to school (I should qualify the word 'rode': sometimes the animal would take to flight and I would take to the ground when a prairie chicken alighted under its belly). By the time I left my country school to go live with my grandparents while attending high school, I was already steeped in the Doukhobor customs, traditions and constraints that would 'taunt and haunt' me for decades to come.

Doukhobors were definitely different! I was struck by the stark contrast between the beliefs of other Canadians I encountered at high school and the 'bread, salt and water' symbolising our belief in 'toil and peaceful life' or our desire to follow the basic priorities of 'natural living'. The high school taught patriotism and nationalism in place of the pacifism and internationalism professed by our community; and competition and individualism in place of co-operation and collectivism. English and French-speaking students talked of 'contacts' and 'family power' in politics, commerce, trade, academia and the professions, whereas our families encouraged more pastoral inclinations, farming, teaching and (above all) staying out of the public eye.

The contrasts came to a head when at age 22 I decided to make my first attempt to run for public office with a federal political party: an indignant Doukhobor elder tried to get me excommunicated for 'non-Doukhobor behaviour'.2 In short, I was being buffeted by the conflicting and uncomplementary forces of the need to seek achievement in the public forum on the one hand, and the need to seek advancement through private inner peace on the other.

I find it surprising that no Doukhobor sage ever suggested to me, then, what I am suggesting to you now — namely, that 'in order to keep youth, we must let youth go', and that inner peace and fulfilment are not inconsistent with outward achievement and empowerment! You must be daring with your potential if you are to stretch it to its limits! Being satisifed with containment is sometimes another way of saying 'I'm afraid to fly'! We all have fear, but how we channel that fear is crucial to our 'flight' as Doukhobors.

When I enrolled at the University of Saskatchewan in 1955 it was necessary to indicate one's religious affiliation on the application form. I boldly put down 'Doukhobor', but three of my Doukhobor friends indicated they were Baptist, Mennonite and Lutheran. In time even these 'revolving-door' Doukhobors conquered their fear of being rebuffed by their colleagues and openly returned to the fold.3 I was simply too brazen to hide my background. Eventually my openness led to invitations to speak about Doukhoborism at the three universities I attended in Canada and abroad.

It was not all smooth sailing! In 1959, while on a scholarship at the Dalhousie Law School in Halifax, I found this 'elegant' Valentine's Day message taped to the door of my residence room:

> Douky, Douky, Icky Douky
> Yours is yours and mine is mine
> You can strip and burn your house
> But you'll never be my valentine!

I never was!

It was during my time at Dalhousie that I proposed (by longdistance!) to that English-Scottish beauty of high cheekbones and brilliant warm eyes whose desk I had fallen over the previous year in university. I daringly chose to throw caution to the winds and to forget she was one of those 'oppressors' who 'dominated Canadian power circles'. That act has won me, to date, a thirty-eight-year relationship with that same beauty (Delva) and three extremely talented and individualistic children (Noral, Nowlan and Nicole).

I will not 'fudge' the facts, however: both sets of parents were adamantly opposed to the proposed 'union'. When Delva informed her parents that I was of Russian extraction — and a Doukhobor to boot — her father, an impassioned man, threatened to 'beat me to a bloody pulp' right on Second Avenue (one of the main streets of Saskatoon, where they lived). His argument was that in addition to being 'communist' (a totally incorrect stereotype he and many others held), I would probably come 'naked' to my own wedding (another stereotype, with only a minimal basis in fact).

Delva's mother reacted less dramatically: she simply took shelter in the family bathroom and refused to come out whenever I happened to be in the house. The only member of Delva's family to support me unconditionally was the family cat, who developed an attachment to my feet. The long and the short of it is that we eloped to Sweden, married in Stockholm, took advantage of scholarships and fellowships and broadened our horizons with travel, talk and trade.

I credit this daring of mine with having created for me a global awareness and an independence of thinking and action that has had a positive influence on my life to this day. I encourage others to do the same by marrying or bonding with the affair of their hearts without being intimidated by linguistic, cultural, religious or ethnic differences. Building on the 'commonalities' keep a couple close, and learning the other's language, customs, traditions and philosophical values will serve as a springboard to discover the greater 'self' within. The true universalism that underlies the Doukhobor view of life is a creed without geographical, cultural or demographic constraints.

Doukhoborism is an attitude that transcends divisiveness. 'Brotherhood is not boundaried; sisterhood is not stunted.' Acceptance of such a mind-set sets one on the road to external and internal peace — a peace which comes from harmony, a state of grace induced by love: love of humankind, love of nature, love of creation itself.

Love is probably the most articulate of all forms of expression. A child in trouble still feels his mother's love and forgiveness. This feeling is a language — clear even when unspoken. I certainly felt it with my mother, who had an inexhaustible reservoir of love for her brood in good times and in bad — a love that was tapped, tested and tried, but never dried up. Fathers express it too! A child in despair from some personal failure can feel his father's faith in his eventual restoration and revival.

I have explored many of the world's faiths — from mosque to temple, synagogue to church — but through all the sacred sites of the world I have never experienced such unabashed adoration of love itself as with the Doukhobors, especially as expressed in their Book of Life.

Witness the following example: 'Where there is counsel, there is light, where there is love, there is God.'4 To the Doukhobors, God is love, and both heaven and hell exist right here in the secular world in the way we live our lives.

As a Doukhobor, I have seen at first hand both heaven and hell. When my good friend Ray, after spending years in torment, frustration and isolation from the love he so craved from others, drove to a secluded spot in the Iowa countryside, put a gun to his temple and blew his skull apart, that was Hell. I shared that Hell — I had heard Ray's cry for help in an all-night talk in another part of the country a short time earlier, yet had failed to prevent the tragic outcome of his despair.

I also witnessed Heaven in the death of my grandfather Efim, who had come to Canada from Russia with the first Doukhobor emigrants in 1899. From his youth he had experienced the same appetite for life, the same thirst for travel and debate that I had, and I loved him without reservation. 'You and I, Kolia, are like fish and water',5 he would say. In his more advanced years he would 'walk with me' wherever in the world I went. Upon my return he would 'bleed' me for accounts of my wanderings until I had told him every last detail, and then we would proceed to 'debate' the merits (or demerits) of those wanderings until my head literally rang with his laughter, admonitions and rejoinders.

His death came some time after my marriage. He passed away in our arms at St Paul's Hospital in Saskatoon, his eyes locked on mine, his voice stilled by the intravenous tubes in his throat, his hand clenching the life in my hands, all the while silently (but eloquently) voicing his great, great elation at having lived. His wistful sadness was at having to finally let human life go, after almost ninety years. Then he was gone, leaving me with the feeling that, if death was so beautiful, so graceful and gracious, could life be anything less?

'Write it in your heart, proclaim it with your mouth', says a Doukhobor maxim.6 Only what you feel in your heart can you articulate with authority. Doukhobors know that. They know that the head can say only what the heart sees. They know about the abasement of today's world by cosmetic proclamations of intent, uttered solely for the purposes of short--term gain. They also know the long-term pain that results from such pretensions — pain that is everywhere around us, felt in massive national debt (while politicians proclaim 'balanced budgets' and 'fiscal responsibility'), monumental strife and violence (while government officials 'gab on' about 'global understanding' and 'peaceful co-existence') and monstrous environmental rape (while corporate executives extol the merits of 'recycling, restoration, conservation and sustainability').

All of this goes to prove that 'for evil to succeed it is only necessary for men (or women) of good will to do nothing'. The Doukhobors of Tomorrow must not only display their love of their planet but act on that love. The world needs them as activists in the cause of universal survival: people who propagate, proselytise and propound on behalf of that cause — even if that activism goes against traditional Doukhobor attitudes. For it is no longer good enough not to worship idols (remember the Doukhobor burning of arms a century ago and the subsequent persecutions they endured). It is necessary now — today and tomorrow — for Doukhobors to articulate the options on which the second millenium can be moulded and to endure the consequences.

To this end Doukhobors must learn the art and science of motivation, management and marketing. They must become proficient in the use of the media. If one voice speaks out but no one hears it, did anyone really speak? Television, mass rallies, syndication of articles, audiotapes and videocassettes, satellite communication, direct-mail appeals, accessing international foundations, lobbying international institutions and much, much more — all these must become the tools of a new wave of Doukhobor activists. With the help of what is known as the 'multiplier effect', they may yet have a positive impact on the world as a whole.

While Doukhobors, numerically speaking, are but a 'pimple' on the face of the world, they could, potentially, become a 'rash' that envelops the world's body. For every Doukhobor who lives and proclaims Doukhobor values, there are multitudes waiting to follow — such is the 'multiplier effect'. The world writhes in a vacuum of unfocussed existence — a mass of 'lemmings' waiting for 'leaders' to advance human progress. Surely the Doukhobor law of leadership — 'What I do not desire for myself, I do not wish for my brother (or sister)' — is the most effective and efficient way to fill that vacuum.

Leadership in troubled and traumatic times, however, requires a high degree of adaptability. Today's sovereign boundaries are defied by 'aids' as well as by aid and trade, which are constantly rewriting the orthodox order of things. International 'joint ventures' are creating a new and favourable climate for business between old enemies, and technological cooperation is in the process of not only 'shrinking' the world, but at the same time 'miniaturising' it.

When we consider the possibility of discovering and cohabiting with our cosmic colleagues out there beyond our current stratospheric reach, we must ask ourselves where in the universe is there a rationale for 'ethnic cleansing'. Surely only the thick-headed and culturally depraved see a future in 'war games'!

I do not pretend to minimise the agony of the moment. I have been where violence was. I have seen the face of danger resulting from distrust, disillusionment, deprivation and denigration. I have conffronted fear when personally accosted and threatened.7 I know the truth in the saying: 'Let a man go hungry for twentyfour hours and he will wriggle with discomfort, but let a man go hungry for a week and he will be ready to wage war!'

Doukhobor adherents must prove adaptable enough to feel 'part' of wherever they live. In claiming their broader heritage as citizens of the world, they will discover their faith is indeed 'portable', one they can take with them even to places where there are no other known Doukhobors. I have carried my ideals with me to India and Sri Lanka, to Ireland and St Lucia, to Liechtenstein and Lapland, to Sweden and Samoa (along with a multitude of other countries) as a diplomat, scholar, lecturer and commentator. I was often alone, but seldom was I lonely. The curiosity in mankind that Doukhoborism instilled in me sustained me socially while the 'direct-dial' to God (no operator!) fuelled my faith.

Doukhobors do not need a 'palace' — nor even a 'temple' — to pray in, nor an intermediary (such as a priest or a fakir) to guide them. Doukhobors are 'self-deliverers' — they are their own 'theological mid--wives', so to speak. Looking into their own hearts, they find their own healer. Religions without pomp, protocol and posturing may be rare, but that is exactly what Doukhoborism is: a religion without recruitment, a movement without an army, a conscience without conscription.

Doukhobors know no 'corrals'. They go where they are needed even if they are not always heeded. By building selfsustaining communities (even in climates that would make polar bears shiver!), they have proved their extraordinary talent for innovation and adaptability. By learning new languages and demographics — and learning how to convert these into instruments of prosperity — they have proved that one's reach can be as wide as one's vision, and is limited only by one's limited vision. Tomorrow's Doukhobors must not fear change. On the contrary, they must court change. It is indeed true that 'change for the better often comes only after one has weathered the worst', and Doukhobors have certainly 'weathered the worst'.

One of my colleagues likes to say that we have experienced not so much 'bad times' as 'bad people' — people who served self not before, but in place of, others; people who have forfeited the future by indebting the present; people who have reached out only to push away instead of to embrace. Doukhobors have the opportunity — yes, the duty — to reverse that order: to include, not exclude; to accept, not reject, to serve, not reserve; to adapt to, not run away from, change.

They must be careful not to be so 'busy' that they forget their true 'business'. They must be audacious, articulate and adaptable to cope with a complacent world, but they must be even more. 'Coping is still groping', my colleague says. 'Teaching is reaching, and that is our true business!'

Doukhobors are considered admirable teachers because they know so well the rewards of education. As the adult-education consultant for the Province of Saskatchewan I once had the occasion to meet Père Murray, the founder of Notre Dame College at Wilcox, the legend who inspired innumerable articles and films (notably Père and The Hounds of Notre Dame). Père Murray was at once the most irreverent and the most devoted Catholic I had ever met.8 He would have made any Pope proud in any age, and yet his ribald and irrepressible behaviour, the vigour of his 'colourful language', his penchant for drink, were enough to raise more than a few eyebrows among the ecclesiastical establishment.9 Asked by a journalist why he took 'bad kids' into his legendary college, Père Murray impaled the poor fellow with a stare and responded: 'I've never met a bad kid, mister. All a bad kid is, is a good kid waiting to come out.'

I have met a lot of 'good kids' waiting to come out. I myself was young once (but as the sage said, 'I gave it up because it was too much hassle'). While there was both good and bad in me, I was fortunate enough to have teachers that were able to bring out the good and beat back the bad.

One teacher in particular stands out to me today. He saved my skin when a friend and I partially blew up the new chemistry laboratory in our high school. As we told him the dreadful news, he turned 'as dark as hail clouds in a prairie storm' and uttered 'Oh, my!' after 'Oh, my!' — but he never 'ratted' on us to our friends or classmates, or even to our parents. He chose an appropriate penance that we were able to discharge with a degree of dignity: he let us 'pay off' the damage in dribs and drabs in a way that neither crippled our allowance nor allowed us an 'easy ride' to his forgiveness. Once our account was settled, he told us both that he believed in us, that life was neither 'easy' nor 'free', and that accountability and opportunity went hand in hand.

Years later I accepted his invitation to go back to his new high school and address his graduating class. Speaking of my Doukhoborism, my dreams, my destiny, I told the class that behind every 'good kid' stands a great mentor — a teacher, a parent, a guardian, someone — that one of my great lessons in life was to learn that 'it's never over 'til it's over, and even then, it's not over. I drew upon Churchill's exhortation: 'Never, never, never, never, never give up! The world is there for our making.' I stated Moses Coady's declaration that 'we truly can be the Masters of our own Destinies'; but, to be masters, we must be accountable for our mistakes and for our mis-starts.

Out of that accountability comes the opportunity to conquer our fear. If I have learnt anything, it is that the inner voice sings more loudly than the braying of innumerable judgemental jackasses. The Doukhobors of Tomorrow must heed their inner voices and lead us beyond the 'braying' to the beckoning melody of the next millenium.

1 'Mixed' in reference to animals, not people!

2 It is ironic that later this same elder was the first Doukhobor straining at his spiritual tether to reach out and shake the hand of the Canadian Minister of Citizenship (whose aide I had become) during a visit to Blaine Lake on St Peter's Day.

3 I do not judge them (as Father Martin once said, 'God has not yet gone on holi-day declaring you or me his substitute'). But my observations have led me to conclude that this repudiation of their past (a past filled with gossip, libel, slander and innuendoes about so-called Doukhobor arsons, bombings, nudity and cupidity) was at the same time crippling their future.

4 From the Zhivotnaia kniga Dukhobortsev [Book of Life of the Doukhobors], compiled and edited by Vladimir Bonch-Bruevich (StPetersburg, 1909). Re-printed: Winnipeg: Regehr's Printing, 1954, p. xxvi.

5 'My s toboi, Kolia, kak ryba s vodoi.' Kolia was short for Nikolai, my Russian Christian name.

6 Bonch-Bruevich, p. 1.

7 After my wife once led me out of danger, a lingering concussion left me speech-less for days. To this day she sometimes describes our marriage as a 'mutual relationship' in which I am expected to be the 'mute'!

8 Reverence, I think, is mostly a matter of awe, while devotion is more a matter of address — addressing the need, the problem, the vacuum, while redressing the wrong.

9 I recall him once repeating: 'Who loves not women, wine or song remains a fool his whole life long.' It was said that he could outdrink a thirsty mule with the nectar he called 'the gift of God that gladdens the hearts of man'.

On Imaging the future

Jon-Lee Kootnekoff

My Doukhobor spiritual and mental mentors and, specifically, my parents and grandparents, taught me to let go of all that does not resonate (or vibrate) with my *true being*. The Doukhobor way of life was and still is committed to the attitude that the time of decision has come. We all must choose. Do we stay in duality? Do we move into oneness?

I was moved to think that my thoughts come directly from the Universal Mind, the God Who is Love, and I am guided at all times toward new concepts for living on Earth.

The Doukhobors' way of life has motivated me to pray, but not to attempt to 'get into' union with God. Prayer is the very acknowledgement — the very expression of — that union.

Doukhoborism has taught me that the presence of God is in the very depths of our being. I know that I do not have to go to a priest, minister, rabbi or church, or belong to a particular religion, cult or political party to talk to God. God is in us, above us, around us, underneath us, and through us.

My parents, my grandparents and the Doukhobor attitude encouraged me to realise that if our thinking and doing are largely linear, analytic and hierarchical, if the self that does that thinking and doing is insular, fearful or manipulative, is it any wonder that our best intentions and problem-solvings soon turn into a 'crazy-quilt' patchwork of 'band-aids'.

Doukhoborism has cautioned me against retreating into fundamentalistic havens, ideological fortresses of 'truth', 'backto-basics' formulas and panaceas that promise to make things real and reliable again while merely sanctifying our stupidity. According to Doukhobor beliefs, the world is too interrelated and interdependent to sustain the further spread of reductionism and myopia.

From one of my teachers I was impressed with the sense that competition needs to be balanced with co-operation and individualism with love. We must develop a new world system guided by a rational master plan for long-term organic growth — a growth shaped by free partnership and held together by a spirit of truly global co-operation. This will require co-operation and teamwork (rather than confrontation) and harmony with nature (rather than its conquest) to become our normative ideals and motivating principles of action.[1]

[1]See also: Kootnekoff, Jon-Lee, *From Kooty with love: Self-discovery through the games of life* (Vancouver, 1990).

Selections from the heart (poems)

Virginia Svetlikov

Silent woman

Woman, bearer of mankind
silent as generals cry death
to her children
suffers unspeaking
the loss of her sons
fighting in wars
with no meaning
or end.

Woman, mother of mankind
tranquil, unseeing
as predators hunt daughters
passive, unfeeling
pain of the helpless
crying in streets
alone
afraid.

Sanction of freedom denied
to her young ones
unheeded questions
her right to decide
to allow destruction of
humans, children
she'd pained giving
birth to
life.Woman, silent woman,
bare me your soul
share with me
your identity
but above all
tell me why
you allow
such atrocities.

The silence was broken, she said
'an unborn child
God created
a miracle
whispered His love
breathed soul in a body
gave mankind pure life
through
woman.

'Listen, look around you
can't you see it, hear it
spirit of life
no colour, hatred, pain
strong as infinity reigns
beautiful as heaven's glow
joins together
mankind to woman.'

Her voice echoed 'cross lands
declaring
'no more will I give you my children
daughters, sons to destroy
away your guns
and violence
enough bloodshed
stealing of souls.

'I've waited, watched
for a glimmer
soon peace would be
part of life
yet soldiers lay dying
children of mine
they can't see, don't know
it's their time.'

Children huddled in fear
'round the woman
whose silence had smouldered
too long
then listened in joy
tears dry forever
as the sound
of her promise
came clear.

'Worlds of this universe
hear me, listen so well
for I am woman
giver of life
He is God giver of soul
these are our children, together
we stand for the right to live
remember this hour
beckoned
I am woman, silent no more.'

Red plaid shirt

Calloused, bruised, were my Father's hands
Nails, blackened with dirt
Sweat rolled down his sun-burned face
His back was bent from toilsome work.

Dad loved the land he broke and farmed
His joy was fields of green
The groans we made when he heard him call
'Come children, the weather, she's mean.'

We cut and raked and stooked the wheat
To send around the world
He said in our own little way we helped
To feed the hungry and cold.

Then the winter came and Father hung
His red plaid shirt on a nail
Fireplace crackling and lamps aglow
He spun his favourite tale.

Of pirates and sailors, and trunks of gold
Buried in every sea
Then he tucked us in and we said our prayers
Papa murmured a special one for me.

'Cause you see I was the only girl
In a house of seven boys
The hand-me-downs were overalls
We played with wooden toys.

And then one day our Daddy watched
Swallowing his pride
The boys all left for greater worlds
My Papa sat and cried.

'Daddy?' I whispered and he raised his head
'I love you, I will stay.'
A funny look came into his eyes
'Go child. Yours is the way.'

The boys and I, and all our clan
Made one last trip today
The gate was closed, the grass uncut
To rest, our Father, we lay.

I once looked back as we drove away
My heart was filled with hurt
And then for one brief second
I glimpsed his red plaid shirt.

It swung on the nail beside the door
The breeze was just enough
It waved and whispered joyously
'Make time for the ones you love.'

The Letter came late

She opened the letter
it read, 'Dear Mama,
I'm sorry for all
that I've done
they've put me away
in a cell of steel
and took away my gun.

'No one believes me
when I say
I didn't know the man
whose dying whisper
was 'I love you'
a crumpled picture of me
in his hand.

'There is so much
I need to know
about the man who died
was he your friend
someone you knew
were you once
his blushing bride.

'They say I'll hang
in the early morn
so the world
will know my guilt
they chained my feet
my neck and hands
a gallows they have built.

'The key has turned
the door has swung
they're dragging me outside
oh, Mama please
I want to run
I'm scared
don't want to die.'

His tears fell hot
on paper white
she knew it was too late
her boy had shot
his own father dead
the postmark read
last year, the date.

Chapter of life

In this world of lights and glitter
Full of pain and violent hatred
We've forgotten life's commitment
Thout shalt love, though shalt not kill.

All the men that have died for honour
To a country, now, don't know
That their death was all for nothing
We still fight, and we still kill.

Once a great man told the story
Of the future of all man
The corruption, the injustice
Of the wars in all the lands.

He said, "'tis not man who has created
All this beauty you destroy
But 'tis man who will have to answer
For each drop of bloody slaying.'

Then as the din of earthly peril
Brilliant lights and glitter ceased
If one listened very closely
One could hear eternal peace.

Like a whisper ever floating
Over desolate, barren lands
It was the ending of life's chapter
As was told to us by Him.

Of all mankind's senseless killing
In this world, you'll never know
That the end was all for nothing
Just a silence, dark and still.

From out of the spirit (poems)

Kathryn Soloveoff Robbie

Dust

If memory infuses dust, what then shall we treasure?

In life my grandmother used a hoe to work the soil
as life worked the ground of her heart, broke it
to a softness that reached out to me
and nurtured this child to take up her own hoe.

How shall I honour the past?

Do I take up the tools my grandmother discarded?
What memory makes beautiful will not be contained
in an old cracked cup...

This treasured, fragile bit of
Royal Albert, never used.
This plaster of paris cat
that held open her door.
This teapot my uncle teased her
about because he said it should
belong to nuns, though she and I
knew it was for gypsies.

Should those things we sacrifice for love
be snatched back by the loved ones?

Yet here I am with my face buried in
my grandmother's old skirts,
alive with memories, her hard
rough hands cracked and strained,
move gently over my head
and my hair
tangles and clings

to her sorrows.

For Sarah

My youngest daughter, who comes behind me
gathering the ashes of my rebellion,
celebrating time and passage with
her deep and reverent memory.

She will clear the path and plant the garden,
she will mend the fence and swing the gate open
and we will all be welcome
at the hearth she is tending.

Picking cherries

plucking, red fingered
victory sweet, the trophy
trickles from my lips

Apricot jam

my knife cuts, blushing
apricot flesh, summer's heat
burning on the shelf

Blackberries

vines with thorns, black fruit
reaching out I am hooked, love
cuts my mouth open

First snow

my daughter in a diaper
lies under catalpa blossoms
summer's blizzard, inverted fragrance
shedding

an avalanche above her.

she keeps still for a season
patient under this hand that shapes
prepares her to stand under so many
harsh hands,

seeing only beauty.

on the way to school one day, she stops
holds her heart like a cup, turns to me

smelling snow.

Unity

One year, I meditated on Unity.
That was the year when everyone fell apart.
All our lives, we strive
adding one to the other… this blending
your job and my job and our expectations.

If we wear matching sweaters — this is a symbol.

Abbreviate the dream.

I find you in a room where you face the corner.
My feet track mud from the garden across the floor.

If we turn toward each other and smile — that is a symbol.

But the dreamer has left the room.

I read our lives with my fingers
feeling for love with my hands,
I boil the water
and peel the potatoes.
How does this gesture unite?
What happens to love
when you burn up the past
and reject the conventions?

Oh rebellious heart

I winnow the days and read
the chaff with my fingers.

The Spirit of '95 (excerpt from a poem)

Larry A. Ewashen

A long time ago, before your mothers and fathers
Were even born, I lived in a distant land; I was
Just a very little child when all of this happened,
I remember it well...
They called themselves
Christians
Your very grandparents
They had seen a lot of killing
All around them
They knew that Jesus had said:
'Thou shalt not kill'.
But how to stop the killing?
There was a simple solution:
Why not not just destroy all of the weapons
That are used to kill?
They gathered all of their swords and guns
And lit them in three huge bonfires...
This was in Russia
A hundred years ago —
The authorities did not like this new
Teaching as taught by Jesus...
Actually, an old teaching
Now the authorities claimed it
As their own...
This old teaching was rediscovered
By your forefathers...
They did not want to be soldiers,
To learn how to kill...

1895 — 28 June
Midnight, the feast day of Peter and Paul,
A traditional day of gathering,
The birthday of Peter V. Verigin —
Our exiled leader...
According to him —

According to our hearts
And not just here in the Wet Mountains of
Transcaucasia
Did we burn all of our weapons,
Our swords and our guns,
All the weapons that we had gathered over the years
As we fell away from our creed of non-violence
And found some accomodation for a deadly weapon
In the name of self-protection
From beasts, both human and of the animal kingdom
And in Kars, and in Elizavetpol
Did the Spirit Wrestlers send their spirits in song
Towards the heavens
As all of the weapons cast their shadows into the
Night sky
To be seen no more...
Just one more weapon that wouldn't kill
Again...

And because of this they sorely abused us,
Abused us till the ground ran red with our blood,
Each strike of their whips cut through our flesh,
Our eyes filled with blood and tears,
Till our flesh dried black...
Those too weak to walk
Stayed behind to come with our wagons and horses...
The rest limped eight miles to Bogdanovka...
We didn't know then that the soldiers
Would occupy our villages
And the greatest abuses were to follow...
Our young women to suffer scars
In private places
That would never heal...
Our elders to lose the dignity and reverence
That comes with age and wisdom...
The wagon brought one who no longer walkes,
No longer breathed,
Trampled to death
By the cruel hooves of the charging force...
We did not know

That fully one fourth of us were to change over
To that different space...
Black broken bodies left for the carrion crow
Before the deliverance of the rest
To a strange land...

As we walked, were driven,
We sang
As we approached the Governor Nakashidze
Bruised and beaten,
Barely crawling,
Suffering the effects of the hail of sharp
Whips — and boots and horseshoes...
We were ordered to halt — and remove our caps,
To which our elder said:
'When the Governor comes and greets us,
Then we will greet him too
As brothers, in the regular manner.'
At this, the blows rained on us once more
And then — in reply , when our young men handed in
Their papers
Of reserve conscription —
His rage was awesome,
And only Prince Ospinsky
Saved the many from being shot in a rage...
Some received 300 lashes —
And the sore abuse went on —
Some were imprisoned,
Others sent to resettlement and exile
To what everyone thought would be a certain death,
Our chattels disposed of...
We didn't want possessions —
But we wanted to be able to live...
That was the plan:
To disperse us all till no life was left —

People have asked:
What possessed sane people
To do such a deed,
A deed that would provoke the wrath

Of Church and State...
And how could it be
That all of a sudden
At three different places
Across the vast steppes of Russia
At the same time
At midnight
The three fires shone out into the night
With our voices...
Know then
That our leader
Banished already for
Eight years —
On false charges
Without trial,
Eight years more to come...
The greatest privation —
The isolation from friends, family and people,
Reward for being chosen as our inspiration
After his years of studies
With our great leader Lushichka,
First in suffering and example,
Our beloved Peter Verigin
Captured and guided our wishes of fulfilment...
And know that — through great privation,
Torment and danger,
Petushka knew all that went on,
And we knew his thoughts and wishes...
Now know the strength of the partners and soulmates,
Those who who braved the Siberian steppes
In peril of their own lives,
At risk of perpetual oblivion banished to the icy wastes,
Through their courage
Our prophetic advisor would know our daily lives...

Those who were called for the lots
Of conscription
Bore the suffering that their refusal brought on
With stoic strength,
A firm example to those of lesser faith

And a force to be feared by all authorities
For the example they were setting,
Not only for fellow Spirit Wrestlers
But for fellow man,
Wherever the military held sway,
Others began to follow their brave stand,
Giving strength to still other humanitarians...
This example was surely to be feared —
What scorn our people raised amongst
Our masters — spiritual and temporal...

What were we — after all?
But bothersome vermin to be swept under and expensive rug
With a Field Marshal's baton perhaps?
And after that —
A sprinkle of Holy Water maybe?
To purify the air where we once were?
How could we even think
That we would be taken seriously?
Ours gave us courage and strength...
No wonder their minds got soft —
A great Russian poet said:
'Be then docile, Muse, to the will of God;
Fear no offence, grasp for no crown,
Learn indifference to both praise and blame
And never stoop to strive with fools.'

As our villages were plundered
And coarse, gleeful Cossacks, drunk
With liberty
Moved into the bedrooms
Of chaste young maidens, some not
Sixteen
And then even into those of the
Mothers of our brave ones...
The final solution had its say —
Sweet children torn from mothers' breasts
To witness their despair...
Men folk into hiding
And into cruel submission when they

Were found
Under a cruel heel topped by a leather
Boot and a harder resolve,
Tears in a strange mixture with
Blood and song,
Strangers in a lnad they loved
But no longer knew
To become stranger still
And now an enquiry
To discover what an enlightened world now
Knew...
Those with will not broken,
Not holding a gun,
Declared criminals
And banished...
A journey of song and joy...
How our heart bleeds as this strange
Motherland eats its innards
And spews them forth in a mixture of
Torment...

We did not need an enquiry
To show us who we were...
Even expensive mirrors
Clouded over in discreet shame
When they looked upon themselves
Through countless enquires for 200 years,
Much obfuscation,
Much missing of the points,
No solutions...
Two diverse points continue to clash:
Too much pride,
Too many peers,
Too much politics,
Too many principles,
Too many police,
Too many prophets,
Too many princes,
Too many predictions,
Too many practicalities,

Too many pistols,
Too many palaces,
Too many priests,
Too many prisons,
Too many prisoners,
Too many prosecutions,
Too many prosecutors
Who were sure they were right...
How could illiterate peasants
Deal with the divine right of kings
And bishops?
But they did —!
So much confusion
Laid to rest
Like leaves covered by first snow...

Let us sum up:
The enquiries,
The Commission,
The truth must out...
First to Signak...
Victims were summoned to testify,
Then to Slavianka,
Then to Kirilovka,
Terpenie,
Throughout the province of Kars...
Other villages...
The enquiry had to bear witness to
The truth
And with each testament
And each fresh violation of human nature
Our deliverance moved closer...

Later that evening, this unusual
Humane and civil Judge
Found the Doukhobors and pressed on them
Two rouble for their dinner
And wished to talk further with the
Doukhobors...
A new convert?

An old philosopher once said he
Would have to travel from morning
Till night for many days with many lamps
Before he would find an honest man.
By becoming honest and decent, the
Doukhobors had ensured that there would
Be a few less scoundrels in the
World?
In this world,
They had little competition.
Heartfelt friends, Tolstoy and Tchertkov,
Now separated by an ocean…
Others banished for their appeal to common
Humanity in helping the Spirit Wrestlers…
Biryukov to a remote area called
Kurland,
Tregubov to the hinterland,
Friend and ally, Chertkov,
Given the chance,
Chose to go to England…
From there he directed a massive
Campaign
To free these prisoners of
Conscience…
Our dear Dedushka, now separated
From his allies,
Waged a valiant
Struggle
Through his wits, talent and
Belief in humanity…

There were others
Through charity or misguided zeal
Who helped —
Leopold Sulerzhitsky!
The single, largest migration
To the Canadian prairies was about
To begin,
One final test of faith
And strength…

Our friend and helpmate
Leopold Sulerzhitsky,
Well organised,
And if he had not taken care of the
Myriad of details
Involved in loading some 2140 of us
Into a ship,
We, who had never seen a ship,
Much less sailed —
And oh, what a frightful storm we had
Before we saw the welcome craggy shore
Of Halifax, Nova Scotia...

Well, that was on 20 January 1899...
The ship — the *Lake Huron* with 2140 Doukhobors...
On the 26th, same month,
The ship called the *Lake Superior* with 2000...
Towards the end of winter, 18 April,
The *Lake Superior* again
With 1036 refugees from Cyprus...
Then 21st June,
2286 from Kars on the *Lake Huron*...
We rushed forward, peering at our new land,
Our first sight of the Canadians that we had never
Seen before...
Of course they were as curious to see us...
Reporters crowded around us
As though we had come from the ends of the earth,
And we had
Physically, though our spiritual journey
They would never know...
Many newspapers came:
'Singing psalms of thanksgiving to Almighty God, over
Two thousand souls freed from Russian tyranny sailed
Into Halifax harbour.
They were thankful for their safe transportation over
The mighty waters of the Atlantic.
They left their country because they refused to take
Up arms, yet they received a warm welcome in a harbour studded
With forts.'

So that is the story of
Why you are here
And how your ancestors
Struggled to make a life of peace...
Let us remember those noble
Ancestors — and their friends
WHo made all this possible...
Our ancestors lighted a beacon of hope
Many years ago
When they lit the fires that burned
That burned the guns...
We must not let that beacon of hope
Extinguish—.

About
the
authors

About the authors of Spirit Wrestlers' Voices

Barnes (*née* Zarchikoff), **Annie**. A retired hospital equipment planner and consultant in Calgary, Alberta, Annie Barnes was born to an independent Doukhobor family in Pelly, Saskatchewan, in 1936. When she was nine years old, she and her recently widowed mother embarked upon a journey that took them into the homes of Community Doukhobors, Sons of Freedom, Ukrainians and non-Doukhobors throughout western Canada, yet she didn't feel as though she belonged anywhere. Annie and her husband Ken now have four children and eight grandchildren and reside in Sundre, Alberta. The opportunity to do a paper on Doukhobor women has opened many doors for her, including writing a play and organising an international conference of Doukhobor women.

Chernoff, Peter F. A retired high school teacher, Peter Chernoff was born to an Independent Doukhobor family in a Saskatchewan colony north of Saskatoon. He is the father of an Olympic athlete. In doing his research on Doukhobor athletes, Peter was surprised to discover a distant relative who became a world champion saddle-bronc rider in 1926.

Deacove, Jim. Born in Kamsack, Sask., to Doukhobor and Polish parents, Jim Deacove worked as an educator and an artist in Winnipeg before moving to Ontario. In the early 1970s Jim created and founded a cottage industry called Family Pastimes Co-operative Games, which he and his wife Ruth (who is also an educator) still run on their farm near Perth (Ont.). Their two daughters Tanya and Christa took their primary school education at a home-based school operated by their parents. Jim has experimented with self-sufficient community living. He has great respect for the teachings of J. Krishnamurti.

Ewashen, Larry A. Born in Alberta of Doukhobor background, Larry Ewashen went on to become a film-maker, playwright, actor, singer and writer. He has played music with such people as Stompin' Tom Connors, Ian Tyson, Gordon Lightfoot and Bob Dylan. His film credits include appearnces with Donald Sutherland and Richard Burton, and in the theatre he has performed with most of Canada's well-known actors. In television he has worked with CTV in Toronto, and in radio on CBC documentaries and plays. Currently, he is associated with Kootenay Creative Consultants, and is also curator of the Kootenay Historical Doukhobor Museum in Castlegar. His wife, Galina Alekseeva, is Head of Academic

Research at the Tolstoy Estate Museum at Yasnaya Polyana south of Moscow.

Grigulevich, Nadezhda I. Nadezhda Grigulevich received her 'Candidate's' degree1 from the Institute of Ethnology and Anthropology of the Russian Academy of Sciences in Moscow. In 1986–90 she participated in ethno-ecological field research on old Russian settlements in Georgia, Armenia and Azerbaidzhan, focusing on the food habits of the population, including the Doukhobors.

Inikova, Svetlana A. An ethnographer with the Russian Academy of Sciences' Ethnology and Anthropology Institute, Svetlana Inikova has participated in several major expeditions, including field research into old Russian settlements in Armenia, Georgia and Azerbaidzhan in the late 1980s and a North American ethnographic expedition on the Doukhobors and related minorities in 1990.

Kabatoff, Jan. Born in the 'zealot' settlement of Krestova, Jan Kabatoff moved around the interior of British Columbia and then finally settled in Bragg Creek, near Calgary (Alberta), with her husband. While she was artistically inclined before, this new location has offered her an opportunity to pursue her art more seriously at the University of Calgary.

Kanigan, Bill. Born to an Independent Doukhobor family in the Kylemore district of Saskatchewan, Bill Kanigan was encouraged to complete his education before going into the furniture business. He has since retired from a successful career and now lives in Saskatoon.

Kanigan, Vera. Vera Kanigan is a Doukhobor activist with the Union of Spiritual Communities of Christ, in Castlegar, B.C., as well as a member of the editorial board of the Doukhobor periodical Iskra. The principles of love, positive effort and peaceful co-existence with others continue to guide her life.

Kolesnikoff, James D. The first Canadian Doukhobor to study in the Soviet Union (he was there five years in the 1960s), Jim Kolesnikoff later obtained his Ph.D. from Simon Fraser University in Burnaby, B.C. While in Russia, he met his Polish wife Nina (see below). Jim was born in the heart of the Doukhobor community in Grand Forks, B.C., where he was active as a youth worker and continues to maintain ties, especially in his involvement in the preservation of archival materials on the Doukhobors. He is currently employed in Toronto with a Russian-Canadian rare gems company.

Kolesnikoff, Nina. Born in Poland, Nina Kolesnikoff now teaches Russian at McMaster University in Hamilton, Ontario. She received her Ph.D. from the University of Alberta, and has written extensively on Polish and Russian literature.

Kootnekoff, Jon-Lee. This athlete, coach, parent, educator and entrepreneur played Olympic-calibre basketball, led the Simon Fraser University Clansmen to six successive championships and taught school in Canada and the United States. Now, as president of the Horizon Positive Self-Image Institute, Jon-Lee Kootnekoff conducts personal-growth seminars for schools, native Indian communities, corporations and government agencies.

Malloff, Steve J. As a high school teacher in Grand Forks, B.C., Steve Malloff initiated a one-level Russian-language programme in 1959, which he eventually expanded to five levels. As chairman of the USCC Russian Schools in the 1970s he was instrumental in negotiating with the B.C. government and three separate school districts for the introduction of daily Russian language instruction into elementary schools in Grand Forks, Castlegar and Nelson. Steve is still an activist with the Community Doukhobors and head of the USCC Video Club, as well as a member of the USCC Migration Committee, the USCCRussia Liaison Committee, the Fructova School Museum and the USCC Friendship Choir.

Nikitina, Serafima E. Having obtained a 'Candidate's' degree in Linguistics and Folklore Studies, Serafima Nikitina went on to become a Senior Researcher with the Russian Academy of Sciences in Moscow, specialising in applied linguistics, ethnolinguistics and folkloristics. Author of a hundred published works, she is currently involved in the study of language acquisition, folklore and religious groups, including the Molokans, Doukhobors and Old Believers.

Peacock, Kenneth. A composer and musicologist residing in Ottawa, Kenneth Peacock was for many years employed by the National Museums of Canada in recording Canada's musical heritage.

Petroff, Fred. A graduate in Agriculture from the University of Saskatchewan in Saskatoon, Fred Petroff farmed in the Canora district of Saskatchewan, where he still resides. For many years he has been active in drainage and flood control programmes. Fred comes from an Independent Doukhobor family: his father is a noted Doukhobor craftsman, while his mother (recently deceased) was once actively involved in traditional textile work.

Plotnikoff (*née* Makaeff), **Vi.** Born to a Doukhobor family in Saskatchewan, Vi Plotnikoff grew up in Grand Forks, B.C. For many years she has lived with her husband Serge in nearby Castlegar, where she worked at the local radio station. While searching her roots, the author enrolled in a writing course at Selkirk College, which led to a rediscovery of herself as a member of the Doukhobor movement. In 1994 she published a successful first novel: *Head Cook at Weddings & Funerals.*

Podovinikoff, Peter P. Peter Podovinikoff was employed with the Sunshine Valley Co-operative in Grand Forks. B.C., before becoming manager of the local Credit Union. He later moved to the west coast, where he has served as the Chief Executive Officer of the B.C. Central Credit Union and continued his work in credit union development. He has been a close observer of Doukhobor co-operative initiatives through the past century.

Popoff, Eli A. Eli Popoff was born in 1921 on a farm near the town of Blaine Lake, Saskatchewan. His father was a veteran of the Doukhobor struggle against militarism in Tsarist Russia in 1895, spending seven years in Siberian exile before coming to Canada in 1905. Eli's publication of a number of anthologies and historical monographs has given him the reputation of a Doukhobor folk historian. He currently resides with his wife Dorothy in Grand Forks, B.C.

Popoff. Peter J. Peter Popoff was born in Saskatchewan in 1907 at a time when the Canadian Government was taking away Doukhobor lands. In 1937 he moved to British Columbia and eventually worked in the sawmill business in Grand Forks. As a member of the Doukhobor Society of Canada, in November 1974 he initiated a series of monthly research symposia in western Canada (sixty-eight in all) on the Doukhobor movement.

Rebin, Norman K. Born to a Doukhobor family in northcentral Saskatchewan, for thirty years Norman Rebin has run an international consulting business known as the Pinehurst Institute. In 1994 Norm and his wife Delva returned to western Canada, where Norm is pursuing his speaking, communications and leadership business. After more than 4,000 speeches, seminars and workshops on four continents, Norm has received 'The Hall of Fame of Speech'. In a 'Discoveries in Doukhoborism' motivational seminar in June 1993, Norm pointed out that Doukhobors have been asleep about their own selfimportance. 'The world sees you as you see yourself. It is up to us to discover what kind of footnote we want in history.'

Robbie (*née* Soloveoff), **Kathryn.** A Doukhobor poet currently residing in Robson, B.C., Kathryn Robbie was born in Penticton to Fred and Mabel Soloveoff, and grew up within the closely knit circle of Doukhobor family and community life in Grand Forks. For the past sixteen years Kathryn has worked at home, raising three daughters.

Semenoff, John J. Popularly known as a 'Doukhobor philosopher', John Semenoff works as a photographer, columnist, and community activist in the area of peace, disarmament, the environment and cultural renewal. He resides in Grand Forks, B.C., where his wife Elizabeth is an educator and former editor of *Iskra*. John is webmaster for the Canadian Doukhobor Society (jsemenof@cln.etc.bc.ca).

Seminoff, Paul J. Paul Seminoff works in the Grand Forks area. He participated in the USCC Senior Commission on the Future, especially as related to cultural exchanges with the Soviet Union, and was active in the Kootenay Branch of the former Canada-USSR Association.

Shockey, Jim. Born to a Ukrainian family, Jim Shockey has become a foremost collector of ethnic furniture in Canada. For many years, his home workshop and Vancouver store, 'FolkArt Interior', has been brim--full with pieces that reflect the history of prairie settlers. His collections have been sold in places far and wide, including Hollywood.

Stushnoff, George. A former farmer, teacher, and federal government employee dealing with issues of Canadian native peoples and multiculturalism, George Stushnoff is currently active with the Doukhobor Society of Saskatchewan and the Doukhobor Society of Saskatoon, where he resides.

Svetlikov, Virginia. Born in Gibson Creek, B.C., Virginia Svetlikoff is currently enrolled in a two-year Journalism/Public Communications programme at Kwantlen University College. For most of her life she has worked as a free-lance writer, and has been active in local theatre. She describes her career as follows: 'While in Moscow in 1982–83 I received my Russian language accreditation; I studied theatre and was able to spend many long hours researching our Doukhobor heritage... Upon my return to Canada, I started working as a Russian interpreter... for various companies in the United States, and on occasion, in Canada, which were beginning to organise joint ventures with the Soviet Union. These contracts took me to most of the continents on this planet — a rewarding experience like none I've ever had. Since the Soviet Union's demise, I have held many contracts in Vancouver, some with the Federal

Government as a communication officer/liaison. Primarily with the Clinton/Yeltsin summit in 1993 in Vancouver.

Tarasoff, Koozma J. Born in Saskatchewan to Doukhobor parents, Koozma Tarasoff is an ethnographer, writer and photographer with special expertise in Doukhobor affairs. He is the author of several books on the Doukhobors, including *Plakun Trava—The Doukhobors* (Grand Forks, 1982). Most recently he has been active in organising the current Doukhobor exhibit at the Canadian Museum of Civilization near Ottawa.

Verigin (*née* Verishine)**, Marilyn.** A homemaker and founding member of the Doukhobor Cultural Association, Marilyn has not forgotten her Saskatchewan Doukhobor roots in traditional hospitality and hard work. This is reflected in her generous community work as well as her devoted toil with Verigin Industries Ltd. of Trail, B.C., which was operated by her husband Elmer until his retirement and his brothers Lawrence and Russell.

Verigin, Michael M. Born in the Doukhobor village of Cowley, Alberta, Michael Verigin has been Secretary-Treasurer of the United Doukhobors of Alberta since 1974. He served six years as a board member of the Christian Community of Universal Brotherhood Trust Fund (representing Alberta), and is currently a member of the Alberta Cultural Heritage Council.

Voykin (*née* Podovinikoff)**, Natalie.** For almost four decades, Natalie Voykin and her husband Bill have raised four children in Slocan Park, B.C. In her own words: 'I love to garden, and have been a vegetarian all my life. Mother Earth provides us with fresh organic vegetables and flowers. Singing in the choir, reading and writing and pursuing the goal of discovering knowledge of my inner-Self is a never-ending adventure. Peace is the word that holds much of the mysteries of the heart. I am a student of Life, where its experiences bring to one's awareness that the whole universe is connected to all, and all are connected to God.... That is what holds much of my attention.'

Weeks, Arnie. Born in Nanaimo, B.C., Arnie Weeks received his B.A. and M.A. degrees in Arts from the University of British Columbia. At UBC he initially founded and later helped reorganise the Slavonic Circle, where he played the balalaika and guitar. In 1965 he began a civil service career in Ottawa with the Department of Energy, Mines and Resources, later working for Employment and Immigration. Now semi-retired, Arnie serves as a computer and immigration consultant in Ottawa, where he and his wife Margita reside.

Woodsworth, John. A native of Vancouver, John Woodsworth holds a B.A. in Russian language from the University of British Columbia as well as an M.A. in Russian linguistics from Simon Fraser University. He has taught Russian language at various universities in Canada and America; since 1982 he has been associated with the University of Ottawa. As an editor and researcher — as well as a Russian/English translator/interpreter for more than thirty years — John has recently been involved in a number of projects concerning the Doukhobors. With experience in audio-visual production, he has produced two cassette albums of his piano improvisations.

[1]*Candidate's degree* — a post-graduate academic degree ranking between an M.A. and a Ph.D.

Suggested readings

BONCH-BRUEVICH, Vladimir Dmitrievich (1909). *Zhivotnaia kniga dukhobortsev* [The Book of Life of the Doukhobors]. St Petersburg. 2nd edition: Winnipeg: Union of Doukhobors of Canada, 1954. Translated into English as *The Book of Life of the Doukhobors*. Saskatoon & Blaine Lake: Doukhobor Societies of Saskatchewan, 1978.

BURNHAM, Dorothy K. (1986). *Unlike the lilies: Doukhobor textile traditions in Canada*. Toronto: Royal Ontario Museum.

DONSKOV, Andrew, ed. (1995). *Leo Tolstoy—Peter Verigin: Correspondence.* With an introduction by Lidia GromovaOpul'skaya. Translated from the Russian by John Woodsworth. Ottawa: Legas.

EWASHEN, Larry A. and Koozma J. TARASOFF (1994). In Search of Utopia: The Doukhobors. Castlegar, B.C.: Spirit Wrestlers Associates. Spirit Wrestlers Book Series, nº 1.

FRIESEN, John W. and Michael M. VERIGIN (1989, 2nd ed. 1996). *The Community Doukhobors: a people in transition.* Ottawa: Borealis Press.

JANZEN, William. (1990). *The Experience of Mennonite, Hutterite, and Doukhobor communities in Canada.* Toronto: University of Toronto Press.

KLIBANOV, A. I. (1965). *Istoriia religioznogo sektantstva v Rossii, 60-e gody XIX v.–1917 g. Moscow.* Translated by Ethel Dunn. Ed. Stephen P. Dunn as *History of religious sectarianism in Russia (1860s–1917).* New York: Pergamon Press, 1982.

PEACOCK, Kenneth (1970). *Songs of the Doukhobors. An Introductory Outline.* Ottawa: Queen's Printer for the National Museums of Canada. Folklore Series: nº 7.

PLOTNIKOFF, Vi (1994). *Head Cook at weddings & funerals and other stories of Doukhobor life.* Vancouver: Polestar.

POPOFF, Eli A. (1992). (1991). *Katya: A Canadian Doukhobor.* Leningrad: Titul & LenArt.

———— *Stories From Doukhobor History.* Grand Forks, B.C.: Iskra.

SULERZHITSKY, Leopold Antonovich (1905). *V Ameriku s dukhoborami.* Moscow: I.N.Kushnerev (publication of Posrednik). Translated by Michael Kalmakoff as *To America With The Doukhobors.* Regina: Canadian Plains Research Centre, 1982 and 1995.

TARASOFF, Koozma J. (1977). *Traditional Doukhobor folkways; an ethnographic and biographic record of prescribed behaviour.* Ottawa: National Museums of Canada. Series: Canadian Centre for Folk Culture Studies, n° 20.

———— (1982). *Plakun Trava: the Doukhobors.* Grand Forks, B.C.: Mir.

———— comp. & ed. (1995). *From Russia with love: the Doukhobors.* Special issue of *Canadian Ethnic Studies,* vol. 27 n° 3.

———— and Larry A. EWASHEN (1994). *In Search of Utopia.* Ottawa & Castlegar: Spirit Wrestlers Associates.

———— and Robert B KLYMASZ , eds. (1995). *Spirit Wrestlers: Centennial Papers in Honour of Canada's Doukhobor Heritage.* Hull, Québec: Canadian Museum of Civilization. Series: Canadian Centre for Folk Culture Studies, n° 67.

TCHERTKOFF, Vladimir (1900; repr. 1993). *Christian Martyrdom in Russia. Persecution of the Doukhobors.* Tula, Russia: PublishingPolygraphic Union of Lev Tolstoy. Ottawa & Castlegar: Spirit Wrestlers Associates. Spirit Wrestlers Book Series, n° 2.

TRACIE, Carl J. (1996). *'Toil and peaceful life' Doukhobor village settlement in Saskatchewan 1899–1918.* Regina: Canadian Plains Research Centre.

WOODCOCK, George & Ivan AVAKUMOVIC (1968). *The Doukhobors.* Toronto: Oxford University Press.

WOODSWORTH, John, comp. (1997). *The Doukhobors: 1895–1943. Annotated, cross-referenced and summarised.* Russian Archival Documents on Canada: Catalogue n° 2. 2nd ed. (revised). Ottawa: Carleton University, Centre for Research on Canadian-Russian Relations.